Aligning Perspectives on Health, Safety and Well-Being

Series Editors

Stavroula Leka, University College Cork, Cork, Ireland

Aditya Jain, Nottingham University Business School and Centre for Organizational Health and Development, University of Nottingham, Nottingham, UK

Gerard Zwetsloot, University of Nottingham, Centre for Organizational Health and Development, Nottingham, United Kingdom, TNO InGerard Zwetsloot Research & Consultancy, Amsterdam, Noord-Holland, The Netherlands

Raising awareness of the interdisciplinary and complementary relationship of different research perspectives on health, safety and well-being is the main aim of the book series Aligning Perspectives on Health, Safety and Well-being. Combined research approaches on health, safety and well-being are becoming more and more popular in several research disciplines across and between the social, behavioural and medical sciences. Therefore, Aligning Perspectives on Health, Safety and Well-being stimulates the publication of interdisciplinary approaches to the promotion of health, safety and well-being. Recognizing a need within societies and workplaces for more integrated approaches to problem solving, the series caters to the notion that most innovation stems from combining knowledge and research results from related but so far separated areas. Volumes will be edited by expert authors and editors and will contain contributions from different disciplines. All authors, and especially volume editors are encouraged to engage in developing more robust theoretical models that can be applied in actual practice and lead to policy development. Editorial Board: Professor Johannes Siegrist, University of Dusseldorf, Germany Professor Peter Chen, University of South Australia Professor Katherine Lippel, University of Ottawa, Canada Professor Nicholas Ashford, MIT, USA Dr Steve Sauter, NIOSH, USA Dr Peter Hasle, Aalborg University, Denmark.

More information about this series at http://www.springer.com/series/10757

Anthony Montgomery • Margot van der Doef •
Efharis Panagopoulou • Michael P. Leiter
Editors

Connecting Healthcare Worker Well-Being, Patient Safety and Organisational Change

The Triple Challenge

Editors
Anthony Montgomery
Department of Education & Social Policy
University of Macedonia
Thessaloniki, Greece

Efharis Panagopoulou
Health Psychology
Aristotle University of Thessaloniki
Thessaloniki, Greece

Margot van der Doef
Health Psychology
Leiden University
Leiden, Zuid-Holland, The Netherlands

Michael P. Leiter
Industrial and Organisational Psychology
Deakin University
Burwood, Australia

ISSN 2213-0497   ISSN 2213-0470 (electronic)
Aligning Perspectives on Health, Safety and Well-Being
ISBN 978-3-030-60997-9   ISBN 978-3-030-60998-6 (eBook)
https://doi.org/10.1007/978-3-030-60998-6

© Springer Nature Switzerland AG 2020
This work is subject to copyright. All rights are reserved by the Publisher, whether the whole or part of the material is concerned, specifically the rights of translation, reprinting, reuse of illustrations, recitation, broadcasting, reproduction on microfilms or in any other physical way, and transmission or information storage and retrieval, electronic adaptation, computer software, or by similar or dissimilar methodology now known or hereafter developed.
The use of general descriptive names, registered names, trademarks, service marks, etc. in this publication does not imply, even in the absence of a specific statement, that such names are exempt from the relevant protective laws and regulations and therefore free for general use.
The publisher, the authors, and the editors are safe to assume that the advice and information in this book are believed to be true and accurate at the date of publication. Neither the publisher nor the authors or the editors give a warranty, expressed or implied, with respect to the material contained herein or for any errors or omissions that may have been made. The publisher remains neutral with regard to jurisdictional claims in published maps and institutional affiliations.

This Springer imprint is published by the registered company Springer Nature Switzerland AG.
The registered company address is: Gewerbestrasse 11, 6330 Cham, Switzerland

Contents

1 Connecting Health Care Worker Well-being, Patient Safety and
  Organizational Change: The Triple Challenge 1
  Anthony J. Montgomery, Margot Van der Doef,
  Efharis Panagopoulou, and Michael P. Leiter

Part I Linking Organisational Factors, Health Care Worker Well-being,
        and Patient Outcomes

2 Job Strain, Burnout, Wellbeing and Patient Safety in Healthcare
  Professionals 11
  Daryl B. O'Connor, Louise H. Hall, and Judith Johnson

3 Missed Nursing Care: The Impact on Patients, Nurses
  and Organisations 25
  Marcia Kirwan and Anne Matthews

4 Linking Organisational Factors and Patient Care:
  Does Healthcare Workers' Well-being Matter? 41
  Kevin Teoh and Juliet Hassard

5 Burnout in Primary Care Workforce 59
  Anli Yue Zhou, Maria Panagioti, Henry Galleta-Williams,
  and Aneez Esmail

Part II Zooming in on the Health Care Context

6 Between Balance and Burnout: Contrasting the Working-Time
  Conditions of Irish-Trained Hospital Doctors in Ireland and
  Australia 75
  John-Paul Byrne, Edel Conway, Aoife M. McDermott,
  Richard W. Costello, Lucia Prihodova, Anne Matthews,
  and Niamh Humphries

7   Doctors Well-being, Quality of Patient Care and Organizational
    Change: Norwegian Experiences............................... 91
    Karin Isaksson Rø, Judith Rosta, Reidar Tyssen, and Fredrik Bååthe

8   The Relationship Between Employee Engagement and
    Organisational Outcomes in the English National Health Service:
    An Analysis of Employee and Employer Data in 28 Healthcare
    Organisations.. 115
    Christian van Stolk and Marco Hafner

9   Governing Health Care Provision: Clinicians' Experiences....... 131
    Berit Bringedal, Inger Lise Teig, and Kristine Bærøe

10 Speaking up about Bullying and Harassment in Healthcare:
    Reflections Following the Introduction of an Innovative
    "Speak Up" Role in NHS England............................. 145
    A. Jones, J. Blake, C. Banks, M. Adams, D. Kelly, R. Mannion,
    and J. Maben

Part III Developing Cultures that Enable Organisational Change

11 Between Taking Care of Others and Yourself: The Role
    of Work Recovery in Health Professionals..................... 165
    Claudia L. Rus, Cristina C. Vâjâean, Cătălina Oțoiu,
    and Adriana Băban

12 Creating Optimal Clinical Workplaces by Transforming
    Leadership and Empowering Clinicians........................ 187
    Paul DeChant and Diane Shannon

13 Compassionate and Collective Leadership for Cultures
    of High-Quality Care... 207
    Michael A. West

14 Workforce and Excellence in Nursing Care: Challenges
    for Leaders and Professionals................................ 227
    P. Van Bogaert, O. Timmermans, S. Slootmans, E. Goossens,
    and E. Franck

15 Mindful Practice: Organizational Change and Health Professional
    Flourishing Through Cultivating Presence and Courageous
    Conversations... 247
    Michael S. Krasner and Ronald Epstein

Part IV Towards Individual- and Organisation-Focused Interventions and Their Effectiveness

16 Training as a Facilitator of Organizational Change in Health Care: The Input-Mediator/Moderator-Outcome-Input Model 263
Megan E. Gregory, Clayton D. Rothwell, and Ann Scheck McAlearney

17 Schwartz Center Rounds: An Intervention to Enhance Staff Well-Being and Promote Organisational Change 281
Jill Maben and Cath Taylor

18 How Healthcare Worker Well-Being Intersects with Safety Culture, Workforce Engagement, and Operational Outcomes 299
Kathryn C. Adair, Kyle Rehder, and J. Bryan Sexton

19 Mindfulness as a Way to Improve Well-Being in Healthcare Professionals: Separating the Wheat from the Chaff 319
Anthony Montgomery, Katerina Georganta, Ashvirni Gilbeth, Yugan Subramaniam, and Karen Morgan

20 Using Transformative Learning to Develop Skills for Managing Conflict: Lessons Learnt over 10 Years 331
Eva Doherty

21 Well-Being, Patient Safety and Organizational Change: Quo Vadis? 345
Anthony J. Montgomery

Chapter 1
Connecting Health Care Worker Well-being, Patient Safety and Organizational Change: The Triple Challenge

Anthony J. Montgomery, Margot Van der Doef, Efharis Panagopoulou, and Michael P. Leiter

There is a growing realisation within healthcare that healthcare worker well-being, patient outcomes and organizational change are symbiotically linked (Montgomery & Maslach, 2019). We have accumulated enough evidence to demonstrate that job burnout has become a major problem within the field of healthcare. It is a response to prolonged exposure to occupational stressors, and it has serious consequences for healthcare professionals (HPs) and the organizations in which they work. Burnout is associated with sleep deprivation (Vela-Bueno et al., 2008), medical errors (Fahrenkopf et al., 2008; Prins et al., 2009; Shanafelt et al., 2010), poor quality of care (Linzer, 2018; Shirom, Nirel, & Vinokur, 2006), and low ratings of patient satisfaction (Vahey et al., 2004). Indeed, for US surgeons, burnout and depression were among the strongest factors related to reporting a recent major medical error (Shanafelt et al., 2011). Contrary to research findings and theory developments, there is growing acceptance among managers and the general public for viewing burnout as an individual failing while de-emphasizing the extent to which the syndrome reflects organizational and healthcare system shortcomings. The most recent meta-analysis in the field of burnout point to the fact there is a need for organisational solutions that address the factors that drive and maintain burnout (Panagioti et al., 2017). Unfortunately, the most common responses have put the responsibility on

---

A. J. Montgomery (✉)
University of Macedonia, Thessaloniki, Greece
e-mail: antmont@uom.edu.gr

M. Van der Doef
Leiden University, Leiden, The Netherlands

E. Panagopoulou
Aristotle University of Thessaloniki, Thessaloniki, Greece

M. P. Leiter
Industrial and Organisational Psychology, Deakin University, Burwood, VIC, Australia

© Springer Nature Switzerland AG 2020
A. Montgomery et al. (eds.), *Connecting Healthcare Worker Well-Being, Patient Safety and Organisational Change*, Aligning Perspectives on Health, Safety and Well-Being, https://doi.org/10.1007/978-3-030-60998-6_1

healthcare professionals to take better care of themselves, become more resilient, and cope with stressors on their own (Montgomery, Panagopoulou, Esmail, Richards, & Maslach, 2019).

This book will delineate the ways in which the key areas, well-being, patient safety and organizational change, are interrelated and contribute to unhealthy workplaces within healthcare. Contributing authors will 'take the temperature' of their subject areas and outline the ways in which we can align these three areas in ways that contribute to a healthy workplace for both healthcare workers and patients. Health care professionals are under increasing pressure to continuously improve quality of care in environments that are not naturally designed to contribute positively to either the health of their employees or to the recipients of care (Montgomery & Maslach, 2019). Improving quality of care requires not only the understanding of the clinical environment, health workers' motivation and commitment, but also patients' needs and literacy, health policy, and the social and political context in which health services are delivered (Montgomery, Tordova, Baban, & Panagopoulou, 2013; Panagopoulou, Montgomery, & Tsiga, 2015). The book has attracted a diverse array of authors from different disciplines that include; primary care, clinical medicine, nursing, occupational psychology, sociology, management, health psychology, clinical governance, health policy and health services research. It has been a rewarding endeavor integrating these different voices and reaching some meaningful conclusions about the challenges in connecting healthcare worker well-being, patient outcomes and organisational change.

The book is divided into four parts. Part I is concerned with linking organizational factors to healthcare worker well-being and patient outcomes. In Chap. 2, O'Connor, Hall and Johnson highlight the links between job strain, burnout, wellbeing and patient safety in order to develop effective interventions. The authors also consider research that has tested interventions in the health professional context, and emphasise the need for us to improve employees' mental health in parallel with the drive for safer work environments. Chapter 3 by Kirwan and Matthews reviews the negative consequences of incomplete nursing care on patient outcomes including higher mortality levels, and outcomes for nurses such as increased levels of burnout and low job satisfaction. The authors examine how greater understanding, awareness, monitoring and addressing of missed care can help overcome the challenges for the nursing profession and healthcare organisations in a context of ever-increasing demands on services. In Chap. 4 Teoh and Hassard bring together organisational factors, well-being and patient care outcomes within a single conceptual model. Within their model, organisational factors are proposed to predict both healthcare workers' well-being and patient care, with healthcare workers' well-being postulated as a mediator. The authors remind us that while there has been considerable focus on improving patient care, there has not been an equal emphasis on improving workers' well-being. In Chap. 5, Zhou et al. review the drivers of burnout in primary care. As the authors note, primary care is responsible for providing over 80% of the patient care across Europe, while general practitioners (GPs) have the highest rates of burnout and turnover across medical specialties. The chapter provides an overview of the challenges for GPs and provides promising examples of interventions to mitigate burnout and promote engagement in primary care.

Part II zooms in for a finer grained look at the healthcare context across the globe. In Chap. 6, Byrne et al. compares the working time conditions of Irish and Australian hospital doctors. The background to their research is how austerity and emigration have shaped the landscape of healthcare services in Ireland. The authors report on the contrasting experiences of participants in Irish and Australian hospitals to illustrate how this context has impacted on the work-time of hospital doctors. Their chapter demonstrates how the work and non-work time of hospital doctors are shaped by institutional and organisational contexts, and how this interdependence of work and non-work time shapes the experience of burnout. In Chap. 7, Isaksson Rø et al. review the experience of Norwegian doctors. The authors discuss the triple challenge from a Norwegian perspective, which includes; healthcare system reforms in Norway, changes in doctors work-life and wellbeing and Norwegian doctors´ understanding of their own the triple challenge (professional well-being, organizational factors and quality of patient care). In Chap. 8, Van Stolk and Hafner look at the concept of employee engagement in the English NHS and draw on two extensive surveys that included large NHS employers (mostly acute hospital trusts). The analyses of the authors suggest that a more holistic approach, which moves beyond single initiatives or interventions are important as various work environment and culture variables show a positive association with staff engagement. In Chap. 9, Bringedal et al. examine the experience of clinicians in the Norwegian health services with regard to the impact of governing instruments on their ability to provide quality care to their patients. The authors highlight how governance will have the opposite effect and that the standardization of clinicians' daily work may give a more transparent and efficient health care service, but that more focus on 'measurable' outcomes will mean other less tangible aspects, equally important, risk being ignored or getting insufficient attention. Chapter 10 reviews a 2016 initiative in the UK NHS aimed at reducing employee silence, named the "Freedom to Speak Up Guardian"(FTSUG) role. Jones and Blake highlight how the FTSUG role was given a broad remit with the hope that it would improve patient safety, but that in practice the majority of FTSUGs time is spent on bullying and harassment concerns, rather than on direct patient safety concerns. The authors recommend the need for FTSUG guidelines to more adequately reflect the fact that employees are using the service to speak up about time-consuming, contentious and antagonistic cases of staff bullying and harassment. The chapter reminds us that employees will not allow us to disconnect clinical performance from employee wellbeing.

Part III explores how developing culture can enable organizational change. In Chap. 11, Rus et al. provide an integrative review of the literature on recovery from work in healthcare professionals. The authors consider the multilevel antecedents and consequences of work recovery, and suggest potential organizational and individual level interventions on work recovery to enhance health professionals' wellbeing and ultimately, patient safety. In Chap. 12, Krasner and Epstein introduce us to Mindful practice, which they describe as moment-to-moment purposeful attentiveness to one's own physical and mental processes during every day work with the goal of practicing with clarity and compassion. The authors argue that Mindful Practice training can cultivate qualities that most clinicians and educators recognize as qualities of excellent practitioners –attentiveness, self-monitoring, curiosity, beginner's mind, commitment, resilience, presence, empathy, acceptance and awareness of one's biases. In Chap. 13, De Chant and Shannon discuss how we can create optimal clinical workplaces by transforming leadership and empowering clinicians. The authors recommend that individual leaders must shift from command-and-control leadership to mentoring, and that healthcare organizations must adopt an inverted organizational chart, which can enable and support servant leadership styles among clinicians. Chapter 14 is a call to embrace compassionate and collective leadership for cultures of high-quality care. West argues that compassion is the key to responding effectively to the triple challenge of ensuring high-quality care for our populations, the well-being of those who provide care, and the effective functioning of health care organizations that provide the context for that care. In Chap. 15, Van Bogaert et al. provide insights on clinical work systems, personal leadership and the nurse practice environment, as well as empirical work investigating associations between nurse work characteristics, such as social capital, decision latitude, workload, work engagement and burnout, and nurses' perception of excellent job satisfaction and care quality. The authors' data show that an environment characterized by balanced work characteristics, including workload, decision latitude and social capital, was associated with higher job satisfaction and self-rated excellence of care quality in staff nurses and midwifes. All the chapters in this part convergence towards a similar conclusion; that changing our models of leadership is the key to changing the cultures of our healthcare organizations.

Part IV reviews the potential for individual and organizational interventions to resolve the triple challenge of the book. In Chap. 16, Gregory et al. reviews the importance of training as a mechanism to facilitate organizational change and explains the mechanisms via the input-mediator/moderator-output-input (IMOI) model. The authors interwove specific examples of two training programs deployed in healthcare settings: teamwork training and cultural competency training. The chapter highlights how well planned training can improve patient safety and worker wellbeing in the context of organizational change. In Chap. 17, Maben and Taylor introduce us to Schwartz Centre Rounds, which are organization-wide forums for healthcare staff which prompt reflection and discussion of the emotional, social or ethical challenges of healthcare work. The authors argue that Schwartz Rounds can help staff see and connect with the bigger picture of how the organization functions, helping to develop organizational cohesiveness and connectedness to the organizational mission and values, and provide a space to process patient cases and learn from mistakes. In Chap. 18, Adair et al. highlight for us how the prevalence, severity and consequential nature of health worker burnout puts institutions at risk for costly patient safety issues and turnover. The authors review a range of brief individual interventions (many at low/no cost) that use reflective practices to improve well-being indicators such as emotional exhaustion, work-life balance, depression and subjective well-being. In Chap. 19, Montgomery et al. examine the evidence base for the effectiveness of mindfulness based interventions (MBIs) among healthcare professionals. There is a general narrative within healthcare that mindfulness has positive impacts on both well-being and clinical practice. The authors question this idea and examine whether grouping MBIs together is scientifically meaningful, whether there is evidence that they affect objective outcomes, and whether these interventions are appropriate tools for healthcare professionals. The chapter highlights the fact that the evidence-base is largely based on female participants from developed countries, which should caution us as to the generalizability of such interventions to health care professionals across the globe. In Chap. 19, Doherty describes in detail how a training programme can be designed and delivered to equip doctors with the knowledge and skills to manage incivility and conflict in their workplace. The author provides extensive detail on how the program can be structured and delivered. Incivility is a common problem within healthcare. Learning how to manage conflict is not routinely taught in education and training programmes for either undergraduate or postgraduate health professionals perhaps because the educators themselves are conflict averse. The chapters in this part provide a range of approaches to addressing worker wellbeing, patient safety and organizational change.

Finally, this book is being written during a time when the world has been dominated by COVID-19 pandemic. Coronavirus Disease 2019 (COVID-19) is disrupting nearly every aspect of everyday life and placing unprecedented demands on our society. Healthcare professionals are at the frontline of this pandemic, and research suggests that healthcare professionals are reporting symptoms of depression, anxiety, insomnia and distress as a direct result of working during COVID-19 conditions (Lai et al., 2020; Zhang et al., 2020). As noted by Kinman, Teoh, and Harriss (2020), there was significant evidence that healthcare workers were already demoralized and mentally and physically depleted, prior to COVID-19. The pandemic has the potential to exacerbate feelings of burnout and disengagement as the burden on healthcare workers increases. It also evident that health workers struggle with having to provide suboptimal care due to high patient numbers, corona restrictions and high emotional burden linked to the isolation of patients on the ICU wards/ and in nursing homes—where patients are dying alone. The pandemic has already created 'new' problems with staff being forced to keep silent about the lack of available resources (Dyer, 2020). These restrictions exacerbate the conflict of providers' professional treatment values with the limitations created by inadequate preparation for pandemics despite many warnings. However, it also represents the possibility to rethink how we organise healthcare and it has brought into sharp focus the connection between health care worker well-being, patient safety and organisational capacity. The current pandemic has forced us to accept that the wellbeing of healthcare workers is an important part of the healthcare equation. The measures being introduced in workplaces to protect workers from contracting COVID-19 may lead to better preparedness in the future for other infections by increases in historically low vaccination rates (Williams et al., 2017), and better personal hygiene at work and work organisation involving greater physical distancing. Additionally, workplace changes introduced due to the COVID-19 crisis, such as the replacement of face-to-face meetings and conferences with online and virtual assemblies can lead to positive environmental effects through less traffic congestion and lower carbon emissions from reduced motor vehicle and aircraft travel (Sim, 2020). However at present, the pandemic has brought huge strains on the health care system and shows its vulnerability; and has huge impacts on the already affected healthcare professionals. This all makes this book all the more relevant in the current time. Hopefully, there is now a momentum to reconsider the organization of healthcare, and take into account and include the suggestions for improvement provided in each chapter.

References

Dyer, C. (2020). Covid-19: Doctors are warned not to go public about PPE shortages. *BMJ, 369*, m1592. https://doi.org/10.1136/bmj.m1592

Fahrenkopf, A. M., Sectish, T. C., Barger, L. K., Sharek, P. J., Lewin, D., Chiang, V. W., et al. (2008). Rates of medication errors among depressed and burnt out residents: Prospective cohort study. *BMJ, 336*, 488–491. https://doi.org/10.1136/bmj.39469.763218.BE18258931

Kinman, G., Teoh, K., & Harriss, A. (2020). Supporting the Well-being of healthcare workers during and after COVID-19. *Occupational Medicine, 70*, 294–296. https://doi.org/10.1093/occmed/kqaa096

Lai, J., Ma, S., Wang, Y., Cai, Z., Hu, J., Wei, N., et al. (2020). Factors associated with mental health outcomes among health care workers exposed to coronavirus disease 2019. *JAMA Network Open, 3*, e203976.

Linzer, M. (2018). Clinician burnout and the quality of care. *JAMA Internal Medicine, 178*, 1331–1332. https://doi.org/10.1001/jamainternmed.2018.370830193370

Montgomery, A., & Maslach, C. (2019). Burnout in health professionals. In S. Ayers, C. McManus, S. Newman, K. Petrie, T. Revenson, & J. Weiman (Eds.), *Cambridge handbook of psychology, health and medicine* (3rd ed.). Cambridge: Cambridge University Press.

Montgomery, A., Panagopoulou, E., Esmail, A., Richards, T., & Maslach, C. (2019). Burnout in healthcare: the case for organisational change. *BMJ, 366*, l4774. https://doi.org/10.1136/bmj.l4774

Montgomery, A., Tordova, I., Baban, A., & Panagopoulou, E. (2013). Improving quality and safety in the hospital: The link between organisational culture, burnout and quality of care. *British Journal of Health Psychology, 18*, 656–662.

Panagioti, M., Panagopoulou, E., Bower, P., Lewith, G., Kontopantelis, E., Chew-Graham, C., et al. (2017). Controlled interventions to reduce burnout in physicians: A systematic review and meta-analysis. *JAMA Internal Medicine, 177*, 195–205. https://doi.org/10.1001/jamainternmed.2016.7674.27918798

Panagopoulou, E., Montgomery, A., & Tsiga, E. (2015). Bringing the Well-being and patient safety research agenda together: Why healthy HPs equal safe patients. *Frontiers in Psychology, 6*, 211. https://doi.org/10.3389/fpsyg.2015.0021

Prins, J. T., van der Heijden, F. M., Hoekstra-Weebers, J. E., Bakker, A. B., van de HBM, W., Jacobs, B., et al. (2009). Burnout, engagement and resident physicians' self-reported errors. *Psychology, Health & Medicine, 14*, 654–666. https://doi.org/10.1080/13548500090331155420183538

Shanafelt, T. D., Balch, C. M., Bechamps, G., Russell, T., Dyrbye, L., Satele, D., et al. (2010). Burnout and medical errors among American surgeons. *Ann Surg, 251*, 995–1000. https://doi.org/10.1097/SLA.0b013e3181bfdab319934755

Shanafelt, T. D., Balch, C. M., Dyrbye, L., Bechamps, G., Russell, T., Satele, D., et al. (2011). Special report: Suicidal ideation among American surgeons. *Archives of Surgery, 146*, 54–62.

Shirom, A., Nirel, N., & Vinokur, A. D. (2006). Overload, autonomy, and burnout as predictors of physicians' quality of care. *Journal of Occupational Health Psychology, 11*, 328–342. https://doi.org/10.1037/1076-8998.11.4.32817059297

Sim, M. R. (2020). The COVID-19 pandemic: Major risks to healthcare and other workers on the front line. *Occupational and Environmental Medicine, 77*, 281–282.

Vahey, D. C., Aiken, L. H., Sloane, D. M., Clarke, S. P., & Vargas, D. (2004). Nurse burnout and patient satisfaction. *Medical Care, 42*(Suppl), II57–II66.

Vela-Bueno, A., Moreno-Jiménez, B., Rodríguez-Muñoz, A., Olavarrieta-Bernardino, S., Fernández-Mendoza, J., de la Cruz-Troca, J. J., et al. (2008). Insomnia and sleep quality among primary care physicians with low and high burnout levels. *Journal of Psychosomatic Research, 64*, 435–442. https://doi.org/10.1016/j.jpsychores.2007.10.01418374744

Williams, W. W., Lu, P. J., O'Halloran, A., Kim, D. K., Grohskopf, L. A., Pilishvili, T., et al. (2017). Surveillance of vaccination coverage among adult populations – United States, 2015. *MMWR Surveillance Summaries, 66*, 1–28.

Zhang, W., Wang, K., Yin, L., Zhao, W. A., Xue, Q. A., Peng, M., et al. (2020). Mental health and psychosocial problems of medical health workers during the COVID-19 epidemic in China. *Psychotherapy and Psychosomatics, 89*, 242–250. https://doi.org/10.1159/000507639

Part I
Linking Organisational Factors, Health Care Worker Well-being, and Patient Outcomes

Chapter 2
Job Strain, Burnout, Wellbeing and Patient Safety in Healthcare Professionals

Daryl B. O'Connor, Louise H. Hall, and Judith Johnson

2.1 Introduction

Over the last three to four decades, there has been a marked increase in media coverage of stress and as a result this has led to increased research and public awareness. Indeed stress is now the most common cause of long-term sick leave and is frequently shown to be a very important factor accounting for in excess of ten million working days lost per annum in the UK (HSE, 2018). In 2017/2018, stress accounted for 44% of all cases of work-related illnesses in the UK (i.e., 595,000 cases). In the United States, the impact of stress is also far reaching, with 66% of Americans reporting that stress is impacting on their physical health and 63% believing the same for their mental health (American Psychological Association, 2012). It is also well established that one of the major sources of stress is associated with one's job. Stress arising from work is known by a range of different labels including occupational stress, job stress, work-related stress, and job strain. As a result a large amount of research has focussed on investigating the effects of work-related stress on a myriad of health, behavioural and occupational outcomes.

Moreover, there is growing evidence that high levels of occupational stress are impacting negatively on health, wellbeing and work-related outcomes in healthcare professionals (e.g., Chang et al., 2006; Louch, O'Hara, Gardner, & O'Connor, 2017;

D. B. O'Connor (✉)
School of Psychology, University of Leeds, Leeds, UK
e-mail: d.b.oconnor@leeds.ac.uk

L. H. Hall
Leeds Institute of Health Sciences, University of Leeds, Leeds, UK

J. Johnson
School of Psychology, University of Leeds, Leeds, UK

Bradford Institute for Health Research, Bradford, UK

© Springer Nature Switzerland AG 2020
A. Montgomery et al. (eds.), *Connecting Healthcare Worker Well-Being, Patient Safety and Organisational Change*, Aligning Perspectives on Health, Safety and Well-Being, https://doi.org/10.1007/978-3-030-60998-6_2

Purcell, Kutash, & Cobb, 2011; Tucker, Weymiller, Cutshall, Rhudy, & Lohse, 2012). Johnson et al. (2018) have recently shown that mental healthcare professionals (HCPs) also report clinical symptoms of psychological distress and burnout. Changes in the organisation and the management of health care provision nationally and internationally, coupled with the nature of medical practice, is likely to have increased the experience of work-related stress in healthcare professionals (Chang et al., 2006; Hall, Johnson, Watt, Tsipa, & O'Connor, 2016; Louch et al., 2017). Elevated levels of occupational stress may also have contributed to the increased prevalence of depression, anxiety and burnout in healthcare professionals (e.g., Adriaenssens, De Gucht, & Maes, 2015; Chang et al., 2006; Singh, Aulak, Mangat, & Aulak, 2016; Woodhead, Northrop, & Edelstein, 2016).

The consequences of work-related stress may be far reaching, not only for the health professionals themselves, but also for the patients within their care. The workload and demands placed on nurses continues to increase and health care organisations are under rising pressure (e.g., Carayon & Gurses, 2008; Gifford, Zammuto, Goodman, & Hill, 2002). Moreover, research has confirmed clear associations between stress and poorer physical and psychological health in nurses together with increased sickness absences, intention to leave and turnover rates, reduced job performance, quality of care and patient safety (e.g., Chang et al., 2006; Heinen et al., 2013). In terms of the latter, a recent daily diary study in hospital nurses found higher levels of chronic stress were associated with poorer perceptions of safety in their hospital wards and being less able to practise safely (Louch et al., 2017). To place in context, in the UK, medical errors are estimated to cost the National Health Service (NHS) over a billion pounds in litigation costs, and £2 billion in additional bed days annually (UK Department of Health, 2000) and it is likely that work-related stress is an important contributing factor. Therefore, there is an urgent need to understand the links between job strain, burnout, wellbeing and patient safety in order to develop effective interventions that can target aspects of the work environment and wellbeing that will help reduce levels of burnout and improve patient safety.

2.2 Work Stress, Patient Safety and Quality of Care

There are a number of psychological models that have dominated the work-related stress area over a long period of time that have attempted to characterise what makes the work environment stressful (e.g., Demerouti, Bakker, Nachreiner, & Schaufeli, 2001; Karasek, 1979; Siegrist, 2002). Of particular note is the job demands-control model or job strain model (Hausser, Mojzisch, Niesl, & Schulz-Hardt, 2010; Heikkila et al., 2013; Karasek, 1979; Van Der Doef & Maes, 1998, 1999). This model incorporates control as a major component in the stress process. The basic axiom of the model is that psychological strain and physical-ill health (and other stress-related outcomes) can be predicted from the synergistic combination of job demands and job control (or decision latitude). The original model argued that a "high strain job" is one characterised by high job demands and low levels of job control (decision latitude). Typical jobs of this type might include being a junior doctor or a nurse in a busy accident and emergency department. A "low strain job" is characterised by low job demand and high levels of decision latitude. Karasek (1979) proposed two fundamental mechanisms underlying the model; the psychological strain and the active learning mechanisms. The former is characterised by the experience of high job demands with simultaneous low levels of latitude over decision-making. The latter is characterised by the experience of high job demands and high levels of decision latitude and is said to promote the development of new behaviour patterns. The model has subsequently been expanded by the addition of social support to form the job demand–control–support model (Johnson & Hall, 1988). Both forms of the model have stimulated considerable research looking at a wide range of physical and psychological outcomes (for reviews see Van Der Doef & Maes, 1998, 1999; de Lange, Taris, Kompier, Houtman, & Bongers, 2003; Hausser et al., 2010; Heikkila et al., 2013).

Relatively early research into stress in health professionals has highlighted the potential links between working in "high strain" work environments and health professional errors and quality of patient care (Firth-Cozens, 1998; O'Connor, O'Connor, White, & Bundred, 2000). For example, it has been argued that high levels of stress in general practice are associated with increased likelihood of clinical mistakes and medical errors (Firth-Cozens; O'Connor et al., 2000). A more recent study by Berland, Natvig, and Gundersen (2008) investigated the effects of work-related stress and patient safety in nurses working in anesthesiology, intensive care and operating rooms (Berland et al., 2008). These authors reported that a demanding work environment together with minimal control and social support from colleagues resulted in increased stress that often negatively impacted on patient safety. Relatedly, in a longitudinal study of hospital physicians, hospital environments with high demands (i.e., social stressors, time pressure and patient demands) were found to directly impact on physician-perceived quality of care (Kramer, Schneider, Spieb, Angerer, & Weigl, 2016). Moreover, the poor care practices then also contributed to increased demands. This study was particularly noteworthy given it was a prospective design with two waves of data collection over a 1-year time lag that utilised cross-lagged path models to test the main hypotheses.

2.3 Job Demands-Resources Model, Burnout and Patient Safety

Another model that has attracted a great deal of empirical investigation is the Job Demand-Resources Model (JD-R; Demerouti et al., 2001). This model extends and improves the JDC model and is particularly relevant to healthcare professionals as it was originally proposed as a model of burnout. The latter is a syndrome consisting of exhaustion, depersonalization and lack of personal accomplishment (Maslach,

1982). Those working in human service occupations (healthcare professionals, social workers, teachers etc.) were assumed to be particularly vulnerable to burnout. However, the concept has since been extended to other occupations, as the core dimensions of exhaustion and disengagement may be found in many professions (Bakker & Demerouti, 2007).

Like the JDC, the JD-R model suggests that stress results from a lack of equilibrium between sets of broadly positive and broadly negative variables. This model focuses on the equilibrium between *job demands* and *resources*. *Job demands* are defined as the 'physical, social, or organizational aspects of the job that require sustained physical and/or psychological (cognitive and emotional) effort or skills and are therefore associated with certain physiological and/or psychological costs' (Bakker & Demerouti, 2007, p. 312). *Job resources*, on the other hand consist of a broad range of aspects of the job that serve to either help the individual to achieve their work goals, help reduce their job demands or facilitate personal growth and development (Bakker & Demerouti, 2007). This may include control and rewards as well as social resources. The model has also been expanded to include personal resources such as optimism and self-efficacy (Xanthopoulou, Bakker, Demerouti, & Schaufeli, 2007).

The model suggests two processes, *the health impairment process* whereby excessive demands may lead to exhaustion and health problems, and the *motivational process* whereby job resources may lead to increased work engagement and performance (Bakker & Demerouti, 2007). A number of studies have now supported these two core processes in relation to psychological burnout and job engagement (e.g., Schaufeli, Leiter, & Maslach, 2009; Xanthopoulou et al., 2007).

In addition to these main effects, the JD-R model, like the JDC model, proposes that interactions between the core variables are also important in predicting strain and motivation. Because of the large number of potential resources and demands, a range of interaction effects are possible whereby specific job resources (control, support, feedback, role clarity etc.) may buffer the impact of different types of demands (Bakker & Demerouti, 2007). Not only may the effects of job resources reduce the negative impact of high demands, but the model also proposes that resources may aid motivation when demands are high.

Moreover, in 2011 a large-scale meta-analysis was published that established clear links between the JD-R model components and different aspects of workplace safety (Nahrgang, Morgeson, & Hofmann, 2011). In particular, they found support for the health impairment process and for the motivational process as mechanisms through which job demands and resources were associated with safety outcomes. Interestingly, these authors also found that across industries, the most consistent job resource was having a supportive work environment and the most consistent job demands were risks and hazards (i.e., perceived risk, level of risk, number of hazards & perceptions of safety) in relation to predicting variability in burnout, engagement, and safety outcomes (i.e., actual accidents & injuries, adverse events and unsafe behaviours). However, this review did not focus on patient safety outcomes or health professionals specifically and the final study included was published in 2010. In addition, therefore, next we review studies that have investigated whether there are links between burnout and patient safety outcomes and also broaden the discussion to include wellbeing.

2.4 Associations Between Healthcare Professionals' Wellbeing and Burnout, and Patient Safety

As outlined earlier, ever increasing numbers of healthcare staff, of all disciplines and across the world, are suffering from high levels of stress, burnout, and poor wellbeing (Gibson et al., 2015; NHS England Survey Coordination Centre, 2018; Reith, 2018). Burnout and poor wellbeing have been cited throughout the literature as contributors to reduced patient safety levels and patient safety incidences (Avery et al., 2012; Salyers et al., 2016; Tawfik et al., 2019; Welp & Manser, 2016). Whilst there has been a wealth of research demonstrating this association exists, the terms burnout and wellbeing are often used interchangeably. This is problematic, because wellbeing and burnout have different causes, symptoms, and potentially differing consequences. Burnout is an effective response to chronic organizational stress, resulting in a 'state of vital exhaustion' (WHO, 2004). Whereas, an individual's wellbeing is affected by all areas of their life, including, but not limited to, their occupation. Poor wellbeing is often characterized by symptoms or diagnoses of mental illnesses (e.g. depression), high levels of stress, and/or a reduced quality of life.

To understand whether it is overall wellbeing, or burnout specifically, that is more strongly associated with patient safety, a systematic review was conducted by Hall et al. (2016). We identified nineteen studies measuring the link between burnout and patient safety, sixteen for wellbeing and patient safety, and eleven measuring both wellbeing and burnout in relation to patient safety. Of those that included a measure of wellbeing (such as quality of life, depression, mental health), the majority (22/27; 82%) found that poorer wellbeing was significantly associated with reduced safety levels (e.g. increased errors, lower ratings of safety). Similarly, within the studies that included a measure of burnout (often the Maslach Burnout Inventory (MBI Maslach et al., 1996)), the majority of these (25/30; 83%) found that higher levels of (at least one subscale of) burnout was significantly associated with decreased safety.

Of particular interest to the question at hand are the eleven studies that measured both burnout and wellbeing. Whilst the majority of these studies (7/11; 64%) found that both variables were significantly associated, in some way, with patient safety, it becomes more complex when you take into account whether self-report or objective measures were used. Of those seven studies that found an association, all bar one used solely self-perceived errors as the patient safety measure. Studies which additionally, or only, used objective measures of safety tell a different story. In these studies, only wellbeing (characterized as stress (Dugan et al., 1996), or depression (Fahrenkopf et al., 2008; Garrouste-Orgeas et al., 2015)) was significantly associated with errors (measured by chart audits). This has implications for the sensitivity of patient safety measures, and may also speak to differences between healthcare professionals' safety *perceptions* versus *behaviours*. It could be that burnt-out HCPs are more likely to perceive their practice as less safe, regardless of actual safety behaviours, due to feelings of low personal accomplishment and exhaustion. Conversely, HCPs with poor wellbeing (e.g. depression) may be more at risk of actual involvement in patient safety incidences, as a consequence of some of the symptoms of poor mental health (e.g. memory and concentration issues, indecisiveness). Given this, future studies should strive to use both subjective and objective measures of safety, alongside measures of wellbeing and burnout, to better understand these nuances.

Since Hall et al.'s (2016) review, four meta-analyses have been published on this topic, allowing effect sizes to be calculated, in addition to describing more recent studies, and expanding the breadth of focus (to include quality of care, professionalism, patient satisfaction, and teamwork) (Panagioti et al., 2018; Salyers et al., 2016; Welp & Manser, 2016). Welp and Manser's meta-analysis of 25 studies measuring wellbeing and patient safety reported a significant association in the expected direction, in the majority of studies, with effect sizes ranging between $OR = 1.09$ and $OR = 8.3$. However, burnout and wellbeing were conflated, with most studies measuring burnout (using the MBI), and not overall wellbeing. Salyers et al.'s (2016) meta-analysis focused solely on burnout, and included measures of quality of care in addition to safety. The 40 articles investigating safety yielded an overall small but significant relationship in the expected direction ($r = -0.23$), despite high levels of heterogeneity. Interestingly, a stronger relationship was found between burnout with *perceptions* of safety ($r = -0.28$), rather than incidents ($r = -0.16$), which has also since been suggested in a survey study amongst General Practitioners in the United Kingdom (Hall, Johnson, Watt, & O'Connor, 2019). Panagioti et al.'s (2018) meta-analysis reported that both physician burnout, and physician depression/emotional distress were associated with being twice as likely to be involved in a patient safety incident. However, similarly to Salyers et al., burnout was only found to be significantly associated with *physician-reported* incidents ($OR = 2.07$), and not for *system-recorded* incidents ($OR = 1.00$). This sub-analysis was not reported for depression/emotional distress.

Considering all of the aforementioned reviews, it is likely that both wellbeing and burnout are important for patient safety. Potential variances between poor wellbeing and burnout may manifest themselves in the differences between perceived safety behaviours and actual incidents, as touched upon throughout this section. Additionally, there is some evidence to suggest that suffering from both burnout and poor wellbeing (specifically depression), presents an even higher risk of making an error than suffering from one or the other (de Oliveira et al., 2013).

An important limitation of the literature is that the majority of studies within these reviews utilize cross-sectional designs. Thus, causality cannot be inferred. Whilst the previous section of this chapter outlines how job strain, job demands and resources etc. could lead to poor patient safety (through increasing stress, depression, and burnout), the reverse is also known to be true, with a breadth of literature on the 'second victim' effect (Seys et al., 2013; Wu, 2012). This gives rise to the notion that burnout, (poor) wellbeing, and patient safety are interconnected in a 'vicious cycle', whereby increases in one leads to the likelihood of increases in another, regardless of which occurred first.

A couple of longitudinal studies attempted to overcome this limitation. West et al. (2006) reported that burnout and error had a circular relationship when measured at three-month intervals. However, whilst self-reported errors predicted subsequent quality of life and screening positive for depression, the reverse was not found to be true. Welp, Meier, and Manser (2016) also measured outcomes at three-month intervals and suggested that clinician burnout leads to reduced interpersonal and cognitive-behavioural teamwork, which then leads to decreased clinician-rated patient safety. Whilst this is a start, it is evident that more prospective studies are needed to better understand the relationships between healthcare professional wellbeing, burnout, and patient safety outcomes. What is clear, however, is that there is indeed a relationship between these variables. As such, it is imperative that healthcare organisations intervene to improve employee wellbeing and burnout levels, for both their workers' and their patients' health and safety.

2.5 Interventions

The final section of the chapter considers research that has tested interventions to reduce burnout, work related stress, and improve wellbeing in the health professional context. Interventions for burnout are usually split into those which are targeted at the 'individual' or 'person' level and those which are focused on organisational-change (Awa, Plaumann, & Walter, 2010; Johnson et al., 2018). They can also be understood as being 'primary', 'secondary' or 'tertiary' in their focus. Primary interventions are those which aim to reduce work stressors; secondary interventions are those which aim to help participants cope with work stressors and tertiary interventions are those which treat individuals who are already suffering with stress due to work (Maslach & Goldberg, 1998). While these taxonomies are distinct there is some overlap, as organisation-directed interventions are often primary interventions, whereas person-directed interventions are often secondary or tertiary interventions.

In healthcare settings, person-directed interventions have included stress-management workshops and mindfulness classes (Goldhagen, Kingsolver, Stinnett, & Rosdahl, 2015; Regehr, Glancy, Pitts, & LeBlanc, 2014). Conceptually, these interventions are context-free; they view workers as stressed individuals and seek to remediate their stress by increasing their capacity to cope. Organisation-directed interventions, in contrast, view workers in context. They conceptualise burnt-out professionals as individuals in environments which are generating stress. Consistent with this view, they seek to reduce the stress which the work environment is causing. In healthcare settings, organisation-directed interventions have included improving inter-professional communications and the introduction of peer support groups (Dreison et al., 2016; Linzer et al., 2015).

Recent years have seen a growing research literature into the evidence-base for burnout interventions in healthcare settings, and three significant reviews of this literature have been published since 2016. The first focused only on interventions in doctors (West, Dyrbye, Erwin, & Shanafelt, 2016). It meta-analysed 15 randomised trials and 37 cohort studies, including 3630 physicians altogether. Results suggested that overall, burnout interventions were effective and decreased burnout on average by 10%, with mean levels dropping from 54% before the intervention to 44% afterwards. The second also focused on studies in doctors. It included 20 randomised trials including a total of 1550 physicians, and similar to the previous review it suggested that overall these resulted in 'small and significant' reductions in burnout (Panagioti et al., 2017). In a departure from the previous two, the third review focused on mental health staff and included studies conducted in all healthcare disciplines (Dreison et al., 2016). It included 13 randomised trials and 14 cohort studies comprising 1894 participants in total, and reported that on average, burnout interventions produced small but significant reductions (Dreison et al., 2016). Taken together, these three reviews suggest that burnout interventions in healthcare professionals are effective, but the level of effectiveness is limited and there is a need to understand how they can be improved.

The issue of intervention type is contentious. Due to increasing demand on healthcare services combined with limited resources, there has been steadily increasing pressure on healthcare professionals to accomplish more with less (Liu, Goryakin, Maeda, Bruckner, & Scheffler, 2017). There is also a growing global healthcare worker shortage, which has led to increased reports of under-staffing and rota gaps in services (Aluttis, Bishaw, & Frank, 2014; RCP, 2018). In this context, many health professionals have rejected person-directed interventions, suggesting they shift blame from government and senior leadership to individual workers (Balme, Gerada, & Page, 2015; Montgomery, Panagopoulou, Esmail, Richards, & Maslach, 2019; Oliver, 2017). Despite this, person-directed interventions have been the most commonly tested in the research literature. For example, in the review by West et al. (2016), person-directed interventions comprised 80% (12 out of 15) of interventions tested in the randomised trials, and 54% (20 out of 37) of the cohort studies. Similarly, in the review by Panagioti and colleagues, 60% of the tested interventions were person-directed (2017). In fact, the only review which suggested that a majority of interventions (70.4%) were organisation-directed was that conducted by Dreison et al. (2016). This variation could be due to an artefact of how 'organisation-directed' interventions were conceptualised. For example, while West et al. (2016) categorised communication training interventions as a form of person-directed intervention, Dreison et al. (2016) grouped these together with other professional training interventions, which they considered to be organisation-directed interventions.

The issue of which type of intervention is most effective is also somewhat controversial. For example, both reviews in doctors provide some indication to suggest that organisation-directed interventions may be more effective than person-directed interventions for reducing burnout. West et al. (2016) reported that organisation-directed interventions had a significantly stronger impact upon reducing overall burnout than person-directed interventions, although there were no significant differences when specific facets of burnout were examined (emotional exhaustion and depersonalisation). Panagioti et al. (2017) only examined the emotional exhaustion facet of burnout. They found that organisation-directed interventions resulted in medium significant reductions in burnout and they were significantly more effective for reducing burnout than person-directed interventions, which only produced small significant effects. In contrast, however, Dreison et al. (2016) found that person-directed interventions were more effective than those targeted at the organisation-level.

These contrasting findings could be misleading and caused by the overly-broad grouping of intervention types. For example, when Dreison and colleagues (2018) broke down the category of organisation-directed interventions into training interventions and non-training interventions, their results changed. Training interventions were the most common subtype of organisation-directed interventions in their study (comprising 44.4%) and when they separated these out, they found that training interventions were in fact more effective for reducing overall burnout scores than person-directed interventions. These findings highlight the limitations in our current approach to conceptualising burnout interventions and indicate that a shift in approach could be needed if more effective interventions are to be developed.

A paradigm shift to this effect is now becoming visible in the literature with researchers calling for a renewed focus on ameliorating the known causes of burnout, rather than rolling out one-size-fits-all programmes (Johnson et al., 2018; Montgomery et al., 2019). This approach requires innovative thinking that transcends the traditional categories of 'organisation-directed' and 'person-directed' interventions. For example, drawing on recent research literature, Montgomery et al. (2019) have called for approaches which consider all aspects of work life—workload, control, reward, community, fairness and values—and consider the 'fit' between individual workers and their workplace on these areas. Similarly, Hall et al. (2017) sought to generate new solutions for burnout in General Practitioners using a focus group design. General Practitioners in the study identified a range of potential interventions, ranging from the use of strategies to improve support from patients, to increasing opportunity for regular tea and coffee breaks. Several of these did not conform easily to the categories of 'person-directed' or 'organisation-directed' interventions, but were instead practical solutions which could be viewed as a mixture of the two. Interestingly, however, they could be interpreted in terms of the JD-R model, with many of the suggested interventions aiming to increase support from colleagues or patients. While reduction in job demands was discussed, General Practitioners viewed this as generally being out of their personal control, and something that could only be affected by the higher organisational levels of UK healthcare.

> **Key Messages for Researchers**
> There is an urgent need to understand the links between the work environment, burnout and patient safety.
> The need to measure healthcare professional wellbeing (i.e. mental health, quality of life, stress) *and* burnout (an affective response to occupational stress), alongside subjective *and* objective measures of safety, is evident: It may be that burnout is only associated with *perceived* safety, whereas wellbeing may be more strongly associated with *actual* safety behaviours.
> Definitions of 'organisational' and 'individual' interventions varies; clearer definitions may enhance the consistency of results between studies.
>
> **Key Messages for Healthcare Delivery**
> Stress arising from the work environment can impact on the health and wellbeing of healthcare professionals *and* can lead to reduced quality of patient care and increased medical errors
> Healthcare organisations should consider what they could do to improve employee wellbeing and prevent burnout, with implications being evident for patient safety outcomes.
> Overall, interventions to reduce burnout in healthcare professionals are effective, supporting their general use in healthcare settings.

References

Adriaenssens, J., De Gucht, V., & Maes, S. (2015). Causes and consequences of occupational stress in emergency nurses, a longitudinal study. *Journal of Nursing Management, 23*, 346–358.

Aluttis, C., Bishaw, T., & Frank, M. W. (2014). The workforce for health in a globalized context – Global shortages and international migration. *Global Health Action, 7*, 23611.

American Psychological Association. (2012). *Stress in America survey.* Retrieved March 25, 2014, from http://www.apa.org/news/press/releases/stress/2012/impact.aspx.

Avery, T., Barber, N., Ghaleb, M., Franklin, B. D., Armstrong, S., Crowe, S., et al. (2012). *Investigating the prevalence and causes of prescribing errors in general practice.* London: The General Medical Council: PRACtICe Study.

Awa, W. L., Plaumann, M., & Walter, U. (2010). Burnout prevention: A review of intervention programs. *Patient Education and Counseling, 78*, 184–190.

Bakker, A. B., & Demerouti, E. (2007). The job demands-resources model: State of the art. *Journal of Managerial Psychology, 22*, 309–328.

Balme, E., Gerada, C., & Page, L. (2015). Doctors need to be supported, not trained in resilience. *British Medical Journal, 351*, h4709.

Berland, A., Natvig, G. K., & Gundersen, D. (2008). Patient safety and job-related stress: A focus group study. *Intensive and Critical Care Nursing, 24*, 90–97.

Carayon, P., & Gurses, A. P. (2008). Nursing workload and patient safety—A human factors engineering perspective. In R. Hughes (Ed.), *Patient safety and quality: An evidence–based handbook for nurses [internet].* Agency for Healthcare Research and Quality: Rockville, MD. Available from http://archive.ahrq.gov/professionals/clinicians-providers/resources/nursing/resources/nurseshdbk/CarayonP_NWPS.pdf

Chang, E. M., Daly, J. W., Hancock, K. M., Bidewell, J., Johnson, A., Lambert, V. A., et al. (2006). The relationships among workplace stressors, coping methods, demographic characteristics, and health in Australian nurses. *Journal of Professional Nursing, 22*, 30–38.

de Lange, A. H., Taris, T. W., Kompier, M. A., Houtman, I. L., & Bongers, P. M. (2003). "The very best of the millennium": Longitudinal research and the demand-control-(support) model. *Journal of Occupational Health Psychology, 8*, 282–305.

de Oliveira Jr, G. S., Chang, R., Fitzgerald, P. C., Almeida, M. D., Castro-Alves, L. S., Ahmad, S., et al. (2013). The prevalence of burnout and depression and their association with adherence to safety and practice standards: A survey of United States anesthesiology trainees. *Anesthesia & Analgesia, 117*, 182–193.

Demerouti, E., Bakker, A. B., Nachreiner, F., & Schaufeli, W. B. (2001). The job demands-resources model of burnout. *Journal of Applied Psychology, 86*, 499–512.

Dreison, K. C., Luther, L., Bonfils, K. A., Sliter, M. T., McGrew, J. H., & Salyers, M. P. (2016). Job burnout in mental health providers: A meta-analysis of 35 years of intervention research. *Journal of Occupational Health Psychology, 23*, 18–30.

Dugan, J., Lauer, E., Bouquot, Z., Dutro, B. K., Smith, M., & Widmeyer, G. (1996). Stressful nurses: The effect on patient outcomes. *Journal of Nursing Care Quality, 10*, 46–58.

Fahrenkopf, A. M., Sectish, T. C., Barger, L. K., Sharek, P. J., Lewin, D., Chiang, V. W., et al. (2008). Rates of medication errors among depressed and burnt out residents: Prospective cohort study. *British Medical Jounal, 336*, 488–491.

Firth-Cozens, J. (1998). Individual and organisational predictors of depression in general practitioners. *British Journal of General Practice, 48*, 1647–1651.

Garrouste-Orgeas, M., Perrin, M., Soufir, L., Vesin, A., Blot, F., Maxime, V., et al. (2015). The Iatroref study: Medical errors are associated with symptoms of depression in ICU staff but not burnout or safety culture. *Intensive Care Medicine, 41*, 273–284.

Gibson, J., Checkland, K., Coleman, A., Hann, M., McCall, R., Spooner, S., et al. (2015). *Eighth national GP worklife survey*. Manchester: Policy Research Unit in Commissioning and the Healthcare System Manchester Centre for Health Economics, University of Manchester.

Gifford, B. D., Zammuto, R. F., Goodman, E. A., & Hill, K. S. (2002). The relationship between hospital unit culture and nurses' quality of work life/practitioner application. *Journal of Healthcare Management, 47*, 13–25.

Goldhagen, B. E., Kingsolver, K., Stinnett, S. S., & Rosdahl, J. A. (2015). Stress and burnout in residents: Impact of mindfulness-based resilience training. *Advances in Medical Education and Practice, 6*, 525.

Hall, L. H., Johnson, J., Heyhoe, J., Watt, I., Anderson, K., & O'Connor, D. B. (2017). Strategies to improve general practitioner Well-being: Findings from a focus group study. *Family Practice, 35*, 511–516.

Hall, L. H., Johnson, J., Watt, I., & O'Connor, D. B. (2019). Association of GP wellbeing and burnout with patient safety in UK primary care: A cross-sectional survey. *British Journal of General Practice, 69*, e507–e514.

Hall, L. H., Johnson, J., Watt, I., Tsipa, A., & O'Connor, D. B. (2016). Healthcare staff wellbeing, burnout, and patient safety: A systematic review. *PLoS One, 11*(7).

Hausser, J. A., Mojzisch, A., Niesl, M., & Schulz-Hardt, S. (2010). Ten years on: A review of recent research on the job demand-control (-support) model and psychological wellbeing. *Work & Stress, 24*, 1–35.

Health and Safety Executive. (2018). *Work related stress, anxiety and depression statistics in Great Britain 2017*. London: Crown Copyright.

Heikkila, K., Fransson, E. I., Nyberg, S. T., Zins, M., Westerlund, H., Westerholm, P., et al. (2013). Job strain and health-related lifestyle: Findings from an individual-participant meta-analysis of 118,000 working adults. *American Journal of Public Health, 103*, 2090–2097.

Heinen, M. M., van Achterberg, T., Schwendimann, R., Zander, B., Matthews, A., Kózka, M., et al. (2013). Nurses' intention to leave their profession: A cross sectional observational study in 10 European countries. *International Journal of Nursing Studies, 50*, 174–184.

Johnson, J. V., & Hall, E. M. (1988). Job strain, work place social support and cardiovascular disease: A cross-sectional study of a random sample of the working population. *American Journal of Public Health, 78*, 1336–1342.

Johnson, J., Hall, L. H., Berzins, K., Baker, J., Melling, K., & Thompson, C. (2018). Mental healthcare staff wellbeing and burnout: A narrative review of trends, causes, implications, and recommendations for future interventions. *International Journal of Mental Health Nursing, 27*, 20–32.

Karasek, R. A. (1979). Job demands, job decision latitude and mental strain: Implications for job redesign. *Administration Science Quarterly, 24*, 285–307.

Kramer, T., Schneider, A., Spieb, E., Angerer, P., & Weigl, M. (2016). Associations between job demands, work-related strain and perceived quality of care: A longitudinal study among hospital physicians. *International Journal of Quality in Health Care, 28*, 824–829.

Linzer, M., Poplau, S., Grossman, E., Varkey, A., Yale, S., Williams, E., et al. (2015). A cluster randomized trial of interventions to improve work conditions and clinician burnout in primary care: Results from the healthy work place (HWP) study. *Journal of General Internal Medicine, 30*, 1105–1111.

Liu, J. X., Goryakin, Y., Maeda, A., Bruckner, T., & Scheffler, R. J. (2017). Global health workforce labor market projections for 2030. *Human Resources for Health, 15*, 11.

Louch, G., O'Hara, J., Gardner, P. H., & O'Connor, D. B. (2017). A daily diary approach to the examination of chronic stress, daily hassles and safety perceptions in hospital nursing. *International Journal of Behavioral Medicine, 24*, 946–956.

Maslach, C. (1982). Understanding burnout: Definitional issues in analyzing a complex phenomenon. In W. S. Paine (Ed.), *Job stress and burnout* (pp. 29–40). Beverley Hills, CA: Sage.

Maslach, C., & Goldberg, J. (1998). Prevention of burnout: New perspectives. *Applied and Preventive Psychology, 7*(1), 63–74.

Maslach, C., Jackson, S. E., & Leiter, M. P. (1996). *Maslach burnout inventory manual*. Mountain View, CA: CPP and Davies-Black.

Montgomery, A., Panagopoulou, E., Esmail, A., Richards, T., & Maslach, C. (2019). Burnout in healthcare: The case for organisational change. *British Medical Journal, 366*, l4774.

Nahrgang, J. D., Morgeson, F. P., & Hofmann, D. A. (2011). Safety at work: A meta-analytic investigation of the link between job demands, job resources, burnout, engagement, and safety outcomes. *Journal of Applied Psychology, 96*, 71–94.

NHS England Survey Coordination Centre. (2018). *NHS Staff Survey 2018: National results briefing*. National Health Service England. Retrieved from https://www.nhsstaffsurveys.com/Caches/Files/ST18_National%20briefing_FINAL_20190225.pdf

O'Connor, D. B., O'Connor, R. C., White, B. L., & Bundred, P. E. (2000). The effect of job strain on British general practitioners' mental health. *Journal of Mental Health, 9*, 637–654.

Oliver, D. (2017). David Oliver: When "resilience" becomes a dirty word. *British Medical Journal, 358*, j3604. https://doi.org/10.1136/bmj.j3604%J

Panagioti, M., Geraghty, K., Johnson, J., Zhou, A., Panagopoulou, E., Chew-Graham, C., et al. (2018). Association between physician burnout and patient safety, professionalism, and patient satisfaction: A systematic review and meta-analysis. *Journal of the American Medical Association: Internal Medicine, 178*, 1317–1331.

Panagioti, M., Panagopoulou, E., Bower, P., Lewith, G., Kontopantelis, E., Chew-Graham, C., et al. (2017). Controlled interventions to reduce burnout in physicians: A systematic review and meta-analysis. *Journal of the American Medical Association: Internal Medicine, 177*, 195–205.

Purcell, S. R., Kutash, M., & Cobb, S. (2011). The relationship between nurses' stress and nurse staffing factors in a hospital setting. *Journal of Nursing Management, 19*, 714–720.

RCP. (2018). *Focus on physicians: 2017–18 census (UK consultants and higher specialty trainees)*. Retrieved August 15, 2019, from https://www.rcplondon.ac.uk/projects/outputs/focus-physicians-2017-18-census-uk-consultants-and-higher-specialty-trainees

Regehr, C., Glancy, D., Pitts, A., & LeBlanc, V. (2014). Interventions to reduce the consequences of stress in physicians: A review and meta-analysis. *The Journal of Nervous and Mental Disease, 202*, 353–359.

Reith, T. P. J. C. (2018). Burnout in United States healthcare professionals: A narrative review. *Cureus, 10*(12), e3681.

Salyers, M. P., Bonfils, K. A., Luther, L., Firmin, R. L., White, D. A., Adams, E. L., et al. (2016). The relationship between professional burnout and quality and safety in healthcare: A meta-analysis. *Journal of General Internal Medicine, 32*, 475–482.

Schaufeli, W. B., Leiter, M. P., & Maslach, C. (2009). Burnout: 35 years of research and practice. *Career Development International, 14*, 204–220.

Seys, D., Wu, A. W., Gerven, E. V., Vleugels, A., Euwema, M., Panella, M., et al. (2013). Health care professionals as second victims after adverse events: A systematic review. *Evaluation & the Health Professions, 3*, 135–162.

Siegrist, J. (2002). Effort-reward imbalance at work and health. *Historical and Current Perspectives on Stress and Health, 2*, 261–291.

Singh, P., Aulak, D. S., Mangat, S., & Aulak, M. (2016). Systematic review: Factors contributing to burnout in dentistry. *Occupational Medicine, 66*, 27–31.

Tawfik, D. S., Scheid, A., Profit, J., Shanfelt, T., Trockel, M., Adair, K. C., et al. (2019). Evidence relating health care provider burnout and quality of care: A systematic review and meta-analysis. *Annals of Internal Medicine, 171*, 555–567.

Tucker, S. J., Weymiller, A. J., Cutshall, S. M., Rhudy, L. M., & Lohse, C. M. (2012). Stress ratings and health promotion practices among RNs: A case for action. *Journal of Nursing Administration, 42*, 282–292.

UK Department of Health (2000). An Organisation with a Memory: Report of an Expert Group on Learning from Adverse Events in the NHS Chaired by theChief Medical Officer: The Stationery Office London.

Van Der Doef, M., & Maes, S. (1998). The job demand-control (−support) model and physical health outcomes: A review of the strain and buffer hypotheses. *Psychology and Health, 13*, 909–936.

Van Der Doef, M., & Maes, S. (1999). The job demands-control (−support) model and psychological Well-being: A review of 20 years of empirical research. *Work & Stress, 13*, 87–114.

Welp, A., & Manser, T. (2016). Integrating teamwork, clinician occupational well-being and patient safety–development of a conceptual framework based on a systematic review. *BMC Health Services Research, 16*, 281. https://doi.org/10.1186/s12913-016-1535-y

Welp, A., Meier, L. L., & Manser, T. (2016). The interplay between teamwork, clinicians' emotional exhaustion, and clinician-rated patient safety: A longitudinal study. *Critical Care, 20*(1), 110. https://doi.org/10.1186/s13054-016-1282-9

West, C. P., Dyrbye, L. N., Erwin, P. J., & Shanafelt, T. D. (2016). Interventions to prevent and reduce physician burnout: A systematic review and meta-analysis. *The Lancet, 388*, 2272–2281.

West, C. P., Huschka, M. M., Novotny, P. J., Sloan, J. A., Kolars, J. C., Habermann, T. M., et al. (2006). Association of perceived medical errors with resident distress and empathy: A prospective longitudinal study. *Journal of the American Medical Association, 296*(9), 1071–1078.

Woodhead, E. L., Northrop, L., & Edelstein, B. (2016). Stress, social support, and burnout among long-term care nursing staff. *Journal of Applied Gerontology, 35*(1), 84–105.

World Health Organisation. (2004). *International statistical classification of diseases and related health problems* (Vol. 1). Geneva: World Health Organisation.

Wu, A. W. (2012). Medical error: The second victim. *British Journal of Hospital Medicine (London), 73*(10), C146–C148.

Xanthopoulou, D., Bakker, A. B., Demerouti, E., & Schaufeli, W. B. (2007). The role of personal resources in the job demands-resources model. *International Journal of Stress Management, 14*, 121–141.

Chapter 3
Missed Nursing Care: The Impact on Patients, Nurses and Organisations

Marcia Kirwan and Anne Matthews

3.1 Introduction

Rationing of healthcare is a subject that prompts political debate, both within healthcare professions and amongst members of the public. The term 'rationing' is one that is, largely, morally charged, and is viewed inherently negatively overall, with some arguing that 'rationing', of any kind, is never an acceptable option in healthcare. Others suggest that rationing is justifiable in many cases, and ultimately inevitable due to limited resources. Few would argue that in contemporary societies where healthcare needs are many, and treatment options vast, there is a need to control overall costs, to consider the costs of choices made, and to use available resources for the benefit of both the individual and society. Balancing limited resources to benefit those in greatest need is a challenge for governments and professionals alike. How costs and resources in healthcare are controlled or rationed can be controversial and may be subject to intense public scrutiny. It seems that an equilibrium between limited resources and infinite need is increasingly difficult to achieve, with rapid advancements in treatments, technology and care approaches occurring in a context of changing (ageing) demographics and disease patterns.

Definitions of rationing in healthcare differ widely, with suggestions that the term should only be applied in situations where absolute scarcity exists, such as organs for transplant i.e. organs are scarce, therefore a list is compiled based on compatibility and urgency, and available organs are allocated to the most compatible patient in the most urgent need. Others suggest that rationing takes place around the allocation of most medicines and treatments. This might involve decisions to choose one

---

M. Kirwan (✉) · A. Matthews
School of Nursing, Psychotherapy and Community Health, Dublin City University, Dublin, Ireland
e-mail: marcia.kirwan@dcu.ie

treatment option, rather than another, or to give a particular expensive medication to one patient, but not another. This definition is less palatable overall, with rationing linked to access, to insurance related eligibility, to cost, to restrictions or to waiting lists, and decisions around rationing linked to poverty, race or other forms of discrimination (Bauchner, 2019). Tilburt and Cassel (2013) categorise the former as justifiable rationing where the process ensures organs, blood products or other scarce life-saving resources are distributed to maximise benefit and to patients in greatest need. However they describe the latter as a de facto form of rationing linked to cost and distribution of resources and treatments, suggesting that where costs are curtailed, rationing is an inevitable outcome. The concept of de facto rationing contradicts the view that rationing exists only where explicit decisions to withhold, supported by policy or administrative decisions, are made. Nonetheless, de facto rationing as an outcome of cost containment or resource shortages in healthcare, may in fact be an example of a less explicit, and less visible, form of rationing.

A relative latecomer to the discussion on rationing in healthcare is the rationing of nursing care. This is an example of a less explicit and less visible mechanism for rationing of care. Rationing of nursing care is an implicit process where nurses in direct care delivery make practice-level (often in-the-moment) decisions about which aspects of care it is possible to provide, and which can be left undone or delayed due to lack of resources, frequently nursing staff (Jones, Hamilton, & Murry, 2015; Schubert, Glass, Clarke, Schaffert-Witvliet, & De Geest, 2007). This could equally be seen as the result of de facto healthcare rationing, where higher-level decisions made concerning the nursing workforce (e.g. nursing numbers, skill mix, education levels, salaries etc.), as well as organisational structures and processes, such as intensification and shorter lengths of stay, result in inadequate (or incomplete) nursing care provision at the bedside. It might be argued, based on patterns of nursing care rationed, that such decisions are less 'in-the-moment' and more a result of culturally acceptable omissions, but this point further supports the implicit nature of this form of healthcare rationing. Srulovici and Drach-Zahavy (2017) highlight that when faced with decisions about which care can be provided and which omitted, nurses frequently make decisions based on acceptable care standards within their workplaces. For instance where some aspects of care are deemed less important than others, it is likely that care will be missed if time is short. Unlike other forms of healthcare rationing, the rationing of nursing care is a phenomenon which remains largely invisible to everyone except the nurse who makes the decision. This means that it is likely the same aspects of patient care will be missed repeatedly by different nurses.

Nurses are key players in the delivery of patient care and make up the largest number of healthcare workers across all healthcare systems. They are frequently seen as coordinators of care in both acute and non-acute settings, and are the conduit through which inter-professional endeavours are planned and realised in the provision of patient care. Nurses therefore, due to their proximity to the patient, are somewhat uniquely placed to influence the quality and safety of care provision, and are often the last link in the chain of delivery of care. Nonetheless, when a nurse has more necessary patient care to provide, than time or resources will allow, it is inevitable that some care, or aspects of care, will be omitted, either consciously or unconsciously. Such missed, rationed, undone or unfinished care is commonly associated with insufficient resources or levels of support, as a result of which individual nurses, overwhelmed by circumstances, make in-the-moment decisions about which patient care is urgently needed and which can be left undone (Harvey et al., 2016). These decisions can be seen over time to become patterned and perhaps accepted, whereby care becomes compromised on a more sustained basis. This acknowledged contemporary experience, and the resultant care deficit, has become a focus for nurse researchers over the last 20 years and should be a cause of concern to patients, nurses and organisations. Missed or implicitly rationed nursing care leaves patients vulnerable to reduced quality of overall care and at greater risk of adverse outcomes, including falls, infections, medication errors, pressure ulcers and higher in-patient mortality (Ausserhofer et al., 2013; Kalisch, Tschannen, & Lee, 2012; Lucero, Lake, & Aiken, 2010; Schubert et al., 2008; Schubert, Clarke, Aiken, & de Geest, 2012). Additionally it leaves nurses vulnerable to adverse personal outcomes, and therefore their organisations may also be exposed to adverse outcomes.

Varying terms have been used to describe the phenomenon of implicitly rationed, missed or incomplete nursing care. The diverse definitions put forward by researchers, have led to a level of uncertainty (Jones et al., 2015), and may have obscured the extent of the problem over time. While slight conceptual differences exist, and different tools are used to measure the concepts, it seems incontrovertible that the concepts described variously as missed nursing care, nursing care left undone or implicitly rationed care all aim to describe necessary patient care which remains undone or incomplete, and that this is reported in those studies to be due to lack of resources or time. Researchers note that nurses across all health systems identify this problem in their practice, with studies finding that between 55 and 98% of nurses report that necessary work remains undone by them at the end of a shift due to lack of time (Jones et al., 2015). There are associated ethical aspects of missed care, concerned with how nurses make decisions around which patient care should be prioritised and which can be left undone (Suhonen & Scott, 2018; Vryonides et al., 2018). Within this chapter, we will track the emergence of the problem over the last 20 years, with reference to outcomes for patients, nurses and organisations. We will consider how it might be addressed, monitored and managed within health services in order to minimise the impact on patients, nurses and organisations.

3.2 The Emergence of the Missed Nursing Care Phenomenon

The International Hospital Outcomes Research Consortium (IHORC) first highlighted the issue of incomplete nursing care as a threat to care quality (Aiken et al., 2001) and described it as *nursing care left undone*. That study used a cross sectional approach to primarily examine the work environment of nurses and nurses' assessment of quality of care. It incorporated a list of what the researchers described as necessary nursing tasks. Nurses were asked to report if any of this work remained undone at the end of their most recent shift due to lack of time. Most frequently nurses reported that oral care, skin care, communication, care and discharge planning and patient education were missed. This University of Pennsylvania-led research highlighted this previously unknown phenomenon and reported its prevalence amongst nurses across the state of Pennsylvania, alongside similar results from Canada and Germany. The origins of the tasks included in the list are not clear from the study reports but would seem to have originated through focus groups which examined care quality (Jones et al., 2015). Despite this, it is beyond doubt that this early work raised a hitherto unknown, but pervasive, problem for the nursing profession and that subsequent similar analysis revealed its consistent presence and impact on patient, nurse and organisational outcomes. In later iterations of this survey, care most frequently missed included medication administration, and patient surveillance.

In 2005 Maria Schubert first explored the related concept of 'rationing of nursing care' in a study involving nurses in Switzerland (Schubert et al. 2005). In this work researchers found, similarly to IHORC findings, that nursing care provision was adversely affected by time constraints and poor staffing. Nurses found themselves having to ration care to patients because they ran out of time. Implicit rationing was defined by these researchers as: *'the withholding of, or failure to carry out, necessary nursing measures for patients due to a lack of nursing resources (staffing, skill mix, time)'*. In the absence of an instrument to measure implicitly rationed care, little was known about the extent or the associated outcomes. The Basel Extent of Rationing of Nursing Care (BERNCA) instrument was developed and validated (Schubert et al., 2007) to address this deficit. See Table 3.1 for an abbreviated example of items included. The researchers considered that implicit rationing occurs within the process of care when nursing resources are not sufficient to provide the care considered to be necessary for all patients. The conceptual framework developed takes into account organisational variables (including policy, budget, structures and culture), the nurse practice environment, the philosophy of care and both patient and nurse variables. Nurse decision-making around implicit rationing takes place within the context of all these variables, with resultant outcomes for both patients and nurses.

A third measure of this concept of missed or undone nursing care emerged from research carried out by a team led by Beatrice Kalisch at the University of Michigan (Kalisch and Williams, 2009, Kalisch, Landstrom, & Sue Hinshaw, 2009). Through focus groups with nurses a tool was developed where necessary nursing work was listed and nurses were asked to indicate how frequently these items had been missed. Arguably, this research, and the naming of the phenomenon as 'missed nursing care', for the first time tried to look at reasons that care might be missed. In the MISSCARE Survey instrument nurses were provided with an inventory of nursing care activities, and asked to identify which were missed. In Part B they were asked to

Table 3.1 BERNCA (Schubert et al., 2007): Examples of abbreviated items

1. **Activities of daily living e.g. Provision of assistance or supervision for:**
   - Bathing/skin care/hygiene
   - Oral/dental hygiene
   - Nutritional needs
   - Mobilization/changing positions
   - Toileting
2. **Caring-support:**
   - Emotional or psychosocial support of patients or their families
3. **Rehabilitation/education:**
   - Rehabilitation care
   - Patient or family education
   - Discharge preparation
4. **Monitoring-safety e.g Adequate attention to:**
   - Vital signs
   - Cognitively impaired patients
   - Physician delays
   - Responding to patient calls
   - HS and hygiene
5. **Documentation**
   - Review patient documentation
   - Update of patient care plans
   - Documentation of care provided

Table 3.2 MISSCARE instrument (Kalisch & Williams, 2009): Examples of included items

- Patient ambulation/repositioning
- Assessing response to medication and/or treatment
- Patient hygiene/mouth care/skin care
- Patient education
- Timely PRN medication
- Full documentation of care
- Patient nutrition/fluid balance monitoring
- On time medications
- Timely response to requests for help
- Emotional support/communication with patient and/or family
- IV/central line care
- Preparation for discharge
- Vital signs/blood sugar monitoring
- Reassessment of patient need/care planning
- Hand washing

Table 3.3 MISSCARE instrument: Abbreviated examples of items measuring reasons for missed care

1. Communication
- Tension, communication breakdown, or lack of support within the nursing team
- Lack of communication regarding care not completed
- Tension, communication breakdown, or lack of support linked to medical staff, or other professionals or departments
- Inadequate communication between shifts
- Unbalanced patient allocation to nursing staff

2. Material resources
- Supplies/equipment not available
- Supplies/equipment not functioning properly
- Medications unavailable

3. Labour resources
- Unexpected changes in patient number and/or acuity
- Urgent patient situations
- Inadequate number of nursing staff
- Inadequate number of other personnel (e.g., nursing assistants, technicians, etc.)

estimate the contribution of potential reasons to that care being missed. See example of items included in MISSCARE Survey Table 3.2 and 3.3.

A review by Jones et al. (2015) which examined all three measures of missed or rationed care confirmed that care most likely to be missed across all three conceptualisations can be categorised as emotional or psychological care rather than physiological. This includes patient support, communication and education along with care coordination and planning and discharge planning. In other studies ambulation of patients is frequently missed (Friese, Kalisch, & Lee, 2013; Kalisch, Tschannen, & Lee, 2011). Care with obvious immediate or short term outcomes is more likely to be carried out. The adverse outcomes associated with missed psychological support are unlikely to be immediate, and notably less likely to undergo clinical audit. The time needed to provide this care is not easily predicted, unlike in the case of physical care, and this may contribute to the nurse's decision to leave it undone. The reasons for care rationing or missed care are consistently reported as organisational factors such as staffing levels or lack of material resources.

All conceptualisations of missed care acknowledge the importance of the overall decision-making model that guides nursing care, often termed the nursing process (Jones et al., 2015). This incorporates the Donebedian model of structure, process and outcome (Donabedian, 2005). The process involves prioritisation and decision-making, based on organisational and workforce resources. Nurses make decisions through a process of prioritisation of care needs within a context which either enables them to provide high quality care or does not. Nonetheless, in the context of healthcare today, nurses find their decision-making limited by factors such as work intensification, resource availability and policy decisions outside their sphere of influence. When asked why some nursing care is missed or rationed, nurses tend to point to local issues around staffing levels and time constraints. This fails to recognise the influence of factors far removed from the point of care such as worldwide staff shortages, changing demographics, advances in treatments and government allocation of finance. Nonetheless the impact of missed or rationed nursing care is becoming clearer, with growing evidence on the reality of care rationing pointing to its undermining effect on patient care, and significantly, on the wellbeing of the nurses involved (Ausserhofer et al., 2014; Jones et al., 2015; Tønnessen, Nortvedt, & Førde, 2011).

Researchers interested in why missed or implicitly rationed nursing care occurs have repeatedly found certain organisational or management factors to be significant. Initially, poor nurse to patient ratios or inadequate skill mix, were seen as major contributory factors; however over time other factors such as poor teamwork or communication, poor professional or organisational leadership and support, in addition to increased nurse workload or overall work intensification have been identified as significant (Blackman et al., 2015; Clarke & Aiken, 2003; Henderson, Willis, Toffoli, Hamilton, & Blackman, 2016; Hernández-Cruz, Moreno-Monsiváis, Cheverría-Rivera, & Díaz-Oviedo, 2017; Kalisch et al., 2009; Kalisch & Lee, 2010; Phelan & McCarthy, 2016).

3.3 The Consequences of Missed Care

The outcomes of missed nursing care for patients can be considerable. They include reduced quality of care, increased risk of adverse events, lower patient satisfaction with care provided, avoidable health deterioration, decreased quality of life, and higher mortality rates (Ball et al., 2018; Cho, Mark, Knafl, Chang, & Yoon, 2017; Kalisch et al., 2012; Lake, Germack, & Viscardi, 2016; Needleman et al., 2011; Phelan, McCarthy, & Adams, 2018; Schubert et al., 2012; Sochalski, 2004).

Of concern also are the associated nurse outcomes. These include increased rates of nurse burnout and turnover rates, lower job satisfaction, moral distress and role conflict, and nurses struggling with increased acuity (Clarke & Aiken, 2003; Sochalski, 2004; Kalisch & Lee, 2010; Winters & Neville, 2012; Papastavrou, Andreou, Tsangari, & Merkouris, 2014; Henderson et al. 2017). It is acknowledged that nurses frequently choose to continue to work when their shift is over in order to provide the care that would not otherwise be possible (NHS, 2018; Phelan & McCarthy 2016). These unpaid compensatory work behaviours are not viable over the longer term and are likely to increase the possibility of adverse personal outcomes for nurses.

Missed care has been associated with increased turnover rates in hospitals and intention to leave the hospital by nurses (Tschannen, Kalisch, & Lee, 2010) an outcome which should be of concern to all those concerned with high quality care delivery. Significantly for organisations, quality assurance efforts are often under pressure (Jangland, Teodorsson, Molander, & MuntlinAthlin, 2018; Willis, Harvey, Thompson, & Pearson, 2018) when even basic care needs are rationed. It seems unreasonable to expect nurses to participate in activities to enhance care quality when they apparently struggle to provide what they see as fundamental levels of care. Many of the patient outcomes associated with missed nursing are likely to result in delayed patient discharge. Delayed discharge has been associated with an increase in poor patient outcomes (Rojas García et al., 2018) and this could have a confounding effect on the poor outcomes already associated with missed care. Delayed discharge in itself adds to the already heavy workload of nurses. The economic impact of delayed discharge has been explored also (Rojas-García et al., 2017) and includes concerns about the costs of cancelled elective procedures and other repercussions (Rojas-García et al., 2018). Although not yet explored in relation to missed nursing care the increased possibility of delayed discharge appears to be an organisational outcome which cannot be ignored.

Another less explored outcome of missed care is the impact over time on patient care. de Vries and Timmins (2016, p. 5) describe a process of 'care erosion' as a 'gradual decline in the quality of care' as lower standards become normalised. At the extreme end, such care erosion can result in highly publicised examples of poor nursing care as described in the Mid-Staffordshire inquiry (Francis, 2013). McSherry, Timmins, deVries, and McSherry (2018, p. 1109) reiterate that 'Over time, the team habitualizes these omissions or deviations from good practice and suddenly care erosion is a reality'. So despite reducing staff-patient ratios/staff numbers, increasing levels of patient dependency and complexity of care needs, shorter stays and work intensification, nurses might be presumed to be able to continue to provide high quality care. This assumption leads to covert decision-making by nurses at the point of care about which aspect of care can be foregone in order for other aspects to be provided. No explicit policy directs nurses to make these decisions, they are pragmatic decisions often made in haste in order to get through the day, and get the job done. In challenging environments, nurses find themselves with little or no choice other than to ration care to patients. Nurses, again through no fault of their own, in response to insufficient human or material resources, find themselves having to compromise their own professional standards (Harvey, Thompson, Pearson, Willis, & Toffoli, 2017) and are unable to practice nursing in a manner consistent with their personal or professional values. This vicious circle of understaffing, poor care and further turnover is detrimental to healthcare professionals and patients.

Direct care with immediate outcomes has been found to be less likely to be left undone or rationed by nurses (Kalisch et al., 2009). In this category of care is medication administration, treatments and interventions. Coincidentally this care is associated, through prescription or direction, with other members of the multidisciplinary team such as physicians, physiotherapists, pharmacists, or other. This is significant as it would appear that nurses prioritise the work linked to other team members, rather than work that is exclusively nursing. The consequence of this prioritisation is that the care that is rationed is relatively invisible to others, except, arguably, to patients. The psychological care, compassion, and unique nurse-patient relationship that is an integral part of nursing is therefore at risk of disappearing. Equally patient education and preparation for discharge can be compromised, and their absence can have quite specific effects on patient re-admission rates with resultant patient, nurse and organisational implications.

3.4 Frameworks to Explain Missed Care

Based on their work described above, key authors in the area including Kalisch et al. (2009) and Schubert et al. (2007) have developed frameworks which attempt to explain missed or rationed nursing care as it occurs in response to organisational factors or circumstances that negatively affect nurses' capacity to provide all necessary care to patients. It is also recognised that factors related to the work environment of nurses also have a profound effect on levels of missed care (Aiken et al., 2013; Ausserhofer et al., 2014; Schubert et al., 2013). The importance of nurse leadership, as an element of the work environment has also been highlighted as critical. The impact of effective leadership on patient satisfaction and adverse event occurrence has been established (Wong, Cummings, & Ducharme, 2013). Hegney et al. (2018) outline the positive impact of effective nurse leadership on nurse resilience to cope with increasing intensification of work. However this may be a short term impact, as even effective leadership cannot maintain staff resilience through sustained periods of care rationalisation or work intensification (Harvey et al., 2016; Rees, Breen, Cusack, & Hegney, 2015) where staff burnout and adverse events are seen to increase.

Rationing of nursing care or missed care can be seen as directly connected to work intensification. This occurs where the environment does not support the provision of complete nursing care, either through insufficient nurse numbers, inappropriate skill mix or other lack of resources. Often historical staffing level determination mechanisms do not take into account the changing patient profile or increased acuity seen in modern healthcare settings. Frequently nurse shortages are addressed through overtime and other ad hoc measures. Evidence suggests that in areas where less overtime is required, there are lower levels of missed care (Bruyneel et al., 2015). Griffiths et al. (2014) suggests that where overtime is used routinely to address staff shortages, this may result in overall reduced quality of nursing care. It seems likely that routine use of overtime, while addressing a short term need, may also have some unintended consequences such as keeping exhausted nursing staff working longer hours with increased levels of burnout and overall poor performance. Ultimately the practise of filling gaps with overtime does not really ameliorate missed care.

3.5 Addressing the Hidden Phenomenon of Missed Care

Missed nursing care is a pervasive phenomenon in modern healthcare, and has been an important focus for nursing research. Unfortunately it often goes unacknowledged by the nurses involved (Kalisch et al., 2009) in that they do not openly admit to missing elements of patient care, or pass on the information at handover to the next shift. Nurses individually are aware that they were unable to provide full care, and report that they felt obliged or forced to make in-the-moment decisions to ration care or leave aspects of it undone (which then can become patterned over time). It is known that, generally nurses prioritise what they see as essential or direct care (Kalisch et al., 2009) leaving undone more elusive, or less immediate elements of care (Aiken et al., 2012). There is a danger that where the same elements of care are routinely missed, that this reduced level of nursing could become normalised with resultant irreversible changes to the care provided by nurses (Bagnasco et al., 2017). It seems clear that in order to improve outcomes for patients, nurses and organisations, nurses must be supported to name and discuss openly care that was not completed at the end of a shift (Piscotty & Kalisch, 2014). In this way, incoming nurses will be more vigilant to ensure missed care from the previous shift gets completed. Currently the evidence suggests that nurses ration care in isolation. As missed or rationed nursing care is not an explicit practice, nurses do not appear to consider if the care they choose to ration was also rationed on previous shifts. If openly acknowledged at handover time, nurses are at least aware of the implications of their actions. If nurses remain silent, the problem of rationed nursing care remains hidden. This means that corrective action cannot be carried out, and the possibility is that the same care is seen as a low priority by the incoming shift also. Where patterns of decision-making are perpetuated, and the same care is habitually missed, it seems likely in the first instance that any resultant adverse patient outcomes may be intensified, and secondly that ongoing rationed nursing care could lead to habitual poor practice. Communication within teams may allow for identification of trends, both of types of care being rationed and resultant outcomes. This process is necessary to clarify if solution identification across organisations is to be possible at all (Jones et al., 2015). This requires a culture of trust and open communication, whereby the implicit becomes explicit, and therefore undeniable by managers. However this is often not the reality within healthcare organisations.

It would seem that nurse managers may have an important role to play in making explicit the issue of missed and rationed nursing care within the workplace, by encouraging nurses to pass on information between shifts about care left undone or rationed, without fear of reprisal or punishment. Effective and open communication within teams could result in a reduction in the frequency of missed care events and identification of patterns (Bragadóttir, Kalisch, & Tryggvadóttir, 2016; Kalisch, Xie, & Ronis, 2013; Srulovici & Drach-Zahavy, 2017). Nurses report feelings of moral distress and guilt associated with leaving care undone for patients in their care. These feelings are associated with a perception that they may have failed to live up to both personal and professional values. Nurse managers have a role to play in alleviating these feelings by creating an environment where missed care is acknowledged and made explicit, and is recognised as a potential outcome of staff shortages. By encouraging nurses to acknowledge missed care when it occurs, nurse managers can contribute to both individual and team resilience. However nurse managers can only be effective in this work if they have the support of the organisation to monitor and act on implicitly rationed nursing care. Nurse decision-making around prioritizing care in contemporary healthcare settings can leave patients vulnerable to unmet needs (Jones et al., 2015), therefore there is a need for supported decision-making for nursing staff. Decision making in healthcare is a complex process which sometimes involves consideration of competing factors. Bucknall (2000) suggests that in some acute settings nurses make decisions at a rate of one every 20 seconds. Nibbelink and Brewer (2018) in a recent literature review identified factors contributing to nurses' decision-making. These include experience, confidence, intuition, autonomy, culture, situation awareness, protocols and colleague collaboration. They suggest use of a decision making framework to enhance nurse decision-making. While the support of colleagues around decision-making of nurses is vital, Nibbelink and Brewer (2018) believe a formal framework around the process is required so that nurses seek support from the most relevant colleague in a given situation, rather than seeking out their friends. Such a framework if used effectively should minimise the impact of cultural norms, inexperience or instinct based on habitual practices. Use of a framework would require training for nurses and their managers, with particular emphasis on its use in times of high intensity, staff shortages and increased workload, all situations which can lead to care rationing.

3.6 Conclusions

Health systems internationally grapple with issues of budget constraints and growing costs, and frequently nurse staffing numbers are targeted as a means of controlling spending. It is clear that reduced nurse numbers in the workforce have the effect of placing nurses in a position where they see no alternative other than rationing care provided due to lack of time. In other types of healthcare rationing, the decisions around allocation of scarce resources are made by policy makers or senior physicians, as in organ transplantation, treatment choices etc. In nursing, these decisions are frequently made by the most junior members of nursing staff who may simply be trying to get through a shift without adequate support. This situation is fraught with risks for patients, staff, and organisations alike. As the decisions are often invisible to other nurses, to managers, and therefore to organisations and policy makers, it would seem that this method of coping has become pervasive across all health care systems, with 55–98% of nurses across many different countries and health systems admitting to leaving necessary care undone at the end of their shift (Jones et al., 2015). The challenge of missed or rationed nursing care, with resultant adverse outcomes for patients, nurses and organisations, is currently a focus for nurse researchers in many countries across six continents.

While nurses continue to ration care covertly, managers and policy makers can claim plausible deniability around their actions to reduce nurse numbers. Plausible deniability can be claimed where senior staff deny knowledge about the actions of others within the organisation when there is a lack of evidence that they had knowledge about the actions, even if those actions are a result of decision making by the senior staff. If nurses continue to cope, outwardly at least, with reduced numbers and insufficient skill mix, organisations can continue to ignore the implicit rationing of patient care. Another view might be that managers are aware that the practice of rationing of nursing care is widespread, but they rely on nurses to do what is necessary, including rationing care as required. This would imply that the act of reducing nurse numbers by organisations or health services is in itself an example of covert rationing.

3.7 What is Unique and Important to Address About Rationing of Nursing Care

Rationing in healthcare is inevitable in order to ensure that resources are available to meet the requirements of those in most urgent need. In cases of clear shortages, such as in organ transplantation or blood product transfusion, the decision-making around such rationing is unambiguous. Other non-explicit forms of rationing in healthcare are more open to challenge. If implicit rationing of nursing care is a result of policy decisions on the nursing workforce, it can be seen as a de facto form of health care rationing carried out frequently by junior members of staff, and with resultant consequences for patients, nurses and organisations. Rationing in this case is covert, and as a result it remains largely ignored by those who plan health services. This seems to be a short-sighted approach at a time where the provision of safe, high quality healthcare is a universal priority, and there is a focus on the health workforce across all countries. If practitioner well-being is to be considered a research priority, the consequences of rationing nursing care on those nurses who make the decisions needs to be acknowledged.

Key Messages for Researchers
1. Further studies using observational methods are needed to examine more deeply if the rationing of nursing care is always a result of lack of time or resources or if other explanations are also possible?
2. Further work is needed on interventions and testing of interventions to address missed care.
3. Further exploration is recommended of the organisational level implications including cost to organisations of missed nursing care as measured by nurse-sensitive patient outcomes. Nurse-sensitive patient outcomes are an important quality indicator, and measure the impact of nursing care on patient care and patient outcomes.

Key Messages for Healthcare Delivery (2–3 Points)

1. There is a need for trust and open communication within nursing teams around care which is missed or rationed by nurses due to lack of time- this will enable pick up by the next shift of work left undone.
2. There is a need to document missed care within a safe environment, inside and outside nursing groups, and within organisations, in order that it can be addressed. By framing this challenge within a patient safety framework, greater levels of scrutiny are required along with greater transparency around lessons to be learned.
3. There is a need for policy makers and decision makers to acknowledge this contemporary aspect of nursing practice, and its implications for adverse outcomes; and to acknowledge the link between higher level decisions about staffing levels and actual nursing care delivery.

References

Aiken, L. H., Clarke, S. P., Sloane, D. M., Sochalski, J. A., Busse, R., Clarke, H., et al. (2001). Nurses' reports on hospital care in five countries. *Health Affairs, 20*(3), 43–53. https://doi.org/10.1377/hlthaff.20.3.43

Aiken, L., Sermeus, W., Van den Heede, K., Sloane, D., Busse, R., McKee, M., et al. (2012). Patient safety, satisfaction, and quality of hospital care: Cross sectional surveys of nurses and patients in 12 countries in Europe and the United States. *BMJ, 344*, e1717. https://doi.org/10.1136/bmj.e1717

Aiken, L., Sloane, D., Bruyneel, L., Van den Heede, K., Sermeus, W. for The RN4CAST Consortium. (2013). Nurses' reports of working conditions and hospital quality of care in 12 countries in Europe. *International Journal of Nursing Studies, 50*(2), 143–153. https://doi.org/10.1016/j.ijnurstu.2012.11.009.

Ausserhofer, D., Schubert, M., Desmedt, M., Blegen, M. A., DeGeest, S., & Schwendimann, R. (2013). The association of patient safety climate and nurse-related organizational factors with selected patient outcomes: A cross-sectional survey. *International Journal of Nursing Studies, 50*(2), 240–252. https://doi.org/10.1016/j.ijnurstu.2012.04.007

Ausserhofer, D., Zander, B., Busse, R., Schubert, M., De Geest, S., Rafferty, A. M., et al. (2014). Prevalence, patterns and predictors of nursing care left undone in European hospitals: Results from the multi-country cross-sectional RN4CAST study. *BMJ Quality and Safety, 2*(23), 126–135.

Bagnasco, A., Aleo, G., Timmins, F., Begley, T., Parissopoulos, S., & Sasso, L. (2017). The need for consistent family-centred support for family and parents of children admitted to paediatric intensive care unit. *Nursing in Critical Care, 22*, 327–328. https://doi.org/10.1111/nicc.12327

Ball, J., Bruyneel, L., Aiken, L. H., Sermeus, W., Slone, D. M., Rafferty, A. M., et al. (2018). Post-operative mortality, missed care and nurse staffing in nine countries: A cross-sectional study. *International Journal of Nursing Studies, 78*, 10–15.

Bauchner, H. (2019). Rationing of health care in the United States: An inevitable consequence of increasing health care costs. *JAMA, 321*(8), 751–752. https://doi.org/10.1001/jama.2019.1081. Published online February 13.

Blackman, I., Henderson, J., Willis, E., Hamilton, P., Toffoli, L., Verrall, C., et al. (2015, January). Factors influencing why nursing care is missed. *Journal of Clinical Nursing, 24*(1–2), 47–56. https://doi.org/10.1111/jocn.12688

Bragadóttir, H., Kalisch, B., & Tryggvadóttir, G. (2016). Correlates and predictors of missed nursing care in hospitals. *Journal of Clinical Nursing, 11–12*, 1524–1534. https://doi.org/10.1111/jocn.13449

Bruyneel, L., Li, B., Ausserhofer, D., Lesaffre, E., Dumitrescu, I., Smith, H. L., et al. (2015). Organization of hospital nursing, provision of nursing care, and patient experiences with care in Europe. *Medical Care Research and Review, 72*(6), 643–664. https://doi.org/10.1177/1077558715589188

Bucknall, T. (2000). Critical care nurses' decision-making activities in the natural clinical setting. *Journal of Clinical Nursing, 9*(1), 25–35.

Cho, S. H., Mark, B. A., Knafl, G., Chang, H. E., & Yoon, H. J. (2017). Relationships between nurse staffing and patients' experiences, and the mediating effects of missed nursing care. *Journal of Nursing Scholarship, 49*(3), 347–355.

Clarke, S. P., & Aiken, L. H. (2003). Registered nurse staffing and patient and nurse outcomes in hospitals: A commentary. *Policy, Politics & Nursing Practice, 5*(1), 12–20.

de Vries, J., & Timmins, F. (2016, March). Care erosion in hospitals: Problems in reflective nursing practice and the role of cognitive dissonance. *Nurse Education Today, 38*, 5–8. https://doi.org/10.1016/j.nedt.2015.12.007

Donabedian, A. (2005). Evaluating the quality of medical care. *The Milbank Quarterly, 83*(4), 691–729.

Francis, R. (2013). *Report of the mid Staffordshire NHS foundation trust public inquiry (volume 1–3)*. London: Stationery Office.

Friese, C. R., Kalisch, B. J., & Lee, K. H. (2013). Patterns and correlates of missed nursing Care in Inpatient Oncology Units. *Cancer Nursing, 36*(6), E51–E57. https://doi.org/10.1097/NCC.0b013e318275f552

Griffiths, P., Dall'Ora, C., Simon, M., Ball, J., Lindqvist, R., Rafferty, A. M., et al. (2014). Nurses' shift length and overtime working in 12 European countries. *Medical Care, 52*(11), 975–981. https://doi.org/10.1097/MLR.0000000000000233

Harvey, C., Thompson, S., Pearson, M., Willis, E., & Toffoli, L. (2017). Missed nursing care as an 'art form': The contradictions of nurses as carers. *Nursing Inquiry, 24*(3), e12180. https://doi.org/10.1111/nin.12180

Harvey, C., Willis, E., Henderson, J., Verrall, C., Blackman, I., Aber, L., et al. (2016). Priced to care: Factors underpinning missed care. *Journal of Industrial Relations, 58*(4), 510–526.

Hegney, D., Rees, C., Osseiran-Moisson, R., Eley, L., Winsor, C., & Harvey, C. (2018). Perceptions of nursing workloads and contributing factors, and their impact on implicit care rationing: A Queensland, Australia study. *Journal of Nursing Management, 27*(2), 371–380. https://doi.org/10.1111/jonm.12693

Henderson, J., Willis, E., Toffoli, L., Hamilton, P., & Blackman, I. (2016). The impact of rationing of health resources on capacity of Australian public sector nurses to deliver nursing care after-hours: A qualitative study. *Nursing Inquiry, 23*(4), 368–376. https://doi.org/10.1111/nin.12151

Henderson, J., Willis, E., Xiao, L., & Blackman, I. (2017). Missed care in residential aged care in Australia: An exploratory study. *Collegian, 24*, 411–416

Hernández-Cruz, R., Moreno-Monsiváis, M. G., Cheverría-Rivera, S., & Díaz-Oviedo, A. (2017). Factors influencing the missed nursing care in patients from a private hospital. *Revistalatinoamericana de enfermagem, 25*, e2877.

Jangland, E., Teodorsson, T., Molander, K., & Muntlin Athlin, A. (2018). Inadequate environment, resources and values lead to missed nursing care: A focused ethnographic study on the surgical ward using the Fundamentals of Care framework. *Journal of Clinical Nursing, 27*(11–12), 2311–2321. https://doi.org/10.1111/jocn.14095

Jones, T. L., Hamilton, P., & Murry, N. (2015). Unfinished nursing care, missed care, and implicitly rationed care: State of the science review. *The International Journal of Nursing Studies, 52*(6), 1121–1137.

Kalisch, B. J., Landstrom, G. L., & Sue Hinshaw, A. (2009). Missed nursing care: A concept analysis. *Journal of Advanced Nursing, 65*(7), 1509–1517. https://doi.org/10.1111/j.1365-2648.2009.05027.x

Kalisch, B., & Lee, K. H. (2010). The impact of teamwork on missed nursing care. *Nursing Outlook, 58*(5), 233–241.

Kalisch, B. J., Tschannen, D., & Lee, K. H. (2011). Do staffing levels predict missed nursing care? International. *Journal for Quality in Health Care, 23*(3), 302–308.

Kalisch, B. J., Tschannen, D., & Lee, K. H. (2012). Missed nursing care, staffing, and patient falls. *Journal of Nursing Care Quality, 27*(1), 6–12. https://doi.org/10.1097/NCQ.0b013e318225aa23

Kalisch, B. J., & Williams, R. A. (2009). Development and psychometric testing of a tool to measure missed nursing care. *Journal of Nursing Administration, 39*(5), 211–219. https://doi.org/10.1097/NNA.0b013e3181a23cf5

Kalisch, B. J., Xie, B., & Ronis, D. L. (2013). Train-the-trainer intervention to increase nursing teamwork anddecrease missed nursing care in acute care patient units. *Nursing Research, 62*(6), 405–413. https://doi.org/10.1097/NNR.0b013e3182a7a15d

Lake, E. T., Germack, H. D., & Viscardi, M. K. (2016). Missed nursing care is linked to patient satisfaction: A cross-sectional study of US hospitals. *British Medical Journal Quality & Safety, 25*(7), 535–543.

Lucero, R. J., Lake, E. T., & Aiken, L. H. (2010). Nursing care quality and adverse events in US hospitals. *Journal of Clinical Nursing, 19*(15–16), 2185–2195. https://doi.org/10.1111/j.1365-2702.2010.03250

McSherry, R., Timmins, F., deVries, J. M. A., & McSherry, W. (2018). A reflective qualitative appreciative inquiry approach to restoring compassionate care deficits at one. *United Kingdom Health Care Site, 26*(8), 1108–1123. https://doi.org/10.1111/jonm.12630

National Health Service. (2018). *NHS staff survey 2017*. Accessed online October 15, 2019, from http://www.nhsstaffsurveys.com/Caches/Files/P3088_ST17_National%20briefing_v5.0.pdf

Needleman, J., Buerhaus, P., Pankratz, S., Leibson, C. L., Stevens, S. R., & Harris, M. (2011). Nurse staffing and inpatient hospital mortality. *New England Journal of Medicine, 364*, 1037–1045.

Nibbelink, C. W., & Brewer, B. B. (2018). Decision-making in nursing practice: An integrative literature review. *Journal of Clinical Nursing, 27*(5–6), 917–928.

Papastavrou, E., Andreou, P., Tsangari, H., & Merkouris, A. (2014). Linking patient satisfaction with nursing care: The case of care rationing – a correlational study. *BioMed Central Nursing, 13*(1), 26. https://doi.org/10.1186/1472-6955-13-26

Phelan, A., & McCarthy, S. (2016). *Missed care in community nursing*. Dublin: UCD & INMO.

Phelan, A., McCarthy, S., & Adams, E. (2018). Examining missed care in community nursing. *Journal of Advanced Nursing, 74*(3), 626–636. https://doi.org/10.1111/jan.13466

Piscotty, R. J., & Kalisch, B. J. (2014). "The relationship between electronic nursing care reminders and missed nursing care", computers, informatics. *Nursing: CIN, 32*(10), 475–481. https://doi.org/10.1097/CIN.0000000000000092

Rees, C. S., Breen, L. J., Cusack, L., & Hegney, D. (2015). Understanding individual resilience in the workplace: The international collaboration of workforce resilience (ICWR) model. *Frontiers in Psychology, 6*, 73. https://doi.org/10.3389/fpsyg.2015.00073

Rojas-García, A., Turner, S., Pizzo, E., Hudson, E., Thomas, J., & Raine, R. (2017). Impact and experiences of delayed discharge: A mixed-studies systematic review. *Health Expectations, 21*, 41–56.

Rojas-García, A., Turner, S., Pizzo, E., Hudson, E., Thomas, J., & Raine, R. (2018). Impact and experiences of delayed discharge: A mixed-studies systematic review. *Health expectations: an international journal of public participation in health care and health policy, 21*(1), 41–56. https://doi.org/10.1111/hex.12619

Schubert, M., Ausserhofer, D., Desmedt, M., Schwendimann, R., Lesaffre, E., Li, B., et al. (2013). Levels and correlates of implicit rationing of nursing care in Swiss acute care hospitals—A cross sectional study. *International Journal of Nursing Studies, 50*(2), 230–239. https://doi.org/10.1016/j.ijnurstu.2012.09.016

Schubert, M., Clarke, S. P., Aiken, L. H., & de Geest, S. (2012). Associations between rationing of nursing care and inpatient mortality in Swiss hospitals. *International Journal for Quality in Health Care, 24*(3), 230–238. https://doi.org/10.1093/intqhc/mzs009

Schubert, M., Glass, T. R., Clarke, S. P., Aiken, L. H., Schaffert-Witvliet, B., Sloane, D. M., et al. (2008). Rationing of nursing care and its relationship to patient outcomes: The Swiss extension of the international hospital outcomes study. *International Journal for Quality in Health Care, 20*(4), 227–237.

Schubert, M., Glass, T. R., Clarke, S. P., Schaffert-Witvliet, B., & De Geest, S. (2007). Validation of the Basel extent of rationing of nursing care instrument. *Nursing Research, 56*(6p), 416–424. https://doi.org/10.1097/01.NNR.0000299853.52429.62

Schubert, M., Schaffert-Witvliet, B., De Geest, S., Glass, T., Aiken, L., Sloane, D. S., et al. (2005). *RICH-nursing study: Rationing of nursing care in Switzerland. Effects of rationing of nursing care in Switzerland on patient' and nurses' outcomes* (Final report Grant, Swiss Federal Office of Public Health, Bern, Switzerland). Basel, Switzerland: Institute of Nursing Science, University of Basel.

Sochalski, J. (2004). Is more better? The relationship between nurse staffing and the quality of nursing Care in Hospitals. *Medical Care, 42*(2), 67–73.

Srulovici, E., & Drach-Zahavy, A. (2017). Nurses' personal and Ward accountability and missed nursing care: A cross-sectional study. *International Journal of Nursing Studies, 75*, 163–171. https://doi.org/10.1016/j.ijnurstu.2017.08.003

Suhonen, R., & Scott, P. A. (2018). Missed care: A need for careful ethical discussion. *Nursing Ethics, 25*(5), 549–551.

Tilburt, J. C., & Cassel, C. K. (2013). Why the ethics of parsimonious medicine is not the ethics of rationing. *Journal of the American Medical Association, 309*(8), 773–774. https://doi.org/10.1001/jama.2013.368

Tønnessen, S., Nortvedt, P., & Førde, R. (2011). Rationing home-based nursing care: Professional and ethical challenges. *Nursing Ethics, 18*(3), 386–396.

Tschannen, D., Kalisch, B. J., & Lee, K. H. (2010, December). Missed nursing care: The impact on intention to leave and turnover. *Canadian Journal of Nursing Research, 42*(4), 22–39.

Vryonides, S., Papastavrou, E., Charalambous, A., Andreou, P., Eleftheriou, C., & Merkouris, A. (2018). Ethical climate and missed nursing care in cancer care units. *Nursing Ethics, 25*(6), 707–723.

Willis, E. C., Harvey, S., Thompson, M., Pearson, A., & Meyer, A. (2018). Work intensification and quality assurance: Missed nursing care. *Journal of Nursing Care Quality, 33*(2), E10–E16.

Winters, R., & Neville, S. R. (2012, March). Registered nurse perspectives on delayed or missed nursing cares in a New Zealand hospital. *Nursing Praxis in New Zealand, 28*(1), 19–28.

Wong, C., Cummings, C., & Ducharme, L. (2013). The relationship between nursing leadership and patient outcomes: A systematic review update. *Journal of Nursing Management, 21*(5), 709–724. https://doi.org/10.1111/jonm.12116

Chapter 4
Linking Organisational Factors and Patient Care: Does Healthcare Workers' Well-being Matter?

Kevin Teoh and Juliet Hassard

4.1 Introduction

Worker well-being is an important focus within organisational research, and refers to a multidimensional concept that includes affect, motivation, behaviour, cognition, and psychosomaticism (van Horn, Taris, Schaufeli, & Schreurs, 2004; Warr, 1994). The concept of well-being goes beyond physical or mental health, and exists on a continuum encompassing both negative (e.g., burnout, depression) and positive (e.g., happiness, engagement) constructs (Bakker & Schaufeli, 2008). Within the healthcare sector, well-being is typically posited to function as a mediator between the work environment and patient care (Montgomery, Panagopoulou, Kehoe, & Valkanos, 2011). This is part of a growing recognition that a holistic systems-level perspective is needed to link the areas of working conditions, healthcare workers' well-being, and patient care (Teoh, Hassard, & Cox, 2019).

Two issues exist with the assertion of well-being as a mediator. First, there has been little empirical examination of this. Instead, this assertion is based on separate pools of research that first link working conditions with healthcare workers' well-being (Adriaenssens, De Gucht, & Maes, 2015; Cummings et al., 2010; Lee, Seo, Hladkyj, Lovell, & Schwartzmann, 2013), and, subsequently, link well-being with patient care (Hall, Johnson, Watt, Tsipa, & O'Connor, 2016; Scheepers, Boerebach, Arah, Heineman, & Lombarts, 2015). Second, nearly all of this research investigates such relationships at the individual level, and conceptually and methodologically neglects that all these constructs operate within a wider system and context. This

---

K. Teoh (✉)
Birkbeck, University of London, London, UK
e-mail: k.teoh@bbk.ac.uk

J. Hassard
University of Nottingham, Nottingham, UK

© Springer Nature Switzerland AG 2020
A. Montgomery et al. (eds.), *Connecting Healthcare Worker Well-Being, Patient Safety and Organisational Change*, Aligning Perspectives on Health, Safety and Well-Being, https://doi.org/10.1007/978-3-030-60998-6_4

means that decisions (e.g., funding and resource allocation), events (e.g., seasonal demands), and structures (e.g., staffing, work processes) at the departmental, organisational, sectoral, and national levels all impact on working conditions, workers' well-being, and the quality of care being delivered (Montgomery, Spânu, Băban, & Panagopoulou, 2015; Powell, Dawson, Topakas, Durose, & Fewtrell, 2014). Greater recognition for these wider contextual factors (e.g., organisational structure, organisational culture, external influences) would yield a more realistic understanding of how working conditions, workers' well-being, and patient care are interlinked, and may, in turn, inform the development of more effective interventions and policies.

This chapter, therefore, aims to bring together organisational factors, well-being and patient care outcomes within a single conceptual model. Within this model, organisational factors is proposed to predict both healthcare workers' well-being and patient care, with healthcare workers' well-being postulated as a mediator. It begins by first reviewing the research linking organisational factors to healthcare workers' well-being and patient care before presenting a conceptual model that draws this together. We then highlight limitations in the existing research and reflect on the implications for research and practice.

4.1.1 The Impact of Organisational Factors on Healthcare Workers' Well-Being and Patient Care

A myriad of factors exists at the organisational level that broadly can be separated according to internal (i.e., structure, people) and external factors to the organisation. Structure refers to the organisational setup, such as type of organisation, policies and processes, staffing, and the availability of resources. People refers to, amongst others, senior leadership, culture and decisions made. Finally, external influences focus on the demands (e.g., number of patients) and resources (e.g., funding) that affect how the organisation may be run, and encompasses a wide range contextual factors relevant to the organisation. Recognising the numerous possible external factors, we focus this chapter primarily on the internal factors, although provide a brief overview of some relevant external factors. We first review the research linking organisational factors with healthcare workers' well-being and patient care. Next, we review the research testing the mediating role of healthcare workers' well-being in the relationship between organisational factors and patient care. Through this, we highlight the importance of organisational factors to both healthcare workers' well-being and to patient care.

4.1.2 Organisational Factors and Healthcare Workers' Well-Being

Increased demands on health services place additional strain not only on the system, but on those who work within it. Therefore, it is not surprising to see overcrowding (Chen, Hsieh, Hu, & Lai, 2017), bed occupancy rates (Sizmur & Raleigh, 2018), and high levels of emergency admissions (Teoh, Hassard, & Cox, 2018) associated with lower levels of healthcare workers' well-being. For example, analysis of 10,184 nurses in the United States found that each increase of one patient in each nurse's patient load raised the risk of burnout by 23% and job dissatisfaction by 15% (Aiken, Clarke, Sloane, Sochalski, & Silber, 2002). When hospitals are stretched they lack the capacity to manage their demands highlighting the importance of having sufficient resources (including staff, material and finances) (Royal College of Physicians, 2016). Failure to provide such resources creates a more challenging work environment that impairs staff well-being. This is evidenced by a recent study that observed lower levels of work-related stress and presenteeism in England were associated with higher spending on temporary staff and better staff-to-bed ratio (Sizmur & Raleigh, 2018). Similarly, insufficient and poor quality medical supplies have been linked to high levels of burnout in Greek healthcare workers (Rachiotis et al., 2014) and Italian and Dutch nurses (Pisanti, van der Doef, Maes, Lazzari, & Bertini, 2011).

The type of hospital also matters, with nurses reporting higher levels of burnout in for-profit as compared to public hospitals (Cimiotti, Aiken, Sloane, & Wu, 2012), or in general rather than specialist hospitals (Renzi, Tabolli, Ianni, Di Pietro, & Puddu, 2005). This may be due to differences in how the hospitals are structured or managed. In English hospitals, senior leadership support, and communication are among the organisational factors that predicted the work-related stress of workers (Powell et al., 2014). These all have an impact on the culture within the hospital, with a systematic review (n = 14) finding stronger organisational climate (e.g., hospital management, nurse-physician relationships) and safety climate to be associated with lower rates of musculoskeletal disorders and burnout among nurses (Gershon et al., 2007). Similarly, hospital mergers likely impact on the working conditions of workers. This is evident where job autonomy, job control, and social support have all been found to predict levels of job satisfaction in healthcare workers experiencing hospital mergers (Lim, 2014). It is not surprising then to see lower levels of job satisfaction when hospitals merge—although the same study found that job satisfaction returned to pre-merger levels 1 year later (Lim, 2014).

Consistent evidence of the predictive association of organisational factors and healthcare professionals' well-being is not always observed in the literature. For example, Teoh et al. (2018) found bed occupancy rates and availability did not predict healthcare workers' levels of presenteeism, work engagement, and work-related stress. It is also unlikely that the organisational factors only have a direct impact on well-being, as indirect effects via job demands and job sources (Lim, 2014) does occur. Similarly, better working conditions (Tucker, Jimmieson, & Oei, 2013) and high levels of resilience (García-Izquierdo, Meseguer de Pedro, Ríos-

Risquez, & Sánchez, 2018) could potentially mitigated any detrimental organisational factors. Moreover, both organisational factors and healthcare workers' well-being have implications for patient care, which is reviewed in the next section.

4.1.3 Organisational Factors and Patient Care

Direct relationships have been observed between organisational factors and patient care. There is particularly robust evidence for nurse-to-patient ratios, with a systematic review of 43 studies that demonstrates that more staff are associated with shorter hospital stays, lower failure-to-rescue rates, and lower mortality rates (Lang, Hodge, Olson, Romano, & Kravitz, 2004). The generalisability of these findings is further evident in a study of nurses from 1115 hospitals in 13 countries, where a higher nurse-to-patient ratio predicted better nurse and patient-rated care outcomes (Aiken et al., 2012). In terms of staffing, higher nurse education levels, richer nurse skill mix, and a lower proportion of temporary workers were associated with better mortality outcomes in Canadian hospitals (Estabrooks, Midodzi, Cummings, Ricker, & Giovannetti, 2005).

The consistency with staff-to-patient ratio is not, however, seen with other organisational factors. In a review of 42 studies, 13 different organisational factors were examined in relation to patient safety (Hoff, Jameson, Hannan, & Flink, 2004), with team structures, procedures and guidelines, technology, feedback, and training/education the most commonly examined factors. Crucially, because these studies only empirically examined the relationship between organisational factors and patient safety little is known about the impact on other aspects of patient care, namely clinical excellence and patient experience (Teoh et al., 2019). This therefore raises important questions as to whether there is sufficient evidence to support a relationship between organisational factors and patient care. Nevertheless, considerable evidence is accumulating demonstrating a link between organisational factors with various patient outcomes (Kagan & Barnoy, 2013; Kapinos, Fitzgerald, Greer, & Rutks, 2012). For example, Sizmur and Raleigh (2018) observed spending on temporary staff and low bed occupancy rates in England negatively correlated with 19 different measures of patient experience (e.g., communicating with doctors, staff working well together; confidence and trust in doctors). In particular, having a strong safety culture is associated with better care outcomes, including fewer reported errors (Hofmann & Mark, 2006; Kagan & Barnoy, 2013), adverse events reported (Mardon, Khanna, Sorra, Dyer, & Famolaro, 2010), and lower readmission rates (Hansen, Williams, & Singer, 2011). This is not surprising given that a strong safety culture typically manifests as focusing on systems rather than individuals; emphasising learning rather than apportioning blame; a commitment to safety at all levels; and the provision of sufficient resources (Health Foundation, 2011; Kagan & Barnoy, 2013; Kapinos et al., 2012). Although these studies demonstrate a direct link between organisational factors and patient care, they do not elaborate on the mechanism(s) underpinning this relationship. As such, the subsequent section examines the research investigating well-being as a mediator within this relationship.

4.1.4 Healthcare Workers' Well-Being as a Mediator

Few studies have examined the role of well-being as a mediator in the postulated relationship between organisational factors and patient care. For example, controlling for nurse burnout nullified the previously observed relationships between the nurse-patient ratio (across 161 American hospitals) with rates of urinary tract and surgical site infections (Cimiotti et al., 2012). In Canada, nurse burnout mediated the relationship between various organisational factors and adverse events (i.e., falls, nosocomial infections, medication errors, and patient complaints). These included senior leadership, staff and material resourcing, and policy involvement (Laschinger & Leiter, 2006). A similar model tested among Belgian nurses found that the practice environment (e.g., hospital management and organisational support, nurse management at the unit level) had both direct and indirect effects on unit-level quality of care (Van Bogaert, Kowalski, Weeks, Van Heusden, & Clarke, 2013; Van Bogaert, Meulemans, Clarke, Vermeyen, & Van de Heyning, 2009). The indirect pathways were first mediated by perceived working conditions (e.g., workload, job control) and then by nurses' self-reported levels of burnout. In England, doctors' work engagement mediated the relationship between the number of emergency admissions and doctors' perception of the quality of care provided by the hospital and by themselves (Teoh, 2018). However, neither work-related stress nor presenteeism functioned as a mediator. None of the well-being measures (i.e., work-related stress, presenteeism, work engagement) examined by this study were mediators where bed occupancy was the predictor. These well-being measures also did not mediate any relationship where hospital-level patient care outcomes were used (e.g., mortality, patient satisfaction, safety incidents). While all the studies above provide some indication of how organisational factors may influence burnout (i.e., through perceived working conditions) and that burnout does function as a mediator, further research is needed to explore this relationship in a greater variety of studies. In particular, future research should consider using organisational-level outcome measures, a wider range of healthcare staff types, and more diverse measures of well-being.

4.2 A Conceptual Model Linking Organisational Factors and Patient Care

Based on the research reviewed above, we propose a conceptual model (Fig. 4.1) where organisational factors operate as an antecedent to healthcare workers' well-being and to patient care. While organisational factors can influence patient care directly, it also does so through a number of indirect pathways with healthcare workers' well-being being the primary mediator (Teoh, 2018; Van Bogaert et al., 2013). The importance of well-being is evident as an outcome of a variety of organisational factors (Cimiotti et al., 2012). Based on the available evidence, a key mechanism lies in organisational factors shaping the psychosocial work environment that healthcare workers operate in (Dollard & Bakker, 2010). This could result in a change in the type and levels of job demands (e.g., workload, bullying, role conflict, and work-life conflict) and resources (e.g., social support, job control, autonomy) that healthcare workers are exposed to (Kinman & Teoh, 2018). This matters as there is strong evidence linking healthcare workers' job demands and resources with their well-being (Adriaenssens et al., 2015; Lee et al., 2013).

Continuing down the pathway, the well-being and patient care relationship draws on the premise that healthier and happier workers are generally more productive. While the reality of this assumption is considerably more complex (Teoh, Hassard, & Kinman, 2020), there is some evidence demonstrating a link between healthcare workers' well-being and the quality of patient care—particularly for positive indicators of well-being (e.g., work engagement, job satisfaction) (Hall et al., 2016; Teoh, 2018). Here, well-being influences patient care through two potential pathways—cognitive and motivation. The cognitive pathway is where well-being, and in particular poor health, affects an individual's memory, recognition, and executive functioning. All of these are necessary for task and contextual performance (Dalgleish et al., 2007; Ford, Cerasoli, Higgins, & Decesare, 2011) and will impair the care provided to patients. The motivational pathway focuses on well-being as a resource in itself that begets additional resources (Hobfoll, 2002). The converse occurs where poor well-being facilitates additional resources loss. Here, well-being as resource fulfils one of four functions: (1) being required to complete work tasks (Bakker & Demerouti, 2017); (2) meeting basic psychological needs (e.g., need to belong or competence) that facilitates intrinsic motivation (Deci & Ryan, 1985); (3) buffer the detrimental effects of demands in the workplace (Karasek & Theorell, 1990); and (4) preventing irrational or defensive behaviour to protect resources (Hobfoll, Halbesleben, Neveu, & Westman, 2018). These four functions typically result in better performance that should provide better patient care. It is important to recognise that the definition of well-being at this start of this chapter includes both motivation and cognition (van Horn et al., 2004; Warr, 1994). This is captured in Fig. 4.1 through the shared box that groups positive and negative well-being with cognition and motivation as well as the reciprocal relationships between them.

It is important to note that studies do not always support these relationships, such as where higher levels of nurse burnout were observed in for-profit hospitals than

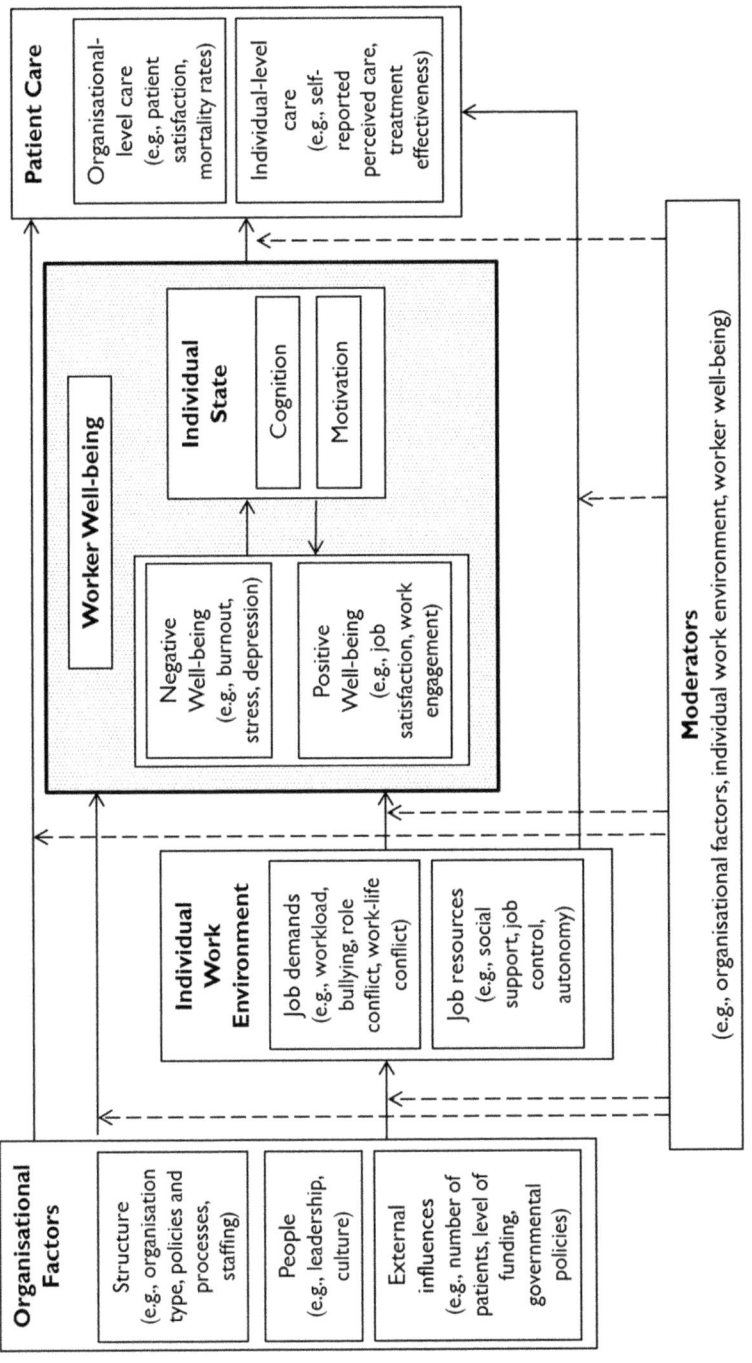

Fig. 4.1 Conceptual model of the direct and indirect effects relationships between organisational factors, worker well-being, and patient care

public hospitals but there were no differences in levels of individual-level job demands and resources (Hansen, Sverke, & Näswall, 2009). This is despite job demands and resources predicting burnout levels. Therefore, the relationships in Fig. 4.1 are likely influenced by other contextual factors. For example, the well-being and patient care relationship could be moderated by the personal values, intrinsic motivation, and occupational background of healthcare workers (Teoh et al., 2020). Similarly, job demands and resources also interact with each other (Bakker & Demerouti, 2017) and with wider organisational factors too (Lowe & Chan, 2010; Teoh, 2018). However, most of these moderations remain postulations and warrant empirical testing in future research.

4.3 Limitations in the Extant Research and Future Research Directions

The extant research has a number of limitations that restrict both the validity and the generalisability of the research reviewed so far. Therefore, in testing the proposed model above and to advance our understanding of this relationship in general, researchers should account and overcome the lack of theory, issues of measurement, and shortcomings in research designs. These are discussed below.

4.3.1 Developing Theory

The conceptual model in Fig. 4.1 does not actually offer a theoretical explanation of why and how these relationships occur. This links in with a wider issue within health services research that is primarily interested in practical factual findings rather than the development of theories (Alderson, 1998). Recognising the interface between relationships at the individual and organisational level, there is the potential to explain these relationships by drawing on existing theories from disciplines including psychology, organisational behaviour, and human resource management. From a psychological perspective, the Job Demands-Resources Theory (Bakker & Demerouti, 2017) maps onto the working conditions, well-being, and performance domains, while Conservation of Resources Theory (Hobfoll & Freedy, 1993) explains how resources (or the lack of them) influence well-being. However, there has been limited consideration of organisational factors within these theories. In contrast, theories from the organisational sciences cover a range of factors such as team dynamics (Dow, DiazGranados, Mazmanian, & Retchin, 2013), culture (Schein, 1985), and change management (Lewin, 1943); although they are less explicit about their impact on workers' well-being. Similarly, while soft human resources management approaches recognise the importance of workers' well-being, it still prioritises the management of workplace performance (Truss, 1999). We, therefore, see a substantial gap in the role of theory and encourage future researchers to embrace an interdisciplinary approach to test, examine, and adapt existing theories from the various disciplines in relation to the pathways postulated in Fig. 4.1.

4.3.2 Using Multilevel Research Designs

Linking organisational-level measures with individual-level measures of workers' well-being present a methodological challenge. As these measures operate at different levels, researchers typically: (1) use the same organisational factor score for all participants from that organisation (i.e., disaggregation); or (2) aggregate the individual scores within an organisation to get an average for the organisation (Heck & Thomas, 2015). This actually violates the need for all variables within a model to function at the same level. This is because disaggregation results in inflated standard error scores that increase the likelihood of Type I errors (i.e., observing a relationship when there is no relationship; (Muthén & Satorra, 1995). In contrast, aggregation not only reduces the number of possible data points, but reduces the level of variability between scores. This, in turn, reduces statistical power and increases the likelihood of Type II errors (i.e., observing no relationship when there is a relationship; (Duncan, Jones, & Moon, 1996; Hox, Maas, & Brinkhuis, 2010). Instead, future research in this area should employ multilevel models that can test for relationships across levels (Heck & Thomas, 2015). By separating the variance of measures into an individual and organisational-level component (Preacher, Zhang, & Zyphur, 2011), multilevel analysis allows organisational-level measures to be modelled against the organisational-level variance components of individual-level well-being and patient care measures. This meets then allows for measures across different levels to be used and provides more statistically robust findings.

4.3.3 Definitions and Operationalising Key Constructs

The research around organisational factors, healthcare workers' well-being and patient care struggles with how these constructs are defined. Within this chapter we have broadly separated organisational factors according to three types: structure, people, and external influences. This requires further refining and testing to see whether they make conceptual and empirical sense. In terms of well-being, the research above highlights the dominance of ill-health indicators and in particular burnout measures (Scheepers et al., 2015). This is an additional issue where different types of well-being mediate the work environment and performance relationship differently (Bakker & Demerouti, 2017). Finally, there is considerable debate around how patient quality is measured and what good quality care represents (Teoh et al.,

Table 4.1 The difficulty measuring quality of care

Quality of care dimension	Example measure	Concerns around validity of the measure
Patient safety	Self-reported errors or events	Having an agreed definition of what an error or adverse event is (Probst & Estrada, 2010). High levels of reporting may represent an environment where healthcare workers feel safe to report and may represent a strong safety culture (Raleigh, Hussey, Seccombe, & Qi, 2009). Reporting could be suppressed in environments where healthcare workers fear blame or reprisals (Snijders, Kollen, van Lingen, Fetter, & Molendijk, 2009). Typically low frequency data which skews data that can be detrimental for analyses (Christian, Bradley, Wallace, & Burke, 2009).
Clinical excellence	Standardised hospital mortality rates	Hospital mortality data is routinely collected and susceptible to mistakes (Howell et al., 2015). Disagreement as to how deaths are coded and what factors should be included or excluded (e.g., should not-for-resuscitation and palliative care deaths should be exempt from calculations; Bottle, Jarman, & Aylin, 2011). Vulnerable to adjustments that present more favourable standards (Mears, 2014). As a comparative indicator changes in patient outcomes in some trusts would impact mortality scores at other trusts as well (Boden et al., 2016).
Patient experience	Patient satisfaction scores	Lack of consistency in conceptualising what this represents, arguably capture the patient's attitudes and expectations about the service received (Crow et al., 2002). Poor links to other forms of quality measures (Salisbury, Wallace, & Montgomery, 2010). Patients can become accustomed to poor practice (McKinstry et al., 2007). Emotional labour and professional standards mean healthcare workers are aware of their limitations and attempt to overcompensate in their delivery (Ratanawongsa et al., 2008) to still deliver, or appear to deliver, appropriate levels of care.

2020) (See Table 4.1 for examples). At the individual level, outcome measures typically refer to belief, attitude, or perception which does not represent actual clinical care outcomes (Teoh et al., 2019). This difficulty in defining and operationalising key constructs affects the validity and generalisability of existing research which means a more critical perspective is required to understand their implications for practice and future research. This includes being clear about what is being measured and how that is defined or understood; recognising the relevance, strengths and limitations of any measures used (e.g., Table 4.1); the suitability of a construct or measure to a particular context; and what the extant research makes known (or not) about the construct or measure of interest.

4.4 Conclusion

This chapter demonstrate that organisational factors are an important antecedent to healthcare workers' well-being and patient care. It further highlights that healthcare workers' well-being can function as a mediator in the organisational factors—patient care relationship. This builds on the recognition that a holistic systems-level perspective is required to address healthcare workers' well-being and patient care (Montgomery et al., 2011). While there has been considerable focus on improving patient care, there has not been an equal emphasis on improving workers' well-being (Royal College of Physicians, 2016). The healthcare workers' well-being and patient care agenda should not operate within separate silos, but recognise that they are interlinked. The conceptual model presented earlier provides a useful framework in which to understand, test, and intervene. For policymakers and practitioners, this means recognising that piecemeal interventions are unlikely to be successful and that wider recognition of contextual and organisational factors is necessary. Equally, decisions in any of these three areas likely have a knock-on effect on the other areas. In reality, many of the organisational factors that influence workers' well-being and patient care are external to the organisation (e.g., number of patients, funding, supply of the medical workforce). Therefore, in addition to managing their own organisation, senior management should take a more active role in lobbying and influencing appropriate stakeholders and decision makers (Landers & Sehgal, 2004) to increase the resources available to them and place more appropriate demands on them. For researchers, a greater awareness of context is required within research design and there is the need to test and validate the model presented in Fig. 4.1. Moreover, the limitations and issues identified in the preceding section, developing theory, using multilevel models, and better operationalisation of constructs are important actions needed to enhance our understanding of this important topic.

Key Messages for Researchers
1. To test the direct and indirect effects between organisational factors, healthcare workers' well-being, and patient care (Fig. 4.1). In particular, to consider organisational-level outcome measures, a wider range of healthcare staff types, and more diverse measures of well-being
2. Research designs with measures at different levels (e.g., the organisation and the individual) should use multilevel designs to reduce the likelihood of Type I and II errors being made.
3. There are differences in how these commonly understood constructs (i.e., organisational factors, workers' well-being, patient care) are defined and operationalised. Researchers should be clearer on how this is done and recognise any corresponding implications.

Key Messages for Healthcare Delivery
1. Organisational factors are important contextual antecedents to workers' well-being and patient care. There should be a great emphasis on recognising that organisations should recognise that the structure, people, and external influences on an organisation have ramifications for staff well-being and patient care.
2. Interventions to improve healthcare workers' well-being should use a systems perspective to make positive changes to factors related tithe structure, people, and external influences on an organisation. This could work alongside interventions that target the individual (e.g. job skills or mindfulness training) to provide a more holistic focus towards the improvement ostaff well-being and patient care.
3. The healthcare workers' well-being and patient care agenda should not be operating in separate silos. While we are not aware of healthcare specific programmes, both the *Total Worker Health Programme* (NIOSH, 2017) and *WHO Healthy Workplace Model* (WHO, 2010) are about preventing worker illness and injury and enhancing sustainable health and wellbeing through the integration of health promotion with occupational safety and health protection.

References

Adriaenssens, J., De Gucht, V., & Maes, S. (2015). Determinants and prevalence of burnout in emergency nurses: A systematic review of 25 years of research. *International Journal of Nursing Studies, 52*(2), 649–661. https://doi.org/10.1016/j.ijnurstu.2014.11.004

Aiken, L. H., Clarke, S. P., Sloane, D. M., Sochalski, J., & Silber, J. H. (2002). Hospital nurse staffing and patient mortality, nurse burnout, and job dissatisfaction. *Journal of the American Medical Association, 288*(16), 1987–1993. https://doi.org/10.1001/jama.288.16.1987

Aiken, L. H., Sermeus, W., Van den Heede, K., Sloane, D. M., Busse, R., McKee, M., et al. (2012). Patient safety, satisfaction, and quality of hospital care: Cross sectional surveys of nurses and patients in 12 countries in Europe and the United States. *BMJ (Clinical Research Ed.), 344* (March), e1717. https://doi.org/10.1136/bmj.e1717

Alderson, P. (1998). The importance of theories in health care. *BMJ, 317*(7164), 1007–1010. https://doi.org/10.1136/bmj.317.7164.1007

Bakker, A. B., Schaufeli, W. B., Leiter, M. P., & Taris, T. W. (2008). Work engagement: An emerging concept in occupational health psychology. *Work & Stress, 22*(3), 187–200.

Bakker, A. B., & Demerouti, E. (2017). Job demands–resources theory: Taking stock and looking forward. *Journal of Occupational Health Psychology, 22*(3), 273–285. https://doi.org/10.1037/ocp0000056

Boden, D. G., Agarwal, A., Hussain, T., Martin, S. J., Radford, N., Riyat, M. S., et al. (2016). Lowering levels of bed occupancy is associated with decreased in hospital mortality and improved performance on the 4-hour target in a UK district general hospital. *Emergency Medicine Journal, 33*(2), 85–90. https://doi.org/10.1136/emermed-2014-204479

Bottle, A., Jarman, B., & Aylin, P. P. (2011). Strengths and weaknesses of hospital standardised mortality ratios. *BMJ (Clinical Research Education), 342*, c7116. https://doi.org/10.1136/bmj.c7116

Chen, K.-C., Hsieh, W.-H., Hu, S.-C., & Lai, P.-F. (2017). A survey of the perception of Well-being among emergency physicians in Taiwan. *Tzu Chi Medical Journal, 29*(1), 30. https://doi.org/10.4103/tcmj.tcmj_12_17

Christian, M. S., Bradley, J. C., Wallace, J. C., & Burke, M. J. (2009). Workplace safety: A meta-analysis of the roles of person and situation factors. *Journal of Applied Psychology, 94*(5), 1103–1127. https://doi.org/10.1037/a0016172

Cimiotti, J. P., Aiken, L. H., Sloane, D. M., & Wu, E. S. (2012). Nurse staffing, burnout, and health care–associated infection. *American Journal of Infection Control, 40*(6), 486–490. https://doi.org/10.1016/j.ajic.2012.02.029

Crow, R., Gage, H., Hampson, S., Hart, J., Kimber, A., Storey, L., et al. (2002). The measurement of satisfaction with healthcare: Implications for practice from a systematic review of the literature. *Health Technology Assessment, 6*(32), 1–244.

Cummings, G. G., MacGregor, T., Davey, M., Lee, H., Wong, C. A., Lo, E., et al. (2010). Leadership styles and outcome patterns for the nursing workforce and work environment: A systematic review. *International Journal of Nursing Studies, 47*(3), 363–385. https://doi.org/10.1016/j.ijnurstu.2009.08.006

Dalgleish, T., Golden, A. M. J., Barrett, L. F., Au Yeung, C., Murphy, V., Tchanturia, K., et al. (2007). Reduced specificity of autobiographical memory and depression: The role of executive control. *Journal of Experimental Psychology: General, 136*(1), 23–42. https://doi.org/10.1037/0096-3445.136.1.23

Deci, E. L., & Ryan, R. M. (1985). *Intrinsic motivation and self-determination in human behavior*. New York, NY: Plenum Publishing.

Dollard, M. F., & Bakker, A. B. (2010). Psychosocial safety climate as a precursor to conducive work environments, psychological health problems, and employee engagement. *Journal of Occupational and Organizational Psychology, 83*(3), 579–599. https://doi.org/10.1348/096317909x470690

Dow, A. W., DiazGranados, D., Mazmanian, P. E., & Retchin, S. M. (2013). Applying organizational science to health care: A framework for collaborative practice. *Academic Medicine, 88*(7), 952–957. https://doi.org/10.1097/ACM.0b013e31829523d1

Duncan, C., Jones, K., & Moon, G. (1996). Health-related behaviour in context: A multilevel modelling approach. *Social Science and Medicine, 42*(6), 817–830. https://doi.org/10.1016/0277-9536(95)00181-6

Estabrooks, C. A., Midodzi, W. K., Cummings, G. G., Ricker, K. L., & Giovannetti, P. (2005). The impact of hospital nursing characteristics on 30-day mortality. *Nursing Research, 54*(2), 74–84. https://doi.org/10.1097/NNA.0b013e318221c260

Ford, M. T., Cerasoli, C. P., Higgins, J. A., & Decesare, A. L. (2011). Relationships between psychological, physical, and behavioural health and work performance: A review and meta-analysis. *Work & Stress, 25*(3), 185–204. https://doi.org/10.1080/02678373.2011.609035

García-Izquierdo, M., Meseguer de Pedro, M., Ríos-Risquez, M. I., & Sánchez, M. I. S. (2018). Resilience as a moderator of psychological health in situations of chronic stress (burnout) in a sample of hospital nurses. *Journal of Nursing Scholarship, 50*(2), 228–236. https://doi.org/10.1111/jnu.12367

Gershon, R. R. M., Stone, P. W., Zeltser, M., Faucett, J., Macdavitt, K., & Chou, S.-S. (2007). Organizational climate and nurse health outcomes in the United States: A systematic review. *Industrial Health, 45*(5), 622–636. https://doi.org/10.2486/indhealth.45.622

Hall, L. H., Johnson, J., Watt, I., Tsipa, A., & O'Connor, D. B. (2016). Healthcare staff wellbeing, burnout, and patient safety: A systematic review. *PLoS One, 11*(7), 1–12. https://doi.org/10.1371/journal.pone.0159015

Hansen, N., Sverke, M., & Näswall, K. (2009). Predicting nurse burnout from demands and resources in three acute care hospitals under different forms of ownership: A cross-sectional questionnaire survey. *International Journal of Nursing Studies, 46*(1), 95–106. https://doi.org/10.1016/j.ijnurstu.2008.08.002

Hansen, L. O., Williams, M. V., & Singer, S. J. (2011). Perceptions of hospital safety climate and incidence of readmission. *Health Services Research, 46*(2), 596–616. https://doi.org/10.1111/j.1475-6773.2010.01204.x

Health Foundation. (2011). *Measuring safety culture. Research scan*. London: Health Foundation. Retrieved from http://www.health.org.uk/sites/health/files/MeasuringSafetyCulture.pdf

Heck, R. H., & Thomas, S. L. (2015). *An introduction to multilevel modeling techniques*. New York, NY: Routledge.

Hobfoll, S. E. (2002). Social and psychological resources and adaptation. *Review of General Psychology, 6*(4), 307–324. https://doi.org/10.1037/1089-2680.6.4.307

Hobfoll, S. E., & Freedy, J. (1993). Conservation of resources: A general stress theory applied to burnout. In W. B. Schaufeli, C. Maslach, & T. Marek (Eds.), *Professional burnout: Recent developments in theory and research* (pp. 115–133). Philadelphia, PA: Taylor & Francis. https://doi.org/10.1680/udap.2010.163

Hobfoll, S. E., Halbesleben, J., Neveu, J.-P., & Westman, M. (2018). Conservation of resources in the organizational context: The reality of resources and their consequences. *Annual Review of Organizational Psychology and Organizational Behavior, 5*(1), 103–128. https://doi.org/10.1146/annurev-orgpsych-032117-104640

Hoff, T., Jameson, L., Hannan, E., & Flink, E. (2004). A review of the literature examining linkages between organizational factors, medical errors, and patient safety. *Medical Care Research and Review : MCRR, 61*(1), 3–37. https://doi.org/10.1177/1077558703257171

Hofmann, D. A., & Mark, B. (2006). An investigation of the relationship between safety climate and medication errors as well as other nurse and patient outcomes. *Personnel Psychology, 59*(4), 847–869. https://doi.org/10.1111/j.1744-6570.2006.00056.x

Howell, A.-M., Burns, E. M., Bouras, G., Donaldson, L. J., Athanasiou, T., & Darzi, A. (2015). Can patient safety incident reports be used to compare hospital safety? Results from a quantitative analysis of the English National Reporting and learning system data. *PLoS One, 10*(12), e0144107. https://doi.org/10.1371/journal.pone.0144107

Hox, J. J., Maas, C. J. M., & Brinkhuis, M. J. S. (2010). The effect of estimation method and sample size in multilevel structural equation modeling. *Statistica Neerlandica, 64*(2), 157–170. https://doi.org/10.1111/j.1467-9574.2009.00445.x

Kagan, I., & Barnoy, S. (2013). Organizational safety culture and medical error reporting by Israeli nurses. *Journal of Nursing Scholarship, 45*(3), 273–280. https://doi.org/10.1111/jnu.12026

Kapinos, K. A., Fitzgerald, P., Greer, N., & Rutks, I. (2012). *The effect of working conditions on patient care: A systematic review* (Evidence-based Synthesis Program No. VA-ESP Project #09–009). Retrieved from http://www.hsrd.research.va.gov/publications/esp/working-conditions-REPORT.pdf

Karasek, R., & Theorell, T. (1990). *Healthy work: Stress, productivity and the reconstruction of working life*. New York, NY: Basic Books. https://doi.org/10.1016/0003-6870(92)90320-U

Kinman, G., & Teoh, K. R.-H. (2018). *What could make a difference to the mental health of UK doctors? A review of the research evidence*. London, UK: Society of Occupational Medicine. Retrieved from https://www.som.org.uk/sites/som.org.uk/files/What_could_make_a_difference_to_the_mental_health_of_UK_doctors_LTF_SOM.pdf

Landers, S. H., & Sehgal, A. R. (2004). Health care lobbying in the United States. *The American Journal of Medicine, 116*(7), 474–477. https://doi.org/10.1016/j.amjmed.2003.10.037

Lang, T. A., Hodge, M., Olson, V., Romano, P. S., & Kravitz, R. L. (2004). Nurse-patient ratios: A systematic review on the effects of nurse staffing on patient, nurse employee, and hospital outcomes. *The Journal of Nursing Administration, 34*(7–8), 326–337. https://doi.org/10.1097/00005110-200407000-00005

Laschinger, H. K. S., & Leiter, M. P. (2006). The impact of nursing work environments on patient safety outcomes: The mediating role of burnout/engagement. *The Journal of Nursing Administration, 36*(5), 259–267. https://doi.org/10.1097/00005110-200605000-00019

Lee, R. T., Seo, B., Hladkyj, S., Lovell, B. L., & Schwartzmann, L. (2013). Correlates of physician burnout across regions and specialties: A meta-analysis. *Human Resources for Health, 11*(1), 48. https://doi.org/10.1186/1478-4491-11-48

Lewin, K. (1943). Psychology and the process of group living. *The Journal of Social Psychology, 17*(1), 113–131. https://doi.org/10.1080/00224545.1943.9712269

Lim, K. K. (2014). Impact of hospital mergers on staff job satisfaction: A quantitative study. *Human Resources for Health, 12*(1), 70. https://doi.org/10.1186/1478-4491-12-70

Lowe, G., & Chan, B. (2010). Using common work environment metrics to improve performance in healthcare organizations. *Healthcare Papers, 10*(3), 43–47. https://doi.org/10.12927/hcpap.2010.21863

Mardon, R. R., Khanna, K., Sorra, J., Dyer, N., & Famolaro, T. (2010). Exploring relationships between hospital patient safety culture and adverse events. *Journal of Patient Safety, 6*, 226–232.

McKinstry, B., Walker, J., Porter, M., Fulton, C., Tait, A., Hanley, J., et al. (2007). The impact of general practitioner morale on patient satisfaction with care: A cross-sectional study. *BMC Family Practice, 8*, 57. https://doi.org/10.1186/1471-2296-8-57

Mears, A. (2014). Gaming and targets in the English NHS. *Universal Journal of Management, 2*(7), 293–301. https://doi.org/http://www.hrpub.org/journals/jour_archive.php?id=21

Montgomery, A., Panagopoulou, E., Kehoe, I., & Valkanos, E. (2011). Connecting organisational culture and quality of care in the hospital: Is job burnout the missing link? *Journal of Health Organization and Management, 25*(1), 108–123. https://doi.org/10.1108/14777261111116851

Montgomery, A., Spânu, F., Băban, A., & Panagopoulou, E. (2015). Job demands, burnout, and engagement among nurses: A multi-level analysis of ORCAB data investigating the moderating effect of teamwork. *Burnout Research, 2*(2–3), 71–79. https://doi.org/10.1016/j.burn.2015.06.001

Muthén, B. O., & Satorra, A. (1995). Complex sample data in structural equation modeling. In P. V. Marsden (Ed.), *Sociological methodology* (pp. 216–316). Washington, DC: American Sociological Association.

NIOSH. (2017). *Total worker health*. Retrieved August 30, 2017, from https://www.cdc.gov/niosh/twh/totalhealth.html

Pisanti, R., van der Doef, M., Maes, S., Lazzari, D., & Bertini, M. (2011). Job characteristics, organizational conditions, and distress/Well-being among Italian and Dutch nurses: A cross-national comparison. *International Journal of Nursing Studies, 48*(7), 829–837. https://doi.org/10.1016/j.ijnurstu.2010.12.006

Powell, M., Dawson, J. F., Topakas, A., Durose, J., & Fewtrell, C. (2014). Staff satisfaction and organisational performance: Evidence from a longitudinal secondary analysis of the NHS staff survey and outcome data. *Health Services and Delivery Research, 2*(50), 1–306. https://doi.org/10.3310/hsdr02500

Preacher, K. J., Zhang, Z., & Zyphur, M. J. (2011). Alternative methods for assessing mediation in multilevel data: The advantages of multilevel SEM. *Structural Equation Modeling: A Multidisciplinary Journal, 18*(2), 161–182. https://doi.org/10.1080/10705511.2011.557329

Probst, T. M., & Estrada, A. X. (2010). Accident under-reporting among employees: Testing the moderating influence of psychological safety climate and supervisor enforcement of safety practices. *Accident Analysis & Prevention, 42*(5), 1438–1444. https://doi.org/10.1016/j.aap.2009.06.027

Rachiotis, G., Kourousis, C., Kamilaraki, M., Symvoulakis, E. K., Dounias, G., & Hadjichristodoulou, C. (2014). Medical supplies shortages and burnout among Greek health care workers during economic crisis: A pilot study. *International Journal of Medical Sciences, 11*(5), 442–447. https://doi.org/10.7150/ijms.7933

Raleigh, V. S., Hussey, D., Seccombe, I., & Qi, R. (2009). Do associations between staff and inpatient feedback have the potential for improving patient experience? An analysis of surveys in NHS acute trusts in England. *Quality & Safety in Health Care, 18*(5), 347–354. https://doi.org/10.1136/qshc.2008.028910

Ratanawongsa, N., Roter, D., Beach, M. C., Laird, S. L., Larson, S. M., Carson, K. A., et al. (2008). Physician burnout and patient-physician communication during primary care encounters. *Journal of General Internal Medicine, 23*(10), 1581–1588. https://doi.org/10.1007/s11606-008-0702-1

Renzi, C., Tabolli, S., Ianni, A., Di Pietro, C., & Puddu, P. (2005). Burnout and job satisfaction comparing healthcare staff of a dermatological hospital and a general hospital. *Journal of the European Academy of Dermatology and Venereology, 19*(2), 153–157. https://doi.org/10.1111/j.1468-3083.2005.01029.x

Royal College of Physicians. (2016). *Underfunded. Underdoctored. Overstretched.* London, UK: RCP. Retrieved from https://www.rcplondon.ac.uk/guidelines-policy/underfunded-underdoctored-overstretched-nhs-2016

Salisbury, C., Wallace, M., & Montgomery, A. A. (2010). Patients' experience and satisfaction in primary care: Secondary analysis using multilevel modelling. *BMJ (Clinical Research Ed.), 341* (oct12_1), c5004. https://doi.org/10.1136/bmj.c5004

Scheepers, R. A., Boerebach, B. C. M., Arah, O. A., Heineman, M. J., & Lombarts, K. M. J. M. H. (2015). A systematic review of the impact of physicians' occupational Well-being on the quality of patient care. *International Journal of Behavioral Medicine, 22*(6), 683–698. https://doi.org/10.1007/s12529-015-9473-3

Schein, E. H. (1985). *Organisational culture and leadership.* John Wiley & Sons, incorporated (vol. 1). San Francisco, CA: Jossey-Bass.

Sizmur, S., & Raleigh, R. (2018). *The risks to care quality and staff wellbeing of an NHS system under pressure.* Oxford, UK: Picker Institute Europe. Retrieved from https://www.picker.org/wp-content/uploads/2014/12/Risks-to-care-quality-and-staff-wellbeing-VR-SS-v8-Final.pdf

Snijders, C., Kollen, B. J., van Lingen, R. A., Fetter, W. P. F., & Molendijk, H. (2009). Which aspects of safety culture predict incident reporting behavior in neonatal intensive care units? A multilevel analysis. *Critical Care Medicine, 37*(1), 61–67. https://doi.org/10.1097/CCM.0b013e31819300e4

Teoh, K. R.-H. (2018). *Hospital working conditions, doctors' work-related wellbeing, and the quality of care provided: A multilevel perspective.* Birkbeck: Birkbeck University of London.

Teoh, K. R.-H., Hassard, J., & Cox, T. (2018). Individual and organizational psychosocial predictors of hospital doctors' work-related Well-being: A multilevel and moderation perspective. *Health Care Management Review, 45,* 162–172. https://doi.org/10.1097/HMR.0000000000000207

Teoh, K. R.-H., Hassard, J., & Cox, T. (2019). Doctors' perceived working conditions and the quality of patient care: A systematic review. *Work and Stress, 33,* 1–29. https://doi.org/10.1080/02678373.2019.1598514

Teoh, K. R.-H., Hassard, J., & Kinman, G. (2020). The healthcare staff wellbeing and patient care relationship: It's not that simple. In A. H. de Lange & L. Lovseth (Eds.), *Healthy healthcare.* Cham: Springer.

Truss, C. (1999). Soft and hard models of human resource management. In L. Gratton, V. H. Hailey, P. Stiles, & C. Truss (Eds.), *Strategic human resource management* (pp. 40–58). New York, NY: Oxford University Press. https://doi.org/10.1093/acprof:oso/9780198782049.003.0002

Tucker, M. K., Jimmieson, N. L., & Oei, T. P. (2013). The relevance of shared experiences: A multi-level study of collective efficacy as a moderator of job control in the stressor-strain relationship. *Work and Stress, 27*(1), 1–21. https://doi.org/10.1080/02678373.2013.772356

Van Bogaert, P., Clarke, S. P., Wouters, K., Franck, E., Willems, R., & Mondelaers, M. (2013). Impacts of unit-level nurse practice environment, workload and burnout on nurse-reported outcomes in psychiatric hospitals: A multilevel modelling approach. *International Journal of Nursing Studies, 50*(3), 357–365. https://doi.org/10.1016/j.ijnurstu.2012.05.006

Van Bogaert, P., Kowalski, C., Weeks, S. M., Van Heusden, D., & Clarke, S. P. (2013). The relationship between nurse practice environment, nurse work characteristics, burnout and job outcome and quality of nursing care: A cross-sectional survey. *International Journal of Nursing Studies, 50*(12), 1667–1677. https://doi.org/10.1016/j.ijnurstu.2013.05.010

Van Bogaert, P., Meulemans, H., Clarke, S. P., Vermeyen, K., & Van de Heyning, P. (2009). Hospital nurse practice environment, burnout, job outcomes and quality of care: Test of a structural equation model. *Journal of Advanced Nursing, 65*(10), 2175–2185. https://doi.org/10.1111/j.1365-2648.2009.05082.x

van Horn, J. E., Taris, T. W., Schaufeli, W. B., & Schreurs, P. J. G. (2004). The structure of occupational Well-being: A study among Dutch teachers. *Journal of Occupational and Organizational Psychology, 77*(3), 365–375. https://doi.org/10.1348/0963179041752718

Warr, P. (1994). A conceptual framework for the study of work and mental health. *Work and Stress, 8*(2), 84–97. https://doi.org/10.1080/02678379408259982

WHO. (2010). *Healthy workplaces: A model for action*. Geneva: WHO.

Chapter 5
Burnout in Primary Care Workforce

Anli Yue Zhou, Maria Panagioti, Henry Galleta-Williams, and Aneez Esmail

5.1 The State of Primary Care Across Europe

Primary care is at the forefront of global healthcare and is responsible for providing over 80% of the patient care across Europe (Starfield, Shi, & Macinko, 2005; Zenasni, Boujut, Woerner, & Sultan, 2012). Primary care is largely viewed as universally accessible service for individuals, families and communities with one of its core missions being the coordination of care provided across several settings. The World Health Organisation has emphasised that health systems should be responsive to the expectations of the population and this is especially true for primary care systems (WHO, 2000). In fact, for most patients, primary care is the point where their health needs are satisfied while in parallel acts as the gatekeeper to the rest of the system. In that respect, primary care plays a crucial role in how patients value health systems as responsive to their needs and expectations (Murante, Seghieri, Vainieri, & Schafer, 2017). People in the general population use primary care more often than any other healthcare setting for health and non-health needs with primary care being the only point in the healthcare system that patients expect to receive continuity of care throughout their lifetime (Starfield, 1998). Primary care is therefore best-placed to put the Evidence Based Medicine into practice with patients and clinicians making treatment choices together after considering the best available evidence, the clinician's experience and the patient's values (Barratt, 2008).

There has been an increasing focus on measuring the quality of primary care especially in response to the aging population and growing burden of chronic

A. Y. Zhou (✉) · M. Panagioti · H. Galleta-Williams · A. Esmail
Division of Population Health, Health Services Research and Primary Care, School of Health Sciences, Faculty of Biology, Medicine and Health, University of Manchester, Manchester Academic Health Science Centre Manchester, Manchester, UK
e-mail: yue.zhou@postgrad.manchester.ac.uk

diseases in the population (OECD, 2016). However, over the past decade, primary care systems across Europe face a serious growing crisis, which is mainly driven by emerging financial constraints, workforce deficiencies and the complexity of electronic systems (Marchand & Peckham, 2017; Roland & Everington, 2016).

The work intensity in primary care combined with negative perceptions of the working life of general practitioners (GPs) appears to be significant factors in the retention and recruitment crisis of GPs in primary care (Dayan, Arora, Rosen, & Curry, 2014). Potential and current GP trainees choose to postpone training or follow an alternate career path. The perception of general practice as a career among medical students has made them less likely to see it as a desirable profession further compounding the risk of staffing shortages in the future (Reid & Alberti, 2018). Medical students have perceived general practice as a less prestigious career choice, negative influences from senior hospital doctors about the role of GPs and the perception that GP being a backup plan (Reid & Alberti, 2018). Those that do complete GP training frequently choose part time, locum or portfolio careers rather than salaried or partner positions (Dale, Russell, Scott, & Owen, 2017). The problem is further compounded by the efflux of experienced practitioners with plans among senior GPs to enter a different line of work or retire early (Sansom, Calitri, Carter, & Campbell, 2016).

There have been government initiatives in the United Kingdom (UK) to combat the primary care crisis by increasing the number of GPs trained, which include pledging to a further 5000 GPs by 2020, but GP numbers are yet to increase (Geurts, Kompier, Roxburgh, & Houtman, 2003). Other European countries have reported the supply of GPs being static over the years (van Loenen et al., 2016) but there have been growing concerns about potential GP shortages in Europe in the future (OECD, 2016).

5.1.1 The Problem of Burnout in Primary Care

It is increasingly recognised that the quality of patient care and the overall efficiency and sustainability of the primary healthcare services largely depend on the function and the well-being of its workforce. The most well-known measure to capture the occupational well-being of people working in healthcare care services is burnout. Burnout is a response to the prolonged exposure to occupational stress encompassing feelings of emotional exhaustion, depersonalisation and reduced professional efficacy (Maslach, Schaufeli, & Leiter, 2001). It is scientifically and clinically established as a work-stress syndrome for more than 30 years and is the primary outcome of the most work-stress interventions worldwide (Dyrbye et al., 2017).

It has been estimated that over 40% of GPs working in primary care across Europe report symptoms of burnout (Goehring, Bouvier Gallacchi, Kunzi, & Bovier, 2005; Linzer et al., 2009; Soler et al., 2008). A recent survey by the British Medical Association in the UK found that nine out of 10 GPs are at high or very high risk of burnout. GPs have been found to have the higher prevalence rates of burnout compared to other specialties (Arigoni, Bovier, & Sappino, 2010; Del Carmen et al., 2019; Dyrbye et al., 2013), especially in relation to emotional exhaustion (Pedersen, Sorensen, Bruun, Christensen, & Vedsted, 2016). Similar findings have also been found in nursing staff and previous research has estimated that up to 44% of primary care nurses have reported symptoms of burnout (Pérez-Francisco et al., 2020).

5.1.2 Contributors of Burnout in Primary Care

There is a recognised need to respond to the needs of the changing population and improve accessibility to primary care (OECD, 2016). The population of most developed countries is aging and has complex medical problems and therefore increasing work demands for primary care workers (Irish & Purvis, 2012; Primary Care Workforce Commission, 2015). In the United Kingdom (UK), investment in primary care has fallen in comparison to hospital investments despite increasing expectations in accessibility, quality of care and the range of services provided in primary care with an increasing shift to services to the community and to reduce potentially avoidable hospital admissions (OECD, 2016; Primary Care Workforce Commission, 2015). Furthermore, there have been diminishing resources coupled within increasing costs of care (Baird, Charles, Honeyman, Maguire, & Das, 2016) and GPs are under pressure to deliver high quality service despite limited resources.

As patients have become more involved in the management of their medical conditions, GPs have an additional role to support patient self-management and decision making (Primary Care Workforce Commission, 2015). This contributes to larger numbers and lengthier consultations per year (Irish & Purvis, 2012; Linzer et al., 2009). These challenging work conditions, low work control, lack of team cohesiveness and high work pace have contributed to burnout (Linzer et al., 2009). Workload is further compounded by high administrative burdens, which in turn can also affect job satisfaction as well as contribute to burnout (Hall, Johnson, Watt, & O'Connor, 2019; van Loenen et al., 2016). There has also been an increasing recruitment crisis in primary care, not just in GPs but also in nursing, whose role may improve access to primary care and also share the GP's workload (Maier, Aiken, & Busse, 2017; Manzano-García & Ayala-Calvo, 2014; Primary Care Workforce Commission, 2015).

5.2 Impact of Burnout in Primary Care

Burnout has profound consequences on the wellbeing of GPs and other primary care workers, adversely affects the quality of patient care and contributes to the ongoing recruitment and retention crisis of the primary care workforce.

5.2.1 Impacts on the Individual Health Professionals

Long periods of excessive work-related stress as well as burnout could have serious consequences on doctors' health (Wallace, Lemaire, & Ghali, 2009) such as substance abuse, depression, poor work-life balance as well as suicidal ideation (Firth-Cozens, 1998; Graham, Albery, Ramirez, & Richards, 2001; van der Heijden, Dillingh, Bakker, & Prins, 2008). It has been suggested that due to the working conditions in primary care, GPs are particularly prone to work-life interference (Firth-Cozens, 1998; Montgomery, Panagopolou, & Benos, 2006), which in turn can impact on their psychological and physical health (Geurts et al., 2003). Emotional exhaustion has been found to be associated with mental health problems and suicidal ideation in GPs (Lheureux, Truchot, & Borteyrou, 2016). Alcohol abuse is well known to be associated with distress and burnout among doctors (Oreskovich et al., 2012; Oreskovich et al., 2015; Pedersen et al., 2016) and in particular, GPs have been found to have a higher than average prevalence of alcohol abuse/dependency in comparison to other specialties (Oreskovich et al., 2015). Moreover, burnout in GPs has also been associated with a higher sickness absenteeism (Soler et al., 2008).

5.2.2 Impacts on Health Care Quality, Workforce Shortages and Economic Costs

There have also been increasing concerns about the impact of GP burnout on the safety and quality of service delivery in primary care (Panagioti et al., 2018). There is evidence that GPs experience burnout were more likely to report medical errors and offer suboptimal services to patients (Panagioti et al., 2018; Williams, Manwell, Konrad, & Linzer, 2007). Burnout is not only associated with negative clinical outcomes, but there have been documented associations between burnout and productivity loss (Dewa, Loong, Bonato, Thanh, & Jacobs, 2014; Wallace et al., 2009). A recent survey suggested that over 25% of GPs reduced their working hours due to stress and mental health issues which worsen the already high decline in the numbers of GPs in the UK (Owen, Hopkins, Shortland, & Dale, 2019). Moreover, GPs reporting high levels of distress, job dissatisfaction and burnout found to have a higher intention to quit the profession and take early retirement (Marchand & Peckham, 2017; Owen et al., 2019; Soler, Yaman, & Esteva, 2007; Wallace et al., 2009). An increasing number of GPs have also left the UK to practice abroad in the past decade and the higher levels burnout might partly explain this (Marchand & Peckham, 2017).

A recent estimation in the United States using reduction in clinical hours and turnover in doctors estimated that over $4 billion dollars was attributable to burnout and therefore reinforces the value of investing in burnout reduction programs for doctors (Han et al., 2019). Furthermore, the economic implications of health inequality in the European Union has been estimated to be approximately 980 billion euros per year and inequality related deaths are estimated to more than 700,000 per year (Mackenbach, Meerding, & Kunst, 2011). GPs play an important role in health service provision with the aim to reduce health inequalities. However, it is known that the distribution of the GP workforce is not equal and with GP workforce shortages, this is likely to impact on isolated and deprived communities and therefore further increasing health inequalities amongst populations (Sibbald, 2005).

5.3 Burnout Inspecific Groups Within Primary Care

Within primary care, there are some groups of doctors who are especially vulnerable to burnout including trainee doctors, female doctors and doctors from ethnic minority groups (Houkes, Winants, & Twellaar, 2008; Kinman & Teoh, 2018).

5.3.1 Trainee Doctors

Trainee doctors are fully qualified doctors engaged in post-graduate training and evidence suggests that trainee doctors experience higher levels of burnout in comparison to senior doctors in various specialities, including in primary care (Del Carmen et al., 2019; Shanafelt et al., 2012). Studies show that burnout in trainee doctors group can be as high as 73.4% (Rodrigues et al., 2018). In a recent national trainees' survey undertaken in the UK, over one-fifth of trainee doctors reported high or very high levels of burnout (Rimmer, 2019). Burnout in trainees can have detrimental personal and professional consequences (Dyrbye & Shanafelt, 2016; Prins et al., 2007) and has been associated with decreased empathy, professionalism concerns, medical errors and suboptimal patient care, as well as concerns around mental health (Dyrbye & Shanafelt, 2016). The underlying factors which drive the high levels of burnout among trainee doctors are not entirely clear but could include high workload (Dyrbye & Shanafelt, 2016; Prins et al., 2007; Sales, Macdonald, Scallan, & Crane, 2016), staff shortages (Rimmer, 2019), concerns regarding career progression and training requirements (Dyrbye & Shanafelt, 2016; Sales et al., 2016) as well as challenging work environments (Starmer, Frintner, & Freed, 2016), lack of support (Martini, Arfken, Churchill, & Balon, 2004) and high work-life conflicts (Dyrbye et al., 2013). Attracting more trainee doctors in primary care is the hope for reversing the current shrinking GP workforce in primary care (Majeed, 2017) and therefore it is of major importance to address factors contributing to burnout in trainee doctors.

5.3.2 Female Doctors

Women make up a significant proportion of doctors in the medical profession and in the UK, women make up nearly 46% of the medical profession (OECD, 2017). Proportions of female doctors worldwide vary between 20.3% in Japan to 74.3% in Latvia (OECD, 2017). Women make up 41–58% of doctors working in primary care (Jefferson, Bloor, & Maynard, 2015; Soler et al., 2008; Vassar, 2019) and similar proportions (54%) have also been found in the UK GP workforce (GP online, 2018). Women therefore play a major role in providing healthcare to the general population. Previous research suggests that female GPs are twice as likely to report burnout compared to males (Rabatin et al., 2016). Key contributory factors to the higher levels of burnout among female GPs are dissatisfaction with their job, difficulties in achieving work-life balance and using fewer stress-regulating measures e.g. exercise and socialising (Dreher, Theune, Kersting, Geiser, & Weltermann, 2019). Work-life balance (Prins et al., 2007; Shadbolt & Bunker, 2009; Shanafelt et al., 2012; Shanafelt et al., 2015) has received particular attention as female GPs were found to more likely prioritise their family life in comparison to other specialties (Buddeberg-Fischer, Stamm, Buddeberg, & Klaghofer, 2008). Poor work-life balance could be attributed to gender differences in domestic activities as female doctors have been found to spend more time on domestic activities and were more likely to have time off work due to childcare arrangements (Jolly et al., 2014). Although research is needed to confirm this, it could be assumed that female GPs are more likely to be trapped into these gender differences compared to other specialities. This could be because of challenging work demands that includes meeting patient demands, low control, high workload and lack of team cohesiveness as well as poor work-life balance and family commitments.

5.3.3 Doctors from Ethnic Minorities

Doctors from ethnic minorities have been estimated to make up around one third of the UK and United States medical workforce (NHS workforce, 2020; Xierali & Nivet, 2018) and are more likely to practice in primary care and in underserved populations (Xierali & Nivet, 2018). There is little research exploring the association between ethnicity and burnout and thus far, a direct association between ethnicity and burnout has not been found (Rabatin et al., 2016). However, there have been concerns of workplace bullying and racial discrimination in doctors from ethnic minority (Esmail, 2007), as well as concerns about isolation and lack of social support, which in turn could impact on career progression (Rich, Viney, Needleman, Griffin, & Woolf, 2016).

Recent data from the UK suggests that GPs received more complaints compared to other specialties and those doctors of ethnic minority and international medical graduates were more likely to receive complaints or to be referred to the medical board for investigation (General Medical Council, 2019b). Workplace factors such as lack of support and effective feedback, isolation and difficulties in transitioning into new work environments, organisational culture and risk of bias and stereotyping have been identified (General Medical Council, 2019a) in doctors from ethnic minority groups. These issues can make this group more vulnerable to complaints and fitness to practice procedures that in turn can impact on mental health in general (Bourne et al., 2015).

5.4 Mitigating Burnout and Promoting Engagement in Primary Care

Cultivating high quality, safe primary care is a challenging target that requires considerable effort, time and resources. Healthcare efficacy in primary care should be seen as the combined consequence of organisational, workforce and patient factors (Rowe, de Savigny, Lanata, & Victora, 2005). Consistent with this view, addressing burnout in primary care should be viewed as a shared responsibility between system, organisation and the individual (West, Dyrbye, & Shanafelt, 2018).

There is increasing evidence that major improvements targeting the function of the healthcare organisation and workforce engagement are needed for achieving high quality healthcare (Benning et al., 2011; Panagioti et al., 2017). For example, recent meta-analyses show that multicomponent organisational interventions are the most effective approaches for mitigating burnout in doctors and healthcare professionals (Panagioti et al., 2017; West, Dyrbye, Erwin, & Shanafelt, 2016). However, such intervention models are rare. Most existing interventions focus on single interventions rather than combined multifaceted approaches and are generally no examined in randomised controlled trial designs, particularly for organisational solutions (West et al., 2018). Furthermore, most studies evaluating the impact of organisational interventions have been found to be of poor quality (DeChant et al., 2019).

There is an increasing expectation for primary care to extend the range of services they provide and therefore there is a need to develop a strong multidisciplinary team to provide these primary care services (Primary Care Workforce Commission, 2015). Promoting effective teamwork has been utilised as an intervention to mitigate burnout by focusing on supporting personnel to reduce administrative burden, expanding team responsibilities and improving communication amongst doctors (DeChant et al., 2019). However, very few studies have utilised a practice-level approach that focuses on the organisational culture and the dynamic relationships of health professionals with their peers (e.g. doctors, allied health professionals and administrators) and their patients (DeChant et al., 2019; Panagioti et al., 2017).

There is paucity of organisational or multicomponent intervention studies for mitigating burnout in European countries (Amis & Osicki, 2018; Giannini et al., 2013; Morrow, Burford, Carter, & Illing, 2014; Quenot et al., 2012; Tucker et al.,

2010) and very few studies have focused on how to monitor and improve workforce engagement in primary care (Cheshire et al., 2017; Cheshire et al., 2017). In the United States, some interventions have been implemented and include workflow redesigns, improving communication, reducing workload, encouraging training and continuing professional development, data-guided interventions and quality improvement projects (DeChant et al., 2019). Extensive research programmes are required to tailor these interventions in different models of care across European countries and undertake evaluations that will provide evidence regarding their feasibility, acceptability and cost-effectiveness. However, the evidence indicates that the core principles of future multicomponent interventions in primary care should focus on (DeChant et al., 2019; Linzer et al., 2009; Montgomery, 2014; Panagioti, Geraghty, & Johnson, 2018, Panagioti et al., 2018; Shanafelt, Dyrbye, & West, 2017; Shanafelt & Noseworthy, 2017; Wallace et al., 2009; West et al., 2018):

- Building a culture of engagement, sense of community and team working
- Effective leadership
- Effective work-life balance within practices
- Promoting peer-support and self-care
- Improving efficiency and workflow of the practice environment
- Involving relevant stakeholders including patients in the design of intervention
- Promoting continuing professional development and quality improvement
- Routinely monitoring dimensions of wellbeing to guide intervention development

Potential interventions in primary could focus on multiple components such as the individual (peer-support and self-care), the work environment (effective leadership and building a culture of community), work processes (quality improvement, workforce development, efficiency improvement) as well as routinely monitoring to ensure any arising issues can be addressed in a timely manner.

5.5 Conclusion

There is ample evidence that burnout has taken the form of an epidemic among doctors and other health care workers. It constitutes a critical threat for primary care because of already ongoing workforce crisis. Substantial financial investments are needed for improving the workforce planning across Europe, a core component of which should be systematic implementation of interventions to mitigate burnout and improve workforce engagement. Multicomponent interventions that will monitor and improve the organisational function of primary care while in parallel with each other, will promote innovative models for effectively engaging health professionals and patients, and have the most realistic potential for improving workforce engagement (Panagioti et al., 2017).

Key Message for Researchers

- Burnout has profound consequences on the wellbeing of General Practitioners and other primary care workers, adversely affects the quality of patient care and contributes to the ongoing recruitment and retention crisis of the primary care workforce.
- There is increasing evidence that major improvements targeting the function of the healthcare organisation and workforce engagement are needed for achieving high quality healthcare
- Extensive research programmes are required to tailor these interventions in different models of care across European countries and undertake evaluations that will provide evidence regarding their feasibility, acceptability and cost-effectiveness.

Key Messages for Healthcare Delivery

- Doctors and healthcare workers in primary care should focus their values to integrate the importance of self-care, work-life balance and effective collaboration with their colleagues to prevent burnout;
- Leaders and policy makers should increase investment on the workforce planning across Europe, a core component of which should be systematic implementation of interventions to mitigate burnout and improve workforce engagement.
- Multicomponent interventions that will monitor and improve the organisational function of primary care and effectively engage health professionals and patients have the most realistic potential for improving workforce wellness.

References

Amis, S. M., & Osicki, T. H. E. (2018). Can patient safety be improved by reducing the volume of "inappropriate prescribing tasks" handed over to out-of-hours junior doctors? *International journal of General Medicine, 11*, 105–112.

Arigoni, F., Bovier, P. A., & Sappino, A. P. (2010). Trend of burnout among Swiss doctors. *Swiss Medical Weekly, 140*, w13070. https://doi.org/10.4414/smw.2010.13070

Baird, B., Charles, A., Honeyman, M., Maguire, D., & Das, P. (2016). *Understanding pressures in general practice*. London: King's Fund.

Barratt, A. (2008). Evidence based medicine and shared decision making: The challenge of getting both evidence and preferences into health care. *Patient Education and Counseling, 73*(3), 407–412. https://doi.org/10.1016/j.pec.2008.07.054

Benning, A., Ghaleb, M., Suokas, A., Dixon-Woods, M., Dawson, J., Barber, N., et al. (2011). Large scale organisational intervention to improve patient safety in four UK hospitals: Mixed method evaluation. *BMJ, 342*, d195.

Bourne, T., Wynants, L., Peters, M., Van Audenhove, C., Timmerman, D., Van Calster, B., et al. (2015). The impact of complaints procedures on the welfare, health and clinical practise of 7926 doctors in the UK: A cross-sectional survey. *BMJ Open, 5*(1), e006687. https://doi.org/10.1136/bmjopen-2014-006687

Buddeberg-Fischer, B., Stamm, M., Buddeberg, C., & Klaghofer, R. (2008). The new generation of family physicians--career motivation, life goals and work-life balance. *Swiss Med Wkly, 138*(21–22), 305–312.

Cheshire, A., Hughes, J., Lewith, G., Panagioti, M., Peters, D., Simon, C., et al. (2017). GPs' perceptions of resilience training: A qualitative study. *The British Journal of General Practice, 67*(663), e709–e715.

Cheshire, A., Ridge, D., Hughes, J., Peters, D., Panagioti, M., Simon, C., et al. (2017). Influences on GP coping and resilience: A qualitative study in primary care. *British Journal of General Practice, 67*(659), e428–e436. https://doi.org/10.3399/bjgp17X690893

Dale, J., Russell, R., Scott, E., & Owen, K. (2017). Factors influencing career intentions on completion of general practice vocational training in England: A cross-sectional study. *BMJ Open, 7*(8), e017143.

Dayan, M., Arora, S., Rosen, R., & Curry, N. (2014). *Is general practice in crisis*. London: The Nuffield Council.

DeChant, P. F., Acs, A., Rhee, K. B., Boulanger, T. S., Snowdon, J. L., Tutty, M. A., et al. (2019). Effect of organization-directed workplace interventions on physician burnout: A systematic review. *Mayo Clin Proc Innov Qual Outcomes, 3*(4), 384–408. https://doi.org/10.1016/j.mayocpiqo.2019.07.006

Del Carmen, M. G., Herman, J., Rao, S., Hidrue, M. K., Ting, D., Lehrhoff, Lenz, S., Heffernan, J., Ferris, T. G. (2019). Trends and factors associated with physician burnout at a multispecialty academic faculty practice organization. *JAMA Network Open, 2*(3), e190554. doi:https://doi.org/10.1001/jamanetworkopen.2019.0554.

Dewa, C. S., Loong, D., Bonato, S., Thanh, N. X., & Jacobs, P. (2014). How does burnout affect physician productivity? A systematic literature review. *BMC Health Services Research, 14*, 325. https://doi.org/10.1186/1472-6963-14-325

Dreher, A., Theune, M., Kersting, C., Geiser, F., & Weltermann, B. (2019). Prevalence of burnout among German general practitioners: Comparison of physicians working in solo and group practices. *PLoS One, 14*(2), e0211223. https://doi.org/10.1371/journal.pone.0211223

Dyrbye, L., & Shanafelt, T. (2016). A narrative review on burnout experienced by medical students and residents. *Medical Education, 50*(1), 132–149. https://doi.org/10.1111/medu.12927

Dyrbye, L. N., Trockel, M., Frank, E., Olson, K., Linzer, M., Lemaire, J., et al. (2017). Development of a research agenda to identify evidence-based strategies to improve physician wellness and reduce burnout. *Annals of Internal Medicine, 166*(10), 743–744. https://doi.org/10.7326/M16-2956

Dyrbye, L. N., Varkey, P., Boone, S. L., Satele, D. V., Sloan, J. A., & Shanafelt, T. D. (2013). Physician satisfaction and burnout at different career stages. *Mayo Clinic Proceedings, 88*(12), 1358–1367. https://doi.org/10.1016/j.mayocp.2013.07.016

Esmail, A. (2007). Asian doctors in the NHS: Service and betrayal. *The British Journal of General Practice, 57*(543), 827–834.

Firth-Cozens, J. (1998). Individual and organizational predictors of depression in general practitioners. *The British Journal of General Practice, 48*(435), 1647–1651.

General Medical Council. (2019a). *Fair to refer?* Retrieved from https://www.gmc-uk.org/about/what-we-do-and-why/data-and-research/research-and-insight-archive/fair-to-refer. (last accessed 10/06/2020).

General Medical Council. (2019b). *The state of medical education and practice in the UK: The workforce report*. Retrieved from https://www.gmc-uk.org/about/what-we-do-and-why/data-and-research/the-state-of-medical-education-and-practice-in-the-uk/workforce-report-2019. (last accessed 10/06/2020).

Geurts, S. A. E., Kompier, M. A. J., Roxburgh, S., & Houtman, I. L. D. (2003). Does work-home interference mediate the relationship between workload and Well-being? *Journal of Vocational Behavior, 63*(3), 532–559. https://doi.org/10.1016/S0001-8791(02)00025-8

Giannini, A., Miccinesi, G., Prandi, E., Buzzoni, C., Borreani, C., & ODIN Study Group. (2013). Partial liberalization of visiting policies and ICU staff: A before-and-after study. *Intensive Care Medicine, 39*(12), 2180–2187.

Goehring, C., Bouvier Gallacchi, M., Kunzi, B., & Bovier, P. (2005). Psychosocial and professional characteristics of burnout in Swiss primary care practitioners: A cross-sectional survey. *Swiss Med Wkly, 135*(7–8), 101–108. https://doi.org/10.4414/smw.2005.10841

GP online. (2018, March). *The rise of women in General Practice*. Retrieved from https://www.gponline.com/rise-women-general-practice/article/1458988. (last accessed 10/06/2020).

Graham, J., Albery, I. P., Ramirez, A. J., & Richards, M. A. (2001). How hospital consultants cope with stress at work: Implications for their mental health. *Stress and Health, 17*(2), 85–89. https://doi.org/10.1002/smi.884

Hall, L. H., Johnson, J., Watt, I., & O'Connor, D. B. (2019). Association of GP wellbeing and burnout with patient safety in UK primary care: A cross-sectional survey. *British Journal of General Practice, 69*(684), e507–e514. https://doi.org/10.3399/bjgp19X702713

Han, S., Shanafelt, T. D., Sinsky, C. A., Awad, K. M., Dyrbye, L. N., Fiscus, L. C., et al. (2019). Estimating the attributable cost of physician burnout in the United States. *Annals of Internal Medicine, 170*(11), 784–790. https://doi.org/10.7326/M18-1422

Houkes, I., Winants, Y. H., & Twellaar, M. (2008). Specific determinants of burnout among male and female general practitioners: A cross-lagged panel analysis. *Journal of Occupational and Organizational Psychology, 81*(2), 249–276.

Irish, B., & Purvis, M. (2012). Not just another primary care workforce crisis. *The British Journal of General Practice, 62*(597), 178–179. https://doi.org/10.3399/bjgp12X635985

Jefferson, L., Bloor, K., & Maynard, A. (2015). Women in medicine: Historical perspectives and recent trends. *British Medical Bulletin, 114*(1), 5–15. https://doi.org/10.1093/bmb/ldv007

Jolly, S., Griffith, K. A., DeCastro, R., Stewart, A., Ubel, P., & Jagsi, R. (2014). Gender differences in time spent on parenting and domestic responsibilities by high-achieving young physician-researchers. *Annals of Internal Medicine, 160*(5), 344–353. https://doi.org/10.7326/M13-0974

Kinman, G., & Teoh, K. (2018). *What could make a difference to the mental health of UK doctors? A review of the research evidence*. London: SOM.

Lheureux, F., Truchot, D., & Borteyrou, X. (2016). Suicidal tendency, physical health problems and addictive behaviours among general practitioners: Their relationship with burnout. *Work and Stress, 30*(2), 173–192. https://doi.org/10.1080/02678373.2016.1171806

Linzer, M., Manwell, L. B., Williams, E. S., Bobula, J. A., Brown, R. L., Varkey, A., et al. (2009). Working conditions in primary care: Physician reactions and care quality. *Annals of Internal Medicine, 151*(1), 28–36., W26-29. https://doi.org/10.7326/0003-4819-151-1-200907070-00006

Mackenbach, J. P., Meerding, W. J., & Kunst, A. E. (2011). Economic costs of health inequalities in the European Union. *Journal of Epidemiology and Community Health, 65*(5), 412–419. https://doi.org/10.1136/jech.2010.112680

Maier, C. B., Aiken, L. H., & Busse, R. (2017). *Nurses in advanced roles in primary care: Policy levers for implementation*. Paris: OECD Publishing.

Majeed, A. (2017). Shortage of general practitioners in the NHS. *BMJ, 358*, j3191. https://doi.org/10.1136/bmj.j3191

Manzano-García, G., & Ayala-Calvo, J. C. (2014). An overview of nursing in Europe: A SWOT analysis. *Nursing Inquiry, 21*(4), 358–367.

Marchand, C., & Peckham, S. (2017). Addressing the crisis of GP recruitment and retention: A systematic review. *British Journal of General Practice, 67*(657), E227–E237. https://doi.org/10.3399/bjgp17X689929

Martini, S., Arfken, C. L., Churchill, A., & Balon, R. (2004). Burnout comparison among residents in different medical specialties. *Academic Psychiatry, 28*(3), 240–242. https://doi.org/10.1176/appi.ap.28.3.240

Maslach, C., Schaufeli, W. B., & Leiter, M. P. (2001). Job burnout. *Annual Review of Psychology, 52*, 397–422. https://doi.org/10.1146/annurev.psych.52.1.397

Montgomery, A. (2014). The inevitability of physician burnout: Implications for interventions. *Burnout Research, 1*(1), 50–56.

Montgomery, A. J., Panagopolou, E., & Benos, A. (2006). Work-family interference as a mediator between job demands and job burnout among doctors. *Stress and Health, 22*(3), 203–212. https://doi.org/10.1002/smi.1104

Morrow, G., Burford, B., Carter, M., & Illing, J. (2014). Have restricted working hours reduced junior doctors' experience of fatigue? A focus group and telephone interview study. *BMJ Open, 4*(3), e004222.

Murante, A. M., Seghieri, C., Vainieri, M., & Schafer, W. L. A. (2017). Patient-perceived responsiveness of primary care systems across Europe and the relationship with the health expenditure and remuneration systems of primary care doctors. *Social Science & Medicine, 186*, 139–147. https://doi.org/10.1016/j.socscimed.2017.06.005

NHS Workforce March 2019. (2020, January). Retrieved from https://www.ethnicity-facts-figures.service.gov.uk/workforce-and-business/workforce-diversity/nhs-workforce/latest#by-ethnicity-and-type-of-role. (last accessed 10/06/2020).

OECD/EU. (2016). *Health at a glance: Europe 2016 – State of health in the EU cycle*. Paris: OECD Publishing.

Oreskovich, M. R., Kaups, K. L., Balch, C. M., Hanks, J. B., Satele, D., Sloan, J., et al. (2012). Prevalence of alcohol use disorders among American surgeons. *Archives of Surgery, 147*(2), 168–174. https://doi.org/10.1001/archsurg.2011.1481

Oreskovich, M. R., Shanafelt, T., Dyrbye, L. N., Tan, L., Sotile, W., Satele, D., et al. (2015). The prevalence of substance use disorders in American physicians. *The American Journal on Addictions, 24*(1), 30–38. https://doi.org/10.1111/ajad.12173

Organisation for Economic Co-operation and Development (OECD). (2017). *Women make up most of the health sector workers but they are under-represented in high-skilled jobs*. Retrieved from https://www.oecd.org/gender/data/women-make-up-most-of-the-health-sector-workers-but-they-are-under-represented-in-high-skilled-jobs.htm. (last accessed 10/06/2020).

Owen, K., Hopkins, T., Shortland, T., & Dale, J. (2019). GP retention in the UK: A worsening crisis. Findings from a cross-sectional survey. *BMJ Open, 9*(2), e026048. https://doi.org/10.1136/bmjopen-2018-026048

Panagioti, M., Geraghty, K., & Johnson, J. (2018). How to prevent burnout in cardiologists? A review of the current evidence, gaps, and future directions. *Trends in Cardiovascular Medicine, 28*(1), 1–7.

Panagioti, M., Geraghty, K., Johnson, J., Zhou, A., Panagopoulou, E., Chew-Graham, C., et al. (2018). Association between physician burnout and patient safety, professionalism, and patient satisfaction: A systematic review and meta-analysis. *JAMA Internal Medicine, 178*(10), 1317–1330. https://doi.org/10.1001/jamainternmed.2018.3713

Panagioti, M., Panagopoulou, E., Bower, P., Lewith, G., Kontopantelis, E., Chew-Graham, C., et al. (2017). Controlled interventions to reduce burnout in physicians: A systematic review and meta-analysis. *JAMA Internal Medicine, 177*(2), 195–205. https://doi.org/10.1001/jamainternmed.2016.7674

Pedersen, A. F., Sorensen, J. K., Bruun, N. H., Christensen, B., & Vedsted, P. (2016). Risky alcohol use in Danish physicians: Associated with alexithymia and burnout? *Drug and Alcohol Dependence, 160*, 119–126. https://doi.org/10.1016/j.drugalcdep.2015.12.038

Pérez-Francisco, D. H., Duarte-Clíments, G., Del Rosario-Melián, J. M., Gómez-Salgado, J., Romero-Martín, M., & Sánchez-Gómez, M. B. (2020). Influence of workload on primary care Nurses' health and burnout, Patients' safety, and quality of care: Integrative review. *Healthcare (Basel), 8*(1). https://doi.org/10.3390/healthcare8010012

Primary Care Workforce Commission. (2015). *The future of primary care: creating teams for tomorrow*.

Prins, J. T., Gazendam-Donofrio, S. M., Tubben, B. J., van der Heijden, F. M., van de Wiel, H. B., & Hoekstra-Weebers, J. E. (2007). Burnout in medical residents: A review. *Medical Education, 41*(8), 788–800. https://doi.org/10.1111/j.1365-2923.2007.02797.x

Quenot, J.-P., Rigaud, J.-P., Prin, S., Barbar, S., Pavon, A., Hamet, M., et al. (2012). Suffering among carers working in critical care can be reduced by an intensive communication strategy on end-of-life practices. *Intensive Care Medicine, 38*(1), 55–61.

Rabatin, J., Williams, E., Baier Manwell, L., Schwartz, M. D., Brown, R. L., & Linzer, M. (2016). Predictors and outcomes of burnout in primary care physicians. *Journal of Primary Care and Community Health, 7*(1), 41–43. https://doi.org/10.1177/2150131915607799

Reid, K., & Alberti, H. (2018). Medical students' perceptions of general practice as a career; a phenomenological study using socialisation theory. *Education for Primary Care, 29*(4), 208–214. https://doi.org/10.1080/14739879.2018.1460868

Rich, A., Viney, R., Needleman, S., Griffin, A., & Woolf, K. (2016). 'You can't be a person and a doctor': The work-life balance of doctors in training-a qualitative study. *BMJ Open, 6*(12), e013897. https://doi.org/10.1136/bmjopen-2016-013897

Rimmer, A. (2019). Trainees are unsure of where to get help with everyday work problems, survey finds. *BMJ: British Medical Journal (Online), 366*, l4587.

Rodrigues, H., Cobucci, R., Oliveira, A., Cabral, J. V., Medeiros, L., Gurgel, K., et al. (2018). Burnout syndrome among medical residents: A systematic review and meta-analysis. *PLoS One, 13*(11), e0206840. https://doi.org/10.1371/journal.pone.0206840

Roland, M., & Everington, S. (2016). Tackling the crisis in general practice. *BMJ, 352*, i942. https://doi.org/10.1136/bmj.i942

Rowe, A. K., de Savigny, D., Lanata, C. F., & Victora, C. G. (2005). How can we achieve and maintain high-quality performance of health workers in low-resource settings? *Lancet, 366*(9490), 1026–1035. https://doi.org/10.1016/S0140-6736(05)67028-6

Sales, B., Macdonald, A., Scallan, S., & Crane, S. (2016). How can educators support general practice (GP) trainees to develop resilience to prevent burnout? *Education for Primary Care, 27*(6), 487–493. https://doi.org/10.1080/14739879.2016.1217170

Sansom, A., Calitri, R., Carter, M., & Campbell, J. (2016). Understanding quit decisions in primary care: A qualitative study of older GPs. *BMJ Open, 6*(2), e010592. https://doi.org/10.1136/bmjopen-2015-010592

Shadbolt, N., & Bunker, J. (2009). Choosing general practice – a review of career choice determinants. *Australian Family Physician, 38*(1–2), 53–55.

Shanafelt, T. D., Boone, S., Tan, L., Dyrbye, L. N., Sotile, W., Satele, D., et al. (2012). Burnout and satisfaction with work-life balance among US physicians relative to the general US population. *Archives of Internal Medicine, 172*(18), 1377–1385. https://doi.org/10.1001/archinternmed.2012.3199

Shanafelt, T. D., Dyrbye, L. N., & West, C. P. (2017). Addressing physician burnout: The way forward. *JAMA, 317*(9), 901–902. https://doi.org/10.1001/jama.2017.0076

Shanafelt, T. D., Hasan, O., Dyrbye, L. N., Sinsky, C., Satele, D., Sloan, J., et al. (2015). Changes in burnout and satisfaction with work-life balance in physicians and the general US working population between 2011 and 2014. *Mayo Clinic Proceedings, 90*(12), 1600–1613. https://doi.org/10.1016/j.mayocp.2015.08.023

Shanafelt, T. D., & Noseworthy, J. H. (2017). Executive leadership and physician Well-being: Nine organizational strategies to promote engagement and reduce burnout. *Mayo Clinic Proceedings, 92*(1), 129–146. https://doi.org/10.1016/j.mayocp.2016.10.004

Sibbald, B. (2005). Putting general practitioners where they are needed: An overview of strategies to correct maldistribution. Secondary Putting general practitioners where they are needed: an overview of strategies to correct maldistribution.

Soler, J. K., Yaman, H., & Esteva, M. (2007). Burnout in European general practice and family medicine. *Social Behavior and Personality, 35*(8), 1149–1150. Retrieved from <go to ISI>://WOS:000251603100015. https://doi.org/10.2224/sbp.2007.35.8.1149.

Soler, J. K., Yaman, H., Esteva, M., Dobbs, F., Asenova, R. S., Katic, M., et al. (2008). Burnout in European family doctors: The EGPRN study. *Family Practice, 25*(4), 245–265. https://doi.org/10.1093/fampra/cmn038

Starfield, B. (1998). *Primary care*. New York: Oxford University Press.

Starfield, B., Shi, L., & Macinko, J. (2005). Contribution of primary care to health systems and health. *The Milbank Quarterly, 83*(3), 457–502.

Starmer, A. J., Frintner, M. P., & Freed, G. L. (2016). Work-life balance, burnout, and satisfaction of early career pediatricians. *Pediatrics, 137*(4), e20153183. https://doi.org/10.1542/peds.2015-3183#

Tucker, P., Brown, M., Dahlgren, A., Davies, G., Ebden, P., Folkard, S., et al. (2010). The impact of junior doctors' work time arrangements on their fatigue and Well-being. *Scandinavian Journal of Work, Environment & Health, 36*, 458–465.

van der Heijden, F., Dillingh, G., Bakker, A., & Prins, J. (2008). Suicidal thoughts among medical residents with burnout. *Archives of Suicide Research, 12*(4), 344–346. https://doi.org/10.1080/13811110802325349

van Loenen, T., van den Berg, M. J., Heinemann, S., Baker, R., Faber, M. J., & Westert, G. P. (2016). Trends towards stronger primary care in three western European countries; 2006-2012. *BMC Family Practice, 17*(1), 59. https://doi.org/10.1186/s12875-016-0458-3

Vassar, L. (2019). *How medical specialties vary by gender, 2015*. Retrieved from: https://www.ama-assn.org/residents-students/specialty-profiles/how-medical-specialties-vary-gender#:~:text=While%20many%20factors%20influence%20what,and%20where%20future%20physicians%20practice.&text=Based%20on%20key%20findings%2C%20women,Family%20medicine%20(about%2058%20percent) (last accessed 10/06/2020).

Wallace, J. E., Lemaire, J. B., & Ghali, W. A. (2009). Physician wellness: A missing quality indicator. *Lancet, 374*(9702), 1714–1721. https://doi.org/10.1016/S0140-6736(09)61424-0

West, C. P., Dyrbye, L. N., Erwin, P. J., & Shanafelt, T. D. (2016). Interventions to prevent and reduce physician burnout: A systematic review and meta-analysis. *The Lancet, 388*(10057), 2272–2281.

West, C. P., Dyrbye, L. N., & Shanafelt, T. D. (2018). Physician burnout: Contributors, consequences and solutions. *Journal of Internal Medicine, 283*(6), 516–529. https://doi.org/10.1111/joim.12752

Williams, E. S., Manwell, L. B., Konrad, T. R., & Linzer, M. (2007). The relationship of organizational culture, stress, satisfaction, and burnout with physician-reported error and suboptimal patient care: Results from the MEMO study. *Health Care Management Review, 32*(3), 203–212. https://doi.org/10.1097/01.HMR.0000281626.28363.59

World Health Organization. (2000). *The world health report 2000. Health systems: Improving performance*. Geneva, World Health Organization. Retrieved from: http://www.who.int/whr/2000/en/. (Last accessed 10/06/20).

Xierali, I. M., & Nivet, M. A. (2018). The racial and ethnic composition and distribution of primary care physicians. *Journal of Health Care for the Poor and Underserved, 29*(1), 556–570. https://doi.org/10.1353/hpu.2018.0036

Zenasni, F., Boujut, E., Woerner, A., & Sultan, S. (2012). Burnout and empathy in primary care: Three hypotheses. *The British Journal of General Practice, 62*(600), 346–347.

Part II
Zooming in on the Health Care Context

Chapter 6
Between Balance and Burnout: Contrasting the Working-Time Conditions of Irish-Trained Hospital Doctors in Ireland and Australia

John-Paul Byrne, Edel Conway, Aoife M. McDermott, Richard W. Costello, Lucia Prihodova, Anne Matthews, and Niamh Humphries

6.1 Introduction

> I met a guy once who did the ED [Emergency Medicine] scheme in Ireland... Before the 18 months were finished he was a dropout.... he just couldn't do it anymore. His mental health couldn't take it... He still wanted to do ED, but he had to quit the scheme. The other option would've been to completely burnout... (P28/IRL).

> That's the choice that I know I'm going to be faced with...go home [Ireland] for family, or stay here for what would be better work, better work-life balance... (P4/AUS).

Ireland is currently experiencing a medical workforce crisis characterised by high rates of doctor emigration (Humphries, Connell, Negin, & Buchan, 2019), burnout and occupational stress (Hayes, Prihodova, Walsh, Doyle, & Doherty, 2019). Austerity-related restructuring of the health services in Ireland involved significant cuts to public healthcare funding, health workforce numbers, hospital resources, and pay-cuts for new entrants, prompting a medical recruitment and retention crisis (Burke, Thomas, Barry, & Keegan, 2014; Humphries et al., 2019). Along with the growth in demand for services because of an ageing population, austerity restrictions have stretched hospital resources, placing a strain on the working conditions of

---

J.-P. Byrne (✉) · R. W. Costello · L. Prihodova · N. Humphries
Royal College of Physicians of Ireland, Dublin, Ireland
e-mail: JohnPaulByrne@RCPI.IE

E. Conway
DCU Business School, Dublin, Ireland

A. M. McDermott
Cardiff Business School, Cardiff University, UK

A. Matthews
Dublin City University, Dublin, Ireland

© Springer Nature Switzerland AG 2020
A. Montgomery et al. (eds.), *Connecting Healthcare Worker Well-Being, Patient Safety and Organisational Change*, Aligning Perspectives on Health, Safety and Well-Being, https://doi.org/10.1007/978-3-030-60998-6_6

hospital doctors in Ireland (Humphries, Crowe, & Brugha, 2018). Research has consistently highlighted the importance of work and employment conditions in understanding poor workplace wellbeing among hospital doctors (McGowan, Humphries, Burke, Conry, & Morgan, 2013) and decisions to emigrate (Humphries, McAleese, Matthews, & Brugha, 2015). This context of significant resource cuts, strained working conditions, and high emigration raises several challenges for the working lives of hospital doctors who often find themselves having to choose between working in a health system under strain (risking burnout) or emigrating to access better (balanced) work and employment conditions. For the purpose of this chapter, we focus on a key feature of work which underpins experiences of intensity, flexibility, balance, and burnout: time.

Time is a 'fundamental dimension of organizational life' (Butler, 1995, p. 925) used to organize and divide the labour process (Holt & Johnsen, 2019). Researchers have recognised the importance of exploring workers subjective experiences of time (Orlikowski & Yates, 2002) and implications for work-life balance (Berg, Appelbaum, Bailey, & Kalleberg, 2004). However, temporal demands are often depicted as a 'challenge' stressor which workers must overcome to achieve goals, rather than a 'hindrance' stressor (e.g. role ambiguity, bureaucracy) which obstruct goal attainment and growth (LePine, Podsakoff, & LePine, 2005). Here, time is considered a 'personal' resource which lies within the agency of the individual (ten Brummelhuis & Bakker, 2012; Wallace, Edwards, Arnold, Frazier, & Finch, 2009). We explore the contrasting structures of time for hospital doctors to illustrate how the experience of time is *beyond* the control of individual doctors (Holt & Johnsen, 2019). This psychosocial approach can help us understand how the experience of time illustrates the '...difference between "having control" and "being in control"' (Lund, Hvid, & Kamp, 2011, p. 256) and can subsequently impact on well-being outcomes.

Drawing on semi-structured interviews with 51 Irish-trained doctors who have emigrated to work in Australia, the chapter compares these hospital doctors' experience of work-time in Ireland and Australia. Australia is one of the most popular destinations for emigrant Irish doctors (Humphries et al., 2019). As participants had emigrated from Ireland and remained in Australia, they may have used the interview to justify this decision. However, this highly skilled diaspora is in a unique position to compare their experiences in two contexts (IRL and AUS) and identify the key factors shaping the nature and impact of work-time. In the findings section, statements are referenced by participant number and the context discussed (e.g. P6/IRL refers to participant six discussing an Irish experience and P9/AUS refers to participant nine discussing an Australian experience). Using a psychosocial work environment (PWE) lens (see Fig. 6.1), we explore the differences in the temporal experiences of work in Irish and Australian hospitals and present a framework which delineates the features of time which comprise contrasting contexts of balance and burnout. These contexts have different expectations and rules for how hospital doctors can allocate, spend and control their work-time, illustrating how institutional and organisational structures shape temporal experiences and impact on work-life balance and well-being.

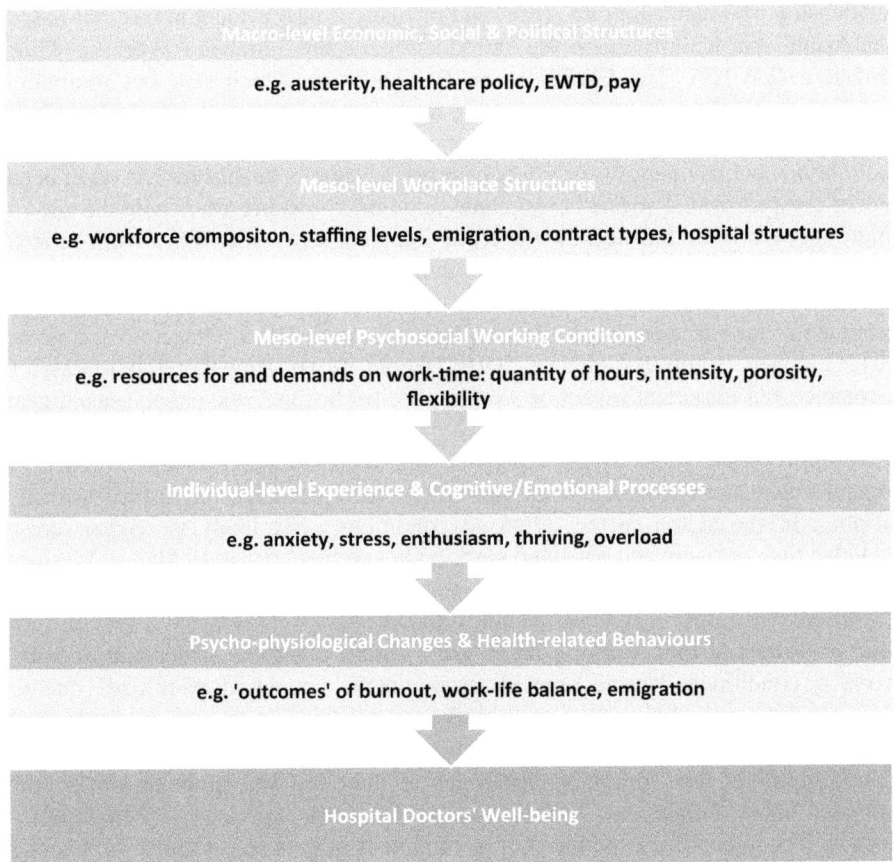

Fig. 6.1 PWE Framework Adapted from Rugulies (2019)

6.2 Time, Balance and Burnout

Hartmut Rosa (2015) depicts modern society as one defined by the acceleration and intensification of time, generated by the interlocking structures of technological acceleration, the acceleration of social change, and the pace of life. Rosa's theory links poor mental well-being outcomes to modern forms of alienation as the acceleration and intensification of time induces a loss of control within work and non-work lives. A sense of control is fundamental to the experience of work and the relationship between working conditions and well-being (Karasek, 1979). However, those in high-autonomy professions who traditionally have more control of their work-time often experience the highest levels of 'time-poverty' and work intensity as wide-ranging and incessant demands, obligations, and responsibilities extend the time and attention required for work (Schieman, Whitestone, & van Gundy, 2006; Strazdins, Welsh, Korda, Broom, & Paolucci, 2016). This complex relationship between autonomy, time, and intensity is also evident in hospital-based healthcare—particularly since the introduction of the European Working Time Directive (EWTD). The EWTD is an EU Directive which sets out minimum standards for the organisation of working time (European Parliament, 2003). Originally set out as a labour law to protect workers' health and safety through maximum work hours and rest periods, its effect on working time in healthcare has often been one of compression. The EWTD regulates and limits working hours with the aim of improving work-life balance. However, in doing so, it also intensifies work-related time pressures, hinders the continuity of care for patients through increased handovers, and impinges on doctors' training time and opportunities—which regularly occur after 'normal' work hours (Brown, Egan, & Lewis, 2019; Fitzgerald & Caesar, 2012; Lambert, Smith, & Goldacre, 2016; Temple, 2010). Time therefore represents a complex but important aspect of working life for hospital doctors and healthcare workers.

A report on job stress by the Economic and Social Research Institute (ESRI) in Ireland noted that the respondents most likely to report stress were professionals working in the health sector. Working conditions most likely to trigger stress included time pressure and extended working hours (40+) (Russell, Maître, Watson, & Fahey, 2018). Due to the diffuse nature of medical work which comprises '…different tempos, schedules, routines and deadlines' (Atkinson, 1995, p. 52), time pressure and long working hours are a common feature of hospital doctors' working conditions. Frantic clinical environments, increased workloads due to understaffing, and high turnover of staff lead to difficult and pressurised work environments for hospital doctors (Humphries et al., 2014). McGowan et al. (2013) highlight the workplace challenges of intensive and irregular workloads, extended hours, fatigue, and limited time, on the work experiences of Irish junior doctors. The intensified experience of work-time is often a consequence of hospital doctors' attempts to balance the efficiency required to see large numbers of patients with a patient-centred approach to ensure quality of care provision for individual patients (Byrne et al., 2019). This consistent time pressure can result in a feeling of work overload; '…having too much to do, in too little time, at too high a pace, with too few resources' (Wichert, 2002, p. 97).

Research has highlighted how intensified working patterns and long working hours may provoke fatigue, exhaustion, and distress, leading to burnout. The Maslach Burnout Inventory (MBI) (Maslach, Jackson, & Leiter, 1996) is built on the three factors of emotional exhaustion (withered emotional resources), depersonalisation (lack of empathy, cynicism), and personal accomplishment (self-evaluation). However, Schaufeli, Bakker, Hoogduin, Schaap, and Kladler (2001) note that most burnout definitions involve elements of work-related fatigue symptoms (mental or emotional exhaustion) and unusual physical distress symptoms which lead to impaired effectiveness and performance. In a national cross-sectional survey of hospital doctors in Ireland, Hayes et al. (2019) found that doctors of all grades reported high work stress, and just under one-third experienced burnout. Those reporting significantly more working hours had a higher prevalence of occupational stress and burnout. Internationally, research has found associations between long working hours and work-life conflict, and burnout for hospital doctors (Amoafo, Hanbali, Patel, & Singh, 2015; Gopal, Glasheen, Miyoshi, & Prochazka, 2005). In a US survey comparing the general population with physicians, Shanafelt et al. (2015) found that between 2011 and 2014 burnout and satisfaction with work-life balance worsened for physicians, highlighting the impact of the high quantity and unpredictable nature of working hours in hospital care. The challenge of time-management has extended beyond the hospital to the entire working life of a doctor, with levels of dissatisfaction associated with the amount of time available to do the job (Dugdale, Epstein, & Pantilat, 1999). In the Hayes et al. (2019) study, only one in five hospital doctor respondents felt their work left them with enough time for personal or family time, indicating how long and unpredictable hours can translate into work-life conflict.

This literature emphasises how hospital doctors' experience of work is shaped by both the intensification (time pressure and intensity) and extensification (long hours, weak boundaries/porosity) of work time which can impact on work-life balance and lead to burnout. The psychosocial characteristics of work (e.g. intensity, demands, long hours) are hugely influential in determining its impact on mental well-being (Butterworth et al., 2011). However, these temporal conditions, experiences, and outcomes are themselves shaped by their institutional and organisational context. Montgomery, Panagopoulou, Esmail, Richards, and Maslach (2019) call for a reconceptualization of burnout following the World Health Organisation's recognition of it as an 'occupational phenomenon', viewing it as an outcome of healthcare systems across doctors' careers rather than an issue with any individual. Similarly, Shanafelt et al. (2015) note the significant role of the organisation in optimising doctors' time and facilitating better work-life integration. These approaches emphasise the role of structural context in shaping the experience and impact of work for hospital doctors. The following section draws on theories of the psychosocial work environment (PWE) to illustrate not only the impact of working time on burnout but also how it is shaped by a range of macro and meso level features which configure the working conditions of hospital doctors.

6.3 The Psychosocial Work Environment: Shaping the Experience of Work-Time

The PWE provides a conceptual frame to help us understand the configuration and impact of work-time across different national contexts. The PWE comprises the structures, resources, demands, and interactions which influence the psychological functioning of workers (Knudsen, Busck, & Lind, 2011). As such it focuses on the conditions which determine whether, on balance, work-time is experienced as a resource which aids control within working life, or a constant demand which induces a loss of control within working life. An array of psychosocial features of work (autonomy, intensity, balance, insecurity) have been theorised to influence work-strain (Bakker & Demerouti, 2007; Karasek, 1979; Siegrist, 1996). For the purposes of this chapter, we use Rugulies (2019) conceptual framework for research on the PWE which outlines the links between macro-level institutional structures and workers' well-being. Figure 6.1 adapts this framework to illustrate the interconnectedness of the following: macro-level healthcare reform and European Working Time Directive (EWTD); meso-level contracts, staffing, and organisation of the medical workforce; time pressure as a critical psychosocial work condition, and; hospital doctors' well-being via the interplay of individual-level experiences, and subsequent psycho-physiological changes and health related behaviours (e.g. work-life balance, burnout, or emigration). The purpose here is to demonstrate the complexity and variety of the conditions which shape the experience and impact of work-time.

This conceptual framework emphasises two important points: firstly, that structural context matters for the experience of working time, and secondly that these temporal experiences influence well-being outcomes. Figure 6.1 also depicts how the context of hospital doctors in Ireland is shaped by emigration through the link between deficits in meso-workplace structure and health-related behaviour levels (e.g. leisure-time, hobbies, drinking, smoking etc.). High rates of doctor migration deplete workforce composition and staffing levels, subsequently shaping the pressurised working conditions experienced, and influencing the decisions of Irish doctors to emigrate (Humphries et al., 2018, 2019). For the purposes of this chapter, we focus on the meso-level temporal conditions underpinning participants' experiences of work intensity, flexibility, balance, and burnout.

Analysing data from semi-structured interviews with Irish-trained hospital doctors who have left the Irish health system to work in Australia, we demonstrate how different national contexts shape the experience and impact of work-time for the same hospital doctors. Rather than establishing the prevalence of outcomes such as burnout, we use the PWE approach to distinguish the *temporal conditions* which enable balance within working life or increase the likelihood of burnout. As such, the discussion focuses mainly on the link between the 'meso-level psychosocial working conditions' and 'individual level experience and cognitive and emotional processes' (Fig. 6.1) to explore the experience of different temporal conditions of working life for hospital doctors in Irish and Australian hospitals. We present a model (Fig. 6.2) which delineates the key facets of work-time used by participants to contrast their experiences in Ireland and Australia—quantity, quality, predictability, and flexibility.

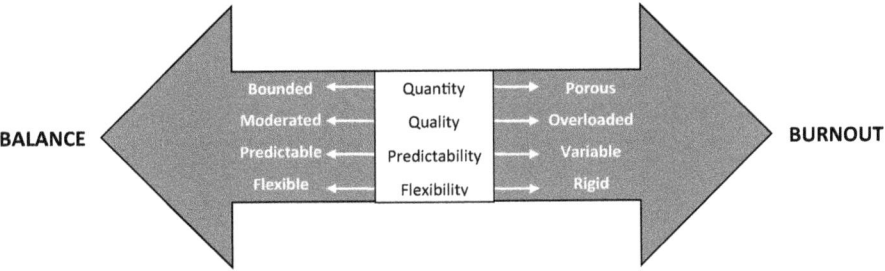

Fig. 6.2 The Temporal Conditions of Balance and Burnout

6.4 Findings

6.4.1 The Contrasting Quantity and Quality of Work-Time

6.4.1.1 The Quantity of Hours

Participants described the number of working hours as the most obvious difference between working as a hospital doctor in Ireland and Australia. Working hours in Ireland were viewed as more excessive and more variable than Australia with weekly working hours of anywhere between 80 and 100 h; 'You were just there all the time' (P37/IRL). During their intern year, 100-h weeks were commonplace for several participants. One doctor described how their inability to 'handle' 36-h shifts was the main reason for emigrating; '...I hated it' (P17/IRL). In contrast, participants emphasised the shorter working week in Australian hospitals; '...there's just no comparison. I laughed...76 hours a fortnight.... I've been working 76 hour a week in Ireland' (P14/AUS). For most participants, emigrating to work in Australia resulted in an immediate reduction in working hours; '...I had 15 extra hours in my week... (P17/AUS). In contrast to the excessive and unpredictable hours of Irish hospitals, participants highlighted the positive impact of the bounded nature of work time in Australian hospitals.

> I have very, very controlled hours, which I don't think are excessive.... I go into work at a reasonable hour and I come out at reasonable hour... (P16/AUS).

> The hours are more contained...you work your hours here, and then you go home (P51/AUS).

Participants used terms like 'controlled' and 'contained' when discussing working hours in Australian hospitals, emphasising clear boundaries between work and non-work time. For one doctor, this limiting of hours meant a better quality of life; '...we have better quality of life.... I'm never home late...in Ireland, you work late more often' (P35/AUS). These temporal boundaries provided participants with a better quality of work and non-work time in Australia.

6.4.1.2 Time Provided and Time Stolen: The Quality of Work and Non-Work Time

> ...having burnt out in my early 30s I realize...When I'm more balanced I'm actually much better at my job...I have more time here...I'm not under constant pressure...I'm not exhausted all the time, I'm actually much better with patients here (P4/AUS).

In Australia, participants felt they had a better quality of time within, and outside of, work. The statement above indicates how the provision of adequate time can lead to a greater sense of balance and more efficacy on the job. For this doctor, having adequate non-work time in Australia has led to a better performance *at* work. With less demands made of time in work, and less incidences of work-time creeping into non-work time, the doctors felt their ability to engage with patients was improved. One doctor described getting time with a patient as the essence of being a doctor; '...you get to spend more time with your patients. Which is one of the reasons you become a doctor' (P17/AUS). Due to staffing and resource levels (meso-level workplace structures in Fig. 6.1) in Australian hospitals, participants noted how they had more time to spend on the 'floor'.

In contrast, experiences in Irish hospitals were determined by a sense of frantic pace, constant interruptions, and limited resources which left participants without the time, 'ability or space' (P14/IRL) to fully engage with all patients. One participant provided an example in highlighting the difference in the average time spent discharging new mothers from maternity care, noting that in Irish hospitals as little as 10 min is available for this task, as the doctor would often be required to do six checks per hour. By contrast, in Australian hospitals these discharges usually take 30–45 min per patient; '...because they have the time' (P37/AUS). This sense of a 'fraught' workplace (P51/IRL) led to experiences of consistent time pressure and overload with one doctor describing how there was; '...too much being asked of you all the time' (P4/IRL). High intensity, long hours and limited resources, were perceived as a threat to doctors' health and well-being; '...Irish medicine is you keep on working until you drop....' (P34/IRL). Paradoxically, despite spending extended amounts of time in work, participants felt they spent less time with patients in Irish hospitals. The contrasting contexts of time-quality were typified by the need to steal time in Ireland and the provision of time in Australia.

> There's two birthdays at work today. There's cake...there's time made to celebrate the good things...it's time. We have time to meet and time to talk... (P24/AUS).

> ...you have time to supervise your juniors. You have time to look at what they're doing, whereas back home you would just give them jobs and hope to Christ that it got done (P49/AUS).

In Australian hospitals, participants portrayed the importance of time for communication with senior colleagues, enhanced teaching and learning environments, and more collegial workplaces. One participant emphasised the importance of being able to contact a senior consultant with questions; '...I can call him.... I'm not...taking his time away....' (P38/AUS). In Irish hospitals, time was a pressurised and rare commodity which most people didn't have and were therefore unwilling to give up easily. Time needed to be stolen from colleagues in Irish hospitals, as colleagues shunned collaboration because of already heavy workloads. The statements above illustrate how collaboration, support, supervision, and engagement are intertwined with the experience of work-time. The distinction between a time stolen and a time provided emphasises participants perception of time as a resource in Australia and a stressor in Ireland, as extended and intense working hours could lead to work overload which negatively impacts on well-being;

> *The actual workload and the stress... it was just too much... People would kind of have a mental breakdown* (P28/IRL).

> *...as an intern. The first week was 80-90 hours.... We did 24/30-hour shifts...I missed myself being extremely unwell. Really, really unwell. And that was a real wake-up call...* (P38/IRL).

Australian hospitals offered; '....just more time for me' (P17/AUS). This also extended to non-work time where participants felt they had more time with their children; '...you definitely get an opportunity to spend more time with your family than you probably would have at home' (P11/AUS). In Irish hospitals, work-time seemed to creep into non-work time, affecting time available to spend with families; '...if I go home [to Ireland] now, I'll never see my children...' (P24/IRL). The quality of work, and non-work, time in Australia allowed these doctors to feel '...more involved in our patients, [and] in our kids' lives (P25/AUS). These experiences were reinforced by different capacities for maintaining work-life balance—a balance shaped by the predictability of work-time and the flexibility of employment.

6.4.2 The Predictability and Flexibility of Work-Life Balance

6.4.2.1 Predictable Boundaries

Australia provided participants with a 'phenomenal' (P45/AUS) work-life balance. In contrast to the porosity of work-time in Ireland, the doctors highlighted how work-time that was bounded, predictable and flexible provided a sense of control within working life in Australia. This related to expectations around daily working time, and the ability to work part-time without damaging one's career prospects. The 'controlled' hours of Australian hospitals provided predictability and certainty for participants in planning and demarcating non-work time and activities; '...allowing me to have leisure time has been, really, a big thing...' (P14/AUS).

> *It doesn't compare...just with knowing...you just know that you'll be free in the evenings. Or you know what hours you'll be working* (P19/AUS).

> *...I know I can plan to meet friends in the evening because I know when I'm going to get out of work...* (P21/AUS).

The predictability ('knowing') of work-time, and therefore non-work time, was important to participants' sense of controlling their own work-life balance. This predictability reinforced the boundaries between work and non-work time, enabling a balance which ensured time with family; 'Our son is two years now, I get to spend a lot of time with him' (P50/AUS). Highlighting the professional (expectations, responsibilities) and organisational (resources, staffing) influences on work-time, participants contrasted the predictable and balanced experience of time in Australia with boundaryless work time in Ireland which impacted on family life; 'I value what I do...but at the same time I don't want to be stuck in at seven o'clock in the evening...I want to be at home playing with my kids before they go to bed' (P16/IRL). Extended and unpredictable working time increased the likelihood of work-life conflict. One doctor described the inability to secure consistent family time as key to the decision to emigrate (P1/IRL). Another participant remarked on how many hours a colleague in Ireland with young kids worked; '...two kids under two. He often doesn't see them for a week at a time...They're just in bed.... he goes to work at 6 o'clock and doesn't get back till 9 o'clock' (R50/IRL). Bounded and predictable work time in Australia meant participants did not have to worry about the constant potential for weekend or late evening work. As a result, they had time to decompress, felt less stressed, and found it easier to 'switch off' from work when at home.

> ...if you don't bring your work home with you then you can just go enjoy the rest of your life...in Ireland you come home, and you practically need a therapy session... (P8/IRL).

> ....better work life balance...There was a stage last year where I wasn't sure if I actually wanted to do medicine. But I think that was all just to do with stress.... (P18/IRL).

6.4.2.2 Flexible Work-Time

The sense of balance experienced by participants in Australia was reinforced by the potential for flexible contracts (i.e. part-time working). Several female participants noted how, after having a baby, the ability to work part-time provided the flexibility required to balance medicine with care-giving responsibilities. This was contrasted with the Irish context where there were minimal opportunities for part-time working. In Ireland, female doctors were either at work or on leave in a full-time capacity with little scope for combing the two flexibly. Furthermore, those individuals out on parental leave were generally not replaced and often resented for the subsequent understaffing. One doctor recalled an instance where an intern who was a single mum with an infant was derided by colleagues for saying that she needed to leave at five o'clock (which was already longer than she was contracted to do) to pick her child up from day-care (P21/IRL). All-or-nothing work-time expectations in Irish hospitals resulted in PWEs with little opportunity for, or acceptance of, flexibility—even for childcare responsibilities. The sessional nature of work organisation for hospital doctors in Australia meant that they had the capacity to shift to part-time work during the first 5 years of their child's life. The hospital would hire someone to cover the rest of the time to ensure the role was fully covered. Both male and female doctors acknowledged the work-life balance opportunities afforded in Australia. In Ireland there are regulations providing for the reduction of work-time (parental leave, term time), however this is regularly in a rigid full-time-work or full-time-leave form and is often not compensated by appointing staff cover. Flexible working hours were perceived as acceptable in Australia and both improbable and career-damaging in Ireland—further emphasising the contrast in control over work and non-work time in both countries which can lead to a sense of balance or burnout; '...bringing in flexible part-time contracts to retain females and not burn them out...' (P7/IRL).

> ...there's a lot of flexibility.... you are entitled to five years after having your baby of having essentially part-time work...(P7/AUS).

> ...my Irish friends...they have to continue to work full time after they've had their babies, whereas I was able to work two days a week for five years, without being looked down on.... my recollection in Ireland was that my female consultants were taking this term time and family leave...which meant they were never really there...workloads weren't being covered properly... (P10/AUS).

> As a working Mum, as a surgeon with three small kids...I was able to have a very flexible work pattern. They really value what you can give, and they will accept you... That's the difference (P25/AUS).

6.5 Discussion

The findings illustrate the value of focusing on work-time as a key constituent of the PWE (Fig. 6.1) which makes a real difference to working lives and well-being. The contrasting experiences of work-time affect the working lives of hospital doctors in terms of how work-time is allocated, spent, and more importantly, controlled, whilst working in Ireland and Australia. Figure 6.2 summarises the findings and provides a framework which distinguishes the *temporal conditions* which enable balance within working life or increase the likelihood of burnout.

Participants drew on four features of work-time to contrast their experiences as hospital doctors in Ireland and Australia: the quantity of hours, the quality of work and non-work time, the predictability of work-time, and the flexibility of contracts (Fig. 6.2). The quantity of working hours in Irish hospitals was described as extensive and porous whereas Australian hospitals had more bounded hours. These more limited hours in Australian hospitals were also experienced as moderated and engaged, unlike Irish hospitals which were depicted as overloaded and intense. These contrasts in the quantity and quality of work-time also had an impact on non-work time with Australian working hours much more predictable and therefore easier to arrange and maintain a social and personal life outside of work. The clear demarcation between work and non-work time in Australia also provided participants with a sense of balance which helped them feel more engaged in work.

Finally, these experiences of work-time extended to the employment relationship. The ability to work part-time after the birth of children, without it impeding on career prospects, was considered as an important advantage to working in Australia. According to participants, working in Ireland did not provide such flexibility due to the rigid—full-time or absent—nature of contracts which offered limited opportunity for flexible working, increasing the strain placed on hospital doctors and the likelihood of work-life conflict. These contrasting experiences portray a work-time in Ireland that is characterised by conditions linked to burnout (intensity, extended hours, unpredictability, work-life conflict), and a work-time in Australia typified by conditions which provide a sense of balance (bounded and predictable hours, moderated intensity, flexibility).

The framework in Fig. 6.2 outlines these temporal antecedents of work-life balance and burnout, illustrating the conditions under which time operates as a 'hindrance' rather than 'challenge' stressor (LePine et al., 2005) as individual efforts and coping strategies are perceived as incapable of meeting incessant temporal demands. Underpinning the contrasting experiences is the importance of a sense of control over work and non-work time and the impact this can have on balance and well-being (Rosa, 2015). The experience in Irish hospitals was one of consistently losing time (work and non-work) to work demands. Extreme time pressure and high workloads inhibited opportunities to use job resources, access supports, or collectively solve problems, thereby exacerbating the temporal demands of work. Intensified and extensified (porous, unpredictable) patterns of work-time resulted in stressed, frustrated doctors all trying to 'steal' each other's time in a 'fraught' medical environment, as well as the increased likelihood of work-life conflict. These are working conditions which have been associated with burnout in doctors (Amoafo et al., 2015; Gopal et al., 2005; Shanafelt et al., 2015). Furthermore, this intensification and extensification of time seemed to be mutually reinforcing as participants described feeling constantly pressed for time while in work, leading to regularly work late into the evening and weekends, and therefore never being sure of when they would finish work, or be able to completely switch off at home. The experience in Australian hospitals was marked by an ability to maintain control over work, and therefore non-work, time due to 'contained' and predictable hours. The predictability provided by 'knowing' when they would *not* be in work fostered participants' sense of work-life balance and promoted engagement whilst at work. Predictability and clarity also typified the employment relationship in Australia as the availability of part-time contracts enabled participants to manage periods when flexible working-time was required without damaging their careers.

The chapter demonstrates how time is critical in shaping the working lives of hospital doctors. The findings presented demonstrate how the work and non-work time of hospital doctors are shaped by institutional and organisational contexts. The contrasting experiences in Ireland and Australia were distinguished by the quantity of hours, quality of work and non-work time, predictability of working hours, and the flexibility of contracts (Fig. 6.2). These disparate experiences reveal the interdependence of work and non-work time which significantly shapes conditions of balance or burnout and is underscored by: (1) the relationship between intensified and extensified work-time, and; (2) the importance of predictability and flexibility for work-life balance and engagement at work. Time, which is '...maybe the most precious of all medical resources' (Davidoff, 1997, p. 483), is shaped by its context, and influences the experience of balance and burnout within the working lives of hospital doctors.

6.6 Conclusion

Over the last decade, austerity and emigration have shaped the landscape of healthcare services in Ireland. The contrasting experiences of participants in Irish and Australian hospitals illustrate how this context has impacted on the work-time of hospital doctors. We present a model (Fig. 6.2) which delineates the conditions which determined the impact of work-time for participants working in Irish and Australian hospitals, highlighting how the interdependence of work and non-work time shape temporal contexts of balance or burnout. For hospital doctors, the experience of work-time is central to the shaping of working lives and well-being outcomes. Alleviating conditions which are conducive to burnout requires a focus on the link between workforce planning, the flexibility and predictability of scheduling, and doctors' ability to manage the boundaries separating work and non-work time.

Key Messages for Researchers
1. To understand the prevalence of burnout amongst hospital doctors we need to investigate the structural and temporal conditions which shape their experience of work and have implications for the reproduction of healthcare workforces and the quality of patient care.
2. Hospital doctors' work-time requires a constant negotiation of work-life boundaries. Future research could focus on the relationship between the intensification and extensification of temporal experiences for hospital doctors and the impact this has on their working lives.
3. A qualitative approach can help unpack the complexity of temporal experiences for hospital doctors to investigate which aspects of time are perceived as challenge or hindrance stressors.

Key Messages for Healthcare Delivery
1. The quantity, quality, predictability, and flexibility of work-time shape the experience and impact of work for hospital doctors.
2. Intense, unpredictable, and porous work-time represents a key stressor for hospital doctors.
3. The antecedents of burnout for hospital doctors are institutional and organisational. Health policy and reform strategies must address work-time experienced as extended, intense, unpredictable and inflexible.

References

Amoafo, E., Hanbali, N., Patel, A., & Singh, P. (2015). What are the significant factors associated with burnout in doctors? *Occupational Medicine, 65*, 117–121. https://doi.org/10.1093/occmed/kqu144

Atkinson, P. (1995). *Medical talk and medical work: The liturgy of the clinic*. London: Sage Publications.

Bakker, A. B., & Demerouti, E. (2007). The job demands-resources model: State of the art. *Journal of Managerial Psychology, 22*(3), 309–328. https://doi.org/10.1108/02683940710733115

Berg, P., Appelbaum, E., Bailey, T., & Kalleberg, A. L. (2004). Contesting time: International comparisons of employee control of working time. *ILR Review, 57*(3), 331–349. https://doi.org/10.1177/001979390405700301

Brown, C., Egan, R. J., & Lewis, W. (2019). The hidden curriculum: Requiem for a surgical dream. *BMJ Postgraduate Medical Journal, 95*(1123), 237–239. https://doi.org/10.1136/postgradmedj-2018-136076

Burke, S., Thomas, S., Barry, S., & Keegan, C. (2014). Indicators of health system cover age and activity in Ireland during the economic crisis 2008–2014–from 'more with less' to 'less with less'. *Health Policy, 117*, 275–278. https://doi.org/10.1016/j.healthpol.2014.07.001

Butler, R. (1995). Time in organizations: Its experience, explanations and effects. *Organization Studies, 16*(6), 925–950. https://doi.org/10.1177/017084069501600601

Butterworth, P., Leach, L. S., Strazdins, L., Olesen, S. C., Rodgers, B., & Broom, D. H. (2011). The psychosocial quality of work determines whether employment has benefits for mental health: Results from a longitudinal national household panel survey. *Occupational & Environmental Medicine, 68*(11), 806–812. https://doi.org/10.1136/oem.2010.059030

Byrne, J. P., Power, R., Kiersey, R., Varley, J., Doherty, C. P., Saris, A. J., et al. (2019). The rhetoric and reality of integrated patient-centered care for healthcare providers: An ethnographic exploration of epilepsy care in Ireland. *Epilepsy & Behavior, 94*, 87–92. https://doi.org/10.1016/J.YEBEH.2019.02.011

Davidoff, F. (1997). Time. *Annals of Internal Medicine, 127*(6), 483–485. https://doi.org/10.7326/0003-4819-127-6-199709150-00011

Dugdale, D. C., Epstein, R., & Pantilat, S. Z. (1999). Time and the patient-physician relationship. *Journal of General Internal Medicine, 14*(Suppl 1), S34–S40. https://doi.org/10.1046/j.1525-1497.1999.00263.x

European Parliament, Council of the European Union. (2003). Directive 2003/88/EC of the European Parliament and of the Council of 4 November 2003 concerning certain aspects of the organisation of working time. *Official Journal* L 299, 18/11/2003, pp. 0009–0019. https://eur-lex.europa.eu/legal-content/EN/ALL/?uri=CELEX:32003L0088

Fitzgerald, J. E. F., & Caesar, B. C. (2012). The European working time directive: A practical review for surgical trainees. *International Journal of Surgery, 10*(8), 399–403. https://doi.org/10.1016/j.ijsu.2012.08.007

Gopal, R., Glasheen, J. J., Miyoshi, T. J., & Prochazka, A. V. (2005). Burnout and internal medicine resident work-hour restrictions. *Archives of Internal Medicine, 165*(22), 2595–2600. https://doi.org/10.1001/archinte.165.22.2595

Hayes, B., Prihodova, L., Walsh, G., Doyle, F., & Doherty, S. (2019). Doctors don't do-little: A national cross-sectional study of workplace Well-being of hospital doctors in Ireland. *BMJ Open, 9*, e025433. https://doi.org/10.1136/bmjopen-2018-025433

Holt, R., & Johnsen, R. (2019). Time and organization studies. *Organization Studies, 40*(10), 1557–1572. https://doi.org/10.1177/0170840619844292

Humphries, N., Connell, J., Negin, J., & Buchan, J. (2019). Tracking the leavers: Towards a better understanding of doctor migration from Ireland to Australia 2008–2018. *BMC Human Resources for Health, 17*, 36–46. https://doi.org/10.1186/s12960-019-0365-5

Humphries, N., Crowe, S., & Brugha, R. (2018). Failing to retain a new generation of doctors: Qualitative insights from a high-income country. *BMC Health Services Research, 18*(1), 144–153. https://doi.org/10.1186/s12913-018-2927-y

Humphries, N., McAleese, S., Matthews, A., & Brugha, R. (2015). "Emigration is a matter of self-preservation. The working conditions . . . are killing us slowly": Qualitative insights into health professional emigration from Ireland. *BMC Human Resources for Health, 13*, 35–48. https://doi.org/10.1186/s12960-015-0022-6

Humphries, N., Morgan, K., Conry, M. C., McGowan, Y., Montgomery, A., & McGee, H. (2014). Quality of care and health professional burnout: Narrative literature review. *International Journal of Health Care Quality Assurance, 27*(4), 293–307. https://doi.org/10.1108/IJHCQA-08-2012-0087

Karasek, R. (1979). Job demands, job decision latitude, and mental strain: Implications for job redesign. *Administrative Science Quarterly, 24*(2), 285–308. https://doi.org/10.2307/2392498

Knudsen, H., Busck, O., & Lind, J. (2011). Work environment quality: The role of workplace participation and democracy. *Work, Employment & Society, 25*(3), 379–396. https://doi.org/10.1177/0950017011407966

Lambert, T. W., Smith, F., & Goldacre, M. J. (2016). The impact of the European Working Time Directive 10 years on: Views of the UK medical graduates of 2002 surveyed in 2013–2014. *Journal of the Royal Society of Medicine Open, 7*(3), 1–8. https://doi.org/10.1177/2054270416632703

LePine, J. A., Podsakoff, N. P., & LePine, M. A. (2005). A meta-analytic test of the challenge stressor – Hindrance stressor framework: An Explanationfor inconsistent relationships among stressors and performance. *Academy of Management Journal, 48*(5), 764–775. https://doi.org/10.5465/AMJ.2005.18803921

Lund, H. L., Hvid, H., & Kamp, A. (2011). Perceived time, temporal order and control in Boundaryless work. In P. Vink & J. Kantola (Eds.), *Advances in occupational, social, and organizational ergonomics*. Boca Raton: Taylor and Francis.

Maslach, C., Jackson, S. E., & Leiter, M. P. (1996). *Maslach burnout inventory* (3rd ed.). Palo Alto, CA: Consulting Psychologists Press.

McGowan, Y., Humphries, N., Burke, H., Conry, M., & Morgan, K. (2013). Through doctors' eyes: A qualitative study of hospital doctor perspectives on their working conditions. *British Journal of Health Psychology, 18*(4), 874–891. https://doi.org/10.1111/bjhp.12037

Montgomery, A., Panagopoulou, E., Esmail, A., Richards, T., & Maslach, C. (2019). Burnout in healthcare: The case for organisational change. *BMJ, 366*, l4774. https://doi.org/10.1136/bmj.l4774

Orlikowski, W. J., & Yates, J. (2002). It's about time: Temporal structuring in organizations. *Organization Science, 13*, 684–700. https://doi.org/10.1287/orsc.13.6.684.501

Rosa, H. (2015). *Social acceleration: A new theory of modernity*. New York: Columbia University Press.

Rugulies, R. (2019). What is a psychosocial work environment. *Scandinavian Journal of Work, Environment and Health, 45*(1), 1–6. https://doi.org/10.5271/sjweh.3792

Russell, H., Maître, B., Watson, D., & Fahey, É. (2018). *Job stress and working conditions: Ireland in comparative perspective*. Dublin: Economic and Social Research Institute (ESRI) Research Series Number 84. https://www.esri.ie/system/files/media/file-uploads/2018-11/RS84.pdf.

Schaufeli, W. B., Bakker, A. B., Hoogduin, K., Schaap, C., & Kladler, A. (2001). On the clinical validity of the Maslach burnout inventory and the burnout measure. *Psychology & Health, 16*(5), 565–582. https://doi.org/10.1080/08870440108405527

Schieman, S., Whitestone, Y. K., & van Gundy, K. (2006). The nature of work and the stress of higher status. *Journal of Health and Social Behaviour, 47*(3), 242–257. https://doi.org/10.1177/002214650604700304

Shanafelt, T. D., Hasan, O., Dyrbye, L. N., Sinsky, C., Satele, D., Sloan, J., et al. (2015). Changes in burnout and satisfaction with work-life balance in physicians and the general US working population between 2011 and 2014. *Mayo Clinic Proceedings, 90*(12), 1600–1613. https://doi.org/10.1016/j.mayocp.2015.08.023

Siegrist, J. (1996). Adverse health effects of high-effort/low-reward conditions. *Journal of Occupational Health Psychology, 1*(1), 27–41. https://doi.org/10.1037/1076-8998.1.1.27

Strazdins, L., Welsh, J., Korda, R., Broom, D., & Paolucci, F. (2016). Not all hours are equal: Could time be a social determinant of health? *Sociology of Health and Illness, 38*(1), 21–42. https://doi.org/10.1111/1467-9566.12300

Temple, J. (2010). *Time for training: A review of the impact of the European working time directive on the quality of training.* London: Medical Education England.

ten Brummelhuis, L. L., & Bakker, A. B. (2012). A resource perspective on the work–home interface: The work–home resources model. *American Psychologist, 67*(7), 545–556. https://doi.org/10.1037/a0027974

Wallace, J. C., Edwards, B. D., Arnold, T., Frazier, M. L., & Finch, D. M. (2009). Work stressors, role-based performance, and the moderating influence of organizational support. *Journal of Applied Psychology, 94*(1), 254–262. https://doi.org/10.1037/a0013090

Wichert, I. (2002). Job insecurity and work intensification: The effects on health and Well-being. In B. Burchell, D. Ladipo, & F. Wilkinson (Eds.), *Job insecurity and work intensification*. London: Routledge.

Chapter 7
Doctors Well-being, Quality of Patient Care and Organizational Change: Norwegian Experiences

Karin Isaksson Rø, Judith Rosta, Reidar Tyssen, and Fredrik Bååthe

Changes in the healthcare organization may influence doctors' work-life and well-being and may in turn impact quality of patient care. As part of the surrounding society health care organizations are constantly subject to change in most countries, and there is a continual challenge to understand how this affects doctors' work, and how quality and safety of patient care can be ensured. We will describe and discuss this triple challenge from a Norwegian perspective. We will first give an overview of important organizational reforms in Norwegian health care during the first two decades of the twenty-first century, before we present changes in doctors' work-life and well-being in Norway compared with other countries, relating these to both individual and organizational factors. We will then discuss quality of patient care.

K. I. Rø (✉)
LEFO – Institute for Studies of the Medical Profession, Oslo, Norway

Department of Behavioural Medicine, Institute of Basic Medical Sciences, Medical Faculty, University of Oslo, Oslo, Norway
e-mail: Karin.Ro@legeforeningen.no

J. Rosta
LEFO – Institute for Studies of the Medical Profession, Oslo, Norway

R. Tyssen
Department of Behavioural Medicine, Institute of Basic Medical Sciences, Medical Faculty, University of Oslo, Oslo, Norway

F. Bååthe
LEFO – Institute for Studies of the Medical Profession, Oslo, Norway

Sahlgrenska Academy at Gothenburg University, Gothenburg, Sweden

Sahlgrenska University Hospital, Gothenburg, Sweden

Institute of Stressmedicin, Region Västra Götaland, Gothenburg, Sweden

© Springer Nature Switzerland AG 2020
A. Montgomery et al. (eds.), *Connecting Healthcare Worker Well-Being, Patient Safety and Organisational Change*, Aligning Perspectives on Health, Safety and Well-Being, https://doi.org/10.1007/978-3-030-60998-6_7

Finally, we will consider how the tension between organizational change, doctors' well-being and quality of care can be understood and handled as both patient and physician needs and identities are changing.

7.1 Health Services and Important Organizational Reforms in Health Care

Norway has a comprehensive, tax financed health service system where the basic principle is equal access to services for all residents regardless of personal finances and place of residence. All residents are insured under the National Insurance Scheme. Inpatient care in general hospitals is free of charge, but there are out-of-pocket payments for GP consultations and out-patient consultations to both hospital doctors and specialists who run their own practice with remuneration from the state. However, there is a "ceiling" per year for out-of-pocket expenditures, which in 2019 was NOK 2369 (€243). When this is reached there is no additional payment (Direktoratet for E-helse, 2019).

During the first two decades of the twenty-first century, five important organizational reforms have been implemented in Norwegian health care. "The Regular General Practitioners Scheme" in 2001 introduced a list-patient system whereby all inhabitants in Norway have their assigned general practitioner (Statsministerenskontor, 2001). This reform aimed at enhancing access to general practitioners and continuity in the patient-doctor relationship and also confirmed that General practitioners (GPs) act as gate-keepers for other specialist care. Primary care in Norway is run by specialists in general practice (or family medicine), which is a separate licenced specialty, and the GPs are employed by the municipalities in each county. The implementation of the list-patient system has modified the structure of GPs' remuneration into a combination of three sources: capitation based payment from the local municipality (30%), fee-for-service payment from the National Insurance System (70%), plus direct, relatively small out-of-pocket payments from the patients (NOK 155–370 (€15–37 Euros) (Ringard, Sagan, Sperre Saunes, & Lindahl, 2013). "The Hospital Reform" in 2002 transferred the ownership of hospitals and specialist health services from the county to the state level aiming at better efficiency and effectiveness (cost-control) and quality of services, by building on principles of New Public Management (i.e. efforts to make the public sector more businesslike, to increase value for money, efficiency and reduce costs in the public health sector by implementing ideas and management principles from the private sector, such as financial incentives for deliveries and privatization of parts of the sector etc.). This was organized through central and local health enterprises (Hagen & Kaarbøe, 2006). "The Coordination Reform" from 2012 was intended as an open-ended progressive reform with the goals to give patients *proper treatment—at the right place and right time* by development of integrated patient pathways, improvement of the collaboration between specialist (secondary) and municipal (primary) health care levels and more prevention (Norwegian Ministry of Health and Care Service, 2012). "The Free Choice of Hospital" reform in 2015 gave the patients a free choice of hospital (Ringard, Sperre Saunes, & Sagan, 2016), and "The Future Primary Care—Proximity and Comprehensiveness" reform in 2015 has been implemented to improve patients involvement, prevention, better collaboration between multidisciplinary teams and more decentralized services close to where patients live to reduce costs (Norwegian Ministry of Health and Care Service, 2015; Rørtveit, 2015). The Coordination Reform has lately been criticized by people working in primary care, since it leads to more out-of-hospital care and pressure on the GPs, without necessary increase in local health resources (Trønderopprøret, 2018). Recent studies show that inadequate communication between hospitals and primary care, as well as competence problems in primary care can lead to inadequate patient care and frequent readmissions to hospitals of an increasing number of medically complex patients (Glette, Kringeland, Røise, & Wiig, 2018; Glette, Kringeland, Røise, & Wiig, 2019).

7.2 Doctors' Well-being: Work-Related and Individual Factors

Studies indicate that organizational factors influence the doctors' work-life and well-being and may in turn impact quality of patient care (Firth-Cozens & Greenhalgh, 1997; Angerer & Weigl, 2015, McKinlay & Marceau, 2011, Bååthe et al., 2016, Baathe, Rosta, Bringedal, & Isaksson Rø, 2019). All organizational changes can contribute in both virtuous and vicious ways, and it is not unusual that the same change can be considered successful or detrimental, depending on what perspectives are being investigated, or which "lens" is being used when studying a change. For instance, from a managerial perspective an organizational change may reduce costs and increase effectivity with respect to patient-turnover, whereas a clinician could experience increased time pressure, less adequate time with patients, and threats to the quality of patient care. The different professional identities between managers and doctors can contribute to some role confusion, i.e. difficulties for clinicians to become managers and for leaders to understand the doctors' perspective (Kippist & Fitzgerald, 2009; Spehar, Frich, & Kjekshus, 2015). At the same time research suggests (Baathe & Norback, 2013; Swensen & Shanafelt, 2020) how this chasm can be transformed in order to establish a more fruitful working alliance where doctors are engaged, together with managers and other health personal, in co-creating a work climate that contributes towards provider well-being, budgetary viability and high quality of patient care. Storkholm, Mazzocato, Savage, and Savage (2017) provides an example of how management was able to create clinical engagement for quality improvement by translating the overarching managerial need for organizational change to improve a budgetary situation into a change process that resonated with the professional identities.

In Norway there are several longitudinal data sets on doctors' health, work and quality of life. Since 1994 the Institute for Studies of the Medical Profession (LEFO, www.legeforsk.org) has surveyed a representative panel of active Norwegian doctors every second year with postal questionnaires. The sample represents an unbalanced cohort in that respondents who leave the panel due to retirement, death, or voluntary withdrawal are replaced by younger doctors, while the sample's representative nature is maintained at all times. In the NORDOC study two cohorts of medical students/young doctors have been surveyed regularly for 25 years since they either started their studies in 1993/1994 or finished their studies in 1994 (www.med.uio.no/imb/english/research/projects/nordoc/). In the Villa Sana study, doctors seeking counselling were followed for 3 years after their visit to a Resource Centre for doctors. The counselling centre is a low-threshold initiative aiming to enhance health and life quality, strengthen professional awareness and identity and prevent burnout. This broad approach is meant to encourage doctors to seek collegial help or guidance, preferably when problems have not escalated too far. Consequently there is a broad spectrum of reasons for seeking help, mainly in situations when doctors feel stressed or burned out, often due to a combination of work-related and private reasons. The counselling is not defined as treatment, but a help to sort through problems together with a colleague, and discuss what actions would be wise to take in the future (Isaksson Rø et al., 2010; Isaksson Rø, Gude, & Aasland, 2007; Isaksson Rø, Gude, Tyssen, & Aasland, 2008). These longitudinal studies give us the possibility to study the impact of health care changes over time on different aspects of doctors' work-life and well-being, as well as effects of a counselling intervention for burnout.

Data from 1994 to 2014 found that the number of **weekly working hours** have been stable for all categories of Norwegian doctors working full-time, except for doctors in academia (working at universities, university hospitals or at a combination of these who reported a significant reduction from 51 h in 1994 to 46 h in 2014). In hospitals, work hours for junior hospital doctors/residents (45 h) and for senior hospital doctors (46 h) did not differ significantly. Hospital doctors working in management (48 h) and general practitioners (48 h) had the longest working week. Female hospital doctors (both junior and senior) worked significantly fewer hours (44 h) than their male colleagues (47 h) (Rosta & Aasland, 2014; Rosta & Aasland, 2016). As in other countries most of the Norwegian doctors work full-time. There is, however, a possibility to work part-time. Especially among junior hospital doctors we have seen a trend towards more part-time work, from 3.4% in 1993 to 10.2% in 2012 (Rosta & Aasland, 2014). With regard to the European work time directive, worries have been expressed whether the number of hours worked would be sufficient to obtain specialist competency (Lambert, Smith, & Goldacre, 2016). The majority of Norwegian doctors perceived the present situation with an average of 45 h per week for specialty registrars as sufficient for obligatory postgraduate specialist training, but senior doctors and doctors working in surgical specialties were more likely to want the work-week to be longer (Rosta & Aasland, 2014). When studying work hours in relation to patient care, we found that time spent on direct patient care fell considerably among hospital doctors (from 61 to 46% of total work time) during this period, while the drop was marginal among GPs (73% versus 69%) and practice specialists (75% versus 72%). Growing documentation requirements, structural changes within the health service, inadequate electronic medical record systems, increasingly diverse allocations of functions and tasks to different categories of health personnel following major health service reforms may explain this (Rosta & Aasland, 2016). In addition, some of the doctors are working part-time or they are occupied with other obligations than direct patient work. According to the OECD data, the proportion of practicing doctors per 1000 inhabitants in Norway increased from 2.8% in 1994 to 4.8% in 2018. In 2018, Norway had the second highest country cover of practicing doctors among the 35 OECD-countries (Austria had higher coverage with 5.2, and examples of other countries are 2.9 in the UK, 3.1 in Belgium, 3.2 in Finland, 4.0 in Denmark and 4.3 in Switzerland and Germany) (OECD, 2019). Norwegian doctor workforce statistics indicates a significant increase in number of practicing doctors, under 70 years, from 12,809 in 1995 to 27,187 in 2019 (General statistics on doctors in Norway, 2019). 17.3% of the practicing doctors in Norway have non-Norwegian citizenships, mostly European (Norwegian Medical Association).

Our data showed that **job satisfaction** of the doctors in Norway was stable and high from 1994 to 2002 (5.20) (Nylenna, Gulbrandsen, Forde, & Aasland, 2005) and further increased in the period 2002–2006 (5.20 versus 5.41) (Aasland, Rosta, & Nylenna, 2010) measured by the ten item version of the "Warr-Cook-Wall scale" with scores ranging from 1 (low satisfaction) to 7 (high satisfaction) (Warr, Cook, & Wall, 1979). From 2010 to 2017, however, job satisfaction decreased significantly among both GPs (5.54 versus 5.17) and hospital doctors (5.14 versus 5.00). In 2010, 40% of the doctors reported a high degree of stress associated with recurring reorganisations (Aasland & Rosta, 2011). Perceived psychosocial work stress, measured as Effort-Reward Imbalance (ERI), has increased significantly among GPs during 2010–2019 (Rosta, Bååthe, Aasland, & Isaksson Rø, 2020). Studies showing increased workload for GPs are in line with these findings (Rosta, Aasland, & Nylenna, 2019). The complex relationships between different health care reforms and satisfaction, stress and workload among doctors are difficult to determine, but satisfaction, stress and workload are likely to be partly related to the reforms. For example, following the Coordination Reform, primary care services and the GPs have to take care of earlier discharges and patients with more severe conditions and multi-comorbidity than they did before, and this has increased their stress at work (Glette et al., 2018). Additionally societal reforms have probably lead to doctors expecting better work-home balance, and patients expecting to take a bigger part in the discussion and decisions around their treatment. This can also influence doctors' work stress and satisfaction (Hertzberg, Tyssen, Skirbekk, & Isaksson Rø, 2019).

In sum, this shows that over the last decade, there seems to be a reduction in job satisfaction among Norwegian doctors, most prominent in GPs (Rosta, Aasland, & Nylenna, 2019). For GPs and doctors in hospital, the job satisfaction scores on different aspects of work like "freedom to choose methods", "recognition for good work", "rate of pay" and "work hours" decreased significantly from 2010 to 2017. Also, GPs reported significantly lower scores for "amount of responsibility" and "overall job satisfaction". There was a non-significant change in job satisfaction for other job positions such as doctors in academia, private practice specialists, community medical officers, doctors in administration and doctors in other positions (Rosta, Aasland, & Nylenna, 2019). There was no increase in number of work hours from 1994 to 2014 (Rosta & Aasland, 2014; Rosta & Aasland, 2016). Surveys from 2018 report long working weeks with a wide variety of tasks (Rebnord, Eikeland, Hunskår, & Morken, 2018) and a growth in work demands for GPs (Johnsen et al., 2018). However, Norwegian doctors continue to work relatively few hours per week, as well as few hours in direct patient care, compared to some other Western countries like Germany, Austria, UK, and Switzerland. USA and Canada (between 50 and 90 h a week) (Rosta & Aasland, 2011; Rosta & Aasland, 2014; Rosta & Aasland, 2016; Tyssen, Palmer, Solberg, Voltmer, & Frank, 2013; Voltmer, Rosta, Siegrist, & Aasland, 2012). This is due to strictly regulated work life and work hours in this socio-democratic Nordic country.

We have also measured many **other aspects of doctors' work life** related to well-being.

Stress related to the effect of work demands on the situation at home, so-called work-home interface stress (WHI) is especially high around 10 years after graduating as a doctor and increases the risk of burn-out (Hertzberg et al., 2016). For doctors who sought a counselling intervention for (mental) health issues, exhaustion and burnout, we have found that reducing work-home interface stress is a key measure to improve the situation (Isaksson Rø et al., 2010). Reducing work-home interface stress may also be a preventive measure for doctors at risk for burn-out, as levels of work-home interface stress predict levels of burnout 5 years later (Hertzberg, Skirbekk, Tyssen, Aasland, & Isaksson Rø, 2016b).

Around 10 years after graduation doctors in 2014 (especially female doctors) report less work-home interface stress and more part-time work, than doctors did 10 years after graduation in 2008. This indicates that there is an increased acceptance among colleagues for doctors to utilise the societal reforms giving parents of small children the right to work shorter hours and the offer of easy access to kindergarten child care (Hertzberg et al., 2019). An increase of part-time work among young doctors could mean that we need to increase the number of positions for junior doctors.

Although a substantial proportion of Norwegian doctors experience threats (53%) and real acts (24%) of violence during their whole work-time career, we have not found any increase in reports of perceived work place violence (Johansen, Baste, Rosta, Aasland, & Morken, 2017) from 1993 to 2015. We have not found any increase in perceived bullying at work either (Rosta & Aasland, 2018). There was an increase in reported **unwanted sexual attention** which may reflect a real increase in unwanted attention and/or increased societal awareness of this phenomenon, and thus a changed reporting threshold (Isaksson Rø, Johansen, & Rosta, 2018).

Compared with doctors in several other countries, our studies find that doctors in Norway seem to work in an environment where the weekly working hours (Rosta & Aasland, 2011; Rosta & Aasland, 2016) and the proportion of risky level of psychosocial work stress are lower (Voltmer et al., 2012), and the life (Rosta,

Nylenna, & Aasland, 2009) and job satisfaction (Rosta et al., 2009; Solberg, Tómasson, Aasland, & Tyssen, 2014; Voltmer et al., 2012) are higher. Nevertheless, a study on opinions about professional autonomy, such as having adequate time with patients and possibility to deliver high-quality care, shows that Norwegian (and Canadian) doctors are less satisfied than US doctors (Tyssen et al., 2013). Interestingly, female doctors in both private (USA) and public health (Canada and Norway) systems seem to be least satisfied with professional autonomy. The lower satisfaction among the female doctors is probably due to higher expectations among them towards providing high quality of care. We know that female doctors perform better than male doctors with respect to observed communication skills, and a good doctor-patient relationship requires adequate time (Gude et al., 2017). We also know that female surgeons had a small but statistically significant lower 30 day mortality and similar surgical outcomes (length of stay, complications, and readmissions), compared with those treated by male surgeons (Wallis et al., 2017), and that elderly hospitalized patients treated by female internists have lower mortality and readmission rates compared with those cared for by male internists (Tsugawa et al., 2017).

As for other professions with high socio-economic status, studies showed better somatic health, healthier lifestyle habits and lower overall **mortality**, among doctors in Norway than in the general population (Aasland, Hem, Haldorsen, & Ekeberg, 2011). An exception is suicide, where doctors have higher rates than other graduates and the general population, both among male [43·0, 95% confidence interval (CI) 35·3–52·5] and female (26·1, 95% CI 15·1–44·9) doctors from 1969–2000 (Hem et al., 2005). From 2000 to 2010, the perceived lifetime prevalence of suicidal feelings decreased from 48 to 45%, and in 2010 was comparable with other professionals in Norway and doctors in Germany (Rosta & Aasland, 2013a). Answering a general question about health,, the vast majority of Norwegian doctors rated their **health** as "very good" or "good", in a study based on data from 2010 (Rosta & Aasland, 2014). We do know, from international studies, that physicians' physical health is similar to the general population, and female physicians even tend to be in better health than other women. Depressive symptoms and suicidal thoughts are prevalent, especially early in the career, probably due to heavy on-call work and sleep deprivation (Mata et al., 2015; Tyssen, Vaglum, Gronvold, & Ekeberg, 2001). Despite the higher rates of suicide, we have no recent studies that compare prevalence of mental disorders, i.e. by diagnostic interviews, among doctors with that in the general population. Following the trend in international studies a majority of Norwegian doctors in 2010 reported no **sickness absence** at all last year (Rosta & Aasland, 2014). On the other hand 76% of Norwegian doctors reported sickness presenteeism—going to work with symptoms that you would have recommended your patient to stay at home for (Gustafsson Sendén, Løvseth, Schenck-Gustafsson, & Friedner, 2013). The issues around sickness absence and presenteeism, are, however, important to understand in relation to the inherent complexity of sickness behaviour in the medical profession. We know that doctors "seldom take sick leave, and tend to make less use of primary health care and some screening facilities, whereas self-treatment is common—even for mental problems" (Tyssen, 2007).

Among Norwegian hospital doctors it has been found that factors associated with competitive climate at work, taking compensatory leave (i.e. offering other reasons for being away from work, when sickness was the real cause), self-diagnosis and self-treatment were associated with presenteeism (Gustafsson Sendén et al., 2013). These behaviours can partly be related to a general professional medical culture, expressed by Norwegian doctors saying that «a high degree of attendance in the workplace» and «a high work capacity» were important characteristics of a "good doctor" (Hertzberg, Skirbekk, Tyssen, Aasland, & Isaksson Rø, 2016b). Still, we have reasons to believe that the younger generation of doctors are more positive towards taking sick-leave than their older colleagues (Hertzberg, Skirbekk, Tyssen, Aasland & Isaksson Rø, 2016c), and there is also an increase of part-time work among younger doctors (Hertzberg et al., 2019). It is suggested that sufficient staffing, predictability in employment, adequate communication of formal policies and senior physicians adopting the position of positive role models are particularly important in order to change the medical culture towards taking care of oneself as a doctor (Giæver, Lohmann-Lafrenz, & Løvseth, 2016). Organizational changes that give employment security and predictability, and promote policies regulating physicians' number of hours can lead to less sickness presenteeism (Gustafsson Sendén et al., 2013). On the other hand, there has been little discussion about consequences for the workforce size if the younger doctors take more sick leave and parental leave. This, and an increasing rate of doctors of both sexes who need longer leaves after childbirth, may increase the need for more positions.

The **drinking pattern** of Norwegian doctors has from 2000 to 2010 changed towards more moderate alcohol consumption and less negative alcohol-related consequences. This is in contrast to studies of the Norwegian general population during the same period that suggest more frequent alcohol use combined with more frequent heavy episodic drinking than before (Rosta & Aasland, 2013b). A longitudinal study of hazardous drinking among Norwegian doctors found no direct association with work-related factors; but the drinking was linked to mental distress (anxiety and depressive symptoms), as in the general population (Mahmood, Grotmol, Tesli, Vaglum, & Tyssen, 2017). Still, we believe that the drinking level in doctors in Norway today is on the same level as in other comparable socioeconomic groups (Mahmood, 2019).

In terms of **individual factors** and well-being among doctors, the NORDOC studies have identified some personality factors of particular importance. This applies to neuroticism trait (or self-criticism, low self-esteem) that predicts work stress, burnout, and even severe depressive symptoms in prospective and longitudinal studies (Grotmol, Gude, Moum, Vaglum, & Tyssen, 2013; Isaksson Rø et al., 2008; Tyssen, Vaglum, Gronvold, & Ekeberg, 2005). The combination of neuroticism and conscientiousness traits seems to be especially unfavorable predictors for work stress in young doctors (Røvik et al., 2007). NORDOC has also found a deviant personality trait, reality weakness, to be a risk for severe depressive symptoms and lack of help-seeking in doctors (Tyssen, 2017). Reality weakness is about ideations on the borderline between fantasy and reality, impressions that are associated with insecurity about identity and relationship with others and paranoid thoughts (or severe personality disorders).

7.3 Individual Interventions to Improve Well-being in Norwegian Doctors

In response to the international and national concern about mental health and suicide among doctors in the 1990s, the Norwegian Medical Association (NMA) established two peer support programs for doctors to contact "in times of strain, due to private or professional reasons". A local network of peer counsellors in all the 18 counties of Norway (Isaksson Rø & Aasland, 2016) was organized, as well as a centralized short-term counselling program, called Resource centre Villa Sana (Isaksson Rø et al., 2007). These were designed to be easily accessible services offering "empathic support, advice and counselling". The services are free of charge for all Norwegian doctors, confidential, and offer counselling and not formalized treatment. It thus follows that no medical records are kept. The local counsellors see the help-seeking doctors within very short time (within a couple of work days), and provide up to 3 face-to-face sessions, or if distances are long—phone conversations. At the Resource centre doctors come for either a day of individual counselling—a one-to-one encounter lasting for 6 h—or for a week-long course together with 8 other colleagues. The course includes lectures, discussions, physical activity and an individual counselling session of 1 h for each participant. All of the counselling relates to the specific work- and life situation that the doctor presents. There is time to sort through the different issues in the situation, discuss coping strategies and to focus on both short- and long-time measures to take. In many cases a contact with either a GP or a therapist (psychiatrist or psychologist) for treatment is suggested. Follow-up studies of doctors entering the Villa Sana program show reduction of burnout, job stress and mental distress both one and 3 years later (Isaksson Rø et al., 2008; Isaksson Rø et al., 2010). During the last 5 years we have, in both these services, increasingly observed how young doctors, especially young female doctors, seek help (Nilsen, 2017). This can have many explanations. As in other Western countries there is an increasing number of female doctors in the profession (General statistics on doctors in Norway, 2019). Work-home interface stress seems to be a stronger predictor of the development of burnout among female doctors than among male doctors in a longitudinal study (Hertzberg et al., 2016). Also, as mentioned above, female doctors might have higher demands on themselves related to providing high quality care and giving their patients more time (Tyssen et al., 2013).

There is a long-term follow up RCT of mindfulness based stress reduction in Norwegian young doctors, who have been followed after a 7 weeks course at an undergraduate level (together with psychology students). The participants were provided "booster sessions" every half-year during the follow-up. The effects on stress are most prominent in female students and doctors, the 4 and 6-year follow-ups show that possible mechanisms of stress reduction may be an increase in active ways of coping and reduction of passive or avoidance coping (de Vibe et al., 2018; Solhaug et al., 2019). One reason for this may be stress reduction due to mindfulness, and more vigilance and active attitude to the many problem-oriented tasks that meet young doctors. There was a less significant reduction in avoidance coping also in the control group, possibly due to maturation during these early years of the career. In addition it seems that participants with unfavourable personality traits (as presented above) profit more from mindfulness training (de Vibe et al., 2015), and a recent long-term follow-up study of this cohort even shows a significant reduction in neuroticism trait over time in the intervention group (Hanley, de Vibe, Solhaug, Gonzalez-Pons, & Garland, 2019).

7.4 Quality of Patient Care

Having documented trends in doctor wellness and described important health care reforms and societal change, it is important to see how this relates to quality of patient care.

Quality of care has been measured in several ways. Subjective quality of care has been rated both by doctors and by patients, and several more "objective" measures of quality of care have been developed.

In 2018, a comparison study of health between 36 different European countries was published (Health at a glance, 2018). Norwegian citizens have a relatively high life-expectancy, and the healthcare system performs well on several health quality indicators like low 30-day mortality after admission to hospital for Acute Myocardial Infarction or stroke. However, when it comes to patient-doctor interaction/communication, patients perceived that Norwegian GPs did not spend enough time with patients in consultation, and Norwegian patients feel less involved by the doctor in decisions about care and treatment, than in almost all the other countries measured. Also, waiting times for patients with a hip replacement need were longer in Norway than for example in Denmark, the Netherlands, Italy, Sweden or the UK. Efforts have been made to understand why Norwegian patients report less satisfaction than patients in most of the other countries. Comparisons are challenging since the patient satisfaction data are gathered in different ways in the different countries and it is difficult to ascertain the quality of the data (Saunes, Hansen, Tomic, & Lindahl, 2017). More studies are needed to understand the differences.

Thus, we find that the quality measures are divergent, and that we need more knowledge about the complex relationships between quality of care, physician wellness and organisation.

Since the 1990s there has been an international focus on individual physician wellness, but during the last years this has also come to explore the relation between physician wellness and quality of patient care, patient safety, and organizational factors (West, 2001; Wallace, Lemaire, & Ghali, 2009; Bodenheimer & Sinsky, 2014). Since 2014 there have been a number of international conferences bringing the themes together (for example; International Conference of Physician Health—ICPH, European Association of Physician Health—EAPH, WELLMED, Interactions between health care Providers, Organization and Quality of care—IPOQ, NOVO-symposium). The importance of organizational factors, creating "virtuous or vicious" working conditions for the individual healthcare worker, has also been expanded on in more recent studies looking for ways to handle the reported increase in burnout numbers (Shanafelt & Noseworthy, 2017; Weigl, Hornung, Angerer, Siegrist, & Glaser, 2013). In 2017 the Declaration of Geneva was revised to state that physicians need to take care of their own health in order to be able to take care of their patients' health (Parsa-Parsi, 2017). Furthermore the "Triple aim of healthcare" launched by the Institute for Healthcare Improvement has been challenged to include an additional fourth aim focusing on the care of the provider in order to sustainably deliver high quality patient care (Bodenheimer & Sinsky, 2014).

7.5 Is There a Clear Link Between the Burnout-Concept and Doctors' Impaired Functioning?

There have been many studies on burnout and possible links to lowered patient care. In a review of these relationships, Rathert et al. found that burned out physicians think that they make more errors and deliver lower quality of care, but that the few studies examining clinical outcomes could not verify this (Rathert, Williams, & Linhart, 2018). One study found higher mortality rates among patients treated by burned out doctors and nurses in an ICU (Welp, Meier, & Manser, 2015), and a couple of studies have shown that GPs who are burned out refer patients that normally would be treated in primary care, more frequently to specialist care (Kushnir et al., 2014; Nørøxe, Pedersen, Carlsen, Bro, & Vedsted, 2019). However, some studies show a relationship between depression and medical errors as well as quality of care (Rathert et al., 2018). As burnout has not to date been validated with respect to mental health deterioration or impaired functioning, Rathert et al. point to the importance of studying the relationship between burnout and depression. The most common burnout cut-offs used may be too low to capture really poor patient functioning measured with objective and observed measures (Tyssen, 2018). Some level of work stress does not necessarily entail poor performance, and as most doctors are extremely motivated to be vigilant and focused, patient care is presumably maintained even when doctors feel stressed, according to the Conservation of resources theory (Innstrand, Langballe, Espnes, Falkum, & Aasland, 2008).

Studies that have measured patient satisfaction mostly show a correlation between doctors' burnout and lower satisfaction with care, but the results are somewhat mixed (Rathert et al., 2018). It is important to also remember the more indirect effects of burnout on health services and patient care, from doctors' dissatisfaction, increased turnover, sickness absence among doctors and early retirement due to burnout.

Thus, the relationships between burnout and quality of care could be complex, and include mediating and moderating variables (Rathert et al., 2018). We probably also need more valid ways of measuring both levels of burnout, correlation between levels of burnout and depression, and levels of distress interfering with functioning of doctors in different ways. The instruments for measuring the clinical "exhaustion syndrome" developed in Sweden (Besèr et al., 2014) and Schaufeli et al's measure of clinical burnout (Roelofs, Verbraak, Keijsers, de Bruin, & Schmidt, 2005) are interesting to pursue, including some new dimensions of cognitive and emotional regulation that are in the process of being developed and evaluated (Schaufeli, De Witte, & Desart, 2019).

7.6 Interactions Among Professional Fulfilment, Organizational Factors and Quality of Patient Care: An Exploratory Interview Study with Hospital Doctors to Provide Further Understanding

The authors of this chapter have been following the development of national healthcare services, and for a long time Norwegian doctors have broadly responded with satisfaction when asked about work conditions and organizational changes. As presented above, recent studies indicate that this pattern of well-being and satisfaction among Norwegian doctors' may have changed. In order to provide a deeper understanding of the statistical results presented above, mainly coming from quantitative survey data, we also need qualitative studies. By the use of individual interviews we have aimed to better understand how doctors experience the interplay among professional fulfilment, organizational factors and quality of patient care (see

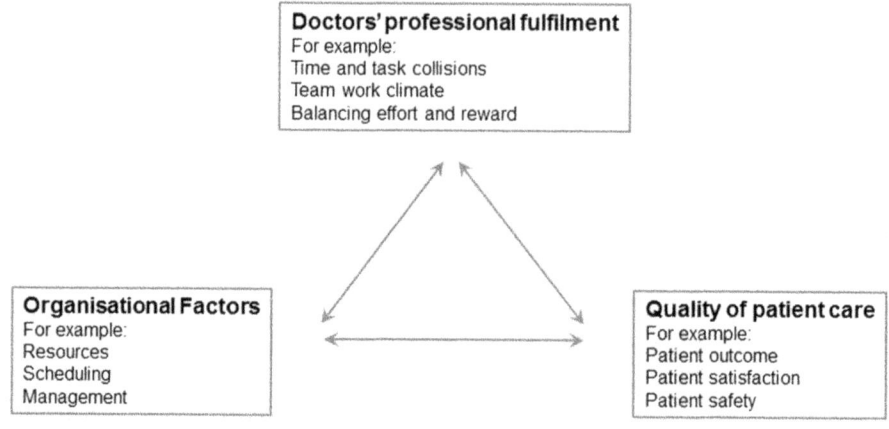

Fig. 7.1 A conceptual framework to explore how doctors experience the interplay among professional fulfilment, organizational factors and quality of patient care

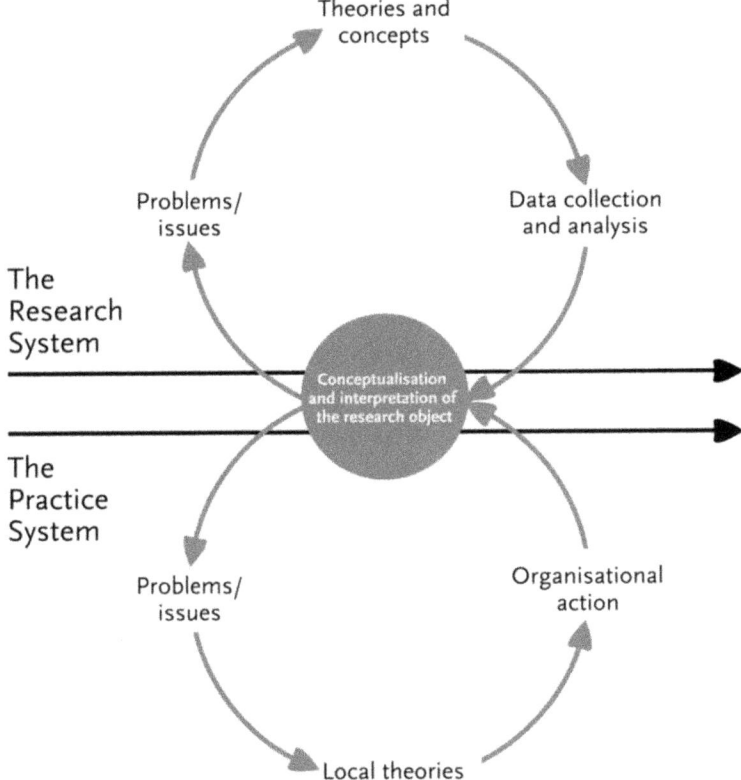

Fig. 7.2 A Model of Knowledge Creation Through Interactive Research (Ellström, 2007)

Fig. 7.1). The triangle depicted below has been used as a conceptual framework when interviewing doctors from two hospitals in Norway and one hospital in the USA.

This multiyear and multisite project has had an interactive research strategy. Knowledgeable about the challenges with engaging physicians in improvement work (Baathe & Norback, 2013; Dickson, 2012), we concluded that interactive research might be a research strategy that could reduce that obstacle. Interactive research is characterised by the aspiration to create a joint learning between the participant and the researchers throughout the entire research process (Ellström, Rönnqvist, & Thunborg, 1994; Greenhalgh, Robert, Macfarlane, Bate, & Kyriakidou, 2004). The dual aim is to conduct a theoretically-related analysis that can contribute with scientific knowledge and publications for the scientific community, while also catering to finding practical knowledge that is relevant and useable for the participants (Svensson, Ellström, & Brulin, 2007). The ambition in interactive research is to conduct research "with the participant" (contrasted to "on the participant"). Figure 7.2 (below) depicts how the research system and the practise system meet each other in feedback/feedforward sessions. There are a number of meetings over time to facilitate learning among the researchers and the practitioners. A typical session would be that researchers present early findings from their analysis of the empirical material from the practise system. The practitioners react to what is being presented, creating confirmation of the early analysis, and/or enabling the researchers to find gaps in the reasoning. A subsequent session would be when researchers have continued the analysis and now also introduce theories and concepts, potentially providing the practitioners with actionable practical strategies tested in a similar setting.

The first published results from this study were based on interviews with Norwegian hospital doctors (Baathe et al., 2019). The following five themes emerged when analysing the interviews and below we will elaborate on the findings to provide additional nuance to how Norwegian doctors' relate to well-being, quality of patient care and organizational change.

1. **Being able to deliver high quality patient care is foundational for professional fulfillment**
2. **The importance of quality of patient care is crowded out by production numbers and economic data**
3. **The accelerating struggle against time impacts doctors' well-being and quality of patient care**
4. **A common strategy is to 'stretch oneself' to deliver quality of patient care despite organizational shortcomings**
5. **Managers do not recognize quality of care challenges and they provide limited support for doctor initiatives**

Our interviews found that doctors' experience of professional fulfillment was closely related to whether their work resulted in good quality of patient care. That **quality of patient care is foundational for professional fulfilment** has been found in many previous studies (Bliss, 1999; Friedberg, Chen, Van Busum, Pham, & Aunon, 2013; West, Guthrie, Dawson, Borrill, & Carter, 2006).

The participants expressed how **conversations about quality of care were crowded out by production numbers and economic data**. They conveyed that the essence of being a professionally fulfilled doctor, creating high quality care for patients, no longer receives sufficient recognition. This finding is in line with research pointing to changes in what society, patients and employers are expecting from a doctor, and how this is starting to create a job situation that is no longer what doctors expect (Edwards, Kornacki, & Silversin, 2002).

The interviewed doctors described how they experienced an **accelerating struggle against time impacting well-being and quality of patient care.** Our participants relate how they have started to consider that quality of patient care, and their own well-being, both could suffer from this way of overextending themselves. While limited time with patients was the primary concern, work–home balance was also an issue that troubled many of the participants. The experience of doctors having less time and more work is aligned with other studies (Dyrbye et al., 2017; Friedberg et al., 2013; Wallace et al., 2009). However, in our study, the participants describe how finding individual workarounds in order to handle organizational shortcomings, no longer is experienced as sustainable. This is in line with recent studies in Sweden and Norway, where young doctors point to the importance of finding a job with a good work–home balance (Hertzberg et al., 2016; Diderichsen, 2017).

The interactions among professional fulfilment, organizational factors and quality of patient care were often experienced as resulting in complex and challenging situations. A doctor could be scheduled to operate while also having to run to the ward to check on patients or run late to pick up children from daycare because shift times between operations ran longer than planned. The interviewed doctors primarily handled this tension individually by finding ways to overcome organizational hindrances. The participants described this experience as '**stretching themselves' to deliver quality care despite organizational shortcomings**. This is in line with recent Norwegian qualitative studies (Glette et al., 2018; Glette et al., 2019).

The last theme emerging from the interviewed Norwegian doctors was an experience of a hierarchical management culture that **did not recognize quality of care challenges and provided limited support for doctor initiatives**. Research suggests that clinical leaders have a crucial role in supporting doctors to find meaning in a changing professional role (Cruess, Cruess, Boudreau, Snell, & Steinert, 2015; McKinlay & Marceau, 2011). The participants expressed frustrations with the limited possibility to participate in developing organizational policies, processes and systems. At the same time, there were few accounts of actual aspirations, or doctors actively working to find solutions to organizational shortcomings.

These findings are in line with research reporting that doctors' engagement in improvement work/clinical development work has been a challenge since it calls on complimentary skills to the bio-medical training (Berwick & Nolan, 1998; Davies, Powell, & Rushmer, 2007; Lee & Cosgrove, 2014). Lindgren, Bååthe, and Dellve (2013) found that doctors were engaged in development work in an abstract sense. More active participation depended on whether development work contributed towards each doctor's experience of professional fulfillment, as much as clinical work did. Davies et al. (2007) suggested that going from an abstract to an active engagement is a key challenge for doctors:

> *In summary, active engagement in quality improvement is likely to entail profound and disconcerting changes, greater uncertainty, and some potential loss of face for individuals and professions in acknowledging other parties, giving up cherished turf and altering everyday routines and established ceremonies. (p. 129)*

For physicians to experience professional fulfilment when participating in healthcare development work (improving healthcare delivery processes), these experiences arguably need to differ qualitatively, to complement, the fulfilling experiences from clinical practice (Bååthe, 2015). The need for experiences of social interaction and relating alongside other professionals, and receiving recognition for work well done, by oneself and others, could be small but powerful nudges embedded in the experience of improvement work to increase doctors' engagement. The need for experiences of social interaction and recognition resonates with Stacey

(2011) who proposed that the fundamental motivator of human behavior is the urge to relate.

7.7 Norwegian Doctors Well-being, Quality of Patient Care and Organizational Change: Key Learnings

Quality of patient care is a key outcome for any healthcare organization. One might consider that statement as self-evident. In particular when working as a doctor in a hospital that is part of the societal infrastructure in Norway, a well-functioning and affluent Nordic country. However, it might be prudent to remind ourselves that the amount of money available to spend on healthcare is limited. This restriction might be even clearer in a tax-financed healthcare system, like the Norwegian. Thus, there is a built-in tension that requires a constant balancing of clinical needs with budgetary means. The inherent tension between an organizational focus on the bottom line and doctors' focus on quality of patient care is found to increase the risk for experiencing meaninglessness, especially in combination with a lack of managerial recognition for work well done (Bailey & Madden, 2016).

Are there overarching societal system effects impacting doctors' opinions of quality of care? A comparison study between Norwegian doctors and US doctors in a private health care system shows that the Norwegian doctors report less adequate time with their patients and less possibility to deliver high quality care than do their American colleagues (Tyssen et al., 2013). On the other hand, Norwegian doctors report higher job satisfaction and less problems with cost containment at the hospitals than Icelandic doctors after the 2008 economic recession (Solberg et al., 2014; Solberg, Tomasson, Aasland, & Tyssen, 2013). Interestingly, our qualitative study on how Norwegian doctors experienced the interplay between professional fulfillment, organizational factors and quality (Baathe et al., 2019) provided deep resonance when presented to American doctors of the same specialty. So it seems as if there are comparable experiences from both Norwegian doctors in a public system and American doctors in a private health system. Therefore, we believe that these opinions and experiences are quite universal among hospital doctors -on a clinical level—at least in relatively affluent Western countries.

Although still relatively high, the satisfaction among both hospital doctors and GPshas been reduced during the last 7–8 years, from around 2010 (Rosta, Aasland, & Isaksson Rø, 2019). GPs have also reported higher levels of stress, with increasing levels of effort and less perceived rewards during several years (Rosta et al., 2019). Internationally there have been many reports of high levels of burnout and loss of satisfaction and meaning amongst doctors in many western societies. There is recent evidence that burnout and reduced well-being in Danish GPs interfere with their functioning. The recent studies by Nørøxe et al. shows that burned out doctors have patients that change GP more often, and that such doctors more often refer patients to hospital specialist care that could have been handled in ambulatory care (Nørøxe,

Pedersen, Carlsen, Bro, & Vedsted, 2019; Nørøxe, Vedsted, Bro, Carlsen, & Pedersen, 2019).

From our empirical material it is interesting to notice that there seem to be signs of a similar negative development also starting to show in the statistical numbers from Norwegian doctors, after 2010. At the same time it seems from the deep probing interviews (and related research), that there are ways to alter the vicious spiral towards a more virtuous development going forward. It is all hinged upon the seemingly simple, but actually foundational premise, of managers needing to ensure that doctors (and other health care workers) are involved when developing organizational policies, processes and clinical systems. In order to support this process, organizational leaders in healthcare need to be attuned to how psychological and social needs relate to doctors' motivation and engagement (Ryan & Deci, 2000; Baathe & Norback, 2013; Herzberg, Skirbekk, Tyssen, Aasland, & Isaksson Rø, 2016c). In a participatory change study, where doctors analyzed work-related problems and created local solutions that were then implemented, working conditions and patients' perceived quality of care both showed positive changes (Weigl et al., 2013). Another study showed that doctors who were actively involved in the process of changing the local ward round experienced better-informed clinical decisions, had fewer follow-up questions from their patients and increased their own professional fulfilment (Baathe, Ahlborg, Lagström, Edgren, & Nilsson, 2014).

To involve doctors in development work, recognizing their ideas and listening to understand what the difficulties are, has been suggested as a central dimension to reduce burnout (Swensen, Kabcenell, & Shanafelt, 2016). A deliberate, collaborative process where managers commit scheduled doctor time for this type of work is key. What a manager says in conversations with the doctors and what a manager does really matter in relation to how clinicians participate in developing clinical policies, processes and systems (Bååthe, 2015; Stacey & Mowles, 2016). Research reminds us that this is a two-way road, managers and doctors need to talk more with each other, and less about each other. "If managers want physicians to engage in improvement work, they must learn to understand and appreciate the mindset of physicians, and physicians must learn to understand and appreciate the mindset of managers" (Baathe & Norback, 2013, p. 490).

By including doctors, the lived experience of the inherent tension among professional fulfilment, organizational factors and quality of patient care could be used in a meaningful way to improve healthcare delivery processes. This is likely to be beneficial for both professional fulfilment and quality of patient care. Furthermore, when clinically active people are engaged in improving healthcare delivery processes from within, there will be a valuable contribution towards the alluring target of meeting the economic needs for healthcare. Healthcare Managers have a tremendous opportunity, and challenge, in evolving healthcare to the better while never losing sight of the three dimensions continuously connected in tensional play; Health care worker well-being, patient safety and organizational change.

Take Home Messages
For researchers:

1. We need further studies on the links between physician well-being and quality of care. We need to understand more about the conceptual issues that are studied—like quality of patient care and physician well-being. What are the levels of reduced physician well-being that impair their patient care? Today there are many definitions and perceptions, and we need more comparative and cross-national studies. This is important in order to integrate knowledge from relevant research fields, and to further international co-operation in research around these important issues.
2. We also need more qualitative research to study this matter more in depth and with nuances. By combining empirical experiences from health care providers, as well as managers, qualitative studies can contribute with a grounded understanding of drivers and solutions.
3. By use of interactive research/collaborative research, where researchers closely and over a prolonged time-horizon collaborate with clinicians and managers, we can study how system changes (co-created by clinicians and managers) impact clinician well-being and quality of care, over time. This might be a fruitful way for researchers, in collaboration with clinicians, supporting the journey to connect health care worker well-being, patient safety and organizational change.

For clinicians and managers:

1. The only long-term sustainable way to handle budgetary dilemmas is to improve the clinical care processes, i.e. the way people in healthcare work together, to meet the needs of patients.
2. Clinicians and managers need to engage in local system changes, aiming for better quality of care and clinician well-being. (team-based)
3. Managers and clinicians need to learn to see/understand both the clinician and the management perspective, in order to better work towards the mutual goal of continuously improving the health care system.

References

Aasland, O. G., Hem, E., Haldorsen, T., & Ekeberg, O. (2011). Mortality among Norwegian doctors 1960–2000. *BMC Public Health, 11*, 173. https://doi.org/10.1186/1471-2458-11-17

Aasland, O. G., & Rosta, J. (2011). Hvordan har overlegene det? (How are senior doctors doing?). *Overlegen, 1*, 47–55.

Aasland, O. G., Rosta, J., & Nylenna, M. (2010). Healthcare reforms and job satisfaction among doctors in Norway. *Scandinavian Journal of Public Health, 38*(3), 253–258.

Angerer, P., & Weigl, M. (2015). Physicians' psychosocial work conditions and quality of care: A literature review. *Professions and Professionalism, 5*(1), 1–20.

Bååthe, F. (2015). *Physicians' engagement: Qualitative studies exploring physicians' experiences of engaging in improving clinical services and processes*. Ph.D. Medical sciences Doctoral thesis, Sahlgrenska Academy at the University of Gothenburg, Gothenburg, Sweden. Retrieved from http://hdl.handle.net/2077/40438

Bååthe, F., Ahlborg, G., Edgren, L., Lagström, A., Nilsson, K., & Lamb, J. (2016). Uncovering paradoxes from physicians' experiences of patient-centered ward-round. *Leadership in Health Services, 29*(2), 168–184.

Baathe, F., Ahlborg, G., Lagström, A., Edgren, L., & Nilsson, K. (2014). Physician experiences of patient-centered and team-based ward rounding – An interview based case-study. *Journal of Hospital Administration, 3*(6), 127–142. https://doi.org/10.5430/jha.v3n6p127

Baathe, F., & Norback, L. E. (2013). Engaging physicians in organisational improvement work. *Journal of Health Organization and Management, 27*(4), 479–497.

Baathe, F., Rosta, J., Bringedal, B., & Isaksson Rø, K. (2019). How do doctors experience the interactions among professional fulfilment, organisational factors and quality of patient care? A qualitative study in a Norwegian hospital. *BMJ Open, 9*(5), e026971. https://doi.org/10.1136/bmjopen-2018-026971

Bailey, C., & Madden, A. (2016). What makes work meaningful – or meaningless. *MIT Sloan Management Review, 57*, 53–61.

Berwick, D. M., & Nolan, T. W. (1998). Physicians as leaders in improving health care: A new series in annals of internal medicine. *Annals of Internal Medicine, 128*(4), 289–292.

Besèr, A., Sorjonen, K., Wahlberg, K., Peterson, U., Nygren, A., & Asberg, M. (2014). Construction and evaluation of a self rating scale for stress-induced exhaustion disorder, the Karolinska exhaustion disorder scale. *Scandinavian Journal of Psychology, 55*(1), 72–82. https://doi.org/10.1111/sjop.12088

Bliss, M. (1999). *William Osler: A life in medicine*. New York: Oxford University Press.

Bodenheimer, T., & Sinsky, C. (2014). From triple to quadruple aim: Care of the patient requires care of the provider. *The Annals of Family Medicine, 12*(6), 573–576.

Cruess, R. L., Cruess, S. R., Boudreau, J. D., Snell, L., & Steinert, Y. (2015). *A schematic representation of the professional identity formation and socialization of medical students and residents: A guide for medical educators* (Vol. 90, pp. 718–725).

Davies, H., Powell, A., & Rushmer, R. (2007). Why don't clinicians engage with quality improvement? *Journal of Health Services Research and Policy, 12*(3), 129–130. https://doi.org/10.1258/135581907781543139

de Vibe, M., Solhaug, I., Rosenvinge, J. H., Tyssen, R., Hanley, A., & Garland, E. (2018). Six-year positive effects of a mindfulness-based intervention on mindfulness, coping and well-being in medical and psychology students; Results from a randomized controlled trial. *PLoS One, 13*(4), e0196053. https://doi.org/10.1371/journal.pone.0196053.eCollection

de Vibe, M., Solhaug, I., Tyssen, R., Friborg, O., Rosenvinge, J. H., Sorlie, T., et al. (2015). Does personality moderate the effects of mindfulness training for medical and psychology students? *Mindfulness, 6*(2), 281–289.

Dickson, G. (2012). *Anchoring physician engagement in vision and values: Principles and framework*. Saskatchewan: Regina Qu'Appelle Health Region.

Diderichsen, S. (2017). *It's just a job: A new generation of physicians dealing with career and work ideals*. (PhD Thesis). Umeå university, Umeå.

Direktoratet for E-helse. (2019). *Frikort for helsetjenester (Exemption card for public health services)*. Accessed May 28, 2019, from https://helsenorge.no/betaling-for-helsetjenester/frikort-for-helsetjenester.

Dyrbye, L. N., Shanafelt, T. D., Sinsky, C. A., Cipriano, P. F., Bhatt, J., Ommaya, A., et al. (2017). *Burnout among health care professionals: A call to explore and address this underrecognized threat to safe, high-quality care*. Washington, DC: NAM Perspectives.

Edwards, N., Kornacki, M. J., & Silversin, J. (2002). Unhappy doctors: What are the causes and what can be done? *BMJ, 324*, 835–838.

Ellström, P. (2007). *Knowledge creation through interactive research: A learning perspective*. Paper presented at the HHS-07 conference, Jönköping University.

Ellström, P. E., Rönnqvist, D., & Thunborg, C. (1994). *Omvärld, verksamhet och förändrade kompetenskrav inom hälso- och sjukvården: En studie av föreställningar hos centrala aktörer inom ett landsting (Environment, operations and changed in demands of competence in healthcare)*. Linköpings: Linköpings Universitet: Institutionen för pedagogik och psykologi.

Firth-Cozens, J., & Greenhalgh, J. (1997). Doctors' perceptions of the links between stress and lowered clinical care. *Social Science & Medicine, 44*(7), 1017–1022. https://doi.org/10.1016/S0277-9536(96)00227-4

Friedberg, M. W., Chen, P. G., Van Busum, K. R., Pham, C., & Aunon, F. M. (2013). *Factors affecting physician professional satisfaction and their implications for patient care, health systems, and health policy: RAND corporation*. Santa Monica, CA: Rand Health, American Medical Association.

General statistics on doctors in Norway. (2019). Accessed May 28, 2019, from https://beta.legeforeningen.no/om-oss/legestatistikk/english/.

Giæver, F., Lohmann-Lafrenz, S., & Løvseth, L. T. (2016). Why hospital physicians attend work while ill? The spiralling effect of positive and negative factors. *BMC Health Services Research, 16*(1), 548. https://doi.org/10.1186/s12913-016-1802-y

Glette, M. K., Kringeland, T., Røise, O., & Wiig, S. (2018, September 19). Exploring physicians' decision-making in hospital readmission processes – a comparative case study. *BMC Health Services Research, 18*(1), 725. https://doi.org/10.1186/s12913-018-3538-3

Glette, M. K., Kringeland, T., Røise, O., & Wiig, S. (2019, August 27). Hospital physicians' views on discharge and readmission processes: A qualitative study from Norway. *BMJ Open, 9*(8), e031297. https://doi.org/10.1136/bmjopen-2019-031297

Greenhalgh, T., Robert, G., Macfarlane, F., Bate, P., & Kyriakidou, O. (2004). Diffusion of innovations in service organizations: Systematic review and recommendations. *The Milbank quarterly, 82*(4), 581–629. https://doi.org/10.1111/j.0887-378X.2004.00325.x

Grotmol, K. S., Gude, T., Moum, T., Vaglum, P., & Tyssen, R. (2013). Risk factors at medical school for later severe depression: A 15-year longitudinal, nationwide study (NORDOC). *Journal of Affective Disorders, 146*(1), 106–111.

Gude, T., Finset, A., Anvik, T., Bærheim, A., Fasmer, O. B., Grimstad, H., et al. (2017). Do medical students and young physicians assess reliably their self-efficacy regarding communication skills? A prospective study from end of medical school until end of internship. *BMC Medical Education, 17*(1), 107–107. https://doi.org/10.1186/s12909-017-0943-y

Gustafsson Sendén, M., Løvseth, L. T., Schenck-Gustafsson, K., & Friedner, A. (2013, August 22). What makes physicians go to work while sick: A comparative study of sickness presenteeism in four European countries (HOUPE). *Swiss Medical Weekly, 143*, w13840.

Hagen, T. P., & Kaarbøe, O. M. (2006). The Norwegian hospital reform of 2002: Central government takes over ownership of public hospitals. *Health Policy, 76*(3), 320–333. https://doi.org/10.1016/j.healthpol.2005.06.014

Hanley, A., de Vibe, M., Solhaug, I., Gonzalez-Pons, K., & Garland, E. (2019). Mindfulness training reduces neuroticism over a 6-year longitudinal randomized control trial in Norwegian medical and psychology students. *Journal of Research in Personality, 82*, 1–6.

Health at a Glance: Europe. (2018). *State of health in the EU Cycle*. Accessed May 28, 2019, from https://ec.europa.eu/health/sites/health/files/state/docs/2018_healthatglance_rep_en.pdf.

Hem, E., Haldorsen, T., Aasland, O. G., Tyssen, R., Vaglum, P., & Ekeberg, O. (2005). Suicide rates according to education with a particular focus on physicians in Norway 1960–2000. *Psychological Medicine, 35*(6), 873–880.

Hertzberg, T. K., Isaksson Rø, K., Vaglum, P. J. W., Moum, T., Røvik, J. O., Gude, T., et al. (2016). Work-home interface stress: An important predictor of emotional exhaustion 15 years into a medical career. *Industrial Health, 54*(2), 139–148. https://doi.org/10.2486/indhealth.2015-0134

Hertzberg, T. K., Skirbekk, H., Tyssen, R., Aasland, O. G., & Isaksson Rø, K. (2016b). The hospital doctor of today – still continuously on duty. *Tidsskrift for Den norske legeforening, 136*(19), 1635–1638. https://doi.org/10.4045/tidsskr.16.0067

Hertzberg, T. K., Skirbekk, H., Tyssen, R., Aasland, O. G., & Isaksson Rø, K. (2016c). The good doctor – Strong and persevering. *Tidsskrift for Den norske legeforening, 136*(19), 1631–1634.

Hertzberg, T., Tyssen, R., Skirbekk, H., & Isaksson Rø, K. (2019). Work-home balance in two cohorts of Norwegian doctors. *Tidsskrift for Den norske legeforening, 139*(19). https://doi.org/10.4045/tidsskr.18.0339

Innstrand, S., Langballe, E., Espnes, G., Falkum, E., & Aasland, O. G. (2008). Positive and negative work-family interaction and burnout: A longitudinal study of reciprocal relations. *Work and Stress, 22*, 1–15.

Isaksson Rø, K., & Aasland, O. G. (2016). Peer counsellors' views on the collegial support scheme for doctors. *Tidsskrift for Den Norske legeforening, 136*(4), 313–316.

Isaksson Rø, K., Gude, T., & Aasland, O. G. (2007). Does a self-referral counselling program reach doctors in need of help? A comparison with the general Norwegian doctor workforce. *BMC Public Health, 7*, 36. https://doi.org/10.1186/1471-2458-7-36

Isaksson Rø, K., Gude, T., Tyssen, R., & Aasland, O. G. (2008). Counselling for burnout in Norwegian doctors; one-year cohort study. *BMJ, 337*, a2004. https://doi.org/10.1136/bmj.a2004

Isaksson Rø, K., Johansen, I., & Rosta, J. (2018). Doctors as targets of unwanted sexual attention. *Tidsskrift for Den norske legeforening, 138*(16).

Isaksson Rø, K., Tyssen, R., Hoffart, A., Sexton, H., Aasland, O. G., & Gude, T. (2010). A three-year cohort study of the relationships between coping, job stress and burnout after a counselling intervention for help-seeking physicians. *BMC Public Health, 10*, 213. https://doi.org/10.1186/1471-2458-10-213

Johansen, I., Baste, V., Rosta, J., Aasland, O. G., & Morken, T. (2017). Changes in prevalence of workplace violence against doctors in all medical specialties in Norway between 1993 and 2014: A repeated cross-sectional survey. *BMJ Open, 7*(8), e017757.

Johnsen, T. M., Berge, V., Høivik, F., Agdestein, C., Grønseth, I. M., & Krogh, H. H., et al. (2018). *Trønderopprørets fastlegeundersøkelse og helsemedarbeiderundersøkelse. (Survey on GPs and co-workers)*, Trondheim. Accessed April 29, 2020, from http://www.flo20.no/undersokelsen/.

Kippist, L., & Fitzgerald, A. (2009). Organisational professional conflict and hybrid clinician managers: The effects of dual roles in Australian health care organizations. *Journal of Health Organization and Management, 23*, 642–655.

Kushnir, T., Greenberg, D., Madjar, N., Hadari, I., Yermiahu, Y., & Bachner, Y. G. (2014). Is burnout associated with referral rates among primary care physicians in community clinics? *Family Practice, 31*(1), 44–50. https://doi.org/10.1093/fampra/cmt060

Lambert, T. W., Smith, F., & Goldacre, M. J. (2016). The impact of the European working time directive 10 years on: Views of the UK medical graduates of 2002 surveyed in 2013–2014. *JRSM Open, 7*(3), 2054270416632703.

Lee, T. H., & Cosgrove, T. (2014). *Engaging doctors in the health care revolution* (Vol. 92, pp. 104–111). Boston: Harvard Business School.

Lindgren, Å., Bååthe, F., & Dellve, L. (2013). Why risk professional fulfilment: A grounded theory of physician engagement in healthcare development. *The International Journal of Health Planning and Management, 28*, e138–ee57.

Mahmood, J. (2019). *Hazardous drinking and life satisfaction in Norwegian medical doctors: Individual and work-related predictors*. Oslo: University of Oslo.

Mahmood, J. I., Grotmol, K. S., Tesli, M., Vaglum, P., & Tyssen, R. (2017). Contextual factors and mental distress as possible predictors of hazardous drinking in Norwegian medical doctors: A 15-year longitudinal, Nationwide study. *European Addiction Research, 23*(1), 19–27. https://doi.org/10.1159/000452442

Mata, D., Ramos, M., Bansal, N., Khan, R., Guille, C., DiAngelantonio, E., et al. (2015). Prevalence of depression and depressive symptoms among resident physicians: A systematic review and meta-analysis. *JAMA, 314*(22), 2373–2383.

McKinlay, J., & Marceau, L. (2011). New wine in an old bottle: Does alienation provide an explanation of the origins of physician discontent? *International Journal of Health Services, 41*(2), 301–335.

Nilsen, L. (2017) *Reality was much tougher than they had thought [in Norwegian: Virkeligheten var mye tøffere enn de hadde forestilt seg]*. Dagens Medisin 5th of September 2017. https:// www.dagensmedisin.no/artikler/2017/09/05/flere-unge-leger-sliter/Seen 13/3-2018.

Nørøxe, K. B., Pedersen, A. F., Carlsen, A. H., Bro, F., & Vedsted, P. (2019). Mental well-being, job satisfaction and self-rated workability in general practitioners and hospitalisations for ambulatory care sensitive conditions among listed patients: A cohort study combining survey data on GPs and register data on patients. *BMJ Qual Saf, 28*(12), 997–1006.

Nørøxe, B. K., Vedsted, P., Bro, F., Carlsen, A. H., & Pedersen, A. F. (2019). Mental Well-being and job satisfaction in general practitioners in Denmark and their patients' change of general practitioner: A cohort study combining survey data and register data. *BMJ Open, 9*(11), e030142–e030142. https://doi.org/10.1136/bmjopen-2019-030142

Norwegian Medical Association. *Statistikk (Statistics)*. Accessed May, 14, 2020, from https://www.legeforeningen.no/om-oss/legestatistikk/english/. Accessed May 28, 2019.

Norwegian Ministry of Health and Care Service. (2012). *The coordination reform*. Accessed May 28, 2019, from www.government.no. Accessed May 28, 2019.

Norwegian Ministry of Health and Care Service. (2015). *Fremtidens primærhelsetjeneste – nærhet og helhet (The future primary care – Proximity and comprehensiveness)*. Oslo: Norwegian Ministry of Health and Care Services.

Nylenna, M., Gulbrandsen, P., Forde, R., & Aasland, O. G. (2005). Unhappy doctors? A longitudinal study of life and job satisfaction among Norwegian doctors 1994-2002. *BMC Health Services Research, 5*, 44. https://doi.org/10.1186/1472-6963-5-44

OECD. (2019). *Doctors*. Accessed November 15, 2019, from https://data.oecd.org/healthres/doctors.htm.

Parsa-Parsi, R. W. (2017). The revised declaration of Geneva: A modern-day physician's pledge. *JAMA, 318*, 1971–1972.

Rathert, C., Williams, E. S., & Linhart, H. (2018). Evidence for the quadruple aim: A systematic review of the literature on physician burnout and patient outcomes. *Medical Care, 56*(12), 976–984. https://doi.org/10.1097/MLR.0000000000000999

Rebnord, I. K., Eikeland, O. J., Hunskår, S., & Morken, T. (2018). *Fastlegers tidsbruk (GPs working time)*. Nasjonalt kompetansesenter for legevaktmedisin, Uni Research Helse: Bergen.

Ringard, Å., Sagan, A., Sperre Saunes, I., & Lindahl, A. (2013). Norway: Health system review. *Health Systems in Transition, 15*(8), 1–162. Accessed April 29, 2020, from https://www.fhi.no/publ/2014/norway%2D%2Dhealth-system-review/.

Ringard, Å., Sperre Saunes, I., & Sagan, A. (2016). The 2015 hospital treatment choice reform in Norway: Continuity or change? *Health Policy, 120*(4), 350–355. https://doi.org/10.1016/j.healthpol.2016.02.013

Roelofs, J., Verbraak, M., Keijsers, G., de Bruin, M., & Schmidt, A. J. M. (2005). Psychometric properties of a Dutch version of the Maslach burnout inventory general survey (MBI-DV) in individuals with and without clinical burnout. *Stress and Health, 21*(1), 17–25.

Rørtveit, G. (2015). Future primary care in Norway: Valid goals without clear strategies. *Scandinavian Journal of Primary Health Care, 33*(4), 221–222.

Rosta, J., & Aasland, O. G. (2011). Work hours and self rated health of hospital doctors in Norway and Germany. A comparative study on national samples. *BMC Health Services Research, 11*, 40.

Rosta, J., & Aasland, O. G. (2013a). Changes in lifetime prevalence of suicidal feelings and suicidal thoughts among norwegian doctors from 2000 to 2010: A longitudinal study based on national samples. *BMC Psychiatry, 13*(322), 1–10.

Rosta, J., & Aasland, O. G. (2013b). Changes in alcohol drinking patterns and their consequences among Norwegian doctors from 2000 to 2010: A longitudinal study based on national samples. *Alcohol and Alcoholism, 48*(1), 99–106.

Rosta, J., & Aasland, O. G. (2014). Weekly working hours for Norwegian hospital doctors since 1994 with special attention to postgraduate training, work–home balance and the European working time directive: A panel study. *BMJ Open, 4*(10), e005704. https://doi.org/10.1136/bmjopen-2014-005704

Rosta, J., & Aasland, O. G. (2016). Doctors' working hours and time spent on patient care in the period 1994–2014. *Tidskrift for Den norske legeforening, 136*(16), 1355–1359.

Rosta, J., & Aasland, O. G. (2018). Perceived bullying among Norwegian doctors in 1993, 2004 and 2014-2015: A study based on cross-sectional and repeated surveys. *BMJ Open, 8*(2), e018161.

Rosta, J., Bååthe, F., Aasland, O. G., & Isaksson Rø, K. (2020). Changes in work stress among doctors in Norway from 2010 to 2019: A study based on repeated surveys. *BMJ Open, 10*(10), e037474. https://doi.org/10.1136/bmjopen-2020-037474

Rosta, J., Aasland, O. G., & Nylenna, M. (2019, September 8). Changes in job satisfaction among doctors in Norway from 2010 to 2017. A study based on repeated surveys. *BMJ-Open, 9*(9), e027891. https://doi.org/10.1136/bmjopen-2018-027891

Rosta, J., Nylenna, M., & Aasland, O. G. (2009). Job satisfaction among hospital doctors in Norway and Germany. A comparative study on national samples. *Scandinavian Journal of Public Health, 37*(5), 503–508.

Rosta, J., Tellnes, G., & Aasland, O. G. (2014). Differences in sickness absence between self-employed and employed Doctors: A cross-sectional study on national sample of Norwegian doctors in 2010. *Health Services Research, 14*(199), 1–8.

Røvik, J. O., Tyssen, R., Gude, T., Moum, T., Ekeberg, O., & Vaglum, P. (2007). Exploring the interplay between personality dimensions: A comparison of the typological and the dimensional approach in stress research. *Personality and Individual Differences, 42*(7), 1255–1266.

Ryan, R. M., & Deci, E. L. (2000). Self-determination theory and the facilitation ofintrinsic motivation, social development, and well-being. *The American Psychologist, 55*, 68–78.

Saunes, I., Hansen, T., Tomic, O., & Lindahl, A. (2017). *Helsei Norge –2017: Kommentarrapporttil OECDs sammenligningavhelseiulike land [Health in Norway–2017: A commentary to OECDs comparison of health in different countries]* retrieved from Oslo.

Schaufeli, W. B., De Witte, H., & Desart, S. (2019). *Manual burnout assessment tool (BAT)*. KU Leuven, Belgium: Unpublished internal report. Accessed May 28, 2019, from http://burnoutassessmenttool.be/project_eng/.

Shanafelt, T. D., & Noseworthy, J. H. (2017). Executive leadership and physician Well-being: Nine organizational strategies to promote engagement and reduce burnout. *Paper presented at the Mayo Clinic Proceedings, 92*, 129–146.

Solberg, I. B., Tómasson, K., Aasland, O., & Tyssen, R. (2014). Cross-national comparison of job satisfaction in doctors during economic recession. *Occupational Medicine (London), 64*(8), 595–600.

Solberg, I. B., Tomasson, K., Aasland, O. G., & Tyssen, R. (2013). The impact of economic factors on migration considerations among Icelandic specialist doctors: A cross-sectional study. *BMC Health Services Research, 13*. https://doi.org/10.1186/1472-6963-13-524

Solhaug, I., De Vibe, M., Friborg, O., Sørlie, T., Tyssen, R., Bjørndal, A., et al. (2019). Long-term mental health effects of mindfulness training: A 4-year follow-up study. *Mindfulness, 10*(8), 1671–1682. https://doi.org/10.1007/s12671-019-01100-2

Spehar, I., Frich, J. C., & Kjekshus, L. E. (2015). Professional identity and role transitions in clinical managers. *Journal of Health Organization and Management, 29*(3), 353–366. https://doi.org/10.1108/JHOM-03-2013-0047

Stacey, R. D. (2011). *Strategic management and organisational dynamics: The challenge of complexity to ways of thinking about organisations*. Harlow: Financial Times Prentice Hall.

Stacey, R. D., & Mowles, C. (2016). *Strategic management and organisational dynamics: The challenge of complexity to ways of thinking about organisations* (Vol. 7). Harlow: Pearson Education.

Statsministerens-kontor. (2001). *The regular general practitioner scheme*. Accessed May 28, 2019, from https://www.regjeringen.no/no/dokumenter/the-regular-general-practitioner-scheme/id419342/#.

Storkholm, M. H., Mazzocato, P., Savage, M., & Savage, C. (2017). Money's (not) on my mind: A qualitative study of how staff and managers understand health care's triple aim. *BMC Health Services Research, 17*(1), 98–98. https://doi.org/10.1186/s12913-017-2052-3

Svensson, L., Ellström, P., & Brulin, G. (2007). Introduction – on interactive research. *International Journal of Action Research, 3*(3), 233–249.

Swensen, S., Kabcenell, A., & Shanafelt, T. (2016). Physician-organizationcollaboration reduces physician burnout and promotes engagement: The mayo clinic experience. *Journal of Healthcare Management, 61*, 105–127.

Swensen, S., & Shanafelt, T. (2020). *12 Actions to create the ideal workplace*. Oxford: Oxford University Press.

Trønderopprøret. (2018). Trønderopprørets fastlegeundersøkelse og helsemedarbeiderundersøkelse (Survey on GPs and health workers) Trondheim. Accessed May 28, 2019, from https://www.flo20.no/wpcontent/uploads/2018/06/TOundersøkelse-2.pdf.

Tsugawa, Y., Jena, A. B., Figueroa, J. F., Orav, E. J., Blumenthal, D. M., & Jha, A. K. (2017). Comparison of hospital mortality and readmission rates for Medicare patients treated by male vs female physicians. *JAMA Internal Medicine, 177*(2), 206–213. https://doi.org/10.1001/jamainternmed.2016.7875

Tyssen, R. (2007). Health problems and the use of health services among physicians: A review article with particular emphasis on Norwegian studies. *Industrial Health, 45*, 599–610.

Tyssen, R. (2017). Personality traits. In K. J. Brower & M. B. Riba (Eds.), *Physician mental health and well-being: Research and practice* (pp. 211–234). Michigan: Springer.

Tyssen, R. (2018 Jun). What is the level of burnout that impairs functioning? *Journal Internal Medicine, 283*(6), 594–596. https://doi.org/10.1111/joim.12769

Tyssen, R., Palmer, K. S., Solberg, I. B., Voltmer, E., & Frank, E. (2013). Physicians' perceptions of quality of care, professional autonomy, and job satisfaction in Canada, Norway, and the United States. *BMC Health Services Research, 13*(1), 516. https://doi.org/10.1186/1472-6963-13-516

Tyssen, R., Vaglum, P., Gronvold, N. T., & Ekeberg, O. (2001). Suicidal ideation among medical students and young physicians: A nationwide and prospective study of prevalence and predictors. *Journal of Affective Disorders, 64*(1), 69–79.

Tyssen, R., Vaglum, P., Gronvold, N. T., & Ekeberg, O. (2005). The relative importance of individual and organizational factors for the prevention of job stress during internship: A nationwide and prospective study. *Medical Teacher, 27*(8), 726–731.

Voltmer, E., Rosta, J., Siegrist, J., & Aasland, O. G. (2012). Job stress and job satisfaction of physicians in private practice: Comparison of German and Norwegian physicians. *International Archives of Occupational and Environmental Health, 85*(7), 819–828.

Wallace, J. E., Lemaire, J. B., & Ghali, W. A. (2009). Physician wellness: A missing quality indicator. *The Lancet, 374*(9702), 1714–1721.

Wallis, C. J., Ravi, B., Coburn, N., Nam, R. K., Detsky, A. S., & Satkunasivam, R. (2017). Comparison of postoperative outcomes among patients treated by male and female surgeons: A population based matched cohort study. *BMJ, 359*, j4366. https://doi.org/10.1136/bmj.j4366

Warr, P., Cook, J., & Wall, T. (1979). Scales for the measurement of some work attitudes and aspects of psychological Well-being. *Journal of Occupational Psychology, 2*(52), 129–148.

Weigl, M., Hornung, S., Angerer, P., Siegrist, J., & Glaser, J. (2013). The effects of improving hospital physicians working conditions on patient care: A prospective, controlled intervention study. *BMC Health Services Research, 13*(1). https://doi.org/10.1186/1472-6963-13-401

Welp, A., Meier, L. L., & Manser, T. (2015). Emotional exhaustion and workload predict clinician-rated and objective patient safety. *Frontiers in Psychology, 5*, 1573–1573. https://doi.org/10.3389/fpsyg.2014.01573

West, E. (2001). Management matters: The link between hospital organisation and quality of patient care. *BMJ Quality & Safety, 10*(1), 40–48.

West, M. A., Guthrie, J. P., Dawson, J. F., Borrill, C. S., & Carter, M. (2006). Reducing patient mortality in hospitals: The role of human resource management. *Journal of Organizational Behavior: The International Journal of Industrial, Occupational and Organizational Psychology and Behavior, 27*(7), 983–1002.

Chapter 8
The Relationship Between Employee Engagement and Organisational Outcomes in the English National Health Service: An Analysis of Employee and Employer Data in 28 Healthcare Organisations

Christian van Stolk and Marco Hafner

8.1 Introduction

There have been concerns around low productivity, poor health and wellbeing and staff engagement for well over a decade in the English National Health Service (NHS). In 2009 the Department of Health commissioned an independent review into the health and wellbeing of NHS led by Dr. Steven Boorman. The Boorman Review as it became known gave an indication of potential savings (mostly through reduced staff absenteeism) that could be made by organisations from adopting more effective ways of managing the health and wellbeing of staff. Especially, it looked at whether hospital boards and senior managers discussed staff health and wellbeing in executive and board meetings, whether they showed role modelling behaviour and whether line managers were trained to look after employee health. Savings to the NHS alone were estimated at £500 million a year (see for instance the Interim Report of the Boorman Review, Boorman & Fellow, 2009). The report also highlighted interesting associations between staff health and wellbeing in the NHS and a range of outcomes such as quality of care lower, mortality rates, and reduced rates of hospital acquired infections. Building on this, the Keogh Review (2013) into patient safety reviewed the quality of care provided by a number of Trusts,[1] and recommended a number of actions to improve patient outcomes. One of the actions was that all NHS organisations seek to understand the positive impact that happy and engaged staff

---

[1] Healthcare organisations in England, especially those delivering community, mental health and acute care, are typically organised as trusts with a degree of independence from national decision-makers. NHS England is a coordinating body that sets the operational plans and provides oversight. However, it does not have direct authority over the independent trusts.

C. van Stolk (✉) · M. Hafner
RAND Europe, Cambridge, UK
e-mail: stolk@randeurope.org

© Springer Nature Switzerland AG 2020
A. Montgomery et al. (eds.), *Connecting Healthcare Worker Well-Being, Patient Safety and Organisational Change*, Aligning Perspectives on Health, Safety and Well-Being, https://doi.org/10.1007/978-3-030-60998-6_8

can have on patient outcomes, including mortality rates, and that this should form a key part of their quality improvement strategy. This focused mainly on involving staff more in decision-making in the health service and indeed decisions regarding the delivery of care.

Wider research on the health service has been seeking to understand the associations between employee experience, health and wellbeing, performance and organisational outcomes in the NHS (Dawson, 2014). Seminal work undertaken by Michael West and Jeremy Dawson (2012) outlined the link between employee experience and positive organisational outcomes (including better financial results, lower rates of hospital acquired infections, and lower mortality rates) and positive patient perceptions on care as measured in patient surveys. While some reviews in the US did not find a clear relationship between employee health and wellbeing and quality of care (Tawfik, Scheid, Profit, et al., 2019), others find that staff wellbeing is also linked to patient outcomes (Maben, Adams, Peccei, Murrells, & Robert, 2012). Dawson also undertook a review of the literature on staff experience and patient outcomes. This study concluded that there is evidence that the experiences of staff, particularly in the form of support received from supervisors and line managers, and staff engagement, are associated with quality of care, patient satisfaction, health outcomes, and ratings of quality of care, as well as staff absenteeism and retention (Dawson, 2014). Other research shows that health professionals who show higher engagement are less likely to make mistakes and produce better patient outcomes (Laschinger & Leiter, 2006). In addition, in the NHS, higher levels of staff engagement are associated with better health outcomes, lower levels of stress and lower presenteeism (the state of being at work but in suboptimal health) (Admasachew & Dawson, 2010). Recent work around presenteeism hints at associations between presenteeism and wider organisational outcomes mainly through lower productivity and reduced engagement with colleagues and the work environment (Lohaus & Habermann, 2019).

In this chapter, we want to look in particular at the concept of employee engagement in the English NHS and build on the Boorman Review and the work of West and Dawson. An issue with some of the reviews has been that they have used secondary data such as NHS administrative data and the NHS staff survey to draw inferences. These sources are not necessarily set up to build a holistic view on the employee experience, health and wellbeing, and the engagement of staff. We will draw on two large surveys that included large NHS employers (mostly acute hospital trusts). These are respectively the Britain's Healthiest Workplace (BHW) and the NHS Healthy Workforce survey administered by RAND Europe in 2016. We expand on how these surveys are conducted below. The main advantages of using these surveys are that they include a wide range of variables in one data set including variables on health and wellbeing, employee engagement and indeed outcome measures. Overall, this study is complementary to the seminal work by West and Dawson (2012) in that it looks at the determinants and outcomes of employee engagement within the NHS, but using a different data source and with a focus on different organisational level interventions (e.g. health and wellbeing interventions, leadership training) beyond the common human resource management (HRM) practices. They offer both an employer as well as an employee perspective by surveying both an employer representative as well as employees. We can also dig a bit deeper below the surface and understand which groups are particularly affected by low staff engagement and the circumstances in which they work. We will discuss the data sources and analysis below.

In this research, we want to investigate a number of hypotheses on the basis of the data.

- There is a relationship between employee engagement and organisational outcomes (H1)
- There is a relationship between employee engagement and specific human resource practice (H2)
- There is a relationship between employee engagement and 'good work' (H3)
- There is a relationship between employee engagement and the health and wellbeing of staff (H4)

8.2 What Is Employee Engagement?

It has proved difficult to conceptualise what we mean by employee engagement. At times, concepts such as health and wellbeing and employee experience are intertwined. This is because some of the reviews mentioned earlier show associations between the health and wellbeing of staff, life satisfaction, job satisfaction, perceptions of the work environment, and employee experience.

The topic of employee engagement gained particular prominence in 2008 when the Secretary of State for Business in the UK commissioned David MacLeod and Nita Clarke to take an in-depth look at employee engagement. The report, 'Engaging for Success' also known as the MacLeod Review explored the potential role of employee engagement to improve organisational competitiveness and productivity in the UK (MacLeod & Clarke, 2009).

This chapter does not aim to provide a comprehensive overview of the literature on employee engagement. There are varying definitions and concepts used. We can broadly distinguish between five approaches. Firstly, Kahn (1990) focuses on personal engagement and sees employee engagement as an expression of the physical, emotional, and psychological self at work. There is an interplay between the self, the role, specific job and environment that a person is in and as such personal engagement is likely to change over time and vary. Higher engagement is then linked to certain number of physical, emotional, and psychological characteristics. Secondly, another body of literature sees employee engagement as the commitment or involvement an individual employee has to or with the objectives and values of an organisation. Commitment and involvement in this sense refer to a psychological state that the individual is in (Robinson, Perryman, & Hayday, 2004). Thirdly, engagement can be seen as a performance construct. So, we would look to a certain set of organisational or social behaviours in an employee that would indicate engagement (West & Dawson, 2012). Within this sit a wide range of concepts: including showing proactive behaviour (Crant, 2000); taking personal initiative (Frese & Fay, 2001); and organizational citizenship behaviour (Organ, 1988). A fourth concept combines the last two and looks at both commitment and involvement as well as behaviours or effort that the employee shows or puts in. Finally, we need to acknowledge some differences in the conceptualisation between practitioners and psychologists. There is a literature that defines engagement as a set of organisational practices and behaviours that are associated with high engagement. This focuses on organisational aspects rather than the individual. It can for instance include involvement in decision-making or processes like consultation (Dickinson & Ham, 2008).

Overall, the characteristics of an engaged staff combine both the individual's psychological state as well as behaviours and effort. It can be described as motivation, satisfaction, involvement, commitment, meaningful work, initiative and pride. There remain key challenges with how engagement is operationalised and different constructs exist to measure staff engagement. In this chapter, we use two concepts of employee engagement that combine both psychological state and behaviours. We provide some more detail below. Our main interest is to show the important associations between the concept of employee engagement and a wider range of variables. Though we draw inferences from the literature, we cannot necessarily be clear about the direction of causality in our analysis.

8.3 Data and Analysis

The NHS Health Workforce Survey was conducted by RAND in 2016 and collected responses from NHS health organisations and their employees through the Organisational Health Assessment (OHA) and the Employee Health Assessment (EHA) respectively. Participating organisations returned the OHA, including general organisational characteristics such as the size and nature of the organisation, the work environment, and information on the organisation's approach to health promotion and well-being interventions. Subsequently, employees were invited to respond to the EHA, which collected socio-demographic information (such as age, gender, income, general background); lifestyle and behavioural and clinical risk factors (including weight, diet, exercise, smoking, alcohol intake, stress, cholesterol and blood pressure); data on the work environment and culture; and information on how often people participate in organisational health and well-being interventions. The EHA had about 150 questions that aimed to provide a holistic picture. We stipulated that a minimum number of employees per organisation had to participate in order to have confidence in the sample. We calculated this number on the basis of the total employees and we wanted a 90% level of confidence and accepted a 5% margin of error. In total, 19 organisations took part in this survey. These were mostly organisations that were participating in a NHS health and wellbeing initiative or similar organisations that were approached for participation in the survey. In terms of the former, it stands to reason that these 11 trusts or primary care organisations were motivated participants as they were already included in a central initiative conducted by NHS England to improve the wellbeing of staff. In terms of the latter, we identified eight trusts that had similar outcomes and profiles to the other 11. The purpose here was to see whether there was something distinct about the 11. Most of our descriptive survey data suggested that there was nothing particularly exceptional about the 11 trusts when compared to the eight or general staff survey. However, on a number of organisational outcomes, the 19 trusts and primary care organisations performed slightly better than average on organisational outcomes when comparing results seen in administrative data and the NHS staff survey.

The organisations have a combined headcount of 105,838 employees and the survey was distributed to 91,872 staff and a complete survey was collected for 7246 employees, resulting in a response rate of about 8%. This response rate is lower than the NHS Staff Survey, which offers a representative sample across all NHS organisations, but our sample was broadly similar across the main demographic variables including age, gender, job category and income levels. We are over-represented in having a large group of mid-career NHS workers and slightly under-represented in the lower income groups and younger and older workers. This is similar to the sample bias in the annual NHS Staff Survey. So despite a lower response rate than in the annual NHS staff survey, we are confident that there is nothing particularly distinct about the bias in our sample. Where we can compare to the general NHS staff survey, our survey shows similar data.

In addition to the NHS Healthy Workforce survey, RAND Europe has conducted Britain's Healthiest Workplace (BHW) survey on an annual basis since 2014. In contrast to the NHS Healthy Workforce Survey, the BHW survey is generally open to all companies, government organisations and other organisations in the UK. For instance, in 2016 it includes nine NHS organisations as well, for which we use data in this study. In this research we combine both surveys. The surveys are about 90% identical and broadly use similar variables. The response rates are also similar (8%) and as before the BHW sample is similar to the NHS Healthy Workforce survey. In total the data sample includes 28 organisations with a combined number of respondents of 9375.

It is important to note that while the participating organisations represent a diverse range of NHS organisations, generalisations of the findings to the wider NHS should only be made with some caution as the sample of participating organisations was not intended to be representative of the entire NHS. The surveys are overweighting secondary care acute trusts. Some community and mental health trusts participated but we have no primary care participation other than one clinical commissioning group. This is not exceptional in NHS surveys as the primary care population is fragmented and hard to survey. Often, the primary care population attracts dedicated surveys. As a result, our findings are mostly relevant to larger health organisations that operate as trusts.

In order to analyse the association between employee engagement and a variety of outcome measures, we complement the information from the NHS Healthy Workforce and BHW surveys with information at the trust level provided by the

NHS. Specifically, we use administrative sickness absence rate data, patient satisfaction surveys for acute and mental health trusts by the Care Quality Commission (CQC)[2] and NHS account data which can be merged at the trust level to the NHS Healthy Workforce survey.

Similar to the study by West and Dawson (2012), we conduct multilevel regression analysis using two engagement constructs across all employees in our sample (from 9 BHW trusts and 19 NHS Healthy Workforce trusts) and examine variables associated with employee engagement. The two constructs that we use are the Utrecht Work Engagement (UWES) nine point scale (Schaufeli, Bakker, & Salanova, 2006) and a composite construct of engagement. The UWES scale focuses on dimensions such as absorption, vigour and dedication. Each dimension has three questions. The use of two constructs was necessary because the surveys used slightly different engagement questions. For the second measure, we followed the approach taken by West and Dawson (2012) that focuses on psychological engagement and involvement in decision-making. For psychological engagement we use the standardised value of job satisfaction and for involvement in decision-making the amount of involvement an employee has at his work as measured through participation in meetings and having knowledge of initiatives, organisational guidance and other organisational dissemination. The correlation coefficient between the engagement indicator and the total UWES scale is 0.58, which suggests a non-perfect but significant correlation. Hence, we are confident that our findings hold across the two samples.

As a first step, the overall engagement score and the UWES-9 overall score are included as dependent variables. In these models, the independent variables include the following:

- **Demographic**: education, ethnicity, age, gender, income;
- **Occupational**: type of NHS occupation, length of tenure;
- **Work environment**: workplace related stress as measured by the Health and Safety Executive management standards (control, relationships, time pressure, etc.), management support, leadership, bullying;
- **Health and lifestyle**: musculoskeletal and chronic health conditions, mental health, sleep and BMI[3];
- **Personal**: children, providing unpaid care, financial concerns;
- **Human capital**: HR practices, provision of health and wellbeing interventions.

In a second step, the overall engagement scores are used to examine the link between engagement and outcome variables, holding other drivers that may determine engagement and the dependent variables simultaneously. Here we are mainly

---

[2] http://www.cqc.org.uk/publications/surveys/adult-inpatient-survey-2016
[3] The assumption that we wanted to test here is that individuals with chronic conditions might inherently have lower work engagement. We also assume that there will be a strong correlation between mental health and employee engagement.

interested in the relationship between employee engagement and the following outcome variables:

- **Absenteeism**: individual level, reported by the employee using the Work Productivity and Activity Impairment scale (WPAI)[4];
- **Presenteeism**: individual level, reported by the employee using WPAI scale;
- **Sickness absence rates**: organisational level;
- **Overall patient satisfaction**: organisational level[5];
- **Staff turnover**: organisational level[6];
- **Financial situation**: organisational level[7];
- **Operational surplus/deficit:** organisational level.[8,9]

The statistical analysis is conducted using STATA Version 15.[10] All results as is common in this type of analysis are presented at the 10% significance level or lower.

8.4 Findings

We present the findings here alongside the hypotheses that we introduced in our introduction. The first hypothesis focuses on the relationship between staff engagement and organisational outcomes. Our analysis consistent with West and Dawson (2012) finds an association between engagement and wider organisational outcomes. Here we combine absenteeism and presenteeism as measured in our surveys using the WPAI with administrative data reported by NHS organisations through administrative data sets (see Table 8.1). These include data on absenteeism and staff turnover. Finally, we look at a wider set of organisational outcomes such as financial situation, patient satisfaction and operational surplus (see Table 8.2). We find that higher staff engagement is associated with better organisational outcomes across the board. These findings hold for variables collected through our surveys or when introducing administrative data. In some cases, we have similar data from multiple

---

[4]The WPAI is a construct that ascertains on a weekly basis the proportion of time that an employee was absent and the extent to which an employee's productivity at work is affected by suboptimal health. As a result, it captures both absenteeism and presenteeism. More information is available at http://www.reillyassociates.net/WPAI_General.html (accessed October 2019).

[5]http://www.cqc.org.uk/publications/surveys/adult-inpatient-survey-2016 (accessed October 2019).

[6]Self-reported from HWS and BHW surveys.

[7]Self-reported from HWS and BHW surveys.

[8]Foundation trusts: https://www.gov.uk/government/publications/nhs-foundation-trust-accounts-consolidation-ftc-files-201617. We use SoCIsubcode 110 for the operational surplus/deficit measure.

[9]Trusts: https://www.gov.uk/government/publications/nhs-trusts-accounts-2016-to-2017. We use the SC 140 subcode for the operational surplus/deficit measure.

[10]https://www.stata.com/new-in-stata/

Table 8.1 Employee engagement and the association with absenteeism, presenteeism and turnover (*, **, and ***) denoting statistically significant outcomes with level of significance increasing with the number of stars)

	(1)	(2)	(3)	(4)	(6)
Outcome variables:	WPAI: Absenteeism	NHS: Sickness absence	WPAI: Presenteeism	Sickness absence (self-reported)	High turnover
Beta	−0.0304	0.0387	−0.0633	−0.2073	−0.0481
se	(0.016)*	(0.017)**	(0.013)***	(0.014)***	(0.012)***
Level of outcome:	Individual	Organisation	Individual	Organisation	Organisation

Source: Authors' calculations

Notes: Robust standard errors (se) in parentheses; *** $p < 0.01$, ** $p < 0.05$, * $p < 0.1$. Analysis based on the combined NHS Healthy Workforce and BHW survey. Rows Beta and Se report the standardized coefficient and corresponding standard error from a regression using the standardized engagement score as predictor variable. Note that WPAI scale is at the employee level and provided in the employee health assessment. It measures the percent of working time lost due to either absenteeism or presenteeism. The NHS sickness absence uses data from the NHS on the rate of annual sickness absence. The outcomes measured in column (4) and (5) come from the organisational assessment of HWS and BHW where organisations are asked whether sickness absence or high staff turnover are an issue in the organisation. Additional control variables include the operational surplus in the previous year (2015) and the total number of employees per organisation. Note that the analysis at the organisational level is weighted by the number of responses by employees

Table 8.2 Employee engagement and the association with patient satisfaction and financial performance (*, **, and ***) denoting statistically significant outcomes with level of significance increasing with the number of stars)

	(1)	(2)	(3)
Outcome variables:	Overall patient satisfaction	Self-reported: Financial situation	Operational surplus/deficit
Beta	0.0501	0.2556	0.0782
se	(0.013)***	(0.008)***	(0.010)***
Level of outcome:	Organisation	Organisation	Organisation

Source: Authors' calculations

Notes: Robust standard errors (se) in parentheses; *** $p < 0.01$, ** $p < 0.05$, * $p < 0.1$. Analysis based on the combined NHS Healthy Workforce and BHW survey. Rows Beta and Se report the standardized coefficient and corresponding standard error from a regression using the standardized engagement score as predictor variable. The overall patient satisfaction values are provided by the CQC for acute and mental health trusts. The HWS and BHW organisational assessment questionnaire asks each organisation about their (self-reported) financial situation based on a scale from 1 (very bad) to 5 (very good). We also complement this self-reported analysis with data from the NHS account data for Foundation trusts and trusts using the operational surplus/deficit as a comparable measure. Note that the self-reported financial situation information and the organisational surplus/deficit measure are correlated with a coefficient of 0.76. Additional control variables include the operational surplus in the previous year (2015) and the total number of employees per organisation. Note that the analysis at the organisational level is weighted by the number of responses by employees sources such as for instance on staff absenteeism. Absenteeism data is collected in the employer survey, the employee survey (using the WPAI) and in NHS administrative data. The relationship holds across the data sources. Importantly, our analysis shows an association between presenteeism and engagement.

The second hypothesis looks at the relationship between engagement and human resource practice. Here, we are mainly interested in variables around the health and wellbeing programme or employer offer to employees and leadership training. These are the variables below in Table 8.3 with a # symbol next to them. Our analysis finds that certain components of the offer are associated with higher staff engagement. Those NHS organisations with a greater number of physical health interventions and those that have health checks in place for staff have higher staff engagement. At the same time, we see an association between leadership (manager) training on employee health and wellbeing and greater staff engagement. Leadership is often seen as a key enabler as it also signals intent to staff that the organisation is willing to change and to engage with the needs of staff. We do not find the same association between a greater number of mental health interventions and staff engagement. The latter is perhaps surprising and an indication we need to understand the relationship between the specific components of a health and wellbeing offer and engagement better.

The third hypothesis considers whether 'good' work is associated with better staff engagement. We first need to consider what good work looks like. Here, we look at proxy indicators (indicated by the * symbol in Table 8.3) such as Health and Safety Executive (HSE) management standards, bullying, flexible working, financial wellbeing and working hours. The HSE management standards focus on relationships at work, control, role, time management, and unrealistic demands. Financial wellbeing is measured by the proportion of individuals who report having financial concerns. Of course, these indicators do not provide a holistic picture of the work environment but it stands to reason that good working environments have lower levels of bullying, allow flexible working, and indeed score better on the HSE management standards. Again, our analysis finds that across the board such proxy indicators are associated with better staff health and wellbeing. Those staff who can work from home and report having flexible hours have higher staff engagement. Clearly, working from home is not available for all NHS staff. All staff can request flexible working but relatively few are aware of the right to flexible working. Management functions have the greatest flexibility followed by clinical groups such as doctors. All HSE management standards are associated with staff engagement. This means that employees who report having a lack of control (control) and are not sure about their role (role) report lower levels of engagement. The same applies for employees reporting high levels of workplace demands (demand), employees that have a lack of peer support (peer support) at the workplace, that are bullied (bullied) and have strained relationships at work (strained relations). These are some of the most significant relationships in our analysis.

Two variables that we may have expected to have an association with staff engagement proved insignificant. Working hours and financial wellbeing were insignificant. This may reflect on the nature of work in the NHS and also the reasons

Table 8.3 Full regression table of all socio-demographic, occupation, work environment, health and wellbeing, and HR practice variables and employee engagement (*, **, and *** denoting statistically significant outcomes with level of significance increasing with the number of stars)

Variables	(1) Beta	(2) Ci: Low	(3) Ci: High	(4) Pval
Education: Medium	−0.0044	−0.032	0.023	0.784
Education: High	0.0122	−0.019	0.043	0.507
% Female	0.0263	0.015	0.038	0.001***
Ethnicity: Asian	−0.0067	−0.019	0.006	0.382
Ethnicity: Black	−0.0038	−0.018	0.010	0.638
Ethnicity: Mixed	0.0007	−0.009	0.010	0.899
Ethnicity: Other	−0.0011	−0.013	0.011	0.879
% Age (55 and under)	−0.0159	−0.022	−0.010	0.000***
% Age^2 (55 and over)	0.0001	0.000	0.000	0.002***
Job: Doctor	0.0065	−0.005	0.018	0.328
Job: Ambulance worker	0.0021	−0.008	0.012	0.721
Job: Public health	−0.0071	−0.021	0.007	0.404
Job: Commissioning	−0.0380	−0.085	0.008	0.175
Job: Registered nurses/midwives	−0.0013	−0.014	0.012	0.864
Job: Nurses/healthcare assistants	0.0140	0.002	0.026	0.051*
% Job: Social care	−0.0105	−0.017	−0.004	0.008***
% Job: Admininstration	−0.0360	−0.051	−0.021	0.000***
Job: Cleaner	−0.0159	−0.032	0.000	0.103
% Job: General management	−0.0166	−0.028	−0.005	0.023**
Job: Other	−0.0105	−0.039	0.018	0.532
*HSE management standards: Control	−0.0581	−0.072	−0.044	0.000***
*HSE: Role	−0.0652	−0.080	−0.051	0.000***
Home Flexitime	0.0178	0.006	0.029	0.013**
Tenure (first 2 years)	−0.0459	−0.079	−0.013	0.024**
Tenure^2 (after 12 years)	0.0468	0.021	0.072	0.004***
*Long working hours	0.0038	−0.010	0.018	0.643
Commute (minutes)	−0.0091	−0.023	0.005	0.281
Having a child	0.0131	−0.001	0.027	0.131
Being a carer	0.0166	−0.001	0.034	0.115
*Having financial concerns	0.0048	−0.007	0.016	0.476
Life satisfaction	−0.0730	−0.083	−0.063	0.000***
@Having musculoskeletal conditions	−0.0146	−0.030	0.001	0.126
@Having a chronic condition	0.0036	−0.016	0.023	0.751
@BMI: Being underweight	−0.0008	−0.012	0.010	0.900
@BMI: Being overweight	0.0046	−0.009	0.018	0.566
@BMI: Being obese	0.0025	−0.011	0.016	0.759
@Sleep: Less than 6 h	0.0072	−0.004	0.019	0.295
@Sleep: More than 9 h	0.0050	−0.008	0.018	0.515
@Sleep quality (lack of)	−0.0330	−0.046	−0.020	0.000***
@Risk of mental health	−0.0749	−0.085	−0.065	0.000***

(continued)

Table 8.3 (continued)

	(1)	(2)	(3)	(4)
*HSE management standards: Unrealistic demands	−0.0227	−0.035	−0.010	0.004***
*HSE: Peer support	−0.0745	−0.092	−0.057	0.000***
*HSE: Strained relations	−0.0549	−0.069	−0.041	0.000***
*HSE: Bullied	−0.0958	−0.109	−0.083	0.000***
#Human capital offer (number of interventions)	0.0242	0.012	0.036	0.002***
#Physical health offer (number of interventions	0.0155	0.001	0.030	0.072*
#Mental health offer (number of interventions)	0.0013	−0.015	0.017	0.892
#Leadership trained in health and wellbeing	0.0093	0	0.023	0.099*

Source: Authors' calculations
Notes: Robust standard errors (Pval) in parentheses; *** $p < 0.01$, ** $p < 0.05$, * $p < 0.1$. Analysis based on the combined NHS Healthy Workforce and BHW survey. Rows Beta and Pval report the standardized coefficient and corresponding p-values from a regression using the standardized variables as predictor variables. Ci low and Ci high represent the 90% confidence interval for beta

why people join the NHS. Generally, it appears that employees do not join the NHS for financial gain and appear proud of the work they do. Antisocial working hours (including shift work, long hours) are perhaps seen as part of the job.

A fourth hypothesis focuses on the link between employee health and wellbeing and employee engagement. Here, we can look at a range of self-reported proxies collected through the EHA including obesity, quality and quantity of sleep, risk of mental health, chronic conditions (any long-term illnesses such as high blood pressure, cancer, diabetes, etc.) and musculoskeletal conditions (@ variables indicated in Table 8.3 below). There exist a number of significant associations between these conditions and engagement. In particular, the risk of mental health is strongly associated with employee engagement in our analysis. We capture this risk through two measures, the Warwick-Edinburgh scale[11] and the Kessler scale.[12] In addition, the self-reported assessment of quality of sleep where respondents rate their quality of sleep from very poor to very good on a Likert scale is associated with engagement. It is notable that few other variables show a significant relationship with engagement. There is for instance no relationship between engagement and musculoskeletal conditions or obesity in our analysis.

Finally, there are a wider range of demographic variables that have a positive association with engagement. Certain demographic and staff groups have lower staff engagement compared to others. For instance, social care workers, administrative support staff and managers tend to have lower engagement than other groups. We do not discuss those associations here in detail. However, it is obvious that healthcare organisations employ different types of staff and as such also have different

---

[11] https://warwick.ac.uk/fac/sci/med/research/platform/wemwbs (accessed October 2019).

[12] The Kessler six instrument is listed in the following link: https://www.hcp.med.harvard.edu/ncs/ftpdir/k6/K6+%20Self%20admin_updated_08-08-11.pdf (accessed October 2019).

sub-cultures. These need to be considered when looking at the issue of staff engagement.

8.5 Conclusions

Our evidence suggests that staff engagement is slightly below average in the NHS compared to other organisations that participate for instance in BHW. However, employee engagement is broadly similar in these NHS organisations when compared to other large employers in BHW and especially when adjusted for age, gender and income. It tends to be lowest in the healthcare assistant, nursing, midwives, and ambulance staff groups. So, employee engagement varies across staff groups and the issue tends to be more pronounced in certain staff groups. These groups also often have other significant wellbeing challenges such as worse mental health, higher rates of obesity and higher incidences of bullying compared to other staff groups.

The NHS in England has been under severe budgetary pressure since the financial crisis of 2008. In this climate, it has proved challenging making substantial progress on the employee experience in the service. Some initiatives have tried to move the debate forward. The Five Year Forward View, published by NHS England in 2014, underscores the importance of staff health and well-being as a crucial factor in improving the performance of the NHS (NHS England, 2014). This led to guidance and frameworks being rolled out across NHS health organisations with the aim to improve the health and wellbeing of staff. In the same year, Public Health England launched the Workplace Well-being Charter, which, for the first time, contains a set of evidence-based national standards for workplace health.[13] In 2015, the National Institute for Health and Care Excellence (NICE) issued guidelines on workplace health (NICE, 2015). The guideline 'covers how to improve the health and well-being of employees, with a focus on organisational culture and the role of line managers'.

The analysis in this chapter is important as it continues to build an understanding of what drives employee engagement and how it impacts organisations. By showing the associations between engagement and a wide set of organisational outcomes it also adds to the business case for health organisations to focus on their staff and work environments. The limitations of our work are several. Our sample focuses mostly on secondary care acute trusts and large NHS organisations. Therefore, we can say little about primary care. We are also limited by the data that we collect as part of the wider survey. As such, there may be variables or concepts that we do not ask about and that may be relevant for further in-depth analysis. Finally, some measurements are not identical across surveys. As such, we had to create some measures to compare outcomes. In terms of bias, we have mostly motivated NHS trusts participating in the surveys as our surveys rely on voluntary participation and

---

[13]The Workplace Wellbeing Charter. As of 22 November 2017: http://www.charter.org.uk

dedicated HR staff rolling out the surveys in their organisations. Respondents of course are under no obligation to participate. However, the results and sample that we obtained are not particularly distinct and mostly similar when compared to other NHS data sources such as the NHS staff survey and NHS administrative data.

This chapter offers some concrete recommendations. The first is that it is important for senior executives in the NHS to know their numbers and understand the issues that they may have in their health organisations. Our surveys are an example of an approach but it is still striking from our experience how few healthcare organisations are aware of employee engagement and health and wellbeing and discuss these issues at board or senior executive level. Our findings also appear to suggest that a more holistic approach, which moves beyond single initiatives or interventions, may be important as work environment and culture variables show a positive association with staff engagement as conceptualised in our analysis. Of course, changing a work environment or culture is a difficult undertaking. The analysis also shows some specific relationships between human resource practice and engagement as well as mental health, quality of sleep and engagement. This offers some entry points for decision-makers and practitioners looking to improve employee engagement in the workplace. In particular, we want to emphasise the interesting associations between the size of the health and wellbeing programme and some specific components and employee engagement as well as the positive relationship between training leadership and line managers to look after the health and wellbeing of staff and employee engagement. Flexible working is also associated with better employee engagement but there remain issues in the NHS with general awareness of flexible working policies and how the wishes of staff are accommodated in working patterns. Bullying remains a toxic issue in the NHS, which on average is significantly higher than in most other organisations that we survey. We also need to consider different sub-cultures in an organisation. Our findings suggest some important differences across staff and demographic groups. So, improvements in staff engagement across a service may also require more tailored or targeted engagement with specific staff and demographic groups. Finally, some of these groups show a range of other challenges including worse mental health and higher rates of obesity than in other groups.

The key message for those involved in healthcare delivery is that improving employee engagement makes business sense as it likely improves a range of organisational outcomes. We suggest some entry points for managers and executives in the health service. Our work hints at some critical components of a strategy that tries to improve employee engagement. However, further research is required to show what aspects of HR practice or changes in work environment are particularly associated with improvements in employee engagement.

Key Messages
For healthcare professionals

- Better staff engagement in a healthcare organisation is associated with better financial and care outcomes
- Even where staff engagement across employees is good as measured on existing scales, there can be substantial differences in specific professional groups
- Employee participation in wellbeing programmes and leadership and line manager training are associated with better staff engagement

For researchers

- Looking at staff engagement in healthcare organisations contributes to a wider understanding of what drives performance in healthcare
- There is evidence on the association between staff engagement and organisational outcomes
- The evidence base around the effectiveness of health and wellbeing programmes is emergent
- As a result, our analysis of what human resource management practices are associated with better staff engagement points to some practices but more research is required

References

Admasachew, L., & Dawson, J. (2010). *Staff engagement in the NHS—A multilevel analysis*. Birmingham: Aston University.

Boorman, S., & Fellow, R. C. N. (2009). *NHS health and Well-being review: Interim report*. NHS Health and Wellbeing Review. London: The Stationery Office.

Crant, J. M. (2000). Proactive behavior in organizations. *Journal of Management, 26*(3), 435–462.

Dawson, J. (2014). *Staff experience and patient outcomes: What do we know. A report commissioned by NHS Employers on behalf of NHS England*. London: NHS Confederation.

Dickinson, H., & Ham, C. (2008). *Engaging doctors in leadership: Review of the literature*. Birmingham: University of Birmingham.

Frese, M., & Fay, D. (2001). 4. Personal initiative: An active performance concept for work in the 21st century. *Research in Organizational Behavior, 23*, 133–187.

Kahn, W. A. (1990). Psychological conditions of personal engagement and disengagement at work. *Academy of Management Journal, 33*, 692–724.

Keogh, B. (2013). *Review into the quality of care and treatment provided by 14 hospital trusts in England: Overview report*. London: NHS England.

Laschinger, H. K. S., & Leiter, M. P. (2006). The impact of nursing work environments on patient safety outcomes: The mediating role of burnout engagement. *Journal of Nursing Administration, 36*(5), 259–267.

Lohaus, D., & Habermann, W. (2019). Presenteeism: A review and research directions. *Human Resource Management Review, 29*(1), 43–58., issn 1053-4822. https://doi.org/10.1016/j.hrmr.2018.02.010

Maben, J., Adams, M., Peccei, R., Murrells, T., & Robert, G. (2012). 'Poppets and parcels': The links between staff experience of work and acutely ill older peoples' experience of hospital care. *International Journal of Older People Nursing, 7*(2), 83–94.

MacLeod, D., & Clarke, N. (2009). *Engaging for success: Enhancing performance through employee engagement: A report to government*. London: Department for Business, Innovation and Skills.

NHS England. (2014). *Five year forward view*. As of 14 November 2017. https://www.england.nhs.uk/wp-content/uploads/2014/10/5yfv-web.pdf

NICE (National Institute for Health and Care Excellence). (2015). *Workplace health: Management practices. NICE guidelines [NG13]*. As of 14 November 2017. https://www.nice.org.uk/guidance/ng13

Organ, D. W. (1988). *Organizational citizenship behavior: The good soldier syndrome*. Lexington: Lexington Books/DC Heath and Com.

Robinson, D., Perryman, S., & Hayday, S. (2004). *The drivers of employee engagement*. Report-Institute for Employment Studies.

Schaufeli, W. B., Bakker, A. B., & Salanova, M. (2006). The measurement of work engagement with a short questionnaire: A cross-national study. *Educational and Psychological Measurement, 66*(4), 701–716.

Tawfik, D. S., Scheid, A., Profit, J., et al. (2019). Evidence relating health care provider burnout and quality of care: A systematic review and meta-analysis. *Ann Intern Med, 171*, 555–567. [Epub ahead of print 8 October 2019]. https://doi.org/10.7326/M19-1152

West, M., & Dawson, J. (2012). *Employee engagement and NHS performance* (Vol. 1, p. 23). London: The King's Fund.

Chapter 9
Governing Health Care Provision: Clinicians' Experiences

Berit Bringedal, Inger Lise Teig, and Kristine Bærøe

9.1 Background

The triple aims of health care are: "improving the experience of care, improving the health of populations, and reducing per capita costs of health care" (Berwick et al., 2008). A number of factors must be in place in order to realize these aims; in this chapter we shall focus on the impact of governance of health care organizations.

Recently, scholars and health care professionals have proposed to expand the triple aim to a quadruple aim, by including the health and wellbeing of health care workers in the list of goals (Bodenheimer, Sinsky, & Bodenheimer, 2014). The background for this suggestion is an observed increase in stress and burnout among health care workers, especially in the US (Shanafelt et al., 2015), a phenomenon which is assumed to imperil the triple aim. Hence, to improve the performance of health care, one must also care for the health workers' wellbeing, is the argument.

Clearly, health care workers represent a crucial link between system requirements and the actual provided care; thus, paying attention to the well-being of health professionals is essential. Whether this should be a goal in itself, or rather considered as a means to good care, can be discussed. Either way, knowledge of how health care workers experience the provision of care and their reflections on requirements for providing good care is crucial. After all, they are the ones who possess first hand knowledge of system factors that support or hinder their possibilities for providing good care.

B. Bringedal (✉)
LEFO – Institute for Studies of the Medical Profession, Oslo, Norway
e-mail: berit.bringedal@legeforeningen.no

I. L. Teig · K. Bærøe
Department of Global Public Health and Primary Care, University of Bergen, Bergen, Norway

Modern health care organizations are increasingly governed by other actors than health professionals themselves (Hasselbladh et al., 2008; Hindhede and Andersen 2019; Waring & Currie, 2009). The days of doctors' autonomous decision-making are gone, now is the time for external steering arrangements like reporting requirements, auditing, incentives, and other systems and means of governance and regulation. The effects are many, and debated (cf. Power, 2007), yet, without taking a stance in the question of whether these changes are for the good or bad, to describe modern health care systems as increasingly complex is uncontroversial. There is a plethora of measures intended to improve the performance of health care, the question is how they contribute to the overall aims of health care.

9.1.1 The Norwegian Health Care System

The Norwegian health care system is a single payer, universal coverage system, funded by the State. Hospital care is organized as regional trusts with independent boards. Yearly contracts are made between the trusts and the Ministry of Health, which decides the total budgets and the expected quantum and quality of care. Primary care is organized as private businesses where GPs receive public funding based on capitation, based on number of patients on the lists, number of consultations and procedures (e.g., lab, ultrasound), and patient co-payment. GPs are gatekeepers to specialist care.

In Norway, as in other countries, recent decades have seen a stronger emphasis on budget control and value for money. A number of reforms are implemented, all with the intention to improve quality, reduce waste, and lead to better priorities. The many reforms and increased focus on budget constraints seem to have led to some skepticism towards some of the reforms among clinicians, in particular fee for service payment arrangements (Bringedal & Carlsen, 2018).

In this chapter, we present and discuss the results of a survey on how medical doctors report different governing instruments to impact on their clinical decisions and whether they believe these instruments contribute to fulfilling the goals of quality and equity, as stated in Norwegian health legislation. The steering instruments we consider are financial and legal measures, clinical guidelines and reporting requirements.

9.2 Material and Methods

9.2.1 Material

In 2016/2017 we surveyed a representative sample of doctors practicing in Norway. The survey was part of a biannual, longitudinal study of a panel of doctors established in 1994, all of them in the form of postal questionnaires. The questions on governance constituted approximately 1/3 of the questionnaire this year, while the remaining parts concerned doctors' working conditions, professional knowledge updating, and ethics (the questionnaire can be provided upon request).

The questions about governance were based on the previous survey of the same panel, in 2014/2015 (Bringedal & Carlsen, 2018), and qualitative interviews of health care personnel in hospitals (Teig & Wester, 2018). The interviews followed up what we found in the 2014/2015-survey. We conducted 15 semi-structured in-depth interviews with doctors, managers and nurses in cardiology at two large Norwegian hospitals autumn 2015 to spring 2016. The aim was to explore the extent to which health care professionals were familiar with a range of legal, political, economic, bureaucratic and professional regulatory instruments in their daily work, as well as their perceptions about how these instruments affected their work—whether they constrained or supported them in their daily practice.

The questions in the present survey were built upon the findings in the interviews, and centered on doctor's perceptions of three subjects: (1) which factors that affect clinical decisions (either positively or negatively), (2) whether all patient groups are equally provided for in the health care system, and (3), the reasons why some patient groups are not provided adequately. See excerpts from the questionnaire in Box 9.1.

9.2.2 Methods

The data were analyzed by descriptive statistics. Most questions are only reported for the whole group of doctors, regardless of e.g., position, gender and age. The reason for this choice is that we were only interested in how doctors in general consider different governing instruments to impact on their decisions, and which patient groups they identify as those who more often risk receiving insufficient care. One group of questions however, namely the questions about specific factors that affect their clinical decision, are reported separately for doctors in primary and specialist care, since their organization and governing are different.

9.3 Results

The following presentation of results reports only the responses from doctors in clinical work (in hospitals, general practice, or other private specialties). Generally We also exclude the category "not valid for me".

Our findings throw light on three subjects: (1) which factors affect clinical decisions; (2) whether there are differences between patient groups regarding priority to care; and (3) if there are unwarranted differences between patient groups, and if so, what are the reasons?

1. *Factors directly affecting clinical decisions.*

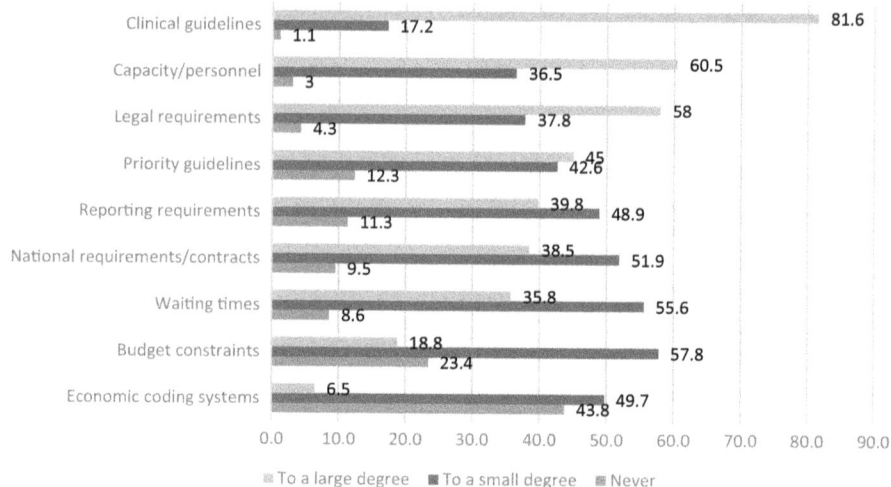

Fig. 9.1 Which of the following non-clinical factors are directly affecting the decisions you make in your main position? Percentage. N = 551–740 (varying numbers of doctors responded to the questions)

The results (Fig. 9.1) show that complying with clinical guidelines is reported as the most prominent factor to directly affect clinical decisions, followed by capacity/personnel and legal requirements. Legal requirements refer to the Patient Rights Act and priority setting guidelines in the Norwegian healthcare legislation. The majority of doctors reported that budget constraints and economic coding systems affected clinical decision making only to a small degree or never.

Since the organization and governing of hospitals and general practices are different, we compared the responses of GPs and hospital doctors. See Table 9.1.

Budget, capacity, national/reporting requirements, and priority guidelines differ the most between GPs and hospital doctors. Budgets are given for hospital doctors, while GPs manage their own businesses. Priority guidelines are part of the Patient Rights' Act, which until recently regulated hospital care only. National contracts and reporting requirements are likewise more prominent in a hospital setting. As expected, the "Not valid for me"- category reflects the differing contexts.

2. *Are all patient groups equally provided for in the health care system?*

Based on the previous studies (survey and interviews), we listed particular patient groups and asked if any of them did not receive the care the doctor considered necessary. Figure 9.2 displays the result.

The specified groups are not mutually exclusive, a specific patient may certainly belong to more than one category, hence, the sum of percentages adds up to more than 100. Still, it gives us a picture of overrepresented groups among those who receives less than sufficient health care, according to the doctors' experiences. Patients with mental health problems and patients with complex health conditions are worst off according to the survey. Other vulnerable groups who receive

9 Governing Health Care Provision: Clinicians' Experiences

Table 9.1 Variations between hospital doctors, n = 783–809 (varying numbers of doctors responded to the questions) and general practitioners (n = 309–317)

	Never/to a small degree		To a large degree		Don't know		Not valid for me	
	Hospital	GP	Hospital	GP	Hospital	GP	Hospital	GP
Economic coding	78.9%	62.1%	5.7%	4.1%	3.5%	2.2%	12.0%	31.5%
Budgets[a]	71.5%	61.1%	16.0%	4.7%	3.9%	1.6%	8.6%	32.6%
Legal[a]	33.3%	39.6%	45.3%	32.0%	10.0%	8.2%	11.4%	20.3%
Priority[a] guidelines	37.7%	46.5%	30.5%	13.8%	12.0%	8.3%	19.8%	31.4%
Reporting requirements[a]	49.3%	32.8%	32.7%	8.0%	2.8%	2.5%	15.2%	56.7%
Clinical guidelines	16.0%	19.0%	73.7%	67.9%	2.9%	2.5%	7.5%	10.8%
Capacity/staff[a]	36.1%	37.0%	55.7%	11.4%	1.6%	1.9%	6.6%	49.7%
Waiting times	50.6%	43.1%	28.4%	17.9%	3.8%	2.2%	17.2%	36.7%
National requirements/ Contracts[a]	44.3%	43.7%	28.0%	12.0%	15.7%	9.4%	12.0%	35.0%

[a]Statistically significant differences

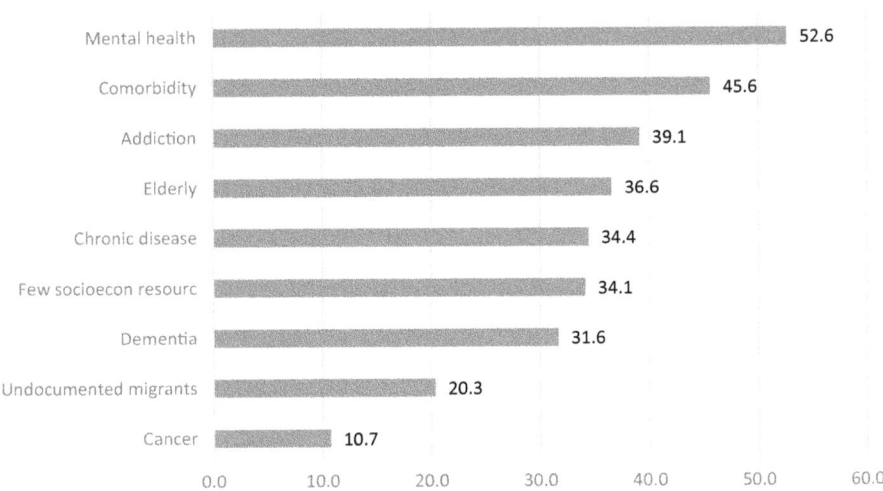

Fig. 9.2 Patient groups not receiving sufficient services according to the doctors' experiences

inadequate help are elderly, patients with an addiction and patients with fewer social resources. The reasons for this situation of differentiated services are diverse and complex.

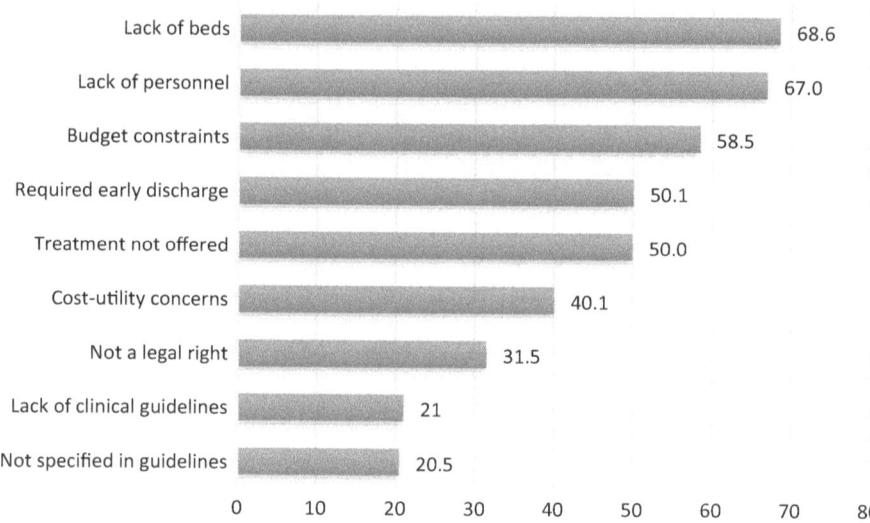

Fig. 9.3 Factors explaining inadequate care for certain patient groups. Percentages (N = 917–1060)

Table 9.2 Reasons given why the doctor considered the discharge as 'too early'. Percentages. (N = 554–593, only those who had experienced too early discharges)	Further medical treatment required	81.8
	Other specialized care required	64.2
	No adequate alternative in area of residence	60.2
	Strain due to change of institution	46.2
	Patient's lack of socioeconomic resources	31.3

3. *The reasons why some patient groups are not provided adequate care* (Fig. 9.3)

Capacity and the personnel situation at the section or unit stand out as the most frequent reasons of inadequate care. Budget constraints and required quality indicators, such as early discharge, are also emphasized. This is probably closely connected to the lack of beds. The alternative "treatment not offered" refers to non-existent services, locally or nationally.

To the question "During the last three months, did you experience that any of your patients was discharged earlier than you considered justifiable?", the respondents divided in two equally sized groups: 50.1% yes and 49.9% no. Among those who responded "yes", they gave the following reasons (Table 9.2).

The main reason for considering discharges as premature was the need for further medical treatment. How does e.g., unwarranted discharging relate to factors on the system level? Figure 9.4 provides the result.

Norwegian health authorities have implemented a number of quality indicators in order to measure the quality of health care services (National Institute of Public Health). One of them, "the number of corridor beds", or, rather, to keep this number as low as possible, is reported as a major reason for premature discharges.

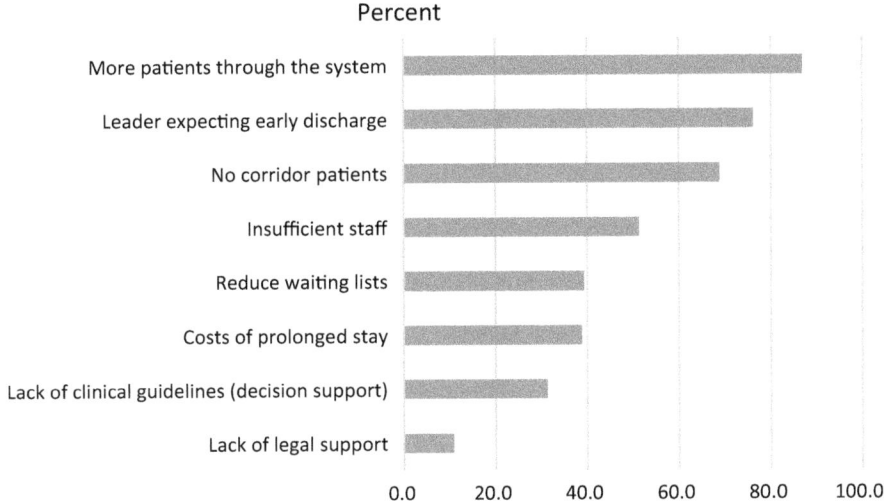

Fig. 9.4 If you prematurely discharged any of your patients during the last 3 months, what were the reasons? Percentages. (N = 379–454)

Compliance with quality indicators is the responsibility of the leader of the department or the hospital, thus a leader's expectations of compliance of organizational performances will significantly influence decisions on discharges.

The questionnaire included an open text field at the end of each group of questions, allowing comments from the respondents. Professional disagreement, lack of competence, inadequate communication, and capacity were added to the factors that affect decisions of early discharges.

These factors point primarily to the respondents' experiences of organisational barriers or lack of possibilities for performing their clinical work adequately. Disagreements or inadequate communication about optimal time for hospitalisation may lead to what some clinicians perceive as premature discharges. The clinician may feel obliged to discharge because of an organizational pressure to comply with the performance criteria and insufficient capacity (in terms of beds and/or staff).

9.3.1 Variations Between Sub-Groups of Doctors

Above we distinguished between GPs and hospital doctors on the question of the significance of particular steering measures, because the two practices are governed by different measures.

On the other questions, we found some statistically significant differences according to gender and position, whilst age had no or only very small effects. On the question of factors that explain limited care for particular groups of patients, more men than women chose responses concerning scarcity: hospital beds, insufficient personnel and treatment not offered. Whether the doctor is a GP or a hospital doctor represented no statistically significant difference in this category.

Significantly more GPs responded, however, that expectations of more patients through the system was a reason for premature discharge. There were no significant gender differences in this category of questions.

9.4 Discussion

Recent years have seen significant changes in the governance of public services, in particular in the provision of education and health care. These changes build upon the idea that quality and efficiency will improve from a combination of incentives, agency, regulation, and provider competition, which New Public Management prescribes (see Hasselbladh et al., 2008; Hindhede & Andersen, 2019 for reports from the Scandinavian countries, and Hull, 2012 from South Africa). Along with these changes, however, professional concerns are voiced. Many professionals claim that the new systems of governance will have the opposite effect than the manifest intentions claim. Standardization of clinicians' daily work may give a more transparent and efficient health care service, but the efforts to controlling health care workers come with a potential downside: Good clinical judgments are based on discretion. Limiting the discretionary space may lead to less individual adaption of general guidelines. To strike a good balance between doctors' descretionary space and health autrorities wish for controlling health care, is, however, a challenge. Too little discretionary space as well as too little governance and control can be detrimental toquality Bringedal, 2015; Lægreid & Christensen, 2011).

The scope of regulation and control of the professions is an important element of this discussion. How detailed should the regulation be, and how much control of individual professionals' conduct is required? These questions concern delegation of professional autonomy and the overall organization and distribution of power, which is open to discussion. Eliot Freidson's change of perspective on this question is noteworthy. In his first account, published in 1970, he was concerned about doctors' "unrestricted" autonomy, and argued in favor of the need to control their power for the sake of societal interests (Freidson, 1970). Thirty years later, his perspective shifted dramatically. He then argued that the medical profession, as well as other professions, experience too little autonomy and may end up between a rock (bureaucracy) and a hard place (the market) (Freidson, 2001).

In this study, we investigated how Norwegian doctors' view the impact of governing instruments to provide good health care services and quality care to their patients in their daily work. We also asked them to identify which patient groups, if any, fall short in the priorities between patients—due to such structural factors.

We found that many reported treatment capacity and national requirements to impact on their decisions. A majority of doctors name capacity issues, requirements of early discharge, low number of corridor patients, and time limits to have significant impact on the decisions for premature discharges. This finding mirrors a paradoxical situation for clinicians when they are expected to process the flow of patients in the hospital, and, at the same time, are required not to use corridor beds and to limit the inpatient days. Perhaps surprisingly, budgets and financial systems, such as DRGs (Diagnosis Related Groups), the financing model for hospitals, or the tariffs/fixed prices for services in primary care, were not considered particularly influential factors.

If the governing instruments are as influential as the doctors report in this study, an important question is whether this leads to decisions in line with the overall goals of health care. Norwegian legislation names quality, efficiency, and equity as the regulating values to govern health care provision (Acts: Spesialisthelsetjenesteloven, Helse- og omsorgstjenestloven).

The Patients Rights Act emphasizes quality and equality especially: ".. equal access to healthcare services of good quality" (§1.1). Although there is room for interpretion of how the aim should be implemented in practice (Bærøe, Kaur, & Radhakrishnan, 2018), the doctors in our study provide information of unjustified inequality. More than 55% (in most cases, between 65 and 75%) have witnessed suboptimal care for certain patient groups (see Fig. 9.2) within the last 3 months, and 50% have experienced premature discharges during the same time. These results indicate that the health care system, to some extent, fails to secure all patients equal possibilities to benefit from health care.

Further, the doctors name the expectation of patient flow and minimum number of corridor patients as direct reasons for premature discharges. Patient flow operates as an important governing instrument because flow is connected to the financing of the hospitals: The more patients the hospital gets through the system, the higher the income. The risk is that leaders put a disproportionate strong attention to patient flow (securing budgets), which may compromise the quality of care. It is particulary unfortunate that one central indicator of quality, i.e., number of corridor patients, is pulling in the same direction as the financing incentives towards early discharge. This may cover up a potential conflict between ensuring quality in terms of avoiding too early discharge on the one side, and the organisational requirement of ensuring a high flow of patients on the other.

On this background, it is, as previously mentioned, somewhat surprising that relatively few doctors name financial systems and budgets among the most influential steering factors. The reason can be that although highly discussed in the public debate, the need for keeping budgets might not be a central topic in the daily practice among hospital doctors, or that GPs only consider the adverse effects of hospital decisions. Financial systems will indirectly influence decisions in both contexts, though not necessarily in the narratives of the doctors themselves– especially since they are asked to consider the direct impact on their decisions.

The doctor (whether a GP or a hospital doctor) operates in the intersection between different roles (Bringedal et al., 2018). S/he is expected to fulfil the role as the patient's advocate, to care for the patient's health, safety, and satisfaction. At the same time the doctor is accountable to society and health care authorities. (See Table 9.3 for an overview of the different roles.)

Table 9.3 Doctors' roles

Role	Administrator and gatekeeper	Professional	Patient's advocate	Private, individual
Accountable to	Society and health authorities.	Medical quality. Professional association. Peers.	Patient and patient's next of kin.	Self (political views, moral values, and personal interests)
Core moral norm (−s)	Act in accordance with laws and system requirements. Take responsibility for population health and for fair distribution of resources.	Adhere to good practice and professional ethics	Ensure care is in line with patient's views and interests	Do not act contrary to political or personal values and interests

The different doctor's roles can come in conflict. Adhering to organisational requirements (e.g., patient flow) on the one hand and securing individual patients good care on the other, can be hard, especially if the system represents hard sanctions if one or the other responsibility suffers. Although clinical guidelines and legal requirements are considered the most influential governing instruments, resource scarcity and measures of technical effectiveness (flow, waiting times) explain breeches of quality- in terms of early discharge and adversely affected groups – according to the respondents. The reasons why the clinical guidelines are less influential than organisational requirements require more research.

In our in-depth interview study (Teig & Wester, 2018) we found that health care professionals establish, maintain and recraft justifiable compromises when faced with emerging role or value conflicts. They do not report that they oppose or circumvent regulations or governing instruments, but will rather search for medical sound compromises in the compound of governing instruments in their daily decisions. For instance, the clinicians described how they acknowledge that some aspects of the patients' hospital stays were not always satisfactory, since the possibility to make optimal clinical decisions varied. Sometimes they compromised with the "human side" of the stay. Nevertheless they insisted that they "did as best they as they could" under the specific circumstances of muliple value conflicts.

It is worth noting that the effect of governing instruments will not only influence on the care of the patients, but health professionals as well. Conflicts between achieving services of good quality on the one side and adherence to organisational instruments on the other, can have a negative impact on their well-being and, in the long run, their health.

The quadruple aims of health care consists of improving the experience of care, improving the health of populations, reducing per capita costs of health care, and ensuring the well-being of healthcare personnel (Bodenheimer et al., 2014). Professional well being is closely connected to the possibility to deliver good medical care, and quality of care arguably includes equity: Unjustified inequalities between patient groups is a breech of a fundamental ethical principle in medicine, namely to treat every patient with equal regard. A system which nudges or requires doctors to act contrary to professional ethics may cause moral stress, contributing to a reduction in their well-being.

Our study indicates that contradictory claims and expectation to their role as a doctor may jeopardize professional values and possibilities to provide quality for all patient groups. Evaluating doctors' daily work according to selected indicators may give a more transparent health care service, but risks producing health care services that are inadequate or insufficient for particular patient groups.

It is the rule rather than the exception that governing systems come with unintended effects. Transparent scoring cards on selected evaluation criteria will draw the attention towards the selected criteria. At the same time, other aspects, equally important, risk being ignored or getting insufficient attention. This is clearly not the intention of the health authorities, yet it can come as an unintended, perhaps also unnoticed, effect of the governing system itself.

The weight on standardisation of flow and measurable quality indicators represents a redirection of health care workers' responsibility from autonomous discretion to accountability and auditability (Power, 2007). It is the individual health care worker who must make daily compromises in order to handle appearently incommensurable governing instruments. One solution may be to engage and involve health care personnel to a larger degree in all stages of planning, producing and evaluating the instruments for governance. Such re-empowering of health care workers may result in better fulfillment of the goals of quality and equity in the health care sector, without breaking budgets or legal requirements.

Measuring and monotoring professional performance is central for governing the health care sector in most countries, but systems with concern for professional work beyond control and sanctions must be developed in order to stimulate learning and improvement in daily health care practice.

Key Messages for Researchers
- Governing instruments may impact negatively on the quality of care. More research is required for better understanding of how governing instruments impact on quality of care.
- Future research should add avoiding inequity, i.e., unjust inequality, to the quadruple aim of health care.
- Future research should explore more closely the scope of how non-clinical factors, such as governing instruments, impact on health care provision.

Key Messages for Healthcare Delivery
- Future health care delivery systems should monitor healthcare personnel's experiences of unjustifiable inequalities in how patient groups are treated to promote equitable treatment of all.
- Future health care delivery systems should be aware that health care personnel's accountability to the authorities may undermine high-quality care and equity. Quality indicators can have effects counter to the intention.

Box 9.1 Excerpts from the Questionnaire

B5	During the last 3 months, have you experienced that certain groups did not receive the care they should have?	Yes	No	Don't know	N/A
B5.1	Patients with psychiatric disease	1	2	3	9
B5.2	Patients with few socioeconomic resources	1	2	3	9
B5.3	Elderly	1	2	3	9
B5.4	Demented	1	2	3	9
B5.5	Chronic disease	1	2	3	9
B5.6	Patients with addicitions	1	2	3	9
B5.7	Comorbidity	1	2	3	9
B5.8	Cancer	1	2	3	9
B5.9	Undocumented immigrants	1	2	3	9
B5.10	Children (below 16 years)	1	2	3	9
B5.11	Other:	1	2	3	9

B6	What factors limited care for these patients?	Yes	No	N/A
B6.1	Treatment not offered	1	2	9
B6.2	Lack of personnel	1	2	9
B6.3	Lack of beds	1	2	9
B6.4	Cost–/utility considerations	1	2	9
B6.5	Budget constraints	1	2	9
B6.6	Not a legal right	1	2	9
B6.7	Not specified in guidelines	1	2	9
B6.8	Lack of clinical guidelines	1	2	9
B6.9	Require dearly discharge	1	2	9
B6.10	Other:	1	2	9

B9	What influenced the decision to discharge patients?	Yes	No	N/A
B9.1	Waiting lists	1	2	9
B9.2	Required no corridor patients	1	2	9
B9.3	Expected more patients through the system	1	2	9
B9.4	Expected early discharge by local leader	1	2	9
B9.5	Lacking personnel	1	2	9
B9.6	Costs of prolonged stay	1	2	9
B9.7	Lack of clinical decision support	1	2	9
B9.8	Lack of legal support	1	2	9
B9.9	Other:	1	2	9

(Translated into the English, original in Norwegian)

References

Bærøe, K., Kaur, J. G., & Radhakrishnan, K. (2018). Lik tilgang og likeverdige tjenester: hvordan styrke realiseringen av disse rettslige formålene. In B. Aasen et al. (Eds.), *Prioritering, styring og likebehandling*. Oslo: Cappelen Akademiske.

Berwick, D. M., Nolan, T., & Whittington, J. (2008). The triple aim: Care, health, and cost. *Health Affairs, 27*(3), 759–769. https://doi.org/10.1377/hlthaff.27.3.759

Bodenheimer, T., Sinsky, C., & Bodenheimer, T. (2014). From triple to quadruple aim: Care of the patient requires care of the provider. *Annals of Family Medicine, 12*(6), 573–576. https://doi.org/10.1370/afm.1713

Bringedal, B. (2015). Guest Editor's introduction. *Professions and Professionalism, 5*(1). https://doi.org/10.7577/pp.1355

Bringedal, B., & Carlsen, B. (2018). How do medical doctors consider different steering instruments' effects on quality and equity in health care? / Norske legers syn på styringsinstrumentenes betydning. In H. S. Aasen, B. Bringedal, K. Bærøe, & A.-M. Magnussen (Eds.), *Prioritering, styring og likebehandling: Utfordringer i norsk helsetjeneste*. Oslo: Cappelen Damm Akademisk.

Bringedal, B., Isaksson Rø, K., Magelssen, M., Førde, R., & Aasland, O. G. (2018). Between professional values, social regulations and patient preferences: Medical doctors' perceptions of ethical dilemmas. *Journal of Medical Ethics, 44*(4), 239–243. https://doi.org/10.1136/medethics-2017-104408

Freidson, E. (1970). *Profession of medicine: A study of the sociology of applied knowledge*. New York: Dodd, Mead & Co.

Freidson, E. (2001). *Professionalism: The third logic. On the practice of knowledge*. Chicago: The University of Chicago Press.

Hasselbladh, H., Bejerot, E., & Gustafsson, R. A. (2008). *Bortom new public management – Institutionell transformation i svensk sjukvård*. Lund: Academia Adacta AB.

Lægreid, P., & Christensen, T. (2011). *The Ashgate research companion to new public management*. Farnham: Ashgate.

Power, M. (2007). *Organized uncertainty: Designing a world of risk management*. Oxford: Oxford University Press.

Shanafelt, T. D., Hasan, O., Dyrbye, L. N., Sinsky, C., Satele, D., Sloan, J., et al. (2015). Changes in burnout and satisfaction with work-life balance in physicians and the general US working population between 2011 and 2014. *Mayo Clinic Proceedings, 90*(12), 1600–1613. https://doi.org/10.1016/j.mayocp.2015.08.023

Teig, I. L., & Wester, G. (2018). Styringsdilemmaer i praksis. Helsepersonells beslutninger om helsehjelp i daglig arbeid (Governance dilemmas in practice. Health care professionals' health care decisions in daily work) Chapter in Aasen, Bringedal, et al.: *Prioritering, styring og likebehandling. Utfordringer i norsk helsetjeneste*. Oslo: Cappelen Akademiske.

Waring, J., & Currie, G. (2009). Managing expert knowledge: Organizational challenges and managerial futures for the UK medical profession. *Organization Studies, 30*(7), 755–778.

Chapter 10
Speaking up about Bullying and Harassment in Healthcare: Reflections Following the Introduction of an Innovative "Speak Up" Role in NHS England

A. Jones, J. Blake, C. Banks, M. Adams, D. Kelly, R. Mannion, and J. Maben

10.1 Introduction

Healthcare organisations reap significant benefits when staff concerns are appropriately listened and responded to, including: improved patient safety and patient experience, reduced costs and improved worker wellbeing and staff morale (Royal College of Physicians, 2015). The obverse is also true, in that patients, employees and the public are significantly disadvantaged when healthcare organisations fail to listen and respond to staff concerns (Jones & Kelly, 2014a, 2014b). Although many employee concerns are dealt with satisfactorily, the act of "speaking up" by employees is no simple issue (Mannion & Davies, 2015). Existing research demonstrates that healthcare employees consider speaking up to be a "high risk, low benefit activity". For example, healthcare employees in the UK and internationally may feel unable to speak up and even when they do speak up, their colleagues and organisations more generally may ignore their concerns or respond inappropriately (Jones & Kelly, 2014b; Morrow, Gustavson, & Jones, 2016). Staff who speak up often suffer

---

A. Jones (✉) · J. Blake · D. Kelly
School of Healthcare Sciences, Cardiff University, Cardiff, UK
e-mail: JonesA97@cardiff.ac.uk

C. Banks · J. Maben
School of Health Sciences, Faculty of Health and Medical Sciences, University of Surrey, Surrey, UK

M. Adams
King's Improvement Science, Health Service & Population Research Department, King's College London, London, UK

R. Mannion
cHealth Services Management Centre, School of Social Policy, University of Birmingham, Birmingham, UK

© Springer Nature Switzerland AG 2020
A. Montgomery et al. (eds.), *Connecting Healthcare Worker Well-Being, Patient Safety and Organisational Change*, Aligning Perspectives on Health, Safety and Well-Being, https://doi.org/10.1007/978-3-030-60998-6_10

deterioration in their relationships with their peers, irrespective of whether the concerns reported are genuine and legitimate (Beckstead, 2005; Ion, Smith, & Dickens, 2017). In some cases, senior staff seek to ostracise and isolate individuals by undermining their concerns. In other cases, employees who have spoken up have been disciplined, suspended or reported for misconduct to professional bodies. Additionally, the formal investigation process is often traumatic for those who are the subjects of concerns, as well as for bystanders (Attree, 2007; Jackson et al., 2010; Moore & McAuliffe, 2012; Peters et al., 2011). A strong fear of repercussions by colleagues and managers and a desire to 'fit in with the team' can often trump the moral courage required to speak up about concerns (Martinez et al., 2017).

In the United Kingdom (UK) National Health Service (NHS), organisational change to improve how employee concerns are raised and responded to has been driven by high-profile incidents where failure to speak up and/or to be listened to, have been implicated in serious patient safety shortcomings (Department of Health, 2013, 2015b; Gosport Independent Panel, 2018). The urgent need for a change in workplace cultures in relation to openness and learning from employee concerns have resulted in a raft of policies and measures seeking to provide legal, structural and social foundations for culture change in the English NHS (Department of Health, 2015a, 2015b; National Advisory Group on the Safety of Patients in England, 2013; NMC, 2015). The recent 'Freedom to Speak Up Review' (Francis, 2015) led to the development and implementation of the Freedom to Speak Up Guardian (FTSUG[1]) role as a means of normalising the raising of concerns.

In this chapter, we explore the work undertaken by FTSUGs across England in light of data showing the role is predominantly used by staff to raise concerns over transgressive or disruptive behaviours by colleagues, including but not limited to misconduct, incivility, unreasonableness, bullying, harassment, and disrespect[2] (Dixon-Woods et al., 2019). Our data show that FTSUGs were surprised and under-prepared to deal with the large numbers of bullying and harassment concerns, indicating an expectation that most concerns would be related to patient care and safety. We situate the work of Guardians as occurring within complex sociotechnical systems (Braithwaite, 2018), and will demonstrate how workarounds, trade-offs and adjustments are deployed by Guardians in order for the everyday activities related to managing bullying and harassment concerns to succeed. We demonstrate differences between the Guardians' work-as-done (WAD) and work-as-imagined (WAI) within policy documents and guidance. Some of these differences are inevitable given the uniqueness and newness of the FTSUG role. However, we argue that a fuller appreciation of the complex overlaps between speaking up and bullying and harassment within the NHS nationally and more locally at the outset of this major organisational change may have avoided some of the challenging issues now

---

[1] Freedom to Speak Up Guardians will be referred to by the acronym FTSUGs, or the shortened term "Guardian/s".

[2] The term 'bullying and harassment' is used by the NHS and by Guardians/NGO to refer to these behaviours and is therefore used throughout this chapter.

being experienced by Guardians. Our intention is to contribute to a better understanding of the important work of FTSUGs by realigning the two perspectives on their work, rather than insisting that one perspective (usually WAI) is right and the other wrong (usually WAD) (Braithwaite, Wears, & Hollnagel, 2017).

10.2 The FTSUG Role and Their Work

One the most significant tragedies in the history of the English National Health Service (NHS)—the failings at Mid Staffordshire NHS Trusts (Department of Health, 2013)—has significantly impacted on healthcare policy in England (Martin & Dixon-Woods, 2014), including the publication of a review of culture and practice around raising concerns (Francis, 2015). The Francis Review collected evidence from a wide range of sources which showed widespread reluctance to speak up among staff, associated to misgivings about retribution by colleagues and to doubts that authorities would listen and act on concerns raised. As a result, the review recommended several measures to foster a culture of speaking up, including the introduction of a highly innovative new role, the 'Freedom to Speak Up Guardian' (FTSUG), in every healthcare provider in England, overseen by the National Guardian's Office for Speaking up (NGO).

The FTSUG role is founded on three interlinked objectives outlined in the Francis Review (Francis, 2015: p. 12) to:

1. Positively influence employees to speak up by creating an environment where speaking up is 'part of the normal routine business of any well led NHS organisation'.
2. Ensure NHS organisations, both individually and collectively, learn from employees who speak up.
3. Promote culture change that reverses the long record of NHS employees being professionally and personally victimised for raising concerns.

However, minimal guidance was available to guide the initial implementation of the role, with organisational leaders charged with the task of designing a FTSUG role that would work in their own organisations. Largely consistent with the role as broadly set out in the national policy 'Freedom to Speak Up' policy document for NHS England (NHS Improvement, 2016), FTSUGs have been deployed as a means of signposting and coordinating workers who wish to speak up, with two important responsibilities: first, providing independent and impartial support and advice, whilst raising awareness of the range of options available to those with concerns, and second, coordinating the management of concerns with access to anyone in the organisation, including the chief executive, or if necessary, outside the organisation.

Although some guidance has been developed (e.g. a generic FTSUG job description National Guardian Freedom to Speak Up, 2018c), the absence of any centralised directive regarding FTSUG role design and only nominal implementation guidance has led to extreme variance in the deployment and allocation of resources for the role. For example, most FTSUGs undertake the role alongside a substantive existing role. A small number of organisations have implemented a full-time FTSUG role, while some organisations opt to appoint multiple FTSUGs. Variance is also present in the appointment of FTSUGs. Some are appointed formally via an application and interviewing process, while others are invited to take up the role within their organisations with little transparent or formal recruitment processes. Role holders are also drawn from a wide range of healthcare professionals (nurses, doctors, physiotherapists, radiographers. Medicine etc.) and corporate staff (Human Resources, Organisational Development) or "other" e.g. hospital chaplaincy, or those recruited externally with no healthcare/NHS experience (National Guardian Freedom to Speak Up, 2020).

Reporting on the impact of the above variation on the role of the FTSUG is beyond the remit of this chapter. Instead the focus will be the third Francis review objective described above, reflecting the many reports of employees suffering 'routine bullying and harassment' (p. 103) as a result of speaking up. Indeed, NHS staff contributions to the Francis Review referred to bullying and harassment more than any other problem, including frustration that no one appeared to be held accountable for bullying and harassment. Of relevance to this chapter and the work of FTSUGs, the Francis Review draws attention to two types of B&H which 'might inhibit speaking up' (Francis, 2015: p. 200): that which occurs as a direct consequences of staff speaking up, and the more prevalent and endemic incidents of B&H which contribute to creating a hostile workplace culture that is ill-disposed to speaking up.

The theme of bullying and harassment is also a prominent feature in a NGO Annual Report (National Guardian Freedom to Speak Up, 2018a), which reports 45% of the 7087 cases of speaking up brought to FTSUGs in NHS Trusts included an 'element of bullying and harassment' (p. 25), compared to 32% which included an 'element of patient safety'. Although the NGO guidance directs FTSUGs to separately categorise 'patient safety/quality' and 'bullying and harassment' cases (National Guardian Freedom to Speak Up, 2018b) their annual report describes bullying and harassment as a 'latent patient safety issue which, left unchecked, can lead to significant harm to both patients and those who care for them' (p. 4).

The remainder of this chapter further explores B&H in relation to speaking up. We initially define the terms before describing some of the consequences of bullying and harassment and interventions designed to reduce such behaviours occurring. The focus then returns to 'speaking up' and what lessons about B&H can be learnt from our evaluation of the FTSUG role.

10.3 Bullying and Harassment in the NHS

10.3.1 Defining Bullying and Harassment

Globally, nursing, midwifery, medicine and dentistry have been shown to be dogged by bullying within the workforce (Lewis & Kline, 2019). Studies have suggested that workforce bullying occurs more frequently in healthcare than in other sectors, possibly because of the interpersonal and emotional nature of healthcare work, the hierarchical structure of healthcare institutions and the conflicting priorities of multidisciplinary team (Lever, Dyball, Greenberg, & Stevelink, 2019). Most of the NHS in the UK is affected by bullying and harassment, with recent conservative estimates suggesting this costs the NHS £2.28 billion per annum in terms of absenteeism, staff turnover and productivity and industrial relations, compensation and litigation costs (Kline & Lewis, 2019). The 2018 NHS Staff Survey indicates that approximately one in five staff report having experienced bullying and harassment from other colleagues (NHS England, 2019). The NHS (NHS Employers, 2019), referring to The Advisory, Conciliation and Arbitration service (ACAS), define bullying and harassment as:

- **Bullying:** may be characterised as offensive, intimidating, malicious or insulting behaviour, an abuse or misuse of power through means intended to undermine, humiliate, denigrate or injure the recipient. It is unwarranted and unwelcome and may be obvious or it may be insidious.
- **Harassment:** unwanted conduct affecting dignity in the workplace with actions or comments that are viewed as demeaning and unacceptable to the recipient.

Although these definitions capture what bullying and harassment behaviours may look like, they do not explain why it occurs, nor do they fully capture all the behaviours and relational dynamics, which may lead individuals to perceive themselves as being a victim of bullying. Indeed, research suggests huge variation with respect to whether individuals perceive and label negative behaviours as 'bullying' (see Notelaers et al., 2006). The academic literature fails to provide conceptual clarity of what counts as bullying and harassment (Einarsen et al., 2011). For example, some scholars argue that for behaviour to be defined as workplace bullying and harassment, victims have to be subject to persistent negative and aggressive behaviours (Leymann, 1996), yet there is disagreement with respect to how long an individual has to endure negative behaviours before it can be classed as bullying. As Einarsen et al. (2011) argue, single episodes of bullying can be just as catastrophic and consequential for victims. Establishing intent can also be difficult if, for example, a whole team are the target of a supervisor's aggressive behaviour (Einarsen et al., 2011; Fevre et al., 2012). Due to the number of ways bullying can manifest itself measuring bullying and harassment within the workplace is, therefore, a difficult task (Fevre et al. 2012), even where instruments are valid and reliable (Carponecchia & Wyatt, 2011). Intervening in such behaviours in the workplace is also difficult given the variability with respect to how perpetrators, victims and bystanders perceive certain behaviours as constituting bullying and/or harassment, or not.

10.3.2 Why Bullying and Harassment Occurs

Explanations as to why workplace bullying occurs also seem to be contested. Psychology research presents workplace bullying as an interpersonal phenomena where bullying behaviours and perceptions of bullying are attributed to certain individual characteristics. For example, Coyne et al. (2000) found that bullying victims were less extrovert, more submissive and averse to conflict; others attribute bullying to differences in the capacities of bullies and their targets to cope with frustration (Baillien et al. 2009). However, for the most part researchers understand bullying as a multifaceted phenomenon, whereby personality traits represent merely one element (Zapf & Einarsen, 2011), with certain organisational characteristics also being associated with higher incidences of bullying and harassment.

Perhaps pertinent for the high incidences of bullying reported by NHS staff, is research which suggests a correlation between higher incidences of bullying and the work environment (Trépanier, Fernet, Austin, & Boudrias, 2016); for example, organisational factors such as continuous organisational change (Illing et al., 2013) and insufficient resources (Baillien et al. 2009). Broadly speaking, constant reorganisation allied to disorderly change management creates fertile ground for bullying to proliferate (Hodson et al., 2009). From this perspective, organisational processes such as performance targets may legitimise and normalise bullying, especially as targets become more stringent. As Bevan and Hood (2006) argue, when people are pressured to meet a target it is inevitable that their behaviour is altered. Others suggest (Shaw, Taylor, & Dix, 2015) that bullying is a key risk of overzealous management of performance measures within organisations and externally by healthcare regulators and government bodies particularly in failing organisations (Shaw et al., 2015).

Bullying also tends to occur in circumstances where there is a power imbalance between the victim and perpetrator. Power differential may be formal (i.e. managers having more power than subordinates) and/or informal (i.e. knowledge, experiences), which may occur "horizontally" between colleagues at the same organisational level, or where colleagues at a lower level exert "bottom-up" power over those immediately above (Hoel and Cooper, 2000). Nonetheless, within the UK literature reports of bullying predominantly refer to top-down bullying by managers and supervisors to subordinates, with managers responsible for between 70 and 80% of incidences. This also means that managers are also likely to be victimised by their own superiors (Hoel et al., 2001), challenging misconceptions that senior managers and executives may be invulnerable to acts of workplace bullying. Irrespective of the perspective that is taken, research clearly demonstrates that workplace bullying is a complicated phenomenon with a recent review of the nursing literature suggesting

Table 10.1 Examples of some of the overlapping transnational, national and local workplace policy initiatives relevant to bullying and harassment operating within NHS England

Trans-national policy interventions (MACRO)	National policy interventions (MESO)	Local/workplace policy interventions (MICRO)
Charter of Fundamental Rights of the European Union (2000/C364/01) European Union framework on harassment and violence at work	NHS England: Tackling bullying in the NHS. A collective call to action NHS employers: Dignity at work policy UK wide professional standards and regulatory guidance on workplace misconduct e.g. codes of conduct for nursing, dentistry, allied health professionals and medicine	NHS employers: Tackling bullying in ambulance trusts. A guide for action Conflict resolution and grievance procedures and policies Dignity at work champions and training Local staff surveys which explore prevalence and experiences of bullying and harassment behaviours

that individual factors contribute to the occurrent of bullying, but on a more modest scale compared to work environment factors (Trépanier et al., 2016).

10.3.3 Interventions

The pervasiveness and complexity of workplace bullying outlined earlier in the chapter is reflected in the multi-level approaches outlined in Table 10.1 to interventions aimed at prevention, ranging from macro-level trans-national policy intervention, meso-level national and local micro level interventions with teams and individual employees.

However, a recent Cochrane review concluded that although organisation and individual interventions occasionally prevent bullying in the workplace, the evidence was of very low quality with no studies evaluating societal or policy level interventions to prevent bullying at work (Gillen, Sinclair, Kernohan, Begley, & Luyben, 2017). Instead, workplace interventions to date, have tended to focus on trade unions and the development of appropriate Human Resource (HR) policies and processes, reflecting the dominant understanding of bullying as an inter-personal phenomenon.

There is also compelling evidence that bullying cultures within the NHS remain deeply resistant to interventions. For example, as discussed earlier, bullying and harassment is a prevalent concern raised with FTSUGs, suggesting that interventions to curb bullying and harassment have been ineffective and that bullying is normative and not amenable to intervention. Moreover, although thousands of NHS workers have raised bullying concerns via FTSUGs, recent data analysis of the NHS staff survey shows that only half of those who experience bullying report it, which suggests that the scale of the problem may be seriously underreported (Carter et al., 2013). Furthermore, Wood, Niven and Braeken (2016) following their analysis of surveys undertaken with 1472 NHS staff suggest that, as a result of NHS policies not being robust enough to curtail bullying by managers, that NHS workers raise concerns via FTSUGs. Speaking up may then reduce rates of bullying and harassment, whilst also increasing workers' confidence to expose bullying rather than, for example, taking sick leave. This viewpoint echoes the Francis Review's focus on FTSUGs having a role in establishing an organisational culture which ensures concerns are welcomed and handled correctly.

Although NGO data usefully show that thousands of NHS workers have spoken up to FTSUGs about bullying there have been no attempts to provide an in-depth exploration and understanding of how Guardians actually deal with these issues in practice. The following sections attempt to address this gap in understanding by drawing on qualitative data from a recent study of FTSUGs. The analysis presented deepens our understanding of the realities of the difficult, contentious and complex work undertaken by Guardians when dealing with bullying concerns They also demonstrate that practitioners' and policy makers' belief that speaking up to FTSUGs may reduce bullying is problematic for several reasons.

10.4 Guardians Views and Experiences of Practically Dealing with Bullying Concerns

During 2018/2019 we sought to sample 70 FTSUGs from Acute Trusts and 30 from Mental Health Trusts from a national population at the time of FTSUGs in 169 Acute trusts and 54 Mental health trusts. However, some organisations had vacancies for their FTSUG roles, or had appointed more than one FTSUG. The final sample for the semi-structured telephone interviews consisted of 87 FTSUGs working in Acute Trusts (n = 64) and Mental Health Trusts (n = 23) in all ten regions of NHS England. Although this is by far the largest dataset collected on the daily working practices of FTSUGs, it is important to bear in mind that FTSUGs are deployed across a number of different types of NHS organisations not captured here (e.g. Ambulance Services) (Table 10.2).

The interviews were collected, following Research Ethics Committee Approval, during one phase of a larger study evaluating the implementation of the FTSUG role across England. Guardians were initially invited to participate in the study via email addresses provided on the register of Guardians which is publicly accessible on the NGO website. Those wishing to participate in the interviews responded to the email

Table 10.2 FTSUG interview response rates

	Total
Total FTSUGs contacted	255
FTSUGs responded	105
FTSUGs interviewed	87
% of total responded	41.2%
% of total interviewed	34.1%
% interviewed after responding	82.9%

indicating their willingness and were then sent further information, in the form of a participant information sheet, by the researchers. A date was then arranged for the telephone interview and verbal consent was provided at the outset of the interview. The interviews were digitally recorded, uploaded to NVivo and thematically analysed.

The qualitative findings presented here both corroborate and provide further depth to the insights provided by the NGO and NHS staff survey data discussed above. For example, interviewees described how most speak up concerns received related to bullying and harassment by colleagues.

> *I thought this role was about patient safety post Mid Staffs. But most concerns are bullying and harassment not patient safety. B&H such a big thing and is such a cultural thing, people raise it more than anything else (WP2: 54)*

> *30% just patient safety, the rest, tend to be behavioural and bullying or cultural issues which also includes some of the patient safety issues. Hundreds of staff in two years have spoken up, general themes are relationships, behaviours, perceptions of bullying and victimization (WP2: 27)*

Providing further depth to the earlier discussed survey data interviewees discussed how staff were fearful of speaking up to FTSUGs, for example:

> *staff are worried about implications of speaking up, particularly when the concern is about a team member or line manager and speak up issue is about bullying behaviours, worried they will fall out of favour and could suffer detriment (WP2: 09)*

> *cultural issues with bullying and harassment are harder to come forward about. People will cope with it or will only come forward if there's more people. Staff will also often report these elsewhere to HR and issues won't be dealt with (WP2: 53)*

Some FTSUGs were surprised by the prevalence of bullying concerns of staff, believing patient safety concerns would, or should be, raised more often. FTSUGs also discussed how bullying concerns were overly and 'incorrectly' occupying their time.

> *Bullying and harassment is the top number of cases every quarter. I do get patient safety concerns but not as much as I should or as often as you would think (WP2: 52)*

> *I feel bullying and harassment has incorrectly taken over the role. The role is there for patient safety, although I acknowledge team bullying can impact on patient safety or quality (WP2: 22)*

Guardians' views differed regarding how to respond to mounting numbers of bullying and harassment concerns. Their role is to support and empower workers to speak up through appropriate channels, not to investigate concerns. However, some were happy to take on these concerns despite acknowledging they could have been dealt with by pre-existing HR processes. As demonstrated in the following quote others felt differently, expressing fears that FTSUGs had to contain their workload by not becoming embroiled with bullying concerns that were better dealt with by HR

> *I will talk to someone about bullying and harassment but will then tend to signpost those experiencing bullying and harassment to HR or to a union rep and following bullying and harassment policy. I don't think people would be able to cope with the Guardian role if they*

dealt with things HR should be dealing with. I feel Guardians are becoming a staff rep and getting involved in HR processes. I wouldn't be able to do the job properly if I spent time dealing with bullying and harassment. There are a whole team of HR staff who are trained to do this. (WP2: 22)

A point frequently made was that bullying concerns could usefully provide intelligence and insights into patient safety concerns, as further illustrated in the following extract

Bullying can be complicated and one of the things I have picked up on is if you have a dysfunctional team, patient safety issues may become issues later on. Poor team dynamics equals a precursor event for patient safety (WP2: 75)

However, echoing the literature reviewed earlier, the following extracts reflect the inherent complications and difficulties of establishing what exactly constitutes bullying behaviours

Is it bullying or is it more just inappropriate behaviour? One person's bullying is another's robust management (WP2: 46)

The majority of them would be what we class as bullying and harassment or management issues but the definition of the categories, I don't know what constitutes bullying and harassment, is it down to what the person feels it is? I don't know (WP2:34)

A lot of the concerns are about people management and people not being treated fairly. But also bad behaviour is tolerated and not addressed, but it's bad people management. Sometimes it's bullying and sometimes it's not, it depends on what the person is experiencing (WP2:20)

The NGO provides guidance to FTSUGs on how to record incidences of bullying and harassment, but Guardians described how this lacked clarity and how they would welcome training opportunities to better count and understand these issues. Questions were also raised about how such difficulties impacted on the quality and accuracy of the bullying and harassment data.

I find the NGO categories challenging, because to me they're a bit indiscriminate and I don't believe we have been properly trained on how to apply them. So I find them a bit arbitrary (WP2:33)

I log as close as I can to the (NGO) guidance, because that's just a framework to follow, but actually there are fine lines between bullying and harassment and behaviours and relationships... and patient safety. So, I think the quality of the data collected is not great across the board (WP2: 04)

I feel that data collected by NGO is not useful in regard to bullying and harassment. I feel we are all reporting it very differently so I am not sure the collation of that information is as accurate as it could be (WP2: 21)

To summarise, more staff concerns about bullying behaviours by staff are received than any other types of concerns raised. Some FTSUGs expressed surprise and personal discontent about dealing with the large number of bullying concerns as these deflected from, in their view, the "true" patient safety remit of the role. In addition, frustration and doubt was expressed about counting bullying concerns separately from other concerns. Some FTSUGs described this as a reductive approach which failed to capture contextual nuances and how, rather than being isolated, such behaviours are often interwoven within daily working life and can be symptomatic of deeper systemic cultural and patient safety issues.

10.5 Discussion and Conclusion

Through the words and experiences of the Guardians interviewed we see a role beset by complexity and emergence. This is particularly the case as the majority of the concerns raised with Guardians relate to often time-consuming, contentious and antagonistic cases of staff bullying and harassment. Researchers undertaking critical analysis of such complex new roles such as FTSUGs often benefit from hindsight unavailable to those implementing such roles. However, in this case, for the reasons outlined earlier in the chapter, it was completely foreseeable that bullying would figure significantly in the daily work of FTSUGs. For example, extensive evidence in the form of international literature on bullying in healthcare, numerous annual staff survey results and the 2015 Francis Review all identified bullying as a major problem that has long been resistant to a variety of interventions. Furthermore, much of the complexity was also highly predictable given that the evidence clearly portrays the act of speaking up about bullying as a multifaceted and intersecting organisational issue.

This makes the absence of specific preparation and guidance puzzling. For example, guidance and training material to prepare FTSUGs to undertake this important role are very general with no direct reference to the considerable individual and organisational challenges presented by bullying cultures, or how to deal with these. The role description for FTSUGs (National Guardian Freedom to Speak Up, 2018c) contains no reference to bullying and harassment despite extensive and disturbing coverage of this in the Speak Up Review which led to the establishment of the role.

The 'Guardian Education and Training Guide' (National Guardian Freedom to Speak Up, 2018b) also contains no specific guidance on dealing with bullying and harassment concerns, providing guidance only in terms of how to count such information for collection and dissemination by the NGO. Some of those we interviewed expressed deep disappointment and discontent when discussing the guidance and support available to them. Similarly, NHS Trusts who are responsible for implementation and deployment of the FTSUG role have provided little or no training and/or guidance and/or little support for Guardians to undertake some of the most difficult and toxic work imaginable. The Guardians interviewed were clear that organisations and bodies at macro (National) and meso (Trust) level are not meeting the needs and expectations of Guardians.

Reflecting and understanding such discrepancies between "work as imagined" (WAI) and "work as done" (WAD) is important for a number of reasons (Braithwaite et al., 2017). For example, the dangerous consequences for patient safety of designing medical devices for an imagined clinical world, rather than for the actual clinical world inhabited by healthcare professionals have been highlighted. Others point to the difficulties and tensions practitioners face when standardised procedures clash with professional judgment (Hannigan, Simpson, Coffey, Barlow, & Jones, 2018; Thomas, Phipps, & Ashcroft, 2016). As Hannigan et al. (2018) outline, this distinction between WAI and WAD is of more than simply abstract interest. Designing policies, standards or guidance for a world of work which is not real has consequences. For example, we have repeatedly identified shortcomings in, or the absence of, speak up guidance and policies and how these impact on the accomplishment of everyday work and the working experiences of Guardians. Operating under such challenging and stressful prevailing circumstance we see Guardians having to frequently interpret and adapt their work activities in order to achieve their goals; thus, divergence is created between their work as imagined (in guidance and policies, for example around what constitutes a B&H concern and how to count concerns) and their work as done (in actual practices, for example B&H and patient safety concerns which do not comfortably fit with guidance on counting concerns). Such strained relationships between practices and procedures can also be understood in terms of organisational resilience (or the lack of), that is, the ability of an organisation or its members to maintain effective and efficient work in the face of challenging contingencies (Thomas et al., 2016).

In addition to the potential organisational costs of bullying, the direct human costs of bullying and harassment are potentially widespread and serious and can be divided into consequences which threaten the overall wellbeing of the individual worker and patients (Layne, Nemeth, Mueller, & Martin, 2019). In terms of individual employees and staff wellbeing, Lever et al.'s (2019) systematic review findings suggest that regular bullying frequently results in adverse consequences for mental and physical health. Unsurprisingly, organisations with high incidences of bullying are likely to suffer from worsening productivity, higher staff turnover, and increased incidences of sickness absence or, conversely, presenteeism (Escartín, 2016). Interestingly, Escartín's (2016) systematic review described how individual consequences can also occasionally spread to the team level, affecting the intention to leave of employees who were not direct targets of bullying. However, there is little or no literature about the individual experiences and personal costs to those who are responsible within organisations for supporting victims and for resolving concerns related to bullying and harassment. This is a significant gap in the literature and of particular relevance given the frequency with which FTSUGs are called on to undertake both of these responsibilities.

In terms of patient safety outcomes, staff who experience diminished psychological safety at work are less likely to seek help, to discuss errors or inform one another of problems (Pearson & Porath, 2009: pp. 81–82). A person who is bullied can feel incompetent and incapable in their work, get flustered and as a result errors may occur, putting the patient at risk. Carter et al. (2013) found that several participants who were bullied commonly reported an inability to think straight and concentrate on procedures and tasks they were undertaking for patients. Even mild rudeness and incivility common in medical practice was shown to have adverse consequences on

Table 10.3 Key messages

Key messages for researchers	Key messages for healthcare delivery
Effects of dealing with bullying and harassment concerns can be corrosive to FTSUGs (and others) wellbeing. More research is required to better understand the support needs of those dealing with such concerns.	More sophisticated change models, support and guidance which better reflects the complex realities of FTSUG work in dealing with bullying and harassment cases are required.
Timely complex interventions, which tackle concerns of bullying and harassment in the workplace at an earlier stage than presently is the case, need to be developed and tested. For example, induction training at the commencement of employment is routinely undertaken, but there is little known about effectiveness of this training or whether/how often it should be repeated to employees.	A "siloed" mind-set which separately counts and reports bullying and harassment concerns to other concerns can prove overly reductive and a barrier to "joined up" learning about concerns. More "joined up" approaches require closer working across disciplinary and organisational boundaries e.g. HR, patient safety teams and clinical leaders need to triangulate and cross-reference data to look for emergent patterns of various transgressive behaviours.
FTSUGs require better information, training and guidance related to dealing with bullying and harassment concerns.	Implementation of speak up initiatives should not merely be based on effective resource planning, but anticipation of a range of possible unexpected or unintended outcomes. For example, organisations who allocate little or no ring-fenced time, or only 1 day a week or less for FTSUGs to undertake their role does not effectively anticipate the complexity of properly dealing with and supporting staff concerns.

the diagnostic and procedural performance of team members, often resulting in profound, if not devastating, effects on patient care (Riskin et al., 2015).

To conclude, the introduction of FTSUGs heralded unprecedented organisational changes to the handing of speaking up cases in NHS England. However, the implementation of the FTSUG role has only been guided in a minimal way by national bodies, a decision that has its origins in the policy document which first introduced the FTSUG role. Specifically, the Francis Review provided little guidance on role implementation, instead leaving executive boards at liberty to 'decide what is appropriate for their organization' (p. 16). Subsequent national guidelines and local implementation approaches have similarly lacked detail and direction. Designing a resilient FTSUG system therefore requires a much deeper understanding and analysis of their work as it is actually carried out. The value of knowing how (and what) Guardians do is crucial for the future success of the role and the wellbeing of those undertaking the role. This chapter contributes a better understanding of the gaps between WAI and WAD and strongly recommends the need for further understanding, discussion and realignment between these two divergent perspectives on the work of FTSUGs (Table 10.3).

Funding Acknowledgement This study/project is funded by the National Institute for Health Research (NIHR) Heath Services and Delivery Research Programme (project reference 16/116/25). The views expressed are those of the author(s) and not necessarily those of the NIHR or the Department of Health and Social Care.

We would like to thank Claire Simpson for her excellent administrative support for this project and all those FTSUGs who agreed to be interviewed.

References

Attree, M. (2007). Factors influencing nurses' decisions to raise concerns about care quality. *Journal of Nursing Management, 15*(4), 392–402. https://doi.org/10.1111/j.1365-2834.2007.00679.x

Baillien, E., Neyens, I., Witte, H. D., & Cuyper, N. D. (2009). A qualitative study on the development of workplace bullying: Towards a three way model. *Journal of Community and Applied Social Psychology, 19*, 1–16. https://doi.org/10.1002/casp.977

Beckstead, J. W. (2005). Reporting peer wrongdoing in the healthcare profession: The role of incompetence and substance abuse information. *International Journal of Nursing Studies, 42*(3), 325–331. https://doi.org/10.1016/j.ijnurstu.2004.07.003

Bevan, G., & Hood, C. (2006). What's measured is what matters: Targets and gaming in the English public health care system. *Public Administration, 84*(3), 517–538. https://doi.org/10.1111/j.1467-9299.2006.00600.x

Braithwaite, J. (2018). Changing how we think about healthcare improvement. *BMJ, 361*, k2014. https://doi.org/10.1136/bmj.k2014

Braithwaite, J., Wears, R., & Hollnagel, E. (2017). Preface in Braithwaite, *J. Resilient Health Care 3:236.* [Vital Source Bookshelf]. https://bookshelf.vitalsource.com/#/books/9781498780575/.

Carponecchia, C., & Wyatt, A. (2011). *Preventing workplace bullying: An evidence-based guide for managers and employees.* London: Routledge.

Carter, M., Thompson, N., Crampton, P., Morrow, G., Burford, B., Gray, C., et al. (2013). Workplace bullying in the UK NHS: a questionnaire and interview study on prevalence, impact and barriers to reporting. *BMJ Open, 3*, e002628. https://doi.org/10.1136/bmjopen-2013-002628

Coyne, I., Seigne, E., & Randall, P. (2000). Predicting workplace victim status from personality. *European Journal of Work and Organizational Psychology, 9*, 335–349. https://doi.org/10.1080/135943200417957

Department of Health. (2013). *Report of the mid Staffordshire NHS foundation trust public inquiry.* http://webarchive.nationalarchives.gov.uk/20150407084003/http://www.midstaffspublicinquiry.com/sites/default/files/report/Volume%201.pdf.

Department of Health. (2015a). *Culture change in the NHS. Applying the lessons of the Francis inquiries.* https://www.gov.uk/government/uploads/system/uploads/attachment_data/file/403010/culture-change-nhs.pdf?utm_source=The+King%27s+Fund+newsletters&utm_medium=email&utm_campaign=5339790_HMP+2015-02-13&dm_i=21A8,36G7I,FLXCFP,BE3O0,1.

Department of Health. (2015b). *Learning not blaming: Response to three reports on patient safety.* https://www.gov.uk/government/publications/learning-not-blaming-response-to-3-reports-on-patient-safety?utm_source=The+King%27s+Fund+newsletters&utm_medium=email&utm_campaign=5931986_HMP+2015-07-17&dm_i=21A8,3J55E,FLXCFP,COENG,1.

Dixon-Woods, M., Campbell, A., Martin, G., Willars, J., Tarrant, C., Aveling, E.-L., et al. (2019). Improving employee voice about transgressive or disruptive behavior: A case study. *Academic Medicine, 94*(4), 579–585. https://doi.org/10.1097/ACM.0000000000002447

Einarsen, S., Hoel, H., Zapf, D., & Cooper, C. L. (2011). The concept of bullying and harassment at work: The European tradition. In S. Einarsen, H. Hoel, D. Zapf, & C. L. Cooper (Eds.), *Bullying and harassment in the workplace: Developments in theory, research, and practice* (2nd ed., pp. 3–39).

Escartín, J. (2016). Insights into workplace bullying: Psychosocial drivers and effective interventions. *Psychology Research and Behavior Management, 9*, 157–169. https://doi.org/10.2147/PRBM.S91211

Fevre, R., Lewis, D., Jones, T., & Robinson, A. (2012). Trouble at work. London: Bloomsbury.

Francis. (2015). *Freedom to speak up. An independent review into creating an open and honest reporting culture in the NHS*. https://freedomtospeakup.org.uk/wp-content/uploads/2014/07/F2SU_web.pdf?utm_source=The+King%27s+Fund+newsletters&utm_medium=email&utm_campaign=5339790_HMP+2015-02-13&dm_i=21A8,36G7I,FLXCFP,BE2C8,1.

Gillen, P. A., Sinclair, M., Kernohan, W. G., Begley, C. M., & Luyben, A. G. (2017). Interventions for prevention of bullying in the workplace. *The Cochrane Database of Systematic Reviews, 1*(1), CD009778–CD009778. https://doi.org/10.1002/14651858.CD009778.pub2

Gosport Independent Panel. (2018). *Gosport war memorial hospital. The report of the Gosport independent Panel*. https://www.gosportpanel.independent.gov.uk/media/documents/070618_CCS207_CCS03183220761_Gosport_Inquiry_Whole_Document.pdf

Hannigan, B., Simpson, A., Coffey, M., Barlow, S., & Jones, A. (2018). Care coordination as imagined, care coordination as done: findings from a cross-national mental health systems study. *International Journal of Integrated Care 18*(3), 12. https://doi.org/10.5334/ijic.3978. http://orca.cf.ac.uk/view/cardiffauthors/A0003188.html, http://orca.cf.ac.uk/view/cardiffauthors/A3265606.html, https://doi.org/10.5334/ijic.3978 file http://orca.cf.ac.uk/113348/8/Hannigan%20et%20al%20%282018%29.pdf

Hodson, G., Hogg, S., & Macinnis, C. (2009). The role of "dark personalities" (narcissism, Machiavellianism, psychopathy), Big Five personality factors, and ideology in explaining prejudice. *Journal of Research in Personality, 43*, 686–690. https://doi.org/10.1016/j.jrp.2009.02.005

Hoel, H., & Cooper, C. L. (2000). *Destructive conflict & bullying at work*. Manchester: Manchester School of Management, University of Manchester, Institute of Science and Technology.

Hoel, H., Cooper, C. L., & Faragher, B. (2001). Workplace bullying in Great Britain: The impact of occupational status. *European Journal of Work and Organisational Psychology, 10*, 443–465.

Illing, J., Burford, B., Morrow, G., Carter, M., Thompson, N., & Crampton, P. (2013). *Evidence synthesis on the occurrence, causes, consequences, prevention and management of bullying and harassing behaviours to inform decision-making in the NHS*. https://www.journalslibrary.nihr.ac.uk/programmes/hsdr/10101201/#/.

Ion, R., Smith, K., & Dickens, G. (2017). Nursing and midwifery students' encounters with poor clinical practice: A systematic review. *Nurse Education in Practice, 23*, 67–75. https://doi.org/10.1016/j.nepr.2017.02.010

Jackson, D., Peters, K., Andrew, S., Edenborough, M., Halcomb, E., Luck, L., et al. (2010). Understanding whistleblowing: Qualitative insights from nurse whistleblowers. *Journal of Advanced Nursing, 66*(10), 2194–2201.

Jones, A., & Kelly, D. (2014a). Deafening silence? Time to reconsider whether organisations are silent or deaf when things go wrong. *BMJ Quality & Safety, 23*(9), 709–713. https://doi.org/10.1136/bmjqs-2013-002718

Jones, A., & Kelly, D. (2014b). Whistle-blowing and workplace culture in older peoples' care: Qualitative insights from the healthcare and social care workforce. *Sociology of Health & Illness, 36*(7), 986–1002. https://doi.org/10.1111/1467-9566.12137

Kline, R., & Lewis, D. (2019). The price of fear: Estimating the financial cost of bullying and harassment to the NHS in England. *Public Money & Management, 39*(3), 166–174. https://doi.org/10.1080/09540962.2018.1535044

Layne, D. M., Nemeth, L. S., Mueller, M., & Martin, M. (2019). Negative behaviors among healthcare professionals: Relationship with patient safety culture. *Healthcare (Basel, Switzerland), 7*(1), 23. https://doi.org/10.3390/healthcare7010023

Lever, I., Dyball, D., Greenberg, N., & Stevelink, S. (2019). Health consequences of bullying in the healthcare workplace: A systematic review. *Journal Of Advanced Nursing, Online Early, 75*, 3195–3209. https://doi.org/10.1111/jan.13986

Lewis, D., & Kline, R. (2019). Tackling bullying and harassment in the NHS: The critical roles played by managers. *British Journal of Healthcare Management, 25*(1), 7–10. https://doi.org/10.12968/bjhc.2019.25.1.7

Leymann, H. (1996). The content and development of mobbing at work. *European Journal of Work and Organizational Psychology, 5*, 165–184. https://doi.org/10.1080/13594329608414853

Mannion, R., & Davies, H. T. O. (2015). Cultures of silence and cultures of voice: The role of whistleblowing in healthcare Organisations. *International Journal of Health Policy and Management, 4*(8), 503–505.

Martin, G. P., & Dixon-Woods, M. (2014). After mid Staffordshire: From acknowledgement, through learning, to improvement. *BMJ Quality & Safety, 23*(9), 706–708. https://doi.org/10.1136/bmjqs-2014-003359

Martinez, W., Lehmann, L. S., Thomas, E. J., Etchegaray, J. M., Shelburne, J. T., Hickson, G. B., et al. (2017). Speaking up about traditional and professionalism-related patient safety threats: A national survey of interns and residents. *BMJ Quality and Safety, 26*, 869–880. https://doi.org/10.1136/bmjqs-2016-006284

Moore, L., & McAuliffe, E. (2012). To report or not to report? Why some nurses are reluctant to whistleblow. *Clinical Governance: An International Journal, 17*(4), 332–342. https://doi.org/10.1108/14777271211273215

Morrow, K., Gustavson, A., & Jones, J. (2016). Speaking up behaviours (safety voices) of healthcare workers: A met synthesis of qualitative research studies. *International Journal of Nursing Studies, 64*, 42–51. https://doi.org/10.1016/j.ijnurstu.2016.09.014

National Advisory Group on the Safety of Patients in England. (2013). *A promise to learn—A commitment to act: Improving the safety of patients in England*. London: Department of Health.

National Guardian Freedom to Speak Up. (2018a). *Annual report 2018*. https://www.cqc.org.uk/sites/default/files/CCS119_CCS0718215408-001_NGO%20Annual%20Report%202018_WEB_Accessible-2.pdf

National Guardian Freedom to Speak Up. (2018b). *Guardian education and training guide*.

National Guardian Freedom to Speak Up. (2018c). *Job description: Freedom to speak up Guardian*. https://www.cqc.org.uk/national-guardians-office/content/publications

National Guardian Freedom to Speak Up. (2020). *Freedom to Speak Up Guardian Survey 2019*. https://www.nationalguardian.org.uk/publications/

NHS Employers. (2019). *Tackling bullying in the NHS*. http://www.nhsemployers.org/retention and staff experience/tackling bullying in the nhs

NHS England (2019) *NHS Staff Survey Results*. Available from https://www.nhsstaffsurveys.com/Page/1085/Latest-Results/NHS-Staff-Survey-Results/

NHS Improvement. (2016). *Freedom to speak up: Raising concerns (whistleblowing) policy for the NHS*. https://improvement.nhs.uk/resources/freedom-to-speak-up-whistleblowing-policy-for-the-nhs/

NMC. (2015). *Raising concerns. Guidance for nurses and midwives*. https://www.nmc.org.uk/globalassets/sitedocuments/annual_reports_and_accounts/raising-concerns-10-june-2015-2.pdf

Notelaers, G., Einarsen, S., Witte, H. D., & Vermunt, J. K. (2006). Measuring exposure to bullying at work: The validity and advantages of the latent class cluster approach. *Work and Stress, 20*, 289–302. https://doi.org/10.1080/02678370601071594

Peters, K., Luck, L., Hutchinson, M., Wilkes, L., Andrew, S., & Jackson, D. (2011). The emotional sequelae of whistleblowing: Findings from a qualitative study. *Journal of Clinical Nursing, 20*(19–20), 2907–2914. https://doi.org/10.1111/j.1365-2702.2011.03718.x

Riskin, A., Erez, A., Foulk, T. A., Kugelman, A., Gover, A., Shoris, I., et al. (2015). The impact of rudeness on medical team performance: A randomized trial. *Pediatrics, 136*(3), 487–495. https://doi.org/10.1542/peds.2015-1385

Royal College of Physicians. (2015). *Work and wellbeing in the NHS: Why staff health matters to patient care*. https://www.rcplondon.ac.uk/guidelines-policy/work-and-wellbeing-nhs-why-staff-health-matters-patient-care

Shaw, J., Taylor, R., & Dix, K. (2015). *Uses and abuses of performance data in healthcare*. Dr Foster. https://www.patientlibrary.net/tempgen/29702.pdf

Thomas, C. E. L., Phipps, D. L., & Ashcroft, D. M. (2016). When procedures meet practice in community pharmacies: Qualitative insights from pharmacists and pharmacy support staff. *BMJ Open, 6*(6), e010851. https://doi.org/10.1136/bmjopen-2015-010851

Trépanier, S.-G., Fernet, C., Austin, S., & Boudrias, V. (2016). Work environment antecedents of bullying: A review and integrative model applied to registered nurses. *International Journal of Nursing Studies, 55*, 85–97. https://doi.org/10.1016/j.ijnurstu.2015.10.001

Wood, S., Niven, K., & Braeken, J. (2016). Managerial abuse and the process of absence among mental health staff—Stephen Wood, Karen Niven, Johan Braeken, 2016. *Work, Employment and Society, 30*(5), 783–801.

Zapf, D., & Einarsen, S. (2011). Individual antecedents of bullying: Victims and perpetrators. In S. Einarsen, H. Hoel, D. Zapf, & C. L. Cooper (Eds.), *Bullying and harsassment in the workplace: Developments in Theory, Research, and Practice* (pp. 177–200). London: Taylor & Francis.

Part III
Developing Cultures that Enable Organisational Change

Chapter 11
Between Taking Care of Others and Yourself: The Role of Work Recovery in Health Professionals

Claudia L. Rus, Cristina C. Vâjâean, Cătălina Oțoiu, and Adriana Băban

11.1 Introduction

Patient safety pertains to more than just the competent medical act in itself. The World Health Organization defines it as "the prevention of errors and adverse effects to patients associated with health care". Ever since 1999, when the Institute of Medicine (IOM) released the extensively cited "To Err is Human: Building a Safer Health System", patient safety has been the focus of numerous studies that have tried to explain both the potential impact of errors in health care on patient safety, and potential ways to counteract their damaging effect (Lawati, Dennis, Short, & Abdulhadi, 2018).

As such, existing literature to date comprises of a large number of studies that discussed antecedents to patient safety. Their focus, however, varies. Most concentrate on individual level factors such as burnout and stress levels (Chuang, Tseng, Lin, Lin, & Chen, 2016), fatigue and recovery (Blasche, Bauböck, & Haluza, 2017), or individual judgments on risk assessment (Chipps et al., 2011; Faye et al., 2010). Other studies, look into team level factors like communication (Botti et al., 2009), implicit and explicit coordination (Kolbe et al., 2014), leadership (Clarke, Lerner, & Marella, 2007), collective vigilance (Jeffs, Lingard, Berta, & Baker, 2012). And finally, an important trend in the existing literature is an investigation of organizational level factors such as safety culture (Lawati et al., 2018; Verbakel, Langelaan, Verheij, Wagner, & Zwart, 2016) and management systems, tools and procedures (Harrison et al., 2015). Because of this variety in research directions, there have been calls in more recent studies to better integrate the existing knowledge and offer a framework that could lead to a better understanding of how patient safety can be

---

C. L. Rus · C. C. Vâjâean · C. Oțoiu · A. Băban (✉)
Babeș-Bolyai University, Cluj-Napoca, Romania
e-mail: adrianababan@psychology.ro

reached (Welp & Manser, 2016). In their systematic review on teamwork, clinician wellbeing and patient safety, Welp and Manser (2016) argue that there are inconsistencies in the way that these concepts (especially patient safety) are operationalized and measured, and they propose a framework to help integrate the relationships between them. One of their more important arguments is that the relationship between clinician wellbeing and patient safety is in fact reciprocal, and not just one sided from wellbeing to patient safety. They explain that this particular relationship is studied mostly in terms of negative ties between the two, with two major reasoning lines concerning these ties. First, some of the research they reviewed showed that high levels of strain, stress and burnout lead to a number of increased medical errors, which in turn lead to low patient safety outcomes. On the other hand, committing an error (which means low patient safety) leads to increased emotional distress levels for clinicians. Existing evidence supports both lines of reasoning, which suggests one could enter a vicious cycle where lowered wellbeing consistently leads to lower patient safety, which in turn has further damaging effects on wellbeing.

We propose to develop their argument by introducing the concept of recovery from work as a potential process that can break this cycle.

The cognitive, emotional and physical resources one individual can invest in their work are limited and should be replenished daily, after work, by engaging in activities that require a different set of resources (Sonnentag, Venz, & Casper, 2017). When this does not happen, each subsequent workday drains furthermore on the existing resources and requires additional effort from the individual to deal with work tasks. This, in time, leads to stress, chronic fatigue, and burnout (Elfering, Grebner, Semmer, & Gerber, 2002). Work recovery is exactly about replenishing ones' resources so that the individual is protected from the adverse effects of occupational stress on ones' wellbeing. Furthermore, recovering from work not only helps individuals by repairing negative strain effects, but can also catalyze the activation of job resources. In a daily diary study that simultaneously examined the relationship between job resources and recovery on the between-person level and the within-person (day) level, Niks, Gevers, de Jonge, and Houtman (2016) found that detachment from work in the evening is positively related to the state of being recovered at the beginning of the working day, and that the state of being recovered is positively related to the level of job resources. Job resources were considered as the aggregated score of cognitive (i.e., the opportunity to determine a variety of task aspects and to use problem-solving skills), emotional (i.e., emotional support from colleagues or supervisors), and physical (i.e., instrumental support from colleagues and supervisors, or ergonomic aids at work) job resources.

The focus of this chapter is to integrate the literature on work recovery in healthcare settings. However, we keep in mind that by doing this we can better understand the role that recovery from work has in the relationship between clinicians' wellbeing and the outcome of patient safety.

In the last decade, research interest in recovery and unwinding from work demands has shown a substantial increase (Sonnentag & Fritz, 2018). Several reviews and meta-analyses in samples of employees from various organizational contexts discussed and evidenced the benefits of work recovery on various individual, group and organizational-level outcomes (Bennett, Bakker, & Field, 2018; Sonnentag & Fritz, 2018; Steed, Swider, Keem, & Liu, 2019). There is, however, no integration of the research conducted on the topic of recovery from work in medical contexts, although studies have shown that healthcare professionals report longer working hours, less leisure time, shorter amounts of sleep than average working adults (Cranley, Cunningham, & Pandac, 2015) and high levels of burnout (Alexandrova-Karamanova et al., 2016). There is evidence that work-related variables such as these can hinder recovery from work in healthcare professionals (Fritz & Crain, 2016; Poulsen, Poulsen, Khan, Poulsen, & Khan, 2015). As such, healthcare professionals seem to be more prone to job strain and, at the same time, they may experience fewer opportunities to replenish and activate their job resources through work recovery. We believe a systemic, integrated view of recovery from work in medical settings would benefit both research and practice in a few ways. First of all, there have been calls in the literature, to not just focus independently on either antecedents or consequences of a particular construct but to try and bridge them in order to obtain a clearer picture of the mechanisms behind that construct. For example, in a recent discussion on burnout in healthcare Montgomery and his colleagues stress the importance of researching burnout in a systemic manner, where multiple inputs and outputs are considered, and they span over individual, team and organizational levels (Montgomery, Panagopoulou, Esmail, Richards, & Maslach, 2019). Welp and Manser (2016) also suggest integrating fragmented knowledge in such a way that we can explore more than just one-way effects and look into reciprocal effects between constructs. As we have explained before, in their systematic review of teamwork, clinicians' wellbeing and patient safety they link team level processes (teamwork processes) with individual level states (wellbeing) and work and organizational outcomes (patient safety). Their framework suggests that there are reciprocal influences between clinicians' wellbeing and patient safety that are not sufficiently explored. We suggest that recovery from work experiences could help improve wellbeing and hence reduce human errors that negatively impact patient safety. We also argue that work recovery experiences could also help healthcare professionals to overcome instances where their work had a negative impact on patient safety and thus prevent incidents at work from affecting their wellbeing too severely. But to be able to find these linkages we need to understand both antecedents and consequences of work recovery, both the strains of the job and the resources that are available. Finally, we need to have a better understanding of the context where healthcare professional work so that we can identify not just individual level effects, but team level and organizational level effects as well. There is a chain of events here that can only be unfolded when one connects the various pieces of information on work recovery available in the literature. The framework we propose answers these calls by integrating multilevel antecedents and consequences of recovery from work. Another benefit of offering an integrated view of work recovery is that it allows us to identify gaps in the literature that should afford ground for developing the theory on recovery from work. Last, but not least, understanding the complex linkages work recovery has with other individual, team level and organizational processes can help us better inform and pinpoint specific interventions on supporting the development and practice of work recovery experiences that are tailored to the specificities of the medical context.

In consequence, the present chapter offers an integrative review of the literature on recovery from work in healthcare professionals by addressing the multilevel antecedents and consequences of work recovery within the complex specificities of medical settings. In developing the model presented in Fig. 11.1, we capitalized on existing frameworks in the field of team effectiveness (e.g., Mathieu, Maynard, Rapp, & Gilson, 2008; Mathieu & Gilson, 2012; Mathieu, Gallagher, Domingo, & Klock, 2019), organizational behavior (e.g., Buchanan & Huczynski, 2017) and the body of research on work recovery highlighting that recovery is influenced by, and influences, both work domain and non–work domain factors (Edwards & Rothbard, 2000; Sonnentag, 2003; Sonnentag & Fritz, 2018). As there are multiple perspectives on work recovery, for the purposes of the present chapter, we consider work recovery only from a process perspective. As such, work recovery refers to leisure activities and non-work experiences that lead to a change in physiological and psychological strain levels (Sonnentag & Fritz, 2018), by facilitating the reduction of strains and replenishment of resources (Sonnentag & Geurts, 2009). Our chapter has a particular focus on work recovery experiences such as psychological detachment, relaxation, mastery experiences, and control.

11.1.1 The Construct of Recovery Experiences

Recovery refers to a process in which individual functional systems, that have been called upon during a stressful experience, return to their pre-stressor levels (Meijman & Mulder, 1998). The recovery process can be seen as opposite to strain. It results in the restoration of impaired mood and action prerequisites, and is often also reflected in a decrease in physiological strain indicators. This definition emphasizes two aspects of the process of recovery from work: *the process itself* (actions) and the results of this process, *the outcome*. Work recovery can be conceptualized as both (Sonnentag & Fritz, 2018; Sonnentag et al., 2017; Steed et al., 2019). When considered as an outcome, work recovery refers to reduced physiological and psychological strain levels after a recovery period, a state or feeling resulting from engagement in non-work activities. As a process, work recovery refers to leisure activities and non-work experiences that lead to a change in physiological and psychological strain levels (Sonnentag & Fritz, 2018), by facilitating the reduction of strains and the replenishment of resources (Sonnentag & Geurts, 2009). In this process perspective on work recovery, some research has focused on specific activities (i.e., particular behaviors) including replenishing and demanding activities, while others have focused on the psychological experiences (i.e., perceptions and psychological processes underlying those behaviors). Besides recovery activities themselves (i.e., what people are doing), their associated experiences and meanings (i.e., how are people experiencing what they are doing) are those that matter more in

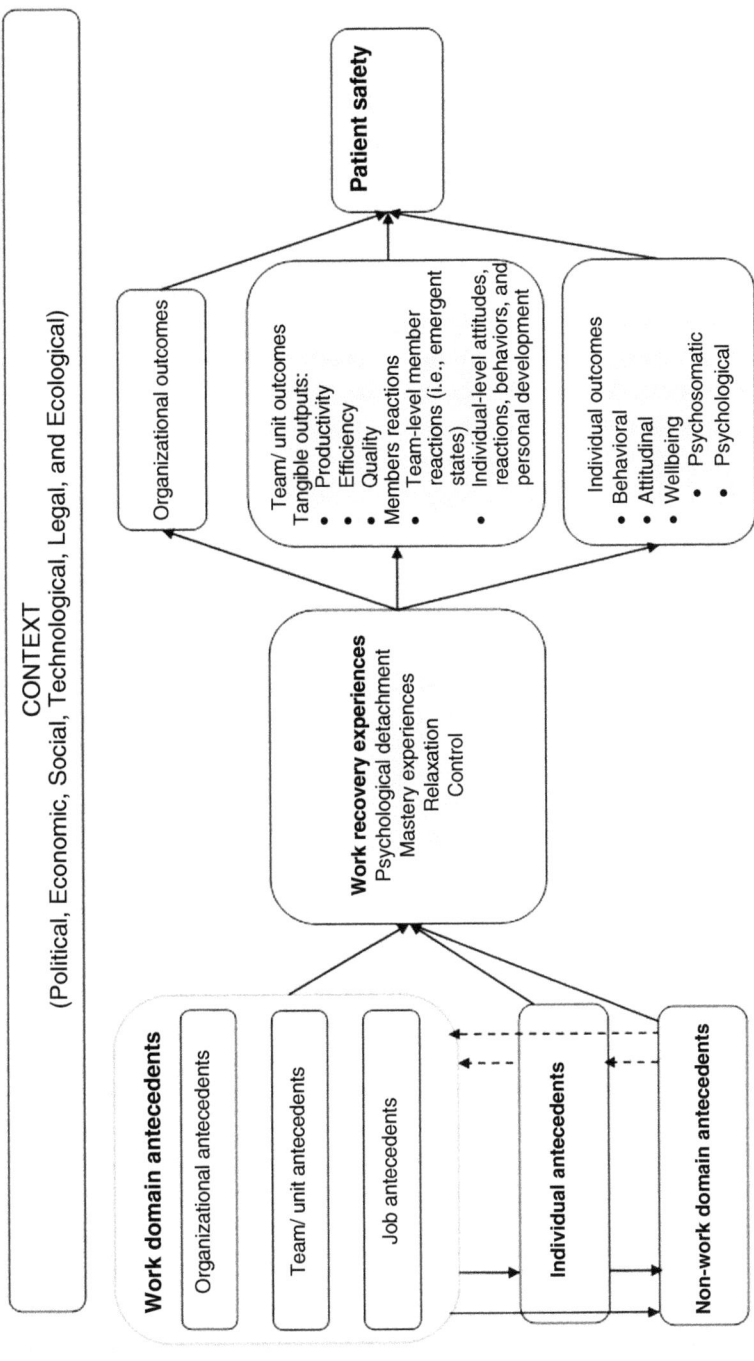

Fig. 11.1 Work recovery experiences model

order to get recovered (Sonnentag & Fritz, 2007). However, specific activities people may pursue during leisure time have an influence on recovery experiences (Sonnentag & Fritz, 2018). Furthermore, empirical research revealed that not just the time spent on off-work activities but also the subjective experience of such activities (i.e., the level of happiness or pleasure felt when performing these activities) play a pivotal role in the way they are linked to recovery (Oerlemans, Bakker, & Demerouti, 2014; van Hooff, Geurts, Beckers, & Kompier, 2011).

Literature reveals a wide range of recovery experiences that a person can engage in to get recovered from work in different settings such as micro-breaks (e.g., short breaks that are less than 10 min; Bennett, Gabriel, & Calderwood, 2019), work breaks (Bosch, Sonnentag, & Pinck, 2018), after work hours, weekends and holidays. The recovery that occurs within the work settings is termed internal recovery (Geurts & Sonnentag, 2006). It can be achieved through formal and informal breaks during the workday. The recovery that occurs outside of work refers to external recovery (Geurts & Sonnentag, 2006). It may take place after work, on weekends, or for longer periods such as holidays (Colombo & Cifre, 2012). In these recovery settings, the four primary recovery experiences that were most studied are: (1) psychological detachment, (2) relaxation, (3) mastery experiences, and (4) control (Sonnentag & Fritz, 2007). These recovery experiences can occur across a wide variety of activities (Sonnentag, Unger, & Rothe, 2016). They are positively related, but empirically different (Bennett, Bakker, & Field, 2018), as they regard discernibly different elements of the recovery process.

Psychological detachment implies being away from work-related duties and mental disengagement from work (Sonnentag & Fritz, 2007), which means refraining from work-related activities, thoughts, and emotions (Sonnentag & Fritz, 2018). Out of all the recovery experiences, psychological detachment appears as the most salient and, so far, it has received the most interest in the literature (see Sonnentag & Fritz, 2015 for a review; Wendsche & Lohmann-Haislah, 2017). *Relaxation* is a state characterized by low mental and physical exertion, an experience that can be obtained both through exercises, such as yoga and meditation, as well through other activities that calm the mind and body, such as reading a book, listening to a concert, watching a movie, taking a walk. *Mastery* experiences refer to off-job activities that distract from the job by providing challenging experiences and learning opportunities in other domains (e.g. philately, apiculture) or broadening one's horizon (e.g., traveling to a foreign country) (Sonnentag & Geurts, 2009). These challenging activities offer opportunities for experiencing competence and proficiency (Sonnentag & Fritz, 2007), without overtaxing the person's capabilities (Sonnentag, Binnewies, & Mojza, 2008). *Control* involves the degree to which a person can decide which activity to pursue during leisure time, as well as when and how to pursue this activity (Sonnentag & Fritz, 2007). Low control of leisure time can be a source of stress and resource consumption. On the other hand, the experience of control during leisure time may satisfy an individual's desire for control by increasing self-efficacy and feelings of competence, which in turn promote wellbeing. In addition, control during leisure time gives the individual the opportunity to choose those specific leisure activities that he or she prefers and that may be especially supportive for the recovery process (Sonnentag & Fritz, 2007).

Considering this conceptualization of work recovery, we integrated the literature that particularly addresses this concept in healthcare professionals by identifying its multilevel antecedents and consequences and focusing on its impact on the wellbeing of healthcare professionals. The literature we considered for integration consists of the results of a search conducted in the following electronic databases: PubMed, EBSCO—Academic Search and Business Source, SAGE, PsychINFO—PsychARTICLES, and Web of Science. The keywords we used were the following: *work recovery, recovery from work, recovery experiences*. To narrow our findings for our intended analysis of work recovery in healthcare settings, all three keywords were paired subsequently with: *health care, health care professionals, health care workers*. We used the model presented in Fig. 11.1 to integrate the results of our search.

11.2 Antecedents of Work Recovery

Research has spent considerable effort on identifying the processes that lead to recovery (Sonnentag & Fritz, 2018). This is also true for the literature on recovery in medical settings. Hence, most of the studies we analyzed considered work recovery experiences as an output and less as a predictor for various individual, team and organizational level outcomes and, ultimately, for patient safety. In addition, few studies examined work recovery experiences as intervening variables (i.e., moderator and mediator) in the relationship between inputs from various domains and multiple-level outcomes. In the following section, we briefly present the antecedents of work recovery experiences we found in our literature integration approach.

11.2.1 Job Specific Antecedents

We only identified a small body of research that examined the influence of various aspects of the job on work recovery experiences. In particular, the relationship between job specific variables and work recovery experiences was highlighted in two studies. In the first one, job specific variables such as shift work, hours worked per week, hours of direct patient care, public versus private work sector, metropolitan versus regional location of main practice, and professional stream were investigated as antecedents of work recovery experiences (Poulsen, Poulsen, Khan, Poulsen, & Khan, 2015). Findings based on multiple regression revealed no relationships between these factors and work recovery experiences. In contrast, another study using rich qualitative and quantitative data found that early career physicians report longer working hours, less leisure time and shorter amounts of sleep than average working adults (Cranley, Cunningham, & Panda, 2015). In addition, other findings of this study indicated that early career physicians do not participate in many resource-replenishing activities while at work, and when out of work, they tend to participate in more passive than active forms of recovery. More than half of the early career physicians surveyed indicated not psychologically detaching from work during their last recovery period and in general from work. Resource-draining activities were identified as requiring much of the early career physicians' non-work time, further limiting recovery. Although these two studies report contradictory findings on the relation between the number of working hours and recovery experiences, they reflect the existing incipient stage of the research on the relationship between job-related variables and recovery experiences in medical settings compared to other organizational settings.

11.2.2 Individual Level Antecedents

The individual level antecedents to work recovery experiences examined in the existing literature are various demographic characteristics, self-reported physical and mental health, and work attitudes.

In one cross-sectional study that involved 573 oncology workers, Poulsen, Poulsen, Khan, Poulsen, and Khan (2015) investigated demographic variables (e.g., gender, age, years of experience, post-graduate qualifications, marital status, having children, income, other-career commitments, participating in strenuous exercise), and self-reported physical and mental health variables including psychological distress, burnout, and work engagement. They found that low recovery experiences were associated with an increase in age, having a postgraduate qualification, being married in contrast to being single or never married, and having career commitments, while participating in strenuous exercise was associated with high recovery. They also showed in their research that there was a negative association between recovery experiences and burnout, as well as psychological distress.

The relationship between work attitudes, in particular passion for work, and recovery experiences outside of regular work hours was investigated by Donahue and colleagues (2012). Passion for work was defined in terms of a strong inclination toward a self-defining activity that one likes (or even loves), finds important (or highly values), and in which one invests time and energy. Two types of passion for work were considered in this study: obsessive and harmonious passion. Obsessive passion refers to a controlled internalization of an activity in one's identity that creates an internal pressure to engage in an activity that the person likes. Harmonious passion refers to an autonomous internalization that leads individuals to choose to engage in an activity that they like (Vallerand et al., 2003). Specifically, data from 118 French-Canadian nurses collected through a prospective design has shown that obsessive passion undermined recovery experiences, while harmonious passion positively predicted recovery experiences.

11.2.3 Non-work Antecedents

Non-work factors (i.e., non-work life and leisure activities) are related to employees' work recovery experiences (Sonnentag & Fritz, 2018). In fact, both foundational and more recent works emphasizing work recovery as a process focused on individual engagement in specific non-work activities to determine whether these activities might replenish resources and curtail demands (Steed et al., 2019). In our search, we found few studies conducted on healthcare professionals that considered individual engagement in off-job recovery activities, including work-related off-job activities, low-effort off-job activities, and cultural activities.

One study highlighted the importance of work-related off-job activities and low-effort off-job activities for healthcare employees' detachment from work. In a two-wave panel study of 230 healthcare employees, de Jonge, Shimazu, and Dollard (2018) examined whether particular recovery activities after-work have an effect on recovery from work (i.e., cognitive, emotional, and physical detachment) and sleep quality. Results of the hierarchical multiple regression analyses revealed that work-related off-job activities were negatively associated with a cognitive and emotional detachment in both the short and long run, whereas low-effort off-job activities were positively related to cognitive detachment in the short run. The long-term findings existed beyond the strong effects of baseline detachment.

Similarly, while looking into individual involvement in off-job cultural activities, Tuisku, Virtanen, Bloom, and Kinnunen (2016) found that employees who reported both receptive (i.e., passive consumption of culture) and creative (i.e., active art-making) cultural activities on a weekly basis had the highest relaxation, mastery and control experiences during time after work. In addition, those with weekly creative activities had beneficial mastery experiences.

The antecedents briefly depicted in this section reveal that the focus of the past research on antecedents of work recovery experiences in healthcare professionals was rather on individual level, job specific and non-work domain factors and less so on team, organizational, and contextual factors. Even so, the body of research that investigated the antecedents of work recovery experiences specifically in healthcare professionals is rather small compared to research that included samples of employees from other professions. Moreover, these studies examined the effects of antecedents alone and not of the interaction between factors from work, non-work and individual domains.

These studies only outline a fragmented and incomplete picture of the work, individual and non-work domains we can capitalize on to facilitate work recovery experiences and, subsequently, the growth of healthcare professionals' wellbeing that will ultimately lead to an increased patient safety. But, of course, this picture can be enhanced, on one side, by using findings from research on work recovery experiences conducted with employees from other professions (e.g., Parker, Sonnentag, Jimmieson, & Newton, 2019; Steed et al., 2019) and, on the other side, by continuing to explore in depth the particularities of work recovery conceptualized either as experiences, activities (e.g., Manomenidis, Panagopoulou, & Montgomery, 2016), and state and its antecedents in healthcare settings.

11.3 Consequences of Work Recovery

Recovery from work experiences, considered individually and together as aggregated score, have been documented to influence a wide variety of outcomes for employees (Colombo & Cifre, 2012; Ouyang, Cheng, Lam, & Parker, 2019; Sonnentag & Fritz, 2018; Steed et al., 2019; Taylor, Snyder, & Lin, 2019; Wendsche & Lohmann-Haislah, 2017), their teams and organizations (Fritz & Sonnentag, 2005). However, the body of research investigating the benefits and pitfalls of work recovery experiences in healthcare professionals is very small. All the studies that we analyzed have only looked into the individual or employee-related outcomes. None of the studies conducted in medical settings documented the influence of work recovery experiences on team and organizational level outcomes. This situation can also be found in the empirical research on work recovery that involved other professions or organizations from other industries. Thus, in the following paragraphs, we will present the range of the individual level outcomes of work recovery experiences in healthcare professionals.

11.3.1 Individual Level Consequences

In healthcare professionals, work recovery experiences have been studied only in relation to individual level outcomes including behavioral and wellbeing outcomes. Also, we found one study that conceptually discussed the impact of job engagement and recovery on dentists' wellbeing (Montasem, 2017).

In terms of behavioral outcomes, work recovery experiences were linked to creative performance. In a day-level study, Niks, de Jonge, Gevers and Houtman (2017) used a within-person design to investigate the role of cognitive and emotional detachment from work during non-work time in relation to equivalent types of job demands and job resources, in the prediction of self-rated employee creativity (e.g., generation of new and useful ideas about work by employees). Survey data were gathered over the course of eight consecutive days from 151 health care employees. Findings from multilevel analyses showed that cognitive detachment was positively related to creativity, irrespective of the level of cognitive job demands and resources, but it did not interact with cognitive demands and/or resources to predict creativity. Furthermore, high emotional job demands in combination with either high levels of emotional job resources or low levels of emotional detachment were positively related to creativity. Thus, these findings indicate that different types of psychological detachment have different effects on producing new (problem solving) ideas about work, sketching the divergent effects of detachment from work, as a recovery experience, on employee creativity.

Work recovery experiences were linked to various aspects of healthcare professionals' wellbeing, including psychosomatic wellbeing (i.e., fatigue at home, state of being recovered) and mental wellbeing (i.e., affect spillover, negative affect at home, emotional exhaustion at work).

Specifically, in a daily diary study in which 96 health-care workers completed surveys three times a day, over the period of one work-week, Sonnentag and Binnewies (2013) tested if psychological detachment from work during evening hours and sleep quality moderate the spillover of positive and negative affect from work to home and, whether affect spillover persists until the next morning. Findings based on the results of hierarchical linear modeling suggested that detachment can impact on spillover processes. While detachment is beneficial in interrupting the spillover of negative affect, it neutralizes potential gains that could be derived from positive affect experienced at work. Again, these findings reveal the divergent effect of psychological detachment on healthcare workers' mental wellbeing.

Donahue and colleagues (2012) found that work recovery experiences and rumination mediated the relationship between passion for work and workers' emotional exhaustion. In turn, recovery experiences protected workers from emotional exhaustion. In another study, Blanco-Donoso, Garrosa, Demerouti and Moreno-Jiménez (2017), using a diary approach and a multilevel design, found that nurses' daily difficulties in emotion regulation have a direct effect on daily emotional exhaustion at work, and on fatigue and negative affect at home at night. They also found that coworker support, psychological detachment and relaxation minimize the unfavorable effects on the wellbeing of difficulties in emotion regulation. These findings were drawn from multilevel analyses conducted on data provided by 74 nurses from various Spanish hospitals and primary health care centers that completed a general questionnaire and a diary booklet over five consecutive workdays at two different moments, after work and at night (N = 370 observations).

As in the case of the antecedents of work recovery, our integration reveals that the focus of the past research on consequences of work recovery experiences in healthcare professionals was rather on individual level outcomes and not on team and organizational outcomes and patient safety. Previous work generally looks into the consequences of work recovery experiences at one level of analysis, neglecting to study the impact that work recovery experiences might have on other levels of analysis such as teams and organizations or, why not, the cross-levels. Furthermore, the types of the consequences we identified in our search efforts emphasize the lack of connecting in a consistent manner work recovery experiences with different dimensions of various concepts relevant for patient safety, such as wellbeing. In addition, we found no studies investigating the role of political, economic, social, technological, legal, and environmental context on work recovery experiences. Focus on this topic might be useful, as recent studies revealed the existence of cultural variability in the association between age and wellbeing (Lawrie, Eom, Moza, Gavreliuc, & Kim, 2019). Using a multilevel approach with an international database (Study 1, N = 64,228), Lawrie and colleagues (2019) found that older age was associated with lower wellbeing in countries higher in uncertainty avoidance but not in countries lower in uncertainty avoidance. Further, this cultural variation was mediated by a sense of control. When, in a second study (Study 2, N = 1025), they focused on the comparison between a culture with low uncertainty avoidance (the United States) and a culture with high uncertainty avoidance (Romania), they found that age was negatively associated with wellbeing in Romania but not in the United States. This cultural difference was mediated by the use of contrasting coping strategies associated with different levels of a sense of control.

In view of these findings, we believe more research is needed in order to identify how work recovery experiences in healthcare settings, via different mechanisms, can lead to patient safety, as well as how interventions dedicated to increase work recovery experiences should be tailored to facilitate it.

11.4 Work Recovery Interventions

In this section, we draw on existing literature and suggest potential organizational and individual level interventions on work recovery to ensure the wellbeing of healthcare professionals and ultimately, patient safety.

11.4.1 Organization Level Interventions

Many work and hospital-specific factors that have an impact on the recovery process are hard to change (Smith, Folkard, Tucker & Evans, 2011). Specifically, a high volume of work, time pressure, or the need for overtime hours are amongst the most common factors that can impair the recovery experiences (Sonnentag & Fritz, 2015). As such, while we would have a hard time trying to build interventions where the aim is to reduce these stressors, we posit that interventions should rather target specific activities to help medical personnel recuperate from working under these conditions. Some of these possible interventions and solutions are straightforward. Micro-breaks during the working day, characterized by social activities (e.g., phoning friends or family members) and relaxation activities (e.g., stretching), but not by cognitive activities, have the potential to reduce the negative effects of work demands such as end-of-workday negative affect (Kim, Park, & Niu, 2017). In addition, the availability of opportunities to relax and recover during the working day is associated with less work–home conflict and indirectly with less emotional exhaustion (Nitzsche et al., 2016). Together, these studies support internal recovery through micro-breaks, daily breaks and 'switching off during work'. They can be regarded as small steps toward enhancing healthcare professionals' wellbeing by preventing states of exhaustion and end-of-workday negative affect. Medical practices should consider including micro-breaks and breaks during a working day of a shift. Daily micro-breaks including social, relaxation, and cognitive activities also have the potential to generate positive affect that leads to a greater job performance for workers with lower general work engagement (Kim, Park, & Headrick, 2018). In parallel, it is also important to create free space and time out at weekends in a targeted way. This can contribute to reduce negative affect, improve the work–home interplay, and to prevent exhaustion and potential burnout.

Also, a high volume of work brings about a number of tasks that remain unfinished at the end of the day. A solution is to establish, at the end of the working day, the way in which the tasks will be solved through the most specific objectives. This method helps to reduce associated negative activation, increases control over tasks, and promotes recovery experiences (Smit & Barber, 2015).

Given the fact that organizational stressors are sometimes difficult to change, a strong emphasis must be put on the medical staff's reactions to stress. In this respect, many cognitive-behavioral programs and relaxation techniques were used in the organizational environment (Richardson & Rothstein, 2008), but recovery experiences were much less used in these programs. In a quasi-experimental study, Hahn et al. (2011) highlighted the benefits of a recovery training program that covered all four recovery experiences in two theoretical and practical sessions. The results of the intervention revealed an increase in mastery experiences, sleep quality and recovery self-efficacy experience. These studies show that recovery experiences can be learned. Furthermore, based on these results, a 1-day workshop intervention conducted on radiation therapists and oncology nurses was developed (Poulsen, Sharpley, Baumann, Henderson & Poulsen 2015). It was found that their intervention had a positive effect on the total recovery experiences and perceived sleep quality, an important component of the recovery process in comparison to the control group.

Sleep, is an important component of the recovery process, and the development of a sleep routine during the daytime and keeping sleep debt to a minimum, is one of the recommendations in guidelines on recovery from the night shifts, for junior doctors. In an intervention to increase work recovery (Hahn et al., 2011), the participants were taught what sleep-hygiene means and rules about sleeping times. After this intervention participants reported a better perceived sleep quality.

The promotion of recovery experiences can start from leaders, primarily through the expectations they have from subordinates. Also, supervisors can discuss with employees about the importance of post-work recovery or draw clear expectations about work-related behaviors (e.g., expectations that employees will respond or not to emails in their spare time). Work-home segmentation expectations are positively associated with psychological detachment after work (Park et al., 2011). More specifically, the perception of work-home segmentation promoted between colleagues or supervisors could influence recovery experiences.

Given the schedule of medical personnel, there are few studies that analyze how many days of recovery it takes to accomplish recovery after work shifts. A study on nurses, suggests that three rest days are necessary to recover after two 12-h day shifts for the full restoration of fatigue and to promote wellbeing (Blasche et al., 2017). When setting up the 12-h work schedule for medical staff, it is important to consider the work-recovery balance, in order to enhance nurses' wellbeing and patient safety.

In a study conducted with medical practitioners, they were asked to write about three good things that happened during the working day (personal or work-related) and to explain why they think those events took place (Bono et al., 2013). The level of stress and wellbeing was assessed before and after the positive reflection intervention, and results demonstrate that participants experienced reduced stress and reported fewer physical and mental health complaints, in comparison with days when they didn't reflect on the positive moments occurring during their day. At the organizational level, the focus should not only be on controlling negative events, but also on reinforcing and revealing positive events. According to the study mentioned above, a brief end-of-workday positive reflection can lead to a decrease in stress levels and improve health in the evening. This practice can be used by supervisors at the beginning of a workday, or at the end, in a meeting. For example, the meeting after the night shifts, aside from discussing the negative events that took place, could also celebrate the colleagues' success or the aspects that went well, and to express gratitude for the effort invested and their engagement in saving people's lives.

More than that, at the organizational level, the focus can be placed on promoting strengths in the working environment, on positive feedback and encouraging productive behaviors, and not on criticisms brought to medical staff. In addition, Schwartz Centre Rounds® can be used to foster healthcare professionals' mastery and reflection with regard to the application of human connection patient-caregiver principle in their practice to improve the quality of caregiving. Rounds are organization-wide forums that prompt reflection and evidence-based interdisciplinary discussion of the emotional, social and ethical challenges of health-care work, with the aim of improving staff wellbeing and patient care (Farr & Barker, 2017; Maben et al., 2018). These rounds provide healthcare professionals with the opportunity to come together in a safe but open environment, to explore the human and emotional impact of their everyday work by sharing their expertise, experience, and a passion for what they do. These rounds last 1 h, typically co-facilitated by a senior doctor and psychosocial practitioner with a panel of up to four presenters and an open audience. Each round begins with short presentations by the panel, on a key theme, scenario or patient case, after which the round is opened for general discussion (Reed, Cullen, Gannon, Knight, & Todd, 2015). Recent empirical studies and scoping reviews highlighted the beneficial role of these rounds among other techniques in the process of team-based reflection (Anderson, Sandars, & Kinnair, 2019; Angelopoulou & Panagopoulou, 2019; Maben et al., 2018). They can lead to improved emotional wellbeing and learning for quality improvement and patient safety. Also, a series of socializing events can be organized according to the work schedule, or during work breaks, meant to increase the wellbeing and the positive emotions between the employees.

11.4.2 Individual Level

While the focus on recovery as an experience aims at better understanding the psychological process underlying recovery from work, a focus on specific recovery activities may provide more focused opportunities for developing interventions. At the individual level, a number of activities have been studied as influencing recovery experiences. Among the activities studied are physical, household activities, such as taking care of children, social activities and also work-related activities. Physical activities have a high ability to distract attention from work problems (Sonnentag, 2001). Social activities also help the recovery process, especially if work-related thoughts are left aside. In a longitudinal study conducted on emergency medical service workers (Fritz & Sonnentag, 2005), social activity during the weekends was negatively associated with the disengagement component of burnout and poor general wellbeing after the weekend. Social activities usually require a lower level of emotional regulation compared to the social interactions at the workplace (Grandey, 2000), helping to restore the invested resources and build new ones. More than that, spending time with others during the weekend was associated with task performance when returning to the workplace.

At the same time, activities that develop new skills, such as various hobbies, have the ability to promote work recovery and also to acquire new resources. In a study that evaluated short and long-term effects of off-job activities on recovery and sleep among healthcare workers (de Jonge, Shimazu, & Dollard, 2018) it has been shown that time spent on high-duty activities like work-related activities has a negative impact on work recovery. On the other hand, activities such as social, creative, physical, and low-effort activities facilitate recovery experiences. Also, cultural activities like going to a concert or performing creative activities like writing or playing an instrument were associated with mastery experiences and control among hospital personnel (Tuisku et al., 2016). These recovery experiences have the potential to create new resources, like feelings of personal accomplishment when acquiring new skills and knowledge, which can then lead to better wellbeing and positive emotions.

Hülsheger, Feinholdt, and Nübold (2015) investigated in a randomized field experiment (with a self-training and a wait-list control group) the effectiveness of a low-dose mindfulness intervention for recovery from work. They also examined the different responses to the treatment in terms of treatment-by-baseline interactions. Recovery from work was conceptualized as psychological detachment, sleep quality, sleep duration, and it was assessed with an event-sampling methodology involving daily measurements over 10 workdays. While growth curve analyses revealed intervention effects on sleep quality and sleep duration, no effects were found for psychological detachment after work. Also, gains in recovery processes, including psychological detachment, due to the intervention were not stronger for participants with low baseline levels.

Poulsen, Sharpley, Baumann, Henderson, and Poulsen (2015) however found, using a sample of 70 oncology care workers, that work recovery experiences can be increased significantly after a one-day educational intervention (workshop) designed to build the recovery-related self-care resources. Workshop participants reported greater mean changes 6 weeks post-workshop for total recovery experiences, self-care satisfaction, and perceived sleep quality. There was a decline in the scores of the control group (that only used written educational materials) over the 6-week period for all measures. Workshop participants not only avoided this decline but also demonstrated increased mean scores, with a significant main effect 6 weeks post-workshop, compared with the control group.

Beyond all of the suggestions offered by literature on setting clear limits on personal and professional life, there are individuals who prefer to dedicate themselves to work even in leisure time. Control over leisure time is an important factor in recovery processes (Sonnentag & Fritz, 2007). An alternative to dropping out of work is to engage in activities that are considered pleasant to reduce the negative effects associated with less pleasant daytime tasks and to orientate cognitive resources to resolve problems at the expense of emotional rumination.

A recent meta-analysis has shown that demands (overload, cognitive, emotional, and physical) were negatively related to work recovery experiences, while resources (contextual-work, contextual-home and personal) were positively related to these experiences (Steed et al., 2019). Thus, interventions dedicated to increase work recovery experiences could target simultaneously reducing the demands of both work and non-work domains and increasing the resources that an employee can access in these domains. These interventions can in particular address recovery that occurs within the work settings through formal and informal breaks during the workday or recovery that takes place after work, on weekends, or for longer periods such as holidays or both.

11.5 Conclusions

It is time to create an organizational culture that encourages healthcare professionals to keep a balance between taking care of others and taking care of themselves, and their personal wellbeing. Focusing attention on how medical personnel manages to restore their work resources will have an impact on both their wellbeing and patient safety. Contrary to first impressions, in order to reduce the overall stress levels, it is not enough to reduce the stress factors associated with the job, but it also requires to highlight the importance of the medical staff's free time. Interventions at the individual level should encourage healthcare professionals to take time after work to engage in low demanding, replenishing or creative cultural off-job activities. These habits can be promoted from leaders to team members.

Taking into account that the medical setting has its particularities, more focused research is needed with regard to the role of recovery from work on health professionals' wellbeing and, subsequently, on patient safety. At the same time, this research should take into account and unpack the various potential individual, team, and organizational factors that can intensify or buffer recovery from work experiences in healthcare professionals. Finally, considering that medical organizations are embedded in the wider society and that they are a critical part of it, it is important to also understand the influence of the political, economic, social, technological, legal and environmental context in intensifying or buffering work recovery experiences.

Key messages for researchers (2–3 points)	*Key messages for healthcare delivery* (2–3 points)
Considering the role of context in shaping organizational outcomes and the lack of studies on the role of context in work recovery, it is important to investigate the role of political, economic, social, technological, legal and environmental context in intensifying or buffering work recovery experiences.	Teach healthcare professionals to identify the signs of stress and recovery needs, and how to effectively address these needs by recognizing when engaging in different work recovery experiences is needed and when not (e.g., psychological detachment from work should be encouraged on days with high levels of negative affect, but not on days with high levels of positive affect).
As there is only a relatively small body of research on recovery experiences of healthcare professionals, in comparison to other domains, it would worth to highlight the particularities of work recovery experiences in healthcare professionals and to further investigate the impact of the individual, team, and organizational factors that can intensify or buffer recovery from work experiences in healthcare professionals. Furthermore, as most of the studies on work recovery experiences in healthcare professionals used cross-sectional and diary studies, it is important to examine longitudinally and from a multilevel perspective how different work recovery experiences are linked to various antecedents from work and non-work domains and consequences, in particular wellbeing and patient safety, and how these variables are reciprocally linked in healthcare settings.	In order to facilitate the occurrence of work recovery experiences during and after work and to achieve the state of feeling and being recovered from work, provide healthcare professionals with: • Opportunities for recovery that takes place during work (e.g., possibility of deciding working hours, the work pace, taking short breaks, deciding when to perform a work task, and having mostly varied work). • Activities to formally and informally share expertise, experience and passion for what they do (e.g., Schwartz Centre rounds®). • Support to engage in replenishing activities during work time (e.g., eating lunch, short time off for relaxation rituals).
Considering that the same daily activities can be either resource replenishing or resource draining, depending on the contexts in which they are experienced (i.e., work and home; Cranley et al., 2015), it is important to examine when (i.e., during work and after work) and how (i.e., the mechanisms) different work recovery experiences lead to individual, team and organizational positive outcomes and reduce the negative ones in healthcare settings.	Support healthcare professionals: • To take time after work to engage in low demanding, replenishing and creative cultural off-job activities. • To build a positive daily cycle of resource replenishment that runs parallel to resource depletion. • To understand how involving in work recovery experiences can be beneficial for them, their units and organizations, and ultimately for patient safety.

References

Alexandrova-Karamanova, A., Todorova, I., Montgomery, A., Panagopoulou, E., Costa, P., Baban, A., et al. (2016). Burnout and health behaviors in health professionals from seven European countries. *International Archives of Occupational and Environmental Health, 89*(7), 1059–1075. https://doi.org/10.1007/s00420-016-1143-5

Anderson, E., Sandars, J., & Kinnair, D. (2019). The nature and benefits of team-based reflection on a patient death by healthcare professionals: A scoping review. *Journal of Interprofessional Care, 33*(1), 15–25. https://doi.org/10.1080/13561820.2018.1513462

Angelopoulou, P., & Panagopoulou, E. (2019). Non-clinical rounds in hospital settings: A scoping review. *Journal of Health Organization and Management, 33*(5), 605–616. https://doi.org/10.1108/jhom-09-2018-0244

Bennett, A. A., Bakker, A. B., & Field, J. G. (2018). Recovery from work-related effort: A meta-analysis. *Journal of Organizational Behavior, 39*, 262–275. https://doi.org/10.1002/job.2217

Bennett, A. A., Gabriel, A. S., & Calderwood, C. (2019). Examining the interplay of micro-break durations and activities for employee recovery: A mixed-methods investigation. *Journal of Occupational Health Psychology, 25*, 126–142. https://doi.org/10.1037/ocp0000168

Blanco-Donoso, L. M., Garrosa, E., Demerouti, E., & Moreno-Jimenez, B. (2017). Job resources and recovery experiences to face difficulties in emotion regulation at work: A diary study among nurses. *International Journal of Stress Management, 24*(2), 107–134. https://doi.org/10.1037/str0000023

Blasche, G., Bauböck, V. M., & Haluza, D. (2017). Work-related self-assessed fatigue and recovery among nurses. *International Archives of Occupational and Environmental Health, 90*(2), 197–205. https://doi.org/10.1007/s00420-016-1187-6

Bono, J. E., Glomb, T. M., Shen, W., Kim, E., & Koch, A. J. (2013). Building positive resources: Effects of positive events and positive reflection on work stress and health. *Academy of Management Journal, 56*(6), 1601–1627. https://doi.org/10.5465/amj.2011.0272

Bosch, C., Sonnentag, S., & Pinck, A. S. (2018). What makes for a good break? A diary study on recovery experiences during lunch break. *Journal of Occupational and Organizational Psychology, 91*(1), 134–157. https://doi.org/10.1111/joop.12195

Botti, M., Bucknall, T., Cameron, P., Johnstone, M. J., Redley, B., Evans, S., et al. (2009). Examining communication and team performance during clinical handover in a complex environment: The private sector post-anaesthetic care unit. *The Medical Journal of Australia, 190*(S11), S157–S160.

Buchanan, D. A., & Huczynski, A. A. (2017). *Organizational behavior* (9th ed.). Harlow: Pearson Education Limited.

Chipps, E., Wills, C. E., Tanda, R., Patterson, E. S., Elfrink, V., Brodnik, M., et al. (2011). Registered nurses' judgments of the classification and risk level of patient care errors. *Journal of Nursing Care Quality, 26*(4), 302–310. https://doi.org/10.1097/NCQ.0b013e31820f4c57

Chuang, C. H., Tseng, P. C., Lin, C. Y., Lin, K. H., & Chen, Y. Y. (2016). Burnout in the intensive care unit professionals: A systematic review. *Medicine (Baltimore), 95*(50), e5629. https://doi.org/10.1097/md.0000000000005629

Colombo, V., & Cifre, E. (2012). The importance of recovering from work: A review of where, how and why. *Papers of the Psychologist, 33*(2), 129–137.

Clarke, J. R., Lerner, J. C., & Marella, W. (2007). The role for leaders of health care organizations in patient safety. *American Journal of Medical Quality, 22*(5), 311–318. https://doi.org/10.1177/1062860607304743

Cranley, N. M., Cunningham, C. L., & Panda, M. (2015). Understanding time use, stress and recovery practices among early career physicians: An exploratory study. *Psychology, Health & Medicine, 21*, 1–6. https://doi.org/10.1080/13548506.2015.1061675

de Jonge, J. D., Shimazu, A., & Dollard, M. (2018). Short-term and long-term effects of off-job activities on recovery and sleep: A two-wave panel study among health care employees.

International Journal of Environmental Research and Public Health, 15(9), 2044. https://doi.org/10.3390/ijerph15092044

Donahue, E. G., Forest, J., Vallerand, R. J., Lemyre, P. N., Crevier-Braud, L., & Bergeron, E. (2012). Passion for work and emotional exhaustion: the mediating role of rumination and recovery. *Applied Psychology. Health and Well-Being, 4*(3), 341–368. https://doi.org/10.1111/j.1758-0854.2012.01078.x

Edwards, J. R., & Rothbard, N. P. (2000). Mechanisms linking work and family: clarifying the relationship Between work and family constructs. *Academy of Management Review, 25*(1), 178–199. https://doi.org/10.5465/amr.2000.2791609

Elfering, A., Grebner, S., Semmer, N., & Gerber, H. (2002). Time control, catecholamines and back pain among young nurses. *Scandinavian Journal of Work, Environment & Health, 28*(6), 386–393. Retrieved October 25, 2020, from http://www.jstor.org/stable/40967229

Farr, M., & Barker, R. (2017). Can staff be supported to deliver compassionate care through implementing Schwartz Rounds in community and mental health services? *Qualitative Health Research, 27*(11), 1652–1663. https://doi.org/10.1177/1049732317702101

Faye, H., Rivera-Rodriguez, A. J., Karsh, B. T., Hundt, A. S., Baker, C., & Carayon, P. (2010). Involving intensive care unit nurses in a proactive risk assessment of the medication management process. *Joint Commission Journal on Quality and Patient Safety, 36*(8), 376–384. https://doi.org/10.1016/s1553-7250(10)36056-9

Fritz, C., & Crain, T. (2016). Recovery from work and employee sleep: Understanding the role of experiences and activities outside of work. In J. Barling, C. M. Barnes, E. L. Carleton, & D. T. Wagner (Eds.), *Work and sleep: Research insights for the workplace* (pp. 55–76). Oxford: Oxford University Press. https://doi.org/10.1093/acprof:oso/9780190217662.003.0004

Fritz, C., & Sonnentag, S. (2005). Recovery, health, and job performance: Effects of weekend experiences. *Journal of Occupational Health Psychology, 10*(3), 187–199. https://doi.org/10.1037/1076-8998.10.3.187

Geurts, S. A. E., & Sonnentag, S. (2006). Recovery as an explanatory mechanism in the relation between acute stress reactions and chronic health impairment. *Scandinavian Journal of Work, Environment and Health, 32*(6), 482–492. https://doi.org/10.5271/sjweh.1053

Grandey, A. A. (2000). Emotional regulation in the workplace: A new way to conceptualize emotional labor. *Journal of Occupational Health Psychology, 5*(1), 95–110. https://doi.org/10.1037/1076-8998.5.1.95

Hahn, V. C., Binnewies, C., Sonnentag, S., & Mojza, E. J. (2011). Learning how to recover from job stress: Effects of a recovery training program on recovery, recovery-related self-efficacy, and wellbeing. *Journal of Occupational Health Psychology, 16*(2), 202–216. https://doi.org/10.1037/a0022169

Harrison, R., Lawton, R., Perlo, J., Gardner, P., Armitage, G., & Shapiro, J. (2015). Emotion and coping in the aftermath of medical error: A cross-country exploration. *Journal of Patient Safety, 11*(1), 28–35. https://doi.org/10.1097/PTS.0b013e3182979b6f

Hülsheger, U. R., Feinholdt, A., & Nübold, A. (2015). A low-dose mindfulness intervention and recovery from work: effects on psychological detachment, sleep quality, and sleep duration. *Journal of Occupational and Organizational Psychology, 88*(3), 464–489. https://doi.org/10.1111/joop.12115

Jeffs, L. P., Lingard, L., Berta, W., & Baker, G. R. (2012). Catching and correcting near misses: The collective vigilance and individual accountability trade-off. *Journal of Interprofessional Care, 26*(2), 121–126. https://doi.org/10.3109/13561820.2011.642424

Kim, S., Park, Y., & Headrick, L. (2018). Daily micro-breaks and job performance: General work engagement as a cross-level moderator. *Journal of Applied Psychology, 103*(7), 772–786. https://doi.org/10.1037/apl0000308

Kim, S., Park, Y., & Niu, Q. (2017). Micro-break activities at work to recover from daily work demands. *Journal of Organizational Behavior, 38*(1), 28–44. https://doi.org/10.1002/job.2109

Kolbe, M., Grote, G., Waller, M. J., Wacker, J., Grande, B., Burtscher, M. J., et al. (2014). Monitoring and talking to the room: Autochthonous coordination patterns in team interaction and performance. *Journal of Applied Psychology, 99*(6), 1254–1267. https://doi.org/10.1037/a0037877

Lawati, M., Dennis, S., Short, S. D., & Abdulhadi, N. N. (2018). Patient safety and safety culture in primary health care: A systematic review. *BMC Family Practice, 19*(1), 104. https://doi.org/10.1186/s12875-018-0793-7

Lawrie, S. I., Eom, K., Moza, D., Gavreliuc, A., & Kim, H. S. (2019). Cultural variability in the association between age and wellbeing: The role of uncertainty avoidance. *Psychological Science, 31*, 51–64. https://doi.org/10.1177/0956797619887348

Maben, J., Taylor, C., Dawson, J., Leamy, M., McCarthy, I., Reynolds, E., et al. (2018). A realist informed mixed methods evaluation of Schwartz center rounds® in England. *Health Services and Delivery Research, 6*(37), 1–260.

Manomenidis, G., Panagopoulou, E., & Montgomery, A. (2016). The 'switch on-switch off model': Strategies used by nurses to mentally prepare and disengage from work. *International Journal of Nursing Practice, 22*(4), 356–363. https://doi.org/10.1111/ijn.12443

Mathieu, J. E., Gallagher, P. T., Domingo, M. A., & Klock, E. A. (2019). Embracing complexity: reviewing the past decade of team effectiveness research. *Annual Review of Organizational Psychology and Organizational Behavior, 6*(1), 17–46. https://doi.org/10.1146/annurev-orgpsych-012218-015106

Mathieu, J. E., & Gilson, L. L. (2012). Criteria issues and team effectiveness. In S. W. Kozlowski (Ed.), *The Oxford handbook of organizational psychology* (Vol. 2, pp. 910–930). New York: Oxford University Press.

Mathieu, J. E., Maynard, M. T., Rapp, T., & Gilson, L. (2008). Team effectiveness 1997-2007: A review of recent advancements and a glimpse into the future. *Journal of Management, 34*(3), 410–476. doi: 0.1177/0149206308316061.

Meijman, T. F., & Mulder, G. (1998). Psychological aspects of workload. In *Handbook of work and organizational: Work psychology* (Vol. 2, 2nd ed., pp. 5–33). Hove, England: Psychology Press/Erlbaum (UK) Taylor & Francis.

Montasem, A. (2017). The impact of job engagement and recovery on dentists' wellbeing. *Journal of the Massachusetts Dental Society, 66*(1), 14–17.

Montgomery, A., Panagopoulou, E., Esmail, A., Richards, T., & Maslach, C. (2019). Burnout in healthcare: The case for organisational change. *BMJ, 366*, l4774. https://doi.org/10.1136/bmj.l4774

Niks, I. M. V., de Jonge, J., Gevers, M. P., & Houtman, I. L. D. (2017). Divergent effects of detachment from work: A day-level study on employee creativity. *European Journal of Work and Organizational Psychology, 26*(2), 183–194. https://doi.org/10.1080/1359432X.2016.1241767

Niks, I. M. V., Gevers, J. M. P., de Jonge, J., & Houtman, I. L. D. (2016). The relation between off-job recovery and job resources: Person-level differences and day-level dynamics. *European Journal of Work and Organizational Psychology, 25*(2), 226–238. https://doi.org/10.1080/1359432X.2015.1042459

Nitzsche, A., Neumann, M., Groß, S. E., Ansmann, L., Pfaff, H., Baumann, W., et al. (2016). Recovery opportunities, work–home conflict, and emotional exhaustion among hematologists and oncologists in private practice. *Psychology, Health & Medicine, 22*(4), 462–473. https://doi.org/10.1080/13548506.2016.1237666

Oerlemans, W. G. M., Bakker, A. B., & Demerouti, E. (2014). How feeling happy during off-job activities helps successful recovery from work: A day reconstruction study. *Work and Stress, 28*(2), 198–216. https://doi.org/10.1080/02678373.2014.901993

Ouyang, K., Cheng, B. H., Lam, W., & Parker, S. K. (2019). Enjoy your evening, be proactive tomorrow: How off-job experiences shape daily proactivity. *Journal of Applied Psychology, 104*(8), 1003–1019. https://doi.org/10.1037/apl0000391

Park, Y., Fritz, C., & Jex, S. M. (2011). Relationships between work-home segmentation and psychological detachment from work: The role of communication technology use at home. *Journal of Occupational Health Psychology, 16*(4), 457–467. https://doi.org/10.1037/a0023594

Parker, S. L., Sonnentag, S., Jimmieson, N. L., & Newton, C. J. (2019). Relaxation during the evening and next-morning energy: The role of hassles, uplifts, and heart rate variability during work. *Journal of Occupational Health Psychology, 25*, 83–98. https://doi.org/10.1037/ocp0000155

Poulsen, M. G., Poulsen, A. A., Khan, A., Poulsen, E. E., & Khan, S. R. (2015). Recovery experience and burnout in cancer workers in Queensland. *European Journal of Oncology Nursing, 19*(1), 23–28. https://doi.org/10.1016/j.ejon.2014.08.003

Poulsen, A. A., Sharpley, C. F., Baumann, K. C., Henderson, J., & Poulsen, M. G. (2015). Evaluation of the effect of a 1-day interventional workshop on recovery from job stress for radiation therapists and oncology nurses: A randomised trial. *Journal of Medical Imaging and Radiation Oncology, 59*(4), 491–498. https://doi.org/10.1111/1754-9485.12322

Reed, E., Cullen, A., Gannon, C., Knight, A., & Todd, J. (2015). Use of Schwartz Centre rounds in a UK hospice: Findings from a longitudinal evaluation. *Journal of Interprofessional Care, 29* (4), 365–366. https://doi.org/10.3109/13561820.2014.983594

Richardson, K. M., & Rothstein, H. R. (2008). Effects of occupational stress management intervention programs: A meta-analysis. *Journal of Occupational Health Psychology, 13*(1), 69–93. https://doi.org/10.1037/1076-8998.13.1.69

Smith, C. S., Folkard, S., Tucker, P., & Evans, M. S. (2011). Work schedules, health, and safety. In J. C. Quick & L. E. Tetrick (Eds.), *Handbook of occupational health psychology (p. 185–204)*. Washington: American Psychological Association.

Sonnentag, S. (2001). Work, recovery activities, and individual wellbeing: A diary study. *Journal of Occupational Health Psychology, 6*(3), 196–210. https://doi.org/10.1037/1076-8998.6.3.196

Sonnentag, S. (2003). Recovery, work engagement, and proactive behavior: A new look at the interface between nonwork and work. *Journal of Applied Psychology, 88*(3), 518–528. https://doi.org/10.1037/0021-9010.88.3.518

Sonnentag, S., & Binnewies, C. (2013). Daily affect spillover from work to home: Detachment from work and sleep as moderators. *Journal of Vocational Behavior, 83*(2), 198–208. https://doi.org/10.1016/j.jvb.2013.03.008

Sonnentag, S., Binnewies, C., & Mojza, E. J. (2008). "Did you have a nice evening?" A day-level study on recovery experiences, sleep, and affect. *Journal of Applied Psychology, 93*(3), 674–684. https://doi.org/10.1037/0021-9010.93.3.674

Sonnentag, S., & Fritz, C. (2007). The recovery experience questionnaire: Development and validation of a measure for assessing recuperation and unwinding from work. *Journal of Occupational Health Psychology, 12*(3), 204–221. https://doi.org/10.1037/1076-8998.12.3.204

Sonnentag, S., & Fritz, C. (2015). Recovery from job stress: The stressor-detachment model as an integrative framework. *Journal of Organizational Behavior, 36*(S1), S72–S103. https://doi.org/10.1002/job.1924

Sonnentag, S., & Fritz, C. (2018). Recovery from work. In D. S. Ones, N. Anderson, & H. K. Sinangil (Eds.), *The SAGE handbook of industrial, work and organizational psychology (Chapter 20)* (pp. 471–482). London: SAGE. https://doi.org/10.4135/9781473914964.n21

Sonnentag, S., & Geurts, S. A. E. (2009). Methodological issues in recovery research. In S. Sonnentag, P. Perrewé, & D. Ganster (Eds.), *Currents perspectives on job-stress recovery* (pp. 1–36). Bingley: Emerald.

Sonnentag, S., Unger, D., & Rothe, E. (2016). Recovery and the work-family interface. In T. D. Allen & L. T. Eby (Eds.), *Oxford library of psychology. The Oxford handbook of work and family (p. 95–108)*. England: Oxford University Press.

Sonnentag, S., Venz, L., & Casper, A. (2017). Advances in recovery research: What have we learned? What should be done next? Journal of Occupational Health Psychology, 22(3), 365–380. https://doi.org/10.1037/ocp0000079

Smit, B. W., & Barber, L. K. (2015) Psychologically detaching despite high workloads: The role of attentional processes. *Journal of Occupational Health Psychology*. Advance online publication. https://doi.org/10.1037/ocp0000019

Steed, L. B., Swider, B. W., Keem, S., & Liu, J. T. (2019). Leaving work at work: A meta-analysis on employee recovery from work. *Journal of Management, XX*(X), 1–31. https://doi.org/10.1177/0149206319864153

Taylor, W. D., Snyder, L. A., & Lin, L. (2019). What free time? A daily study of work recovery and wellbeing among working students. *Journal of Occupational Health Psychology, XX*(X), xxx–xxx. https://doi.org/10.1037/ocp0000160

Tuisku, K., Virtanen, M., De Bloom, J. D., & Kinnunen, U. (2016). Cultural leisure activities, recovery and work engagement among hospital employees. *Industrial Health, 54*(3), 254–262. https://doi.org/10.2486/indhealth.2015-0124

Vallerand, R. J., Blanchard, C., Mageau, G. A., Koestner, R., Ratelle, C., Léonard, M., et al. (2003). Les Passions de l'Âme: On obsessive and harmonious passion. *Journal of Personality and Social Psychology, 85*, 756–767. https://doi.org/10.1037/0022-3514.85.4.756

van Hooff, M. L. M., Geurts, S. A. E., Beckers, D. G. J., & Kompier, M. A. J. (2011). Daily recovery from work: The role of activities, effort and pleasure. *Work & Stress, 25*(1), 55–74. https://doi.org/10.1080/02678373.2011.570941

Verbakel, N. J., Langelaan, M., Verheij, T. J. M., Wagner, C., & Zwart, D. L. M. (2016). Improving patient safety culture in primary care: A systematic review. *Journal of Patient Safety, 12*(3), 152–158. https://doi.org/10.1097/pts.0000000000000075

Welp, A., & Manser, T. (2016). Integrating teamwork, clinician occupational wellbeing and patient safety–development of a conceptual framework based on a systematic review. *BMC Health Services Research, 16*, 281. https://doi.org/10.1186/s12913-016-1535-y

Wendsche, J., & Lohmann-Haislah, A. (2017). A meta-analysis on antecedents and outcomes of detachment from work. *Frontiers in Psychology, 7*, 2072. https://doi.org/10.3389/fpsyg.2016.02072

Chapter 12
Creating Optimal Clinical Workplaces by Transforming Leadership and Empowering Clinicians

Paul DeChant and Diane Shannon

> If doing things that produce healthier work environments pay off for both employees and employers, why don't more companies do it? Jeffrey Pfeffer, Dying for a Paycheck

Clinicians are not faring well in the current health care environment. Physician burnout has been recognized as a public health emergency, in the United States, with prevalence rates running about 50% (Massachusetts Medical Society, Massachusetts Health and Hospital Association, Harvard T.H. Chan School of Public Health, & Harvard Global Health Institute, 2019; Shanafelt, West, et al., 2019).Other health care professionals are also suffering high rates of burnout. Studies of nurse burnout show a prevalence of 34–86% (McHugh, Kutney-Lee, Cimiotti, Sloane, & Aiken, 2011; Mealer, Burnham, Goode, Rothbaum, & Moss, 2009) and turnover among nurses is especially high. Almost 1 in 5 registered nurses leaves their first job within the first year after completion of training; one third leave within 3 years (Kovner, Brewer, Fatehi, & Jun, 2014). Health care leaders are not immune. A recent poll found that 73% of administrators felt some degree of burnout from their jobs (Medical Group Management Association, 2018). Given the nature of the healing interaction between patient and clinician, burnout among doctors and nurses adversely affects patients as well (National Academies of Science, Engineering, and Medicine, 2019; Panagioti et al., 2018; Windover et al., 2018).

Research has demonstrated that professional burnout arises from a problematic work environment rather than an increased susceptibility among individual workers (Maslach & Leiter, 2016). In health care, clinician burnout results when highly motivated clinicians work in chaotic work environments that are rife with barriers

---

P. DeChant (✉)
Paul DeChant, MD, MBA, LLC, San Ramon, CA, USA
e-mail: paul@pauldechantmd.com

D. Shannon
Shannon Healthcare Communications, Chestnut Hill, MA, USA

that prevent them from engaging in meaningful relationships with their patients—the very reason many choose the profession in the first place. In such work environments, clinicians cannot be successful at their work without constant vigilance and use of multiple workarounds to deal with dysfunctional processes.

Most leaders of health care provider organizations are unsure how to address clinician burnout. Many presume the solution requires reducing clinician workloads or adding wellness programs. Reducing workloads would likely result in lower revenues in the private sector and reduce patient access to needed care, resulting in longer waits for clinical services in both the private and public sectors. Adding wellness programs would result in higher expenses. Few health care systems can financially absorb the resulting negative financial impact to their already narrow operating margins.

We believe the alternative, reducing burnout while improving financial performance along with quality and service metrics, is not only possible, but when realized, provides a health care organization with a significant strategic advantage. Organizations can create optimal clinical workplaces while simultaneously achieving their strategic goals by adopting a leadership style based on coaching rather than top-down mandate and implementing a daily management system that empowers clinicians to fix the problems they encounter while aligning clinicians' efforts with organizational goals (Peikes et al., 2019).

Such transformations require leaders to commit to learning and implementing a new approach focused on organizational health. This chapter will describe these transformations and provide examples of organizations that have successfully created healthier clinical workplaces.

It is worth noting that little published research exists on interventions changing the management system or redesigning workflows to reduce administrative burden in health care (DeChant et al., 2019). This is a critically important area for additional study.

12.1 The Problem of Burnout

Some clinician advocates object to the use of the term *burnout*, because it connotes a problem that is a result of individual weakness and suggests that solutions to increase individuals' resilience to workplace stress are sufficient to address the issue (Rowe, Stewart, Farley, & Marchalik, 2019). Terminology arguments notwithstanding, professional burnout, which was first defined in the 1970s, is "a psychological syndrome in response to chronic interpersonal stressors on the job" (Maslach & Leiter, 2016). It is not simply fatigue or lack of time off; and it is not synonymous with depression. Professional burnout includes three components, which manifest in clinicians as: emotional exhaustion ("I've given all I can and have nothing left to give"), depersonalization or cynicism (a self-protective distancing of oneself from administration or patients when one feels as though one has nothing left to give), and perceived lack of self-efficacy (feeling as though one is not making a real difference.)

In 2019, the World Health Organization identified burnout as a diagnosis for the first time, defining it in the ICD-11 as a "workplace phenomenon...resulting from chronic workplace stress that has not been successfully managed" (World Health Organization, 2019). This inclusion may "legitimize" the condition, yet the vague definition represents a missed opportunity to name the cause of the mismanaged stress, namely the workplace and larger organization.

Toxic clinical workplaces and the resultant high rates of burnout among clinicians have a number of potential negative downstream effects.

- Burnout is associated with higher reported intent to a leave current position (Meeusen, Van Dam, Brown-Mahoney, Van Zundert, & Knape, 2011)
- Injury rates among hospital workers are higher than other professions (Occupational Health and Safety Administration, 2013)
- Disruptions in care continuity (Agency for Healthcare Research and Quality, 2017)
- Medical errors, reduced quality of care, lower patient satisfaction (Hamidi et al., 2018; Panagioti et al., 2018; Wallace, Lemaire, & Ghali, 2009; West, Dyrbye, & Shanafelt, 2018)
- Reduced revenues due to physicians restricting clinical hours (Shanafelt et al., 2016)
- Burnout in physicians is associated with substance abuse (Jackson, Shanafelt, Hasan, Satele, & Dyrbye, 2016; Oreskovich et al., 2015) and suicide ideation (Shanafelt et al., 2011); the rate of suicide among physicians is much higher than that of the general population: 40% greater in male physicians and 130% greater in female physicians (Schernhammer, 2005).

These downstream effects result in negative consequences for patients, health care professionals, health care organizations, and society as a whole.

12.2 The Underlying Causes of the Toxic Clinical Workplace

Maslach and Leiter described six underlying drivers of professional burnout (Maslach & Leiter, 2016). These describe the origins of the toxic clinical workplace, although the degree to which each element impacts a specific workplace varies by organization and by clinical unit.

The six drivers of burnout include:

12.2.1 Work Overload

Work overload is simply too many tasks to complete in a set amount of time. Time pressure and chaotic work environments exacerbate the already high workload in health care. There is increasing information overload as well (Kolusu, 2015). Medical knowledge has grown at an exponential rate; it is estimated to *double* in volume every 73 days (Densen, 2011).

12.2.2 Lack of Control

Control is an aspect of autonomy, which is a deeply held value for physicians. In fact, it is one of the intangible rewards physicians seek in pursuing the profession. Several factors have led to a substantial reduction in control in the clinical workplace, especially for physicians. These factors include the increasing corporatization of medicine and physicians moving from private practice to employment, with a significant rise in non-clinician administrators, increased demands on clinicians to achieve outcome metrics, and the imposition of clinical protocols with limited input from clinicians. Prior authorization is another example of lack of control, in that the physician has made a clinical decision that is often then questioned by a non-clinician administrator at an insurance company. Physicians interpret this as a lack of trust of physicians' professional judgement.

12.2.3 Insufficient Reward

In general, financial rewards are not a primary issue for most clinicians. However, the non-financial rewards, like recognition and acknowledgement by patients, peers, and organizational leaders, are too-often lacking. Clinicians value meaningful relationships with patients, and they want connection with colleagues. The need to interact with the electronic health record makes it more difficult to create and maintain these relationships. Relationships with patients may also be less satisfying when there is less time for each patient interaction and with changing expectations from patients who are demanding testing or treatments based on a Google search rather than valuing the physician's professional judgement.

12.2.4 Breakdown of Community

Physicians value collegiality with each other. Work overload, data entry requirements, and time pressure have translated into fewer opportunities for nurses and physicians to meet with colleagues in staff break rooms, the doctors' lounge, or over a meal. In addition, physicians and nurses interact directly less often with each other, now that physicians' orders and communication between clinicians occurs almost exclusively via computerized physician order entry (CPOE). This breakdown of community means individual clinicians may be less likely to feel a sense of support at work.

12.2.5 Absence of Fairness

Fairness is about being treated with dignity and respect regardless of one's demographics or job title. In the workplace, lack of fairness occurs when there is inconsistent handling of promotions and evaluations or when there is inequity in workload or pay (Maslach & Leiter, 2016). As the clinical workforce has increasing gender and ethnic diversity, issues of lack of fairness in hiring, promotion, and firing, are more obvious and adversely affect the work environment. Inequity can lead to burnout because experiencing lack of fairness is exhausting, and it breeds cynicism about the workplace.

12.2.6 Conflicting Values

Today, clinicians increasingly feel that the organization they work for does not share their values, such as prioritizing patient safety. In an era of administrators responding to rapid changes in the external environment, avoiding a conflict of values requires trust and regular communication from leaders to frontline clinicians. For example, organizational leaders may make policy decisions to increase access for patients, but if they fail to communicate the reasons for the resulting changes, clinicians may assume the shifts are motivated by a desire to increase profits. Also, if administrators set an aspirational target of achieving 90th percentile performance yet fail to provide the resources needed to achieve those targets, physicians see this as a conflict of values.

12.3 Aspects of the Health Care Environment That Drive Burnout

We believe that three aspects of the health care environment are especially important in the development of clinician burnout.

- Dysfunctional workflow processes
- Command and control leadership

- Unhealthy organizational culture

Dysfunctional workflow processes can manifest in lack of control and work overload. Command and control leadership can manifest in lack of control and insufficient reward. Unhealthy culture can manifest in breakdown of community, absence of fairness, and conflicting values.

First, health care is rife with dysfunctional work processes. Health care has an error rate that is thousands of times higher that of other high-risk industries, such as aviation and nuclear energy, and much less frequent use of optimal and standard processes (Kapur, Parand, Soukup, Reader, & Sevdalis, 2015; Nolan, Resar, Haraden, & Griffin, 2004). Most clinicians can describe many ways that their daily work experience involves tasks that cannot be completed efficiently, conveniently, and with a low risk of error. The "non-doable" tasks and the attendant chaos of dysfunctional work processes result in work overload.

In addition, over the last 15–20 years there have been numerous changes in the ways in which care is delivered. These changes have significantly altered the clinical workflow, often without the needed redesign to effectively incorporate them. For example, introduction of the electronic health record, without significantly changing patient care workflows from the days of paper charts, has significantly increased the data entry burden for most clinicians, and increases in prior authorization requirements have resulted in more and more physician and nurse time spent on calls to payers. An electronic monitoring study has shown that primary care physicians spend two hours on documentation for every hour of direct patient care (Sinsky et al., 2016). Not only have these changes in care delivery resulted in work overload, they have also directly affected the clinicians' ability to connect with patients (Crampton, Reis, & Shachak, 2016; Ratanawongsa et al., 2016), an essential aspect of the profession that drew them to the field in the first place.

Although electronic health records and administrative burden are often first named by physicians as causes of burnout (Gardner et al., 2019; Kane, 2019), clinical work processes were not ideal prior to the addition of these newer aspects of care delivery. However, the increased focus on cost efficiency, quality, and patient outcomes in recent years has resulted in more metrics to capture, more data to enter, and more results to analyze. Pursuing higher quality, safer care for patients has had an unintended consequence: increased clinician burnout (Spinelli, 2013). The additional work tasks and requirements associated with efforts to improve quality and safety were added onto existing tasks and requirements in most cases without careful consideration of the effect on frontline clinicians and without conscious, proactive redesign of how work is done and which team member is best suited to do each task. Physicians' time has often been viewed as expendable without additional cost to the health system, resulting in doctors' work hours expanding into the evening and weekends (Ofri, 2019).

Second, health care, as with many other industries, has been dominated by a top-down, command-and-control leadership style (de Zulueta, 2015).This approach is characterized by leadership that decides what is to be done, how to do it, and directs the workers to perform specific tasks in specific ways to achieve outcome targets.

Such an approach is problematic when managing knowledge workers such as physicians and nurses, especially when working in dynamic and unpredictable work environments. Clinical care is often intense, carrying high stakes of life and death. Clinicians have highly specialized knowledge and skills that administrators cannot possibly know as well. When non-clinicians make decisions that impact how clinicians are able to care for their patients, it puts the patients at risk and is demoralizing for the clinicians. Examples of this include insurance company prior-authorization requirements and hospital administrators choosing diagnostic equipment.

Clinical workplaces function more effectively when clinicians with specialty expertise are engaged in the process of making decisions about the way they deliver care. While this may appear intuitively obvious, such an approach takes time and includes some risk, so administrators often find it more expedient to make decisions themselves without getting input from all key stakeholders. Examples include having physicians design exam rooms so that they can properly examine a patient as opposed to an administrator choosing a design that reduces building expenses, or allowing each clinical site to schedule a daily huddle when it works best for the staff at that location rather than having the director dictate that all huddles happen at the same time for the convenience of the director.

Third, the organizational and professional culture in which health care is delivered is often unhealthy for workers. Organizational culture, which can be defined as "shared and fundamental beliefs of a group that are so widely accepted that they are implicit and often no longer recognized" (Shanafelt, Schein, et al., 2019) can create, condone, or exacerbate drivers of burnout. Specifically, in an organization where the spoken or unspoken demand for specific performance outcomes is extremely strong, leaders and middle managers will generally focus on the performance of frontline clinicians and push them toward specific outcomes without a concomitant effort to redesign workplaces and work processes that support the delivery of high-quality, safe, clinical care. The focus on performance outcomes at the expense of workplace functioning creates an environment where the accepted norm is "not doable work" for frontline clinicians. In addition, the focus on performance without creating the conditions in which to succeed is a missed opportunity to engage workers and achieve positive outcomes.

Clinicians also operate with a professional culture that includes unhealthy aspects. As one report describes, "Too often, new care providers enter a system in which disrespect for one's peers and coworkers is not only tolerated, it is the norm" (Institute for Healthcare Improvement, 2013). Historically, medical training has emphasized sacrifice, delayed gratification of needs, lack of self-care, independence, not asking for help, and ignoring basic human needs such as sleep. This culture is changing somewhat as millennials enter the clinical workforce in increasing numbers (Frelick, 2019), but aspects of the unhealthy professional culture remain. New nurses entering the workforce struggle for a variety of reasons (Hofler & Thomas, 2016). In their clinical training the workloads are significantly lower than they are expected to manage once they are on the wards, resulting in them feeling overwhelmed as they begin their first nursing jobs. The nursing shortage has left their assigned mentors overburdened, resulting in inadequate orientation and exposure to mentors who are burned out themselves. Twelve-hour shifts, once thought to be a benefit to reduce stress by providing 4 days off a week, have been shown to increase stress and error rates (Stimpfel & Aiken, 2013; Stimpfel, Sloane, & Aiken, 2012).

Ultimately, unhealthy organizational and professional culture adversely affects several drivers of professional burnout, including community, work overload, lack of fairness, and conflicting values.

12.4 Envisioning the Optimal Clinical Workplace

What would an optimal (i.e., functional, non-toxic) clinical workplace look like? By definition, it would be a work setting that negates or minimizes the six drivers of professional burnout and the three aspects of the health care environment that we believe are especially important in the development of clinician burnout. In building the optimal clinical workplace, however, organizational leaders would do well to aim beyond a goal of reducing burnout to the goal of enabling clinicians to thrive in their work.

Here, we consider, as a model for enabling clinicians to thrive, the three components of motivation of the general workforce identified in *Drive: The Surprising Truth About What Motivates Us* by Daniel Pink: autonomy, mastery, and purpose (Pink, 2009). Pink's research was not focused on health care workers, but we believe it is especially applicable because the values of autonomy, mastery, and purpose are deeply ingrained in providing quality patient care (Kane, 2019; Rizk, 2018).

Autonomy is important to all clinicians, especially physicians, whose training often focuses on the ability to make independent decisions and to own the ultimate responsibility for patient outcomes. Enabling autonomy does not mean avoidance of teamwork or eschewing best practices or standardized protocols. Instead, it means that clinicians have the leeway and resources and feel empowered to fix local problems and escalate those they cannot fix themselves. Empowering physicians to fix frustrations at the local level (or "pebbles in your shoe") fosters autonomy in designing the way that care is delivered in the clinical workplace. An example of autonomy in the clinical setting is the ability to vary scheduling and staffing for local needs. Autonomy in this context does not mean that clinicians have complete control to select clinical treatment options that do not align with widely accepted community standards of care.

For clinicians, *mastery* includes direct clinical abilities, such as diagnostic and treatment skills, and other competencies, such as communication and leadership skills. In the past, clinician training has primarily focused on direct clinical competencies, often leaving clinicians underprepared for engaging in ideal communication, team building, leadership, and self-care. These competencies can be addressed through specific training and modeling by leaders.

Finally, *purpose* is all-important to clinicians both individually and collectively. Most health care professionals enter the field because of a desire to be of service to others and reduce suffering. Engaging clinicians in creating shared mission, vision, and values can help to ensure a shared understanding of purpose. However, few physicians think mission, vision, and values statements are important, as evidenced in blog postings by physicians. In many institutions, the disconnect between the C-level leaders and clinicians on the front lines of care leads to distrust and cynicism, which is exacerbated when clinicians see examples of organizations violating their stated values.

As hospital systems and medical groups grow through acquisition, it is increasingly important to ensure that merging entities do actually share core values. This can be made more meaningful by developing a compact—a document that explains how both parties (individuals and the organization) will reciprocally honor each value. For example, if "quality" is a value, physicians will commit to closing care gaps in each encounter, and the organization will commit to providing them the resources needed to do so effectively.

A healthy clinical workplace is one in which clinicians can spend most of their time in direct patient care because the burdens associated with data entry and other administrative requirements are minimized. Such practices provide support to clinicians by hiring additional staff to perform data entry and administrative tasks. For example, the department of Family Medicine at the University of Colorado Health System instituted a team-based model in which medical assistants complete a structured process with patients at the beginning of the visit, remain in the room to perform documentation, and provide patient education and health coaching, allowing the physician to focus on medical decision making (Wright & Katz, 2018). It is also an environment that promotes psychological and physical safety, as well as a strong sense of community. This benefits clinicians by allowing them to do their work efficiently and by reducing the underlying drivers of burnout. It also benefits patients, through more satisfying interactions with their clinicians, easier navigation of a clinical environment, and lower rates of medical error. Physicians can see more patients and be more fulfilled if they spend their time connecting to patients rather than documenting the time spent with patients. The good news for health care organizations is that achieving an optimal clinical workplace is possible while improving the most important organizational performance measures, including financial metrics, reputation in the marketplace, and customer (patient) loyalty.

12.5 Moving from the Vision to Execution

Worldwide, efforts are growing to reduce burnout and improve clinician well-being. However, little research has been conducted to date regarding the effects of leadership style on clinician burnout. The lack of existing evidence must be remedied with ongoing research but should not impede steps toward improvement, when guided by expert opinion and best practices.

The Stanford Model for professional fulfillment categorizes interventions into three domains: personal resilience, efficiency of practice, and culture of wellness (Bohman et al., 2017). Much effort has gone into enhancing personal resilience to help individuals cope with the dysfunctional workplace, but these interventions do not address the root causes of burnout.

Organizational leaders are increasingly focusing on improving efficiency of practice by redesigning dysfunctional workflows and eliminating non-clinical tasks or assigning them to support staff, allowing clinicians to better focus on the patient. Leaders must engage and empower the frontline clinicians and non-clinical staff to effectively identify and fix these workflows, because these individuals are best situated to know what is broken and how to fix it.

Engaging and empowering clinicians is critical for improving the culture of wellness. Senior leadership must commit to transforming the management system and organizational culture. In this section, we will describe the key components necessary for such a transformation: servant leadership style, organizational structure that supports mentoring, and a daily management system that empowers the frontline and facilitates efficient, cross-organization communication.

12.5.1 Servant Leadership

Creating a healthy, functional workplace requires a shift from a top-down, command-and-control style of leading to servant leadership. While servant leadership is rare in practice (Aij & Rapsaniotis, 2017; Pfeffer, 2018; Trastek, Hamilton, & Niles, 2014), its features are widely described in business books (Chapman & Sisodia, 2015; Schein & Schein, 2018; Suchman, Sluyter, & Williamson, 2018).

This style of leading is characterized by mutual respect and by mentoring not managing ("mentor people to manage processes"). It results in workers that are empowered and aware of and aligned with larger organizational goals. As a result, the organization achieves better performance on a variety of metrics, including financial, quality, safety, customer service, patient engagement, access to services, and employee engagement.

Servant leadership is not passive. It is a proactive, hands-on approach that often requires personal change for those in top leadership positions. If a leader actively engages in servant leadership, middle managers will view this change as important and adopt a similar style. If top leadership does not actively engage, middle managers who are not inclined to change will not transform.

For most top leaders, who were educated in command-and-control leadership, shifting from a commander to a mentor role requires guidance and support from an executive coach. Leaving the known for the new is challenging for everyone, including leaders who have held the belief that mandating and dictating equate to strong leadership and whose identity has been tied to solo decision-making.

Servant leadership is also effective for health care professionals who are not in executive C-suite positions. Managers and frontline clinicians can pursue change within their specific sphere of influence by applying these principles to areas over which they have control. After securing approval from superiors, they can try a pilot project in a service line or clinical unit. After making small tests of change they can seek opportunities to share best practices with other clinical units.

To maximize the benefits of a servant leadership style, leaders need two key elements: an organizational structure that enables and encourages mentoring rather than managing and a management system that empowers front-line problem solving.

12.5.2 Organizational Structure That Supports Mentoring

The ideal organizational structure for servant leadership supports mentoring and creates the framework for an effective daily management system. This structure clarifies which individuals are responsible for each role and task. It can be described as an "inverted org chart," in that the focus is on supporting and empowering the frontline workers who provide the actual value delivered to customers (i.e., clinicians providing patients with health care services). The manager's role is to support the frontline worker, and upper management's role is to support both managers and frontline workers.

This organizational structure addresses demand and capacity issues for each role, through the use of strategy deployment, which is a process for assigning responsibility to implement strategic and performance improvement initiatives. This is developed in a process of "catchball" in which those assigning tasks and those accepting the task agree that the expectations are achievable, providing the opportunity for workers, managers, and leaders to be successful. (For more information, see the resource list at the end of the chapter.) Simply rearranging roles on paper is insufficient, however; the ideal structure requires redesign of work processes and the removal of some tasks ("de-selecting") when new ones are added (Fig. 12.1).

In contrast with the traditional organizational chart, the inverted org chart places the front line worker at the top of the chart, and each successive layer of management below the next layer, indicating that upper and middle management *support* those who report to them.

Leaders who engage in personal transformation, which requires openness to change and coaching, will be most successful. This organizational structure and coaching enable the personal changes that every individual at each level of the

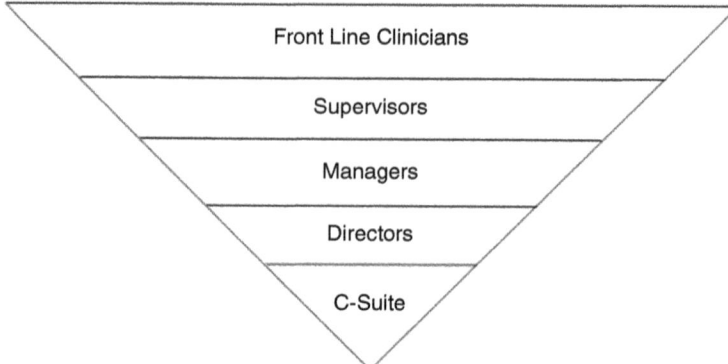

Fig. 12.1 Inverted organizational chart

organization must adopt for the clinical workplace to become functional and optimized. Similarly, organizations that undergo culture change will be more effective at creating optimal workplaces (Pourbarkhordari, Zhou, & Pourkarimi, 2016; Troy, 2008).

12.5.3 Management System That Empowers Front-Line Problem Solving

Several authors have provided the theoretical basis for leadership that empowers frontline workers (Pfeffer, 2018; Pink, 2009). However, they have not provided specific details on a management process that would support and enable such empowerment. We believe an essential component of an effective management process is a daily management system with tiered, structured huddles with visual management for team communication, such as white boards in each clinical unit that show current performance and planned work for the day (Ulhassan, von Thiele Schwarz, Westerlund, Sandahl, & Thor, 2015).

These huddles have a different focus at each level of the organization. At the frontlines, huddles focus on daily needs to provide care. Key components of such huddles include:

- Preparing for the day—identifying any potential supply-demand mismatch (based on the schedule or census, assessing whether there are enough staff, the supplies are sufficient, and the equipment needed is functioning properly)
- Identifying and developing a plan to fix small problems that happened the previous day ("pebbles in your shoe"), to prevent them from recurring
- Tracking metrics at the local level that are aligned with the organization's targets
- Acknowledging team members for special effort or notable life events (birthdays, children's achievements, etc.)

At the manager and leader levels, huddles focus on assessing resources and demands and removing barriers escalating issues that were raised at the frontline huddles which cannot be resolved with the resources or authority of the frontlines workers.

Effective management processes have numerous benefits for leaders, including reduced time spent in meetings and responding to inbound communications, more time to strategize rather than put out fires and to visit the clinical workplace and observe gaps and successes firsthand. When such huddles are tiered up to the C-suite, the CEO has much greater awareness of any operational challenges early on and is rarely surprised by a problem not being resolved. (To learn more about management processes that enable empowered frontline workers, see the resource list at the end of the chapter.)

An effective daily management system, along with servant leadership and an organizational structure that supports mentoring, creates an organization that is more resilient and can respond more rapidly and effectively to changes in the external environment, such as strategic threats, technology advances, or new regulatory requirements.

12.6 Connecting the Dots: Leadership Style and Clinician Well-Being

Leadership style has a direct impact on clinician well-being. Researchers at the Mayo Clinic have shown that negative leadership behaviors directly correlate with the risk of burnout among physicians supervised by that leader. These behaviors include failure to hold career development conversations, not treating the physician with dignity and respect, and failure to keep the physician informed about changes taking place in the organization (Shanafelt et al., 2015). Leaders who lead by mentoring resist providing solutions to problems, but instead support the clinical teams—the individuals who best know the nature of the problems at the locus of care delivery—to develop solutions. Mentoring empowers and engages. The personal experience of one of us (P.D.) as CEO of the Sutter Gould Medical Foundation demonstrated that this style of leadership mitigates the six drivers of clinician burnout:

- Teams are able to redesign work processes to remove waste and reduce *work overload*.
- Clinicians experience greater autonomy, are empowered to make local changes to improve work efficiency, care quality, and patient safety, addressing *lack of control*.
- Clinical teams show greater appreciation for each other, which is one component of addressing *insufficient reward*.
- Clinical teams working together to redesign workflows and solve local problems experience collaboration, counteracting *breakdown of community*.

- The collaboration that ensues when clinical teams work to identify and address local problems increases their understanding of others' perspective and priorities, thus improving mutual respect among team members and reducing the sense of *absence of fairness*.
- When teams are aligned around improving performance on frontline metrics that align to the organization's strategy and goals, and the C-level leaders are communicating these to the frontlines, the risk of *conflicting values* decreases significantly.

Servant leadership and the associated culture change not only reduce the drivers of clinician burnout, but also result in several other positive outcomes that are important to health care organizations, leaders, clinicians, patients, and society. First, it has been our experience that by reducing burnout, servant leadership can reduce its negative downstream effects, including lack of engagement, medical errors, lower patient satisfaction, high staff turnover, and inadequate billing (lower reimbursement due to lower performance-based compensation and lower productivity in clinicians with burnout). Second, servant leadership can reduce waste and delays. It is estimated that one third of health care in the US represents waste (Institute of Medicine, 2013; Lalleman, 2012). By proactively engaging the front line as problem-solvers, servant leadership can reduce costs by eliminating wasted time, goods, and services.

Third, servant leadership is better suited for the current health care arena. Frontline clinicians are knowledge workers with specific training and skill sets that managers often do not have. In this world, it is ineffective for managers and leaders to expect improved performance without collaborating with clinicians and providing the needed support, resources, and work environment.

Finally, servant leadership enables the health care organization to be more adaptable to changes in the external environment, such as new patient safety challenges, changes in technology, changes in financing, and greater awareness of equity and access issues. By mentoring managers rather than dictating mandates to them, by opening communication channels with frontline clinicians, by fostering problem solving by those most closely involved in care delivery, servant leadership helps create an organization better poised to make rapid adjustments to external stressors.

12.7 Challenges to Spreading Servant Leadership

Over the past few decades, many leadership experts, including Simon Sinek, Bob Chapman, and Jeffrey Pfeffer have recommended a servant leadership style, or one with similar attributes. However, servant leadership is the exception and not the rule (Stoller, 2015). If this style of leading has been identified by experts as advantageous, why aren't more organizations adopting it, especially in the for-profit sector where there is tremendous pressure from shareholders to improve financial performance?

Shifting from the traditional, command and control style of leadership to servant leadership is challenging for a host of reasons. First, any change invokes fear and resistance, because it involves moving from the status quo. Fear of change is personal; people worry about the potential effects on their career and livelihood (Maurer, 2010). Adopting a new and unfamiliar style of leadership requires internal change within the leader. Seeing the benefits of change generally takes time—the shift must build momentum, which is not instantaneous.

Second, for a variety of reasons, health care as an industry is conservative and risk averse. The service provided involves life and death. Health care operates in a VUCA environment (volatility, uncertainty, complexity, and ambiguity) making any change more risky. There are valid concerns about maintaining viable financial margins, which are significantly narrower for most health care organizations than in other industries, making the stakes associated with a misstep greater. Given the significant challenges of attempting to fix the current work processes, reduce waste, and increase the efficiency of operations, many leaders opt to prioritize instead mergers and acquisitions, which increase market power and expand sources of revenue, mitigating the need for organizational change.

Third, senior leaders often have business expertise but are not well-versed in frontline clinical issues. They are focused on "running a business" and may not consider mentoring or closely communicating with clinicians to be part of their realm. In addition, many senior leaders trained in top-down management have achieved their status through traditional leadership behaviors and have bought into the hierarchy inherent in most health care organizations. Their personal success has been achieved using top-down management, so they question the need to change.

Leaders adopting servant style leadership accept that everyone in the organization may have information to share that can improve service delivery, cost, efficiency, and other key performance metrics. Top leaders are ready to listen to new ideas and potential solutions, whether they originate in the C-suite, among middle managers, frontline clinicians, or housekeeping or other support staff.

12.8 Taking Action: Adopting Servant Leadership and Creating Optimal Clinical Workplaces

When a leader accepts the theory that problems with performance should be addressed with workplace redesign and empowering the frontline to identify and solve problems, he or she may find it challenging to execute on this theory in the current market, where there is overwhelming pressure to demonstrate improvement in performance outcomes in the short term. Having the support of the board of directors is essential. If the board members are able to focus on long-term success, rather than the next quarter, they are more likely to support decisions that drive sustainable improvements, including investing in the changes needed to redesign the workplace.

Culture and leadership style can change more quickly when higher level leaders are engaged. A single leader cannot achieve these changes alone. Instead, leaders across the organization must be engaged in order to inculcate the organization with the new version of "how we do things here." To read about organizations that have adopted a coaching and mentoring style of leadership, see the case studies in the resource list at the end of the chapter.

12.9 Conclusion

Clinician burnout is a widespread problem caused by toxic, dysfunctional clinical workplaces. Clinicians are adversely affected, as are patients, leaders, private and public payers, and society overall. Optimal clinical workplaces are designed to ensure clinicians can connect compassionately with their patients, and effectively and efficiently care for them.

Creating optimal workplaces will require both individual and organizational change. Individual leaders must shift from command-and-control leadership to mentoring. Managers must shift from managing people to managing the process. Clinicians must participate in change processes and engage in identifying and fixing workflow problems. Organizations must invest in leadership development, adopt an inverted org chart, enable and support servant leadership, and implement strategy deployment, process improvement, and an effective daily management system.

Toxic workplaces are a significant driver of clinician burnout. Now is the time for health care leaders to transform themselves and their organizational cultures to create optimal clinical workplaces. A leader who embraces a servant leadership style, engages with and empowers frontline staff, and prioritizes clinician well-being can create a healthier clinical workplace, ultimately benefiting clinicians, patients, and the organization, as well as realizing greater personal and professional fulfillment themselves.

Key messages for researchers
More study is needed to identify the most effective approaches to improving the clinical workplace, such as management systems, workplace culture, leadership attributes, and workflow redesign opportunities. – Determine optimal metrics to better assess individual thriving, clinician wellbeing, effective teams, and reducing hassle factors – Develop more effective approaches to measuring the cost of burnout beyond turnover, and the return on investment of burnout reduction interventions – Identify root causes that hold leaders back from fully engaging in burnout reduction work and effective interventions to drive leaders to engage more fully
A strong body of literature exists regarding servant leadership in other industries. More research on servant leadership in healthcare would be beneficial. – Develop case studies on servant leadership in health care to provide examples other leaders can emulate

(continued)

– Identify outcomes associated with servant leadership in health care
– Identify features or capabilities of leaders best exemplify servant leadership in health care
– Identify best practices for how these competencies can be learned
– Recommend changes to masters in business administration (MBA) and Health Care Administration (HCA) programs to reinforce servant leadership

Key messages for health care delivery

Health care organizations should:
– Invest significantly more resources in designing practice workflows to enhance efficiency, with the potential for substantial improvement in all performance metrics
– Focus more attention on improving their management system and culture of wellness, and expanding these efforts organization-wide rather than only at the local units or departments level
– Implement an organization-wide daily management system that aligns and empowers frontline clinicians
– Consider a hybrid or pilot approach for leadership change: select a part of the organization (i.e., "a model cell") to shift into a mentoring style of leadership; demonstrated improvement in the model cell can help engage the rest of the organization
– Seek out opportunities to observe organizations that have made changes in leadership style and culture, through study trips and site visits
– Connect with other organizations pursuing optimal workplaces. For example, consider joining the Health Care Value Network or the Association for Manufacturing Excellence.
– Review the literature on change management. (See the resources list at the end of the chapter.)

Executive leaders should:
– Shadow clinicians to learn firsthand about the challenges they face
– Prioritize efforts to design workflows that provide clinicians more time to directly engage with patients and less time engaged with administrative work. These design efforts should be led by clinicians with administrative support
– Focus more intensively on improving organizational culture away from traditional "command and control" and towards servant leadership, recognizing the challenges described in this chapter
– Engage an executive coach to help guide the shift, unless leaders have led successful organizational culture change in the past. One key advantage of external coaches in this setting is that they do not have management responsibility in the organization and can be considered a safe confidant with whom a senior leader can express concerns

Boards of Directors should:
– Include and prioritize clinician well-being as a key performance indicator
– Shadow clinicians to learn firsthand about the challenges they face

References

Agency for Healthcare Research and Quality. (2017). *Physician burnout*. Retrieved September 11, 2019, from https://www.ahrq.gov/prevention/clinician/ahrq-works/burnout/index.html.

Aij, K. H., & Rapsaniotis, S. (2017). Leadership requirements for Lean versus servant leadership in health care: a systematic review of the literature. *Journal of Healthcare Leadership, 9*, 1–14.

Bohman, B., Dyrbye, L., Sinsky, C.A., Linzer, M., Olson, K., Babbott, S., et al. (2017). Physician well-being: the reciprocity of practice efficiency, culture of wellness, and personal resilience. Retrieved September 15, 2019, from https://catalyst.nejm.org/physician-well-being-efficiency-wellness-resilience.

Chapman, B., & Sisodia, R. (2015). *Everybody matters: The extraordinary power of caring for your people like family*. New York: Random House.

Crampton, N. H., Reis, S., & Shachak, A. (2016). Computers in the clinical encounter: a scoping review and thematic analysis. *Journal of the American Medical Information Association, 23*(3), 654–665.

DeChant, P. F., Acs, A., Rhee, K., Boulanger, T. S., Snowdon, J. L., Tutty, M. A., et al. (2019). The effect of organization-directed workplace interventions on physician burnout: a systematic review. *Mayo Clinic Proceedings: Innovations, Quality, and Outcomes, 3*(4), 384–408.

Densen, P. (2011). Challenges and opportunities facing medical education. *Transactions of the American Clinical and Climatological Association, 122,* 48–58.

de Zulueta, P. C. (2015). Developing compassionate leadership in health care: an integrative review. *Journal of Healthcare Leadership, 8,* 1–10.

Frelick M. (2019). *Most residents say work/life balance is first priority in job hunt.* Retrieved August 26, 2019, from https://www.medscape.com/viewarticle/916701.

Gardner, R. L., Cooper, E., Haskell, J., Harris, D. A., Poplau, S., Kroth, P. J., et al. (2019). Physician stress and burnout: the impact of health information technology. *The Journal of the American Medical Informatics Association, 26*(2), 106–114.

Hamidi, M. S., Bohman, B., Sandborg, C., Smith-Coggins, R., de Vries, P., Albert, M. S., et al. (2018). Estimating institutional physician turnover attributable to self-reported burnout and associated financial burden: a case study. *BMC Health Services Research, 18*(1), 851.

Hofler, L., & Thomas, K. (2016). Transition of new graduate nurses to the workforce: challenges and solutions in the changing health care environment. *North Carolina Medical Journal, 77*(2), 133–136.

Institute for Healthcare Improvement. Lucian Leape Institute. (2013). *Through the eyes of the workforce: creating joy, meaning, and safer health care.* Boston, MA: National Patient Safety Foundation.

Institute of Medicine. (2013). *Best care at lower cost: the path to continuously learning health care in America.* Washington, DC: The National Academies Press.

Jackson, E. R., Shanafelt, T. D., Hasan, O., Satele, D. V., & Dyrbye, L. N. (2016). Burnout and alcohol abuse/dependence among U.S. medical students. *Academic Medicine, 91*(9), 1251–1256.

Kane, L. (2019). Medscape national physician burnout, depression & suicide report 2019. Retrieved December 14, 2019, from https://www.medscape.com/slideshow/2019-lifestyle-burnout-depression-6011056.

Kapur, N., Parand, A., Soukup, T., Reader, T., & Sevdalis, N. (2015). Aviation and healthcare: a comparative review with implications for patient safety. *JRSM Open, 7*(1):2054270415616548.

Kolusu, H. R. (2015). *Information overload and its effect on healthcare.* Retrieved September 8, 2019, from Scholar Archive website: http://digitalcommons.ohsu.edu/etd/3599

Kovner, C. T., Brewer, C. S., Fatehi, F., & Jun, J. (2014). What does nurse turnover rate mean and what is the rate? *Policy, Politics & Nursing Practice, 15*(3–4), 64–71.

Lalleman, N. C. (2012). *Reducing waste in health care.* Retrieved September 11, 2019, from https://www.healthaffairs.org/do/10.1377/hpb20121213.959735/full.

Maslach, C., & Leiter, M. P. (2016). Understanding the burnout experience: recent research and its implications for psychiatry. *World Psychiatry : Official Journal of the World Psychiatric Association (WPA), 15*(2), 103–111.

Massachusetts Medical Society, Massachusetts Health and Hospital Association, Harvard T.H. Chan School of Public Health, & Harvard Global Health Institute. (2019). A crisis in health care: A call to action on physician burnout. Retrieved September 11, 2019, from https://cdn1.sph.harvard.edu/wp-content/uploads/sites/21/2019/01/PhysicianBurnoutReport2018FINAL.pdf.

Maurer, R. (2010). *Beyond the wall of resistance.* Austin, TX: Bard Press.

McHugh, M. D., Kutney-Lee, A., Cimiotti, J. P., Sloane, D. M., & Aiken, L. H. (2011). Nurses' widespread job dissatisfaction, burnout, and frustration with health benefits signal problems for patient care. *Health Affairs (Millwood), 30*(2), 202–210.

Mealer, M., Burnham, E. L., Goode, C. J., Rothbaum, B., & Moss, M. (2009). The prevalence and impact of post traumatic stress disorder and burnout syndrome in nurses. *Depression and Anxiety, 26*(12), 1118–1126.

Medical Group Management Association. (2018) *MGMA Stat poll shows majority of healthcare leaders feel at least somewhat burnt out at their job*. Retrieved August 26, 2019., from https://www.mgma.com/resources/resources/human-resources/mgma-stat-poll-shows-majority-of-healthcare-leader.

Meeusen, V. C. H., Van Dam, K., Brown-Mahoney, C., Van Zundert, A. A. J., & Knape, H. T. A. (2011). Understanding nurse anesthetists' intention to leave their job: How burnout and job satisfaction mediate the impact of personality and workplace characteristics. *Health Care Management Review, 36*(2), 155–163.

National Academies of Sciences, Engineering, and Medicine. (2019). *Taking action against clinician burnout: A systems approach to professional well-being* (pp. 71–72). Washington, DC: The National Academies Press.

Nolan, T., Resar, R., Haraden, C., & Griffin, F.A. (2004). *Improving the reliability of health care*. IHI Innovation Series white paper. Boston: Institute for Healthcare Improvement.

Occupational Health and Safety Administration. (2013). *Facts about hospital worker safety*. Retrieved September 11, 2019, from https://www.osha.gov/dsg/hospitals/documents/1.2_Factbook_508.pdf.

Ofri, D. (2019). The business of health care depends on exploiting doctors and nurses. *New York Times*. Retrieved September 3, 2019, from https://www.nytimes.com/2019/06/08/opinion/sunday/hospitals-doctors-nurses-burnout.html.

Oreskovich, M. R., Shanafelt, T., Dyrbye, L. N., Tan, L., Sotile, W., Satele, D., et al. (2015). The prevalence of substance use disorders in American physicians. *American Journal on Addictions, 24*(1), 30–38.

Panagioti, M., Geraghty, K., Johnson, J., Geraghty, K., Johnson, J., Zhou, A., et al. (2018). Association between physician burnout and patient safety, professionalism, and patient satisfaction: a systematic review and meta-analysis. *JAMA Internal Medicine, 178*(10), 1317–1330.

Peikes, D. N., Swankoski, K., Hoag, S. D., Duda, N., Coopersmith, J., Taylor, E. F., et al. (2019). The effects of a primary care transformation initiative on primary care physician burnout and workplace experience. *Journal of General Internal Medicine,34*(1):49–57.

Pfeffer, E. (2018). *Dying for a paycheck: how modern management harms employee health and company performance—and what we can do about it*. New York: HarperCollins.

Pink, D. (2009). *Drive: The surprising truth about what motivates us*. New York: Random House.

Pourbarkhordari, A., Zhou, E. H., & Pourkarimi, J. (2016). Role of transformational leadership in creating a healthy work environment in business setting. *European Journal of Business and Management, 8*(3):57–70.

Ratanawongsa, N., Barton, J. L., Lyles, C. R., Wu, M., Yelin, E. H., Martinez, D., et al. (2016). Association between clinician computer use and communication with patients in safety-net clinics. *JAMA Internal Medicine, 176*(1), 125–128.

Rizk, R. (2018). What is the force behind people who work hard (and love what they do)? Retrieved January 2, 2020, from University of Michigan Medical School website: https://rafrizk.med.umich.edu/daniel-pink-explains-drive-2-0-in-a-best-seller.

Rowe S., Stewart, M. T., Farley, H., & Marchalik, D. (2019). Defending the term "burnout": a useful tool in the quest to ease clinician suffering. *NEJM Catalyst*. Retrieved December 13, 2019, from https://catalyst.nejm.org/doi/full/10.1056/CAT.19.0631.

Schein, E. H., & Schein, P. A. (2018). *Humble leadership: the power of relationships, openness, and trust*. Oakland, CA: Barrett-Koehler Publishers.

Schernhammer, E. (2005). Taking their own lives—the high rate of physician suicide. *The New England Journal of Medicine, 352*(24), 2473–2476.

Shanafelt, T. D., Balch, C. M., Dyrbye, L., Bechamps, G., Russell, T., Satele, D., et al. (2011). Special report: Suicidal ideation among American surgeons. *Archives of Surgery, 146*(1), 54–62.

Shanafelt, T. D., Gorringe, G., Menaker, R., Storz, K. A., Reeves, D., Buskirk, S. J., et al. (2015). Impact of organizational leadership on physician burnout and satisfaction. *Mayo Clinic Proceedings, 90*(4), 432–440.

Shanafelt, T. D., Mungo, M., Schmitgen, J., Storz, K. A., Reeves, D., Hayes, S. N., et al. (2016). Longitudinal study evaluating the association between physician burnout and changes in professional work effort. *Mayo Clinic Proceedings, 91*(4), 422–431.

Shanafelt, T.D., Schein E., Minor L.B., Trockel, M., Schein, P., &Kirch, D. (2019). Healing the professional culture of medicine. *Mayo Clinic Proceedings, 94*(8), 1556–1566.

Shanafelt, T. D., West, C. P., Sinsky, C., Trockel, M., Tutty, M., Satele, D. V., et al. (2019). Changes in burnout and satisfaction with work-life integration in physicians and the general U.S. working population between 2011 and 2017. *Mayo Clinic Proceedings, 94*(9), 1681–1694.

Sinsky, C., Colligan, L., Li, L., Prgomet, M., Reynolds, R., Goeders, L., et al. (2016). Allocation of physician time in ambulatory practice: a time and motion study in 4 specialties. *Annals of Internal Medicine, 165*(11), 753–760.

Spinelli, W. M. (2013). The phantom limb of the triple aim. *Mayo Clinic Proceedings, 88*(12), 1356–1357.

Stimpfel, A. W., & Aiken, L. H. (2013). Hospital staff nurses' shift length associated with safety and quality of care. *Journal of Nursing Care Quality, 28*(2), 122–129.

Stimpfel, A. W., Sloane, D. M., & Aiken, L. H. (2012). The longer the shifts for hospital nurses, the higher the levels of burnout and patient dissatisfaction. *Health Affairs, 31*(11), 2501–2509.

Stoller, J. (2015). *The lean CEO: Leading the way to world-class excellence.* New York: McGraw Hill.

Suchman, A. L., Sluyter, D. J., & Williamson, P. R. (Eds.). (2018). *Leading change in healthcare: transforming organizations using complexity, positive psychology and relationship-centered care.* London: Radcliffe.

Trastek, V. F., Hamilton, N. W., & Niles, E. E. (2014). Leadership models in health care—a case for servant leadership. *Mayo Clinic Proceedings, 89*(3), 374–381.

Troy, M. H. (2008). The cross-cultural leader: the application of servant leadership theory in the international context. Retrieved September 8, 2019, from https://www.semanticscholar.org/paper/The-Cross-cultural-Leader-%3A-the-Application-of-in-Troy/bf7722843e63c79a59317c1209ad30e133b229d2.

Ulhassan W., von Thiele Schwarz U., Westerlund H., Sandahl C., & Thor J. (2015). How visual management for continuous improvement might guide and affect hospital staff: a case study. *Quality Management in Health Care, 24*(4):222–228.

Wallace, J. E., Lemaire, J. B., & Ghali, W. A. (2009). Physician wellness: a missing quality indicator. *The Lancet, 374*(9702), 1714–1721.

West, C. P., Dyrbye, L. N., & Shanafelt, T. D. (2018). Physician burnout: contributors, consequences and solutions. *Journal of Internal Medicine, 283*(6), 516–529.

Windover, A. K., Martinez, K., Mercer, M. B., Neuendorf, K., Boissy, A. M., & Rothberg, B. (2018). Correlates and outcomes of physician burnout within a large academic medical center. *JAMA Internal Medicine, 178*(6), 856–858.

World Health Organization. (2019). Burn-out an "occupational phenomenon." In: *International classification of diseases.* Retrieved August 26, 2019, from https://www.who.int/mental_health/evidence/burn-out/en.

Wright, A. A., & Katz, I. T. (2018). Beyond burnout—redesigning care to restore meaning and sanity for physicians. *The New England Journal of Medicine, 378*(4), 309–311.

Chapter 13
Compassionate and Collective Leadership for Cultures of High-Quality Care

Michael A. West

13.1 Introduction

Human societies function by having shared values that guide decision-making, resource allocation and relationships (Peterson & Seligman, 2004). A central value in all societies, countries and cultures is compassion—a value that shapes our reaction to those who are suffering and in need of help. Compassion is elicited when we perceive another's suffering with the intention to act to help.

Recent research has demonstrated that compassion is a powerful element of health care, affecting both patient outcomes and clinician well-being (Trzeciak & Mazzarelli, 2019). In this chapter, we explore how understanding compassion is key to responding effectively to the triple challenge of ensuring high-quality care for our populations, the well-being of those who provide care, and the effective functioning of health care organisations that provide the context for that care.

The chapter begins by describing the global workforce crisis we face and the current challenges for healthcare before drawing on large scale studies and data sets from research in the UK National Health Service (NHS). This research shows how organisational culture is at the heart of meeting the triple challenge and the key elements that must be present for cultures of high-quality care, staff well-being and organisational effectiveness. Ensuring these cultural elements are in place is in turn dependent on the leadership of health care organisations—leadership at every level.

The research evidence suggests that compassionate leadership is both highly effective and key to creating cultures of high-quality and compassionate care (West & Chowla, 2017). Given the nature of the health care workforce, both highly

---

M. A. West (✉)
Lancaster University Management School, Lancaster, UK

The King's Fund, London, UK
e-mail: M.West@kingsfund.org.uk

motivated and highly skilled, hierarchical leadership is not only inappropriate but counter-productive. It is vital to ensure there is collective leadership (West, Lyubovnikova, Eckert, & Denis, 2014).

The chapter describes the rationale and research evidence for both compassionate and collective leadership. A programme for achieving this at practice and at scale at national level is described along with data on the success of this programme across the UK and internationally.

13.2 The Workforce Challenge in Healthcare

We begin by describing the workforce challenges that confront almost every country in the world, requiring an urgent response to the triple challenge by researchers, policy makers and practitioners.

Most countries in the world are facing a crisis in healthcare resulting from difficulties recruiting and retaining the staff they need to provide health care services effectively to their populations (Britnell, 2019). In a study of 183 countries the World Health Organization and Global Workforce Alliance found that all had staff shortages (Global Health Workforce Alliance and World Health Organization, 2014) and that existing ageing staff were not being replaced by sufficient recruitment. Some of the figures from around the world illustrate the problem: China needs 200,000 more paediatricians, 161,000 GPs, and 40,000 psychiatrists (Britnell, 2019). India needs 1.5 million doctors and 2.5 million nurses to match the average population coverage of healthcare professionals globally. Japan is seeking to recruit a quarter of a million more nurses despite tripling the numbers over the last 4 years. Germany is projected to have a shortage of 300,000 nurses by 2030. Estimates from the United States suggest that between 2014 and 2022, there will be 1.2 million nurse vacancies.

Many health care staff are leaving because of the chronically high stress levels they experience, largely a result of excessive workloads. Some illustrative data from UK doctors are provided below but these are representative of similar problems in most countries (West & Coia, 2019). Research in the UK suggests that nearly half of doctors working in hospitals and other secondary care organisations in England are considering leaving the organisations in which they work (47%) while nearly one in five (17%) are considering leaving the NHS altogether.

Why is this happening? In the 2018 English National Staff Survey, 37% of doctors indicated that they had been unwell as a result of work-related stress in the previous year (https://www.nhsstaffsurveys.com/Page/1064/Latest-Results/2018-Results/). Nearly one in four UK doctors in training and one in five trainers (practicing doctors who also educate trainee doctors) said they are burnt out because of their work (West & Coia, 2019). Nearly half of UK doctors in training work beyond their rostered hours, while one in five said that their working pattern had left them short of sleep.

The 2018 General Medical Council (GMC) National Training Survey (NTS) of all doctors in training and trainers across the UK employed such an internationally used and validated measure of burnout (the Copenhagen Burnout Inventory—Kristensen, Borritz, Villadsen, & Christensen, 2005) and this showed that nearly one in four UK doctors in training and one in five trainers were burnt out because of their work. Nearly one in five say they don't have energy for family and friends. In the 2018 English National Staff Survey, 37% of doctors indicated that they had felt unwell as a result of work-related stress in the previous year.

The English National Health Service has run an annual staff survey for 15 years, with responses from over 250,000 staff every year. The data has been analysed carefully and linked to outcomes such as patient care, financial performance, staff absenteeism and intention to quit, infection rates and patient mortality (Dawson, 2014, 2018; West & Dawson, 2011, 2012). The size of the data set (including nearly 300 organizations made it possible to control for many potentially confounding factors including resources available to organizations, teaching hospital status, type of health care organization (community care, mental health, acute hospital, specialist hospital such as children, cancer etc.), geographical region and size). Overall, the evidence is clear that healthcare staff have chronically high levels of stress in their work which is affecting turnover, absenteeism, presenteeism and performance—and of course the quality of patient care (see for a summary West & Coia, 2019). How then do we create the conditions that enable staff to deliver high-quality care and to thrive and be well in the process? The answer is ensuring an appropriate culture in their organizations, because culture is the most powerful factor shaping behaviour in organizations (Schneider, González-Romá, Ostroff, & West, 2017). We now turn to research investigating culture in NHS organisations.

13.3 Culture and Outcomes in the UK National Health Service (NHS)

Organizational culture exerts a profound influence on the behaviour of all who work in or interact with an organization (Martin, 1992; Pettigrew, 1979; Schein, 1992; Schneider et al., 2017). It is a gestalt of "... the values and beliefs that characterize organizations, as transmitted by socialization processes that newcomers have, the decisions made by management, and the stories and myths people tell and retell about their organizations" (Schneider & Barbera, 2014, p. 10). What are the core cultural characteristics needed to respond to the triple challenge and deliver high performance in the specific context of health care along with the well-being of staff?

The answers to these questions in this chapter are informed by two major programs of study. The first is a study of cultures of quality and safety in the English National Health Service (Dixon-Woods et al., 2014) involving 107 interviews with key, senior level stakeholders from across the NHS and beyond; 197 interviews with executive and board level leaders of NHS primary care and acute organisations through to frontline clinicians where staff care for patients; over 650 h of ethnographic observation in hospital wards, primary care practices, and accident and emergency units; 715 survey responses from patient and carer organisations; focus groups and interviews with patient and carer organisations; team process and performance data from 621 clinical teams, drawn from the acute, ambulance, mental health, primary care and community trust sectors; 793 sets of minutes from the meetings of 71 NHS trust boards from multiple sectors over an 18-month period, including detailed analysis of eight boards' minutes.

The second (West et al., 2011) involved analysis of NHS national staff survey data from 350+ organizations surveyed each year from 2004 to 2018, sampling the national workforce of 1.4 million employees. Responses were received each year from a sample of 150,000–250,000 staff, with response rates varying from 55 to 60%. The data from these surveys were linked to national patient satisfaction surveys, mortality data, data on quality of care, financial performance, staff absenteeism and staff turnover.

This research (see Dixon-Woods et al., 2014 for more detail) suggested that five key elements are necessary for sustaining cultures that ensure high-quality, compassionate care for patients: inspiring visions operationalized at every level; clear aligned objectives for all teams, departments and individual staff within a feedback-rich environment; supportive and enabling leadership and people management ensuring high levels of staff engagement; learning and quality improvement embedded in the practice of all staff; and effective team and inter-team working (West, 2013). We consider each of these factors in turn.

13.3.1 Visions of High-Quality Care

The research showed that leaders in the best performing health care organizations (high quality care, good financial performance, and good staff outcomes including high levels of employee engagement and low levels of absenteeism and intention to quit) prioritized a compassionate vision and developed a strategic narrative focused on high-quality, compassionate care. In the best performing health care organizations, all leaders (from the top to the front line) made it clear that high-quality compassionate care was the core purpose and priority of the organization (Dixon-Woods et al., 2014).

Targets, productivity, cost cutting, efficiency and meeting the requirements of health service regulators are obviously important but high-quality, compassionate care was the top priority in the best performing organizations. While cost effectiveness is vital given the demands on health services, the case studies suggested leaders must be vigilant in ensuring that their concern with cost effectiveness does not appear to staff in practice to trump a concern with delivering high-quality, safe and compassionate care.

Visions must also be translated into leadership actions because the messages that leaders send about their priorities are communicated more powerfully through their actions than their words. Leadership authenticity is revealed by what leaders monitor, attend to, measure, reward and reinforce and this in turn regulates and shapes the efforts of staff (Avolio & Gardner, 2005). If leaders focus more on targets, cost efficiencies, productivity and costs (vital though these are) than patient experience, quality of care and patient safety, it undermines trust in the organizational vision and shapes the culture accordingly.

The NHS research also showed that in the poorer performing organizations, senior leaders were more likely to ignore staff concerns, dismiss staff stress, avoid discussing workload pressures and to fail to deal with systems problems, such as blockages in patient pathways, unnecessary bureaucracy, and inter-departmental conflicts (Dixon-Woods et al., 2014).

13.3.2 Clear Objectives

The second key cultural component for high-quality care cultures is clear objectives at every level. This models a compassionate concern for staff well-being among leaders. Staff in the English NHS report often feeling overwhelmed by tasks and unclear about their priorities resulting in stress, inefficiency and poor-quality care (Dixon-Woods et al., 2014). Creating cultures that are focused on high-quality care requires clear, aligned and challenging objectives at all levels in the organization that ensure such care is the priority (for example, a primary health care team committing to reducing smoking among their patients by 40% within 5 years). This is not the same as the institution of target-driven cultures (such as governments imposing a mandatory maximum four hour wait for patients attending Emergency Departments) that are used to drive change in the system with, the evidence suggests, not great success (Ham, 2014).

When people and teams have clear, challenging objectives at work, they are generally motivated to work harder and to innovate (Locke & Latham, 2013). Such clear objectives begin with the top management team having clear purpose and five or six clear objectives (Wageman, Nunes, Burruss, & Hackman, 2008). This clarity of objectives must then be replicated at every level so that each directorate, department, team and individual (the latter via their appraisal process) has clear objectives aligned with the purposes, vision, mission and values of the organization. West et al. (2011) found that where staff reported such clear goals, patients reported better care—patient satisfaction was higher in organizations where staff indicated there were clear goals at every level.

13.3.3 People and Performance

The third key cultural element is compassionate people management which is particularly significant in service sectors because of the well-established relationships between staff management, customer service satisfaction and financial performance, demonstrated in the commercial service sector (Schneider, Ehrhart, Mayer, Saltz, & Niles-Jolly, 2005; Schneider, White, & Paul, 1998; Yagil, 2014). The research evidence suggests that where health service staff report that they are well led and that they have high levels of satisfaction with their immediate supervisors, patients report that they, in turn, are treated with respect, care and compassion (Dawson, 2018).

Health care staff who are engaged are likely to deliver high-quality care, to be focused on improving services and to have more capacity for compassion (Bakker, 2011; Bakker, Schaufeli, Leiter, & Taris, 2008; Bakker, van Emmerik, & Euwema, 2006). Survey data reveals that staff engagement is the best overall predictor of NHS organizational outcomes. The average level of staff engagement in health service organizations in the NHS predicts (positively) care quality and financial performance (based on independent audit body ratings), staff health and well-being, patient satisfaction, and (negatively) patient mortality, staff absenteeism and stress (West, Lyubovnikova et al., 2014). The results are consistent across the different health care sectors: primary care, ambulance, mental health and acute hospital services.

13.3.4 Learning and Quality Improvement

The landmark report by the Institute of Medicine's "To Err Is Human" led to a major movement in the United States to improve the quality and safety of health care (Kohn, Corrigan, & Donaldson, 2000). Following the failures in Mid Staffordshire NHS Trust, a report by Don Berwick in 2013 in the UK, advocated culture changes in health care with a strong emphasis on embedding learning and quality improvement throughout health care organizations.

Chassin and Loeb (2013) provide specificity to these recommendations by proposing that health care organizations incorporate high-reliability science, based on practices in commercial aviation and nuclear power. In such industries, there are hazardous conditions, but safety levels are generally much better than those in health care. There are now many examples in the UK where such approaches have been used highly successfully (e.g., Wrightington, Wigan and Leigh Foundation NHS Trust, Salford Royal NHS Foundation Trust) as well as in the United States (e.g., Virginia Mason—Pisek, 2014).

13.3.5 Team Working

There is much evidence that team work is a vital contributor to health care quality. Health care staff must work together across professional boundaries to deliver high-quality care, particularly as the complexity of health care increases and co-morbidity becomes more common (West, 2012; West & Lyubovnikova, 2012). The data from the NHS national staff survey reveal that most NHS staff (91%) report working in a team. Follow up questions that are intended to test for the existence of basic elements of team work (team objectives, interdependent working, regular meetings) reveal that only around 40% of staff work in teams with these three characteristics (Lyubovnikova, West, Dawson, & Carter, 2015). Analyses reveal that the more staff who work in teams with those characteristics, the lower the levels of errors, injuries to staff, harassment, bullying and violence against staff, staff absenteeism and patient mortality.

Health care teams that take time to review performance and adapt their processes (termed 'team reflexivity') appear to be much more productive, effective and innovative than other teams (Schippers, West, & Dawson, 2015; Widmer, Schippers, & West, 2009), especially in the high work demands characteristic of health care. Reflexivity enables interdisciplinary health care teams to understand how well they are meeting patient needs, and therefore to identify what they need to change about their ways of working. A meta-analysis (Tannenbaum & Cerasoli, 2013) suggested that teams that take time to review, de-brief etc. are, on average, 38% more productive.

We now take our argument an important step forward by exploring the characteristics of leadership that we propose are necessary for nurturing the cultural characteristics described above, and which we propose are fundamental to ensuring the delivery of continually improving, high-quality and compassionate care. Compassionate and collective leadership, we propose, are vital for achieving such cultures.

13.4 Changing Culture: The Role of Compassionate and Collective Leadership

Organizational culture is shaped by the nature of its leadership. It is the behaviour of leaders, top to bottom and end to end, individually and collectively, in health care organizations that powerfully determine whether care quality is the priority; all staff have clear objectives; there is enlightened people management; there are high levels of staff engagement; learning and quality improvement are embedded; and good team and inter-team working is endemic.

Research on climate and culture in health care internationally suggests that leadership cultures of command and control are less effective than more engaging and compassionate leadership styles in health care systems across the world (Dickinson, Ham, Snelling, & Spurgeon, 2013; West, Topakas, & Dawson, 2014) and implies that compassionate and collective leadership approaches are likely to be most effective. We begin by describing the role of compassionate leadership.

Compassionate Leadership Caring for the health and well-being of others is an intrinsically compassionate behaviour that is at once an act and an expression of the core human value of compassion. Virtually all those people who work in health and care services have dedicated a large part of their lives to caring for others. Compassion is important to them and the extent to which their organizations also mirror in practice that value of compassion will influence the value 'fit' between health care workers and their organizations. The stronger that fit—the alignment of individual and organizational values—the higher the levels of staff members' commitment, engagement and satisfaction (Greguras & Diefendorff, 2009).

Compassion (in an organizational context) can be understood as having four components: attending, understanding, empathising and helping (Atkins & Parker, 2012). In the context of an interaction between a health care professional and a patient in distress, compassion involves:

1. Paying attention to the other and noticing his or her suffering—attending
2. Understanding what is causing the other's distress, by making an appraisal of the cause, ideally through a dialogue with the patient—understanding
3. Having a felt empathic response, to some extent mirroring the other's distress—empathising
4. Taking thoughtful, skilled and appropriate action to help relieve the other's suffering or at least to help them cope more effectively with it—helping or serving.

Compassionate leadership involves the same four behaviours but understood and applied in the context of leading others.

Attending The first element of compassionate leadership is being present with and attending to those we lead. Leaders who attend will model being present with those they lead and 'listening with fascination' (Kline, 2002). Listening is probably the most important skill of leadership (West et al., 2015) and involves taking the time to listen the challenges, obstacles, frustrations, and hurts staff experience as well as the successes and pleasures.

Understanding The second component involves leaders appraising the situation those they lead are struggling with to arrive at a measured understanding. Ideally, leaders arrive at their understanding through dialogue with those they lead and perhaps have to reconcile conflicting perspectives rather than imposing their own understanding. In the context of highly pressured work situations, staff often feel they are not listened to and that their leaders do not understand the situations they face (West, Dawson, Admasachew, & Topakas, 2011).

Empathising The third component of compassionate leadership is empathising. Compassionate leadership requires being able to feel the distress or frustration of those we lead without being overwhelmed by the emotion and therefore unable to help. Putting oneself in the other's shoes means taking their perspective which increases understanding of the sources and context of the difficulties they face (Gilbert, 2010).

Helping The fourth and final component is taking thoughtful and intelligent action to help the other. Probably the most important task of leaders in health care is to help those they lead to deliver the high-quality, compassionate care they want to provide.

Leadership, according to all definitions, includes helping and supporting others. The helping element can be seen as having four components: scope—breadth of resources offered; scale—the volume of resources; speed—the timeliness of the response; and specialization—the extent to which the response meets the real needs of the other (Lilius, Kanov, Dutton, Worline, & Maitlis, 2011).

These four elements of compassionate leadership are particularly relevant in health care, where the work force is composed of highly skilled and motivated professionals, intent on doing their jobs to the highest possible standard. They require support rather than direction and enabling rather than controlling interventions from leaders (West, Topakas, et al., 2014). When leaders demonstrate compassion they provide this support in a way that is consistent with the core value orientation of those they lead. But they also legitimate it as a valued and worthwhile way of behaving, thus encouraging those they lead to respond compassionately in the face of suffering (Worline & Boik, 2006).

The affective states of leaders influence the general mood of those they lead, a phenomenon known as mood linkage or emotional contagion (Hatfield, Cacioppo, & Rapson, 1992; Totterdell, 2000; Totterdell, Kellett, Teuchmann, & Briner, 1998). Research shows that positive leader affect is associated with more positive affect among employees (Cherulnik, Donley, Wiewel, & Miller, 2001), enhanced team performance (George, 1995), and higher rates of prosocial behaviours (George, 1990).

Experiencing compassion from others shapes individuals' appraisals about themselves (e.g., seeing themselves as more capable), their peers (e.g., viewing them as kinder) and the kind of organization of which they are a part (Dutton, Workman, & Hardin, 2014). When staff feel valued and cared for (i.e., perceived organizational support), they tend to feel more satisfied in their jobs, and have increased affective commitment to their organizations (Lilius et al., 2011) and there is considerable evidence that this is true in health care organizations and is associated with high levels of patient satisfaction, care quality and even organizational financial performance (West & Chowla, 2017).

Research in the NHS has shown that learning and innovation is more likely to take place in the context of compassionate leadership and psychological safety rather than a blame culture (Edmondson, 1999; West, Eckert, Collins, & Chowla, 2017). Compassionate leadership is linked to psychological safety because psychological safety is more likely in environments where people feel safe to speak up about errors they or others have made, near misses, perceptions of excessive workload, inadequate resources, harassment, bullying or discrimination. Where people believe they will not be ridiculed, punished or abused for speaking up, they feel a stronger sense of psychological safety resulting in a greater likelihood of individual and team learning, innovation and quality improvement. Moreover, a culture of supportive teams with compassionate team leadership is linked with reduced levels of stress, errors, staff injuries, harassment, bullying and violence against staff, staff absenteeism and (in the acute sector) patient mortality (Lyubovnikova et al., 2015).

Intrinsically enfolded in the concept of compassionate leadership is the notion of collective leadership. Where leaders are focused on enhancing the well-being, growth and motivation of those they lead, they are more likely to encourage growth and development, problem solving, delegation, autonomy and control (West & Chowla, 2017). In effect, this promotes collective leadership rather than command and control leadership.

13.4.1 Collective Leadership

Given the challenges health services face in delivering care for patients, we need to enable staff to apply their knowledge, skills, and their capacities for cooperation and coordination across boundaries, to develop and implement new and improved ways of delivering services, promoting efficiency, improving quality and providing patient care. Creating the conditions for innovation requires giving front line teams autonomy to experiment, discover and apply new and improved ways of delivering care (Hirst, Van Knippenberg, Chen, & Sacramento, 2011; Liu, Chen, & Yao, 2011; Somech, 2006). Leadership in this context is more/rather? a collective endeavour than a designated hierarchical status reflecting an organizational chart.

There is a growing literature demonstrating that shared leadership in teams consistently predicts team effectiveness, particularly but not exclusively within health care (Aime, Humphrey, DeRue, & Paul, 2014; Carson, Tesluk, & Marrone, 2007). In summary, we suggest that collective leadership creates the culture in which high-quality, compassionate care can be delivered because all staff accept the distribution and allocation of leadership power to wherever expertise, capability and motivation sit within organizations.

Teams, departments, individuals and leaders within health care organizations must collaborate to provide seamless, coherent, integrated, efficient patient care. Where there are chronic inter-team conflicts, patient care suffers. Throughout health care organizations there are failings as a result of poor integration between teams, departments and services (Dixon-Woods et al., 2014). Collective leadership is an approach to understanding leadership that emphasises the importance of leaders working together in organizations to ensure that there is seamless, coherent, integrated, efficient patient care.

Collective leadership is an approach that requires leaders to adopt a common leadership philosophy in which they overtly, consciously and collectively commit to promote compassion, engagement, participation and involvement as their core leadership behaviours; promote staff autonomy and accountability; ensure staff 'voices' are encouraged, heard and acted on; encourage staff to be responsibly proactive and innovative; avoid domination, command and control except in crisis; take action to address systems problems that hinder staff from providing high-quality care; deal effectively with intimidating behaviour and poor performance by staff towards their patients or colleagues, regardless of seniority; and model compassion in dealing with patients and staff.

This can only be achieved through the development of a collective leadership strategy. The final step in our argument is therefore, that the challenges that face health care organizations can best be met if health care organizations develop such strategies carefully and purposively, to ensure they have both the leaders and the collective leadership culture necessary for creating high-quality care cultures.

13.5 Changing Culture via a Leadership Strategy

A compassionate and collective leadership strategy in health care represents a conscious effort to plan for an integrated, compassionate and collective network of leaders within a health care organization, who embody shared values of compassion and consistent leadership practices focused on providing high-quality and continually improving care (Browning, Torain, & Patterson, 2011; Pasmore, 2014; West, Lyubovnikova et al., 2014).

A compassionate and collective leadership strategy describes the leadership culture needed to nurture the overall organizational culture; it identifies the leadership skills and behaviours required; and plans how to identify, attract, develop and sustain leadership; and plans for how to ensure the diversity of leaders needed to implement and sustain the desired leadership culture. A leadership strategy therefore represents an organizational effort to tackle the challenge of leadership, identifying it as a collective organizational responsibility, and investing the resources needed to produce the cultures, structures and processes that will ensure the delivery of high-quality patient care.

The leadership strategy has two overarching purposes: To identify what kind of leadership the organization needs in order to achieve its strategic goals, and to ensure that this kind of leadership is developed, practiced and maintained. This requires identifying the key leadership positions in the organization such as clinical directors, medical directors, director of people management for example and also the hard to fill positions that may or may not be senior. In an organization with high levels of staff stress, sickness absence and intention to quit, an organization would need to recruit or develop leaders with supportive leadership styles and a focus on staff wellbeing and development. Such a decision-making process therefore focuses both on the numbers of leaders needed as well as the knowledge, skills, abilities and values required (see Table 13.1 for an example and for an extended description of the process see https://improvement.nhs.uk/resources/culture-and-leadership/). leadership development plan then flows from the leadership strategy specifying how skills and behaviours (individual and collective) will be developed and sustained. This contrasts with the way many organizations rely on training packages delivered by outside agencies at locations remote from the organization and with content that does not relate to the desired compassionate culture of the organization.

On an individual level, a compassionate and collective leadership strategy will focus on developing skills and behaviours that all leaders in the organization need in order to create and maintain a compassionate and collective leadership culture. These might include being present with those they lead, reflective listening, empathising and helping. They also include direction setting, agreeing and clarifying

Table 13.1 A leader capability analysis

An analysis of current and future individual leader capabilities might include the following criteria:
- Quantity: How many leaders will be needed over the next 5–10 years, taking into account growth, changes in organisational structure, integration of services, specialty focus, and projected turnover of staff? When will they be needed? Where in the organisation will these leaders be located? At what level in the organisation will they be placed?
- Qualities: The characteristics individual leaders, and leadership overall should possess, such as demographics (age, gender, ethnicity, education, experience)
   - Background: Subject matter expertise
   - Identity (managerial/medical/clinical)
   - Diversity: Ethnic and gender diversity by level and location
- Skills/behaviours: The specific skills, behaviours, knowledge, competencies or abilities leaders need in order to implement organisational strategy—an really important aspect of individual capability for collective leadership, which is only just becoming recognised, is the cognitive capacity of senior leaders to not just understand the complexity and interdependence of the local health economy, but also to build effective collaboration in the best interest of their patients.
   - Generic behavioural competencies that apply to all leaders in the organisation
   - Specific behavioural competencies by level or function e.g., clinical competence, understanding of quality improvement methodologies, dealing with intimidating behaviour and poor performance
   - Generic skills and knowledge required by all leaders in the organisation e.g., nurturing culture, promoting reflexive practice, leading across specialty and organisational boundaries, promoting efficacy, optimism and cohesion, leading for compassion.
   - Skills or knowledge required by level or function e.g., skills of ward manager or clinical director
   - Skills, knowledge or capabilities by location e.g., ICU, midwifery and A&E leaders

Adapted from Eckert, West, Altman, Steward, and Pasmore (2014)

team and individual goals, providing supportive leadership that promotes engagement, encouraging a positive climate, effective conflict resolution, valuing diversity (of professional and demographic backgrounds for example), promoting innovation and quality improvement, and leading teams effectively. A collective leadership strategy will ensure that all groups represented in the organization in terms of age, gender, (dis)ability and ethnicity are involved equally in leadership, thus specifying the appropriate and necessary diversity across and within all organizational levels and functions. Table 13.2 offers a simplified summary of a leadership strategy for a healthcare organization.

The strategy will also specify the *collective capabilities* of formal leaders and all staff members that are needed for compassionate and collective leadership to function. These are the capabilities of leaders when acting together such as modelling the four compassionate leadership behaviours in their daily work; providing a sense of direction; demonstrating alignment with departmental or service goals; generating commitment as a collective leadership team to the success of the organization overall; as well as an awareness of how collective leadership is established and the necessary skills to contribute to it in one's team or department (Morgeson, DeRue, & Karam, 2009).

Table 13.2 A simplified leadership strategy

- Double number of clinical leaders in the next 5 years
- Work with professional bodies to encourage clinicians to take on leadership roles
- Seek potential clinical leaders from wider health service pool
- Understand and remedy causes for females and BMEs to decline leadership opportunities
- Initiate fast-track career development paths
- Diversify leadership development staff to reflect mission
- Make action development projects a priority in terms of time invested
- Promotions to the executive team over the next 5 years must be people capable of role-modelling and powerfully facilitating collective leadership
- Increase proportion of leaders under age 50 in top three levels
- Increase percentage of female and BME leaders at senior levels
- Identify attractive career paths for clinicians
- Achieve 60% of growth in clinical leadership from internal promotion
- Communicate advantages of taking clinical leadership roles to all clinical staff
- Mainstream leadership responsibility into care-giving functions
- Preferred selection of younger, female and BME talent for executive succession plans
- Incorporate behavioural assessments of desired qualities into promotion criteria
- Create focused and effective development experiences to enhance desired skills
- Invest in development of local leaders particularly in midwifery and A&E

Adapted from Eckert et al. (2014)

Table 13.3 A case study of the culture and leadership programme: Manchester University Foundation Trust, England

One example in the UK is Manchester University Hospitals Foundation Trust which was launched after a merger of nine hospitals in 2017. The Director of Organization Design and Development commented that 'The merger provided a once in a lifetime chance to deliver even better services for the people of Manchester. We joined the culture journey in January 2016 and were able to maximise the benefits at a time of significant organisational change. The culture programme was a key element of our pre- and post-merger work and provided a robust framework for understanding, describing and strengthening the leadership and culture of our new organisation. As well as the insight we have gained through the research that underpins the process, the staff and patients have benefitted. I am confident we would not have achieved a CQC (Care Quality Commission—the independent regulator of health and social care in England) rating of 'Good' or seen improvements in our staff survey results 1 year on from such a large merger if we hadn't embarked on this journey.'

In describing the strategy process, we draw on the work of the Center for Creative Leadership (CCL) (Hughes, Beatty, & Dinwoodie, 2013; McGuire & Rhodes, 2009) in working with organizations in health care as well as other industries to develop and implement leadership strategies. The approach used by CCL has three stages: discovery, design, and delivery. This involves a careful examination of existing culture and leadership (the open source materials for achieving this are available at https://improvement.nhs.uk/resources/culture-and-leadership/) and then designing a leadership strategy (again using the open source material) that will deliver the leadership and thereby the culture needed to provide high quality patient care. Table 13.3 provides a summary case study.

The discovery phase involves collecting information about the culture, vision, mission, future challenges, political context, threats and opportunities faced by the organization. This enables those developing the strategy to identify the leadership capabilities they will need in the future and the gap between current and required future capabilities. The design phase involves identifying the means to acquire, develop and sustain those capabilities—the leadership strategy. The design process involves key stakeholders and design groups in sculpting the strategy. Finally, the delivery phase involves both individual leadership development and organizational development, targeting culture, systems and processes, as well as leadership development in an integrated and strategic way.

In 2015, the regulatory body for the NHS in England, NHS Improvement, committed to building a programme of support for NHS organisations to develop collective leadership strategies to ensure cultures of high-quality care across the NHS. The creation of this programme was a direct response to the evidence arising from the research described above. NHS Improvement have invested over £2 million in developing tools that enable NHS organisations to assess their existing cultures and leadership, design strategies to develop leadership that will ensure cultures of high-quality care and implement the strategies. The programme is based on the five cultural elements identified by the research. It is being implemented voluntarily by upwards of 100 NHS trusts in England as well as shaping the national health care leadership strategies in Wales, Northern Ireland and Scotland. Awareness of the programme has been raised by presentations at hospitals and other health care organisations over recent years by the author and by the national regulator. Take up of the programme has been enthusiastic, widespread and almost entirely voluntary. A small number of health care organizations with chronic performance problems have been mandated to begin the programme to help them in their efforts to transform their cultures and care. It is also informing practice in other health care systems around the world including Australia, Sweden, Canada and New Zealand.

13.6 Conclusions

Our aim should be to ensure that our health service organisations support staff by promoting their mental health and well-being. Moreover, their health and well-being is critical to the quality of care they are able to provide for patients and communities, affecting their compassion, professionalism, competence and commitment.

This is the responsibility of the organisations that oversee and provide health care and the role of health service workers themselves. They must work collectively to influence decisions in their organisations and ensure the cultures of those organisations are characterised by a commitment to high quality care and staff well-being. They must ensure they work in effectively functioning multidisciplinary teams that meet regularly to review and improve their performance. And they must work together to ensure that the issue of stress at work, caused for example by excessive workload is constantly addressed and tackled and solutions found.

Table 13.4 Key messages for healthcare delivery

• A critical factor influencing patient care is the well-being of staff • Compassionate leadership helps to create compassionate cultures which in turn impact on care quality, patient satisfaction and patient outcomes • The most important interventions to improve health care is for senior leaders in health and care to ensure that leadership strategies are being implemented that focus on high quality, compassionate care for patients and high quality, compassionate support for staff

Adapted from Eckert et al. (2014)

Table 13.5 Key messages for researchers

• There is a need to develop and evaluate primary interventions focused on improving the workplace factors that influence staff stress and wellbeing • Research is needed on organizational level interventions that aim to improve culture to better ensure the delivery of high quality, compassionate care for patients and high quality, compassionate support for health care staff

Adapted from Eckert et al. (2014)

We have repeatedly referred to the role of compassion or kindness in interactions with those we work with, those we lead and those for whom we provide services. There is now a large and convincing evidence base for the beneficial effects of compassion on patient outcomes and the wellbeing of health and care professionals (Trzeciak & Mazzarelli, 2019). Neglect, incivility, bullying and harassment have quite opposite effects (Porath & Pearson, 2009).

Lawrence and Maitlis (2012) describe an ethic of care in effective teams and organizations which is more likely to occur in organizations "that foster integration, nurture trust and respect the emotional lives of members, and where members have the opportunity to become competent carers" (p. 656). Helping organizations to develop compassionate and collective ways of working will equip health care professionals, their teams and organizations to deal effectively with the challenges they face.

Our call to action is for all health care leaders to practise the skills of compassion in order to create the cultures that health services needs for the future. Where organizations are founded on values and cultures of compassion, they will foster individual, team, inter-organizational, and community well-being characterized by fairness, trust, thriving and wellbeing. And in that way, they will effectively create the conditions for staff well-being, effective organizational performance and thereby better serve the well-being of the patients and communities they serve (Tables 13.4 and 13.5).

References

Aime, F., Humphrey, S., DeRue, D. S., & Paul, J. B. (2014). The riddle of heterarchy: Power transitions in cross-functional teams. *Academy of Management Journal, 57*(2), 327–352.

Atkins, P. W. B., & Parker, S. K. (2012). Understanding individual compassion in organizations: The role of appraisals and psychological flexibility. *Academy of Management Review, 37*(4), 524–546.

Avolio, B. J., & Gardner, W. L. (2005). Authentic leadership development: Getting to the root of positive forms of leadership. *The Leadership Quarterly, 16*(3), 315–338. https://doi.org/10.1016/j.leaqua.2005.03.001.

Bakker, A. B. (2011). An evidence-based model of work engagement. *Current Directions in Psychological Science, 20*(4), 265–269.

Bakker, A. B., Schaufeli, W. B., Leiter, M. P., & Taris, T. W. (2008). Work engagement: An emerging concept in occupational health psychology. *Work & Stress, 22*(3), 187–200.

Bakker, A. B., van Emmerik, H., & Euwema, M. C. (2006). Crossover of burnout and engagement in work teams. *Work and Occupations, 33*(4), 464–489.

Britnell, M. (2019). *Human: Solving the global workforce crisis in healthcare.* Oxford: Oxford University Press.

Browning, H. W., Torain, D. J., & Patterson, T. E. (2011). *Collaborative healthcare leadership: a six-part model for adapting and thriving during a time of transformative change.* Greensboro, NC: Center for Creative Leadership.

Carson, J. B., Tesluk, P. E., & Marrone, J. A. (2007). Shared leadership in teams: An investigation of antecedent conditions and performance. *Academy of Management Journal, 50*(5), 1217–1234.

Chassin, M. R., & Loeb, J. M. (2013). High-reliability health care: getting there from here. *Millbank Quarterly, 91*(3), 459–490.

Cherulnik, P. D., Donley, K. A., Wiewel, T. S. R., & Miller, S. R. (2001). Charisma is contagious: The effect of leaders' charisma on observers' affect. *Journal of Applied Social Psychology, 31*(10), 2149–2159.

Dawson, J. F. (2014). *Staff experience and patient outcomes: What do we know?* London: NHS Employers. [Internet]. Available from: https://www.nhsemployers.org/-/media/Employers/Publications/Research-report-Staff-experience-and-patient-outcomes.pdf

Dawson, J. (2018). *Links between NHS staff experience and patient satisfaction: Analysis of surveys from 2014 and 2015.* Retrieved from NHS England: https://www.england.nhs.uk/wp-content/uploads/2018/06/01-018-edc03-staff-inpatient-survey-report.pdf

Dickinson, H., Ham, C., Snelling, I., & Spurgeon, P. (2013). *Are we there yet? Models of medical leadership and their effectiveness: an exploratory study.* Birmingham, England: NIHR Service Delivery and Organisation Programme.

Dixon-Woods, M., Baker, R., Charles, K., Dawson, J., Jerzembek, G., Martin, G., McCarthy, I., McKee, L., Minion, J., Ozieranski, P., Willars, J., Wilkie, P., & West, M. (2014). Culture and behaviour in the English National Health Service: Overview of lessons from a large multimethod study. *BMJ Quality & Safety, 23*(2), 106–115.

Dutton, J. E., Workman, K. M., & Hardin, A. E. (2014). Compassion at work. *Annual Reviews of Organizational Psychology and Organizational Behaviour, 1*(1), 277–304.

Eckert, R., West, M. A., Altman, D., Steward, K., & Pasmore, B. (2014). *Delivering a collective leadership strategy.* London: Center for Creative Leadership/The King's Fund.

Edmondson, A. (1999). Psychological safety and learning behavior in work teams. *Administrative Science Quarterly, 44*(2), 350–383. https://doi.org/10.2307/2666999

George, J. M. (1990). Personality, affect, and behavior in groups. *Journal of Applied Psychology, 75*(2), 107.

George, J. M. (1995). Leader positive mood and group performance: The case of customer service. *Journal of Applied Social Psychology, 25*(9), 778–794.

Gilbert, P. (2010). *The compassionate mind (Compassion focussed therapy).* London: Constable.

Global Health Workforce Alliance and World Health Organization. (2014). *Workforce, alliance, A universal truth: no health without workforce.* Geneva, Switzerland: World Health Organization.

Greguras, G. J., & Diefendorff, J. M. (2009). Different fits satisfy different needs: Linking person-environment fit to employee commitment and performance using self-determination theory. *Journal of applied psychology, 94*(2), 465–477.

Ham, C. (2014). *Reforming the NHS from within. Beyond hierarchy, inspection and markets*. London: The King's Fund. Available at: http://www.kingsfund.org.uk/sites/files/kf/field/field_publication_file/reforming-the-nhs-fromwithin-kingsfund-jun14.pdf

Hatfield, E., Cacioppo, J. T., & Rapson, L. R. (1992). Primitive emotional contagion. In M. S. Clark (Ed.), *Review of personality and social psychology: Emotion and social behavior* (Vol. 14, pp. 151–177). Newbury Park, CA: Sage.

Hirst, G., Van Knippenberg, D., Chen, C. H., & Sacramento, C. A. (2011). How does bureaucracy impact individual creativity? A cross-level investigation of team contextual influences on goal orientation–creativity relationships. *Academy of Management Journal, 54*(3), 624–641.

Hughes, R. L., Beatty, K. M., & Dinwoodie, D. (2013). *Becoming a strategic leader: your role in your organization's enduring success*. San Francisco, CA: Jossey-Bass.

Kline, N. (2002). *Time to think: Listening to ignite the human mind*. London: Cassell.

Kohn, L. T., Corrigan, J. M., & Donaldson, M. S. (2000). *To err is human: building a safer health system*. Washington, DC: National Academies Press.

Kristensen, T. S., Borritz, M., Villadsen, E., & Christensen, K. B. (2005). The Copenhagen Burnout Inventory: A new tool for the assessment of burnout. *Work & Stress, 19*(3), 192–207.

Lawrence, T. B., & Maitlis, S. (2012). Care and possibility: Enacting an ethic of care through narrative practice. *Academy of Management Review, 37*(4), 641–663.

Lilius, J. M., Kanov, J., Dutton, J. E., Worline, M. C., & Maitlis, S. (2011). Compassion revealed: What we know about compassion at work (and where we need to know more). In K. Cameron & G. Spreitzer (Eds.), *The Oxford handbook of positive organizational scholarship*. New York: Oxford University Press.

Liu, D., Chen, X. P., & Yao, X. (2011). From autonomy to creativity: a multilevel investigation of the mediating role of harmonious passion. *Journal of Applied Psychology, 96*(2), 294–309.

Locke, E. A., & Latham, G. P. (Eds.). (2013). *New developments in goal setting and task performance*. New York: Routledge.

Lyubovnikova, J., West, M. A., Dawson, J. F., & Carter, M. R. (2015). 24-Karat or fool's gold? Consequences of real team and co-acting group membership in healthcare organizations. *European Journal of Work and Organizational Psychology, 24*(6), 929–950.

Martin, J. (1992). *Cultures in organizations: three perspectives*. Oxford: Oxford University Press.

McGuire, J. B., & Rhodes, G. B. (2009). *Transforming your leadership culture*. San Francisco, CA: Wiley.

Morgeson, F. P., DeRue, D. S., & Karam, E. P. (2009). Leadership in teams: a functional approach to understanding leadership structures and processes. *Journal of Management, 36*(1), 5–39.

Pasmore, W. (2014). *Developing a leadership strategy: a critical ingredient for organizational success*. Greensboro, NC: Center for Creative Leadership.

Peterson, C., & Seligman, M. E. (2004). *Character strengths and virtues: A handbook and classification*. Oxford: Oxford University Press.

Pettigrew, A. M. (1979). On studying organizational cultures. *Administrative Science Quarterly, 24*(4), 570–581.

Pisek, P. (2014). *Accelerating health care transformation with lean and innovation: The Virginia Mason experience*. Boca Raton, FL: CRC Press.

Porath, C., & Pearson, C. (2009). How toxic colleagues corrode performance. *Harvard Business Review, 87*(4), 24.

Schein, E. (1992). *Organizational culture and leadership*. San Francisco: Jossey-Bass.

Schippers, M. C., West, M. A., & Dawson, J. F. (2015). Team reflexivity and innovation: The moderating role of team context. *Journal of Management, 41*, 769–788. https://doi.org/10.1177/0149206312441210

Schneider, B., & Barbera, K. M. (Eds.) (2014). *The Oxford handbook of organizational climate and culture*. Oxford: Oxford University Press.

Schneider, B., Ehrhart, M. G., Mayer, D. M., Saltz, J. L., & Niles-Jolly, K. (2005). Understanding organization-customer links in service settings. *Academy of Management Journal, 48*(6), 1017–1032.

Schneider, B., González-Romá, V., Ostroff, C., & West, M. A. (2017). Organizational climate and culture: Reflections on the history of the constructs in the Journal of Applied Psychology. *Journal of Applied Psychology, 102*(3), 468–482. https://doi.org/10.1037/apl0000090

Schneider, B., White, S. S., & Paul, M. C. (1998). Linking service climate and customer perceptions of service quality: tests of a causal model. *Journal of Applied Psychology, 83*(2), 150–163.

Somech, A. (2006). The effects of leadership style and team process on performance and innovation in functionally heterogeneous teams. *Journal of Management, 32*(1), 132–157.

Tannenbaum, S. I., & Cerasoli, C. P. (2013). Do team and individual debriefs enhance performance? A meta-analysis. *Human Factors, 55*(1), 231–245.

Totterdell, P. (2000). Catching moods and hitting runs: mood linkage and subjective performance in professional sport teams. *Journal of Applied Psychology, 85*(6), 848–859.

Totterdell, P., Kellett, S., Teuchmann, K., & Briner, R. B. (1998). Evidence of mood linkage in work groups. *Journal of Personality and Social Psychology, 74*(6), 1504–1515.

Trzeciak, S., & Mazzarelli, A. (2019). *Compassionomics: The revolutionary scientific evidence that caring makes a difference*. Pensacola, FL: Studer Gr.

Wageman, R., Nunes, D. A., Burruss, J. A., & Hackman, J. R. (2008). *Senior leadership teams: what it takes to make them great*. Boston, MA: Harvard Business School Press.

West, M. A. (2012). *Effective teamwork: practical lessons from organizational research* (3rd ed.). Oxford: Blackwell.

West, M. A. (2013). Creating a culture of high-quality care in health services. *Global Economics and Management Review, 18*(2), 40–44.

West, M. A., Armit, K., Loewenthal, L., Eckert, R., West, T., & Lee, A. (2015). *Leadership and leadership development in health care*. London: FMLM and The King's Fund/Brussels: Center for Creative Leadership.

West, M. A., & Chowla, R. (2017). Compassionate leadership for compassionate health care. In P. Gilbert (Ed.), *Compassion: Concepts, research and applications* (pp. 237–257). London: Routledge.

West, M. A., & Coia, D. (2019). *Caring for Doctors Caring for Patients*. London: General Medical Council.

West, M. A., & Dawson, J. F. L. (2011). *NHS staff management and health service quality*. London: Department of Health. Available from: https://assets.publishing.service.gov.uk/government/uploads/system/uploads/attachment_data/file/215454/dh_129658.pdf

West, M., & Dawson, J. (2012). *Employee engagement and NHS performance*. London: King's Fund. Available from: https://www.kingsfund.org.uk/sites/default/files/employee-engagement-nhs-performance-west-dawson-leadership-review2012-paper.pdf

West, M. A., Dawson, J. F., Admasachew, L., & Topakas, A. (2011). *NHS staff management and health service quality: Results from the NHS Staff Survey and related data*. Report to the Department of Health, available at: http://www.dh.gov.uk/health/2011/08/nhs-staff-management/

West, M. A., & Lyubovnikova, J. (2012). Real teams or pseudo teams? The changing landscape needs a better map. *Industrial and Organizational Psychology, 5*(1), 25–28.

West, M. A., Lyubovnikova, J., Eckert, R., & Denis, J. L. (2014). Collective leadership for cultures of high quality health care. *Journal of Organizational Effectiveness: People and Performance, 1*, 240–260. https://doi.org/10.1108/JOEPP-07-2014-0039

West, M. A., Topakas, A., & Dawson, J. F. (2014). Climate and culture for health care performance. In B. Schneider & K. M. Barbera (Eds.), *The Oxford handbook of organizational climate and culture* (pp. 335–359). Oxford: Oxford University Press.

West, M., Eckert, R., Collins, B., & Chowla, R. (2017). *Caring to change. How compassionate leadership can stimulate innovation in health care*. London: The King's Fund.

Widmer, P. S., Schippers, M. C., & West, M. A. (2009). Recent developments in reflexivity research: A review. *Psychology of Everyday Activity, 2*(2), 2–11.

Worline, M. C., & Boik, S. (2006). Leadership lessons from Sarah: values based leadership as everyday practice. In K. Cameron & E. Hess (Eds.), *Leading with values: positivity, virtue, and high performance* (pp. 108–131). Cambridge: Cambridge University Press.

Yagil, D. (2014). Service quality. In B. Schneider & K. M. Barbera (Eds.), *The Oxford handbook of organizational climate and culture* (pp. 297–316). Oxford: Oxford University Press.

Chapter 14
Workforce and Excellence in Nursing Care: Challenges for Leaders and Professionals

P. Van Bogaert, O. Timmermans, S. Slootmans, E. Goossens, and E. Franck

---

P. Van Bogaert (✉)
Department of Nursing and Midwifery Sciences, Centre for Research and Innovation in Care (CRIC), Faculty of Medicine and Health Sciences, University of Antwerp, Wilrijk, Belgium
e-mail: peter.vanbogaert@uantwerpen.be

O. Timmermans
Department of Nursing and Midwifery Sciences, Centre for Research and Innovation in Care (CRIC), Faculty of Medicine and Health Sciences, University of Antwerp, Wilrijk, Belgium

HZ University College of Applied Sciences, Vlissingen, The Netherlands
e-mail: olaf.timmermans@uantwerpen.be

S. Slootmans
Department of Nursing and Midwifery Sciences, Centre for Research and Innovation in Care (CRIC), Faculty of Medicine and Health Sciences, University of Antwerp, Wilrijk, Belgium

Antwerp University Hospital, Edegem, Belgium
e-mail: stijn.slootmans@uantwerpen.be

E. Goossens
Department of Nursing and Midwifery Sciences, Centre for Research and Innovation in Care (CRIC), Faculty of Medicine and Health Sciences, University of Antwerp, Wilrijk, Belgium

Department of Public Health and Primary Care, KU Leuven – University of Leuven, Leuven, Belgium

Research Foundation Flanders (FWO), Brussels, Belgium
e-mail: eva.goossens@uantwerpen.be

E. Franck
Department of Nursing and Midwifery Sciences, Centre for Research and Innovation in Care (CRIC), Faculty of Medicine and Health Sciences, University of Antwerp, Wilrijk, Belgium

Centre of Expertise the Cycle of Care, Karel De Grote University College, Antwerp, Belgium
e-mail: erik.franck@uantwerpen.be

© Springer Nature Switzerland AG 2020
A. Montgomery et al. (eds.), *Connecting Healthcare Worker Well-Being, Patient Safety and Organisational Change*, Aligning Perspectives on Health, Safety and Well-Being, https://doi.org/10.1007/978-3-030-60998-6_14

14.1 Background

Healthcare faces serious challenges due to fast moving transformations in patient characteristics such as growing age, increasing prevalence of comorbidity as well as changes in resources and organizational needs (WHO, 2018). To address these challenges (Soukup et al., 2018), future care will predominately be provided inter-professionally and outside institutions. Moreover, in-hospital care will become even more complex and demanding (Plsek, 2001). Empirical data demonstrating the effectiveness of accreditation strategies in hospitals, in terms of patient safety and quality of care, within an international context, is scarce (Jovanovic, 2005; Shaw et al., 2014). The needs of patients and their family rise beyond standards and demand engaged and empowered healthcare teams having the capacity to use feedback mechanisms to learn, adapt and improve their work system's design and processes through the monitoring and evaluation of care quality, both at individual and patient subgroup level (Van Bogaert et al., 2018). Inter-professional teams need to adapt their work system configurations in order to address these challenges in healthcare.

14.2 Insights on Clinical Work Systems, Personal Leadership and Nurse Practice Environment

14.2.1 Clinical Work Systems as Learning and Adaptive Systems

Implementation science identified key constructs within organizational inner settings, such as culture, leadership engagement, available resources, and access to information and knowledge, as vital components impacting the readiness of teams as settings for adaptation, change and improvements (Damschroder et al., 2009). Moreover, the conceptual model of work systems (Systems Engineering Initiative for Patient Safety or SEIPS 2.0), within the domain of healthcare human factors and ergonomics, described adaptation as a feedback mechanism explaining how dynamic systems evolve in planned and unplanned ways (Holden et al., 2013). Although such theoretical and conceptual models give us insight into factors influencing team adaptation, change and improvements, empirical underpinnings are still limited. Hence, we need empirical insights of practice-oriented theoretical frameworks entailing the dynamics within teams. Such findings provide us an opportunity to guide successful cyclical improvement processes as an answer to previously existing top-down 'one-size-fits-all'-approaches that are founded on a limited evidence base (Van Bogaert & Clarke, 2018).

14.2.1.1 Clinical Work System Design

The design of work systems, as described by the Systems Engineering Initiative for Patient Safety (SEIPS 2.0) model is determined by: (1) tasks or specific actions in care delivery, supported by, (2) necessary tools and technology, (3) effective organization forms such as teamwork, collaboration and coordination, and (4) a physical environment that influences processes and affects patients, care providers and organizational outcomes (Holden et al., 2013). It was hypothesized that balanced care teams have the empowerment and capacity to adapt their work system and processes based on feedback and learning strategies, with the aim of improving care. Understanding work systems through the SEIPS 2.0 model could be helpful in practice but has limited evidence on which aspects of work systems have an influence on respective outcomes (i.e., proximal and/or distal) and how feedback loops from these outcomes could improve work systems and their processes. Work systems itself are a part of clinical microsystems (Nelson, Batalden, & Godfrey, 2011). These microsystems are the smallest replicable units of healthcare delivery where a small group of people, comprising healthcare professionals, care-receiving patients and their families, collaborate in a defined setting on a regular basis (or as needed) to provide care for discrete subpopulations of patients. Examples of clinical microsystems are medical and surgical units, short stay units and day clinics, as well as teams that provide surgical or technical interventions and clinical teams in primary care settings. As a complex, adaptive system, such a microsystem has many functions, including performing the tasks associated with the core aims, meeting member needs, and safeguarding self-maintenance over time as a functioning clinical team. These aspects can, however, change over time.

14.2.1.2 Ambidextrous Work Systems Oriented to Production and Development in Care Delivery

To continuously adapt to changes, healthcare teams have to combine the provision of care with innovation of care (Timmermans, Van Linge, Van Petegem, Van Rompaey, & Denekens, 2013). Consequently, healthcare teams are becoming 'ambidextrous' as they simultaneously have to exploit production-oriented as well as development-oriented processes (Raisch & Birkinshaw, 2008; Timmermans, Van Linge, Van Petegem, Elseviers, & Denekens, 2011). For example, a hospital-based nursing team handles nursing care processes in care delivery, as well as implements processes to prevent clinical deteriorating of patients through and evidence-based standardized observation and communication protocol such as early warning score and SBAR (i.e., situation, background, assessment and recommendation) (Haegdorens et al., 2018). However, to act as ambidextrous teams, healthcare professionals undertake different learning processes, at individual and team level, processing different types of information crossing-over within the team (Timmermans et al., 2011; Timmermans, van Linge, Van Petegem, & Denekens,

2012). Throughout the different types of information that continuously cross over in healthcare teams, innovations are discovered, explored and implemented. Well-balanced care teams are characterized by empowerment and the capacity to innovate their work system and processes based on their feedback and learning strategies. A major stream of the direct care innovations of such teams originates from practices on patient safety and adoption of a new health perspective. Patient safety initiatives introduce incremental innovations such as the early detection of deterioration or the assessment of malnutrition. The adoption of a new perspective on health introduced major innovations on the management of clinical pathways or healthy lifestyle as a treatment. An example of the use of a healthy lifestyle treatment is the provision of lifestyle advices to patients with diabetes, where changes in diet and lifestyle resulted in a decline of medication dependence to zero (Johansen et al., 2017). Moreover, the adoption of a new perspective on health enables healthcare teams to focus not merely on enhancing health for the individual patients they take care of. Adoption of a new perspective makes nursing teams aware of the need to strengthen their self-care (i.e., as employees) and to establish a healthy region. In a healthy region, there is a continuous action of health-promoting activities, transcending from a disease-oriented towards a health-oriented perspective. Furthermore, in a healthy region, teams also promote healthy behavior in the direct workplace and beyond.

14.2.1.3 Mastering Methods Within Clinical Work Systems

In healthcare, the use of quality improvement (QI) methods and tools is growing (Nicolay et al., 2012). Very well-known QI-approaches are Lean Management, Six Sigma and Total Quality Management. The Plan-do-study-act (PDSA) cycle and the concept of iterative testing are central within all these QI-approaches (Reed & Card, 2015; Taylor et al., 2013). Despite the strong growth of quality improvement initiatives, there is only limited knowledge about their effectiveness. Certain studies demonstrated improved patient outcomes, while others showed modest or even no effects (Dixon-Woods, McNicol, & Martin, 2012; Kaplan et al., 2010). These diffuse results can potentially be explained by contextual differences in which such initiatives are implemented (Kaplan et al., 2010). Literature reviews have been published exploring the effectiveness of specific QI methodologies, such as Six Sigma and Lean, which recently became more popular in the entire of healthcare scene (Kringos et al., 2015). Other reviews have looked at broader system-wide QI models or collaborations, and highlighted their context-dependent nature, the degree of overlap between models and the need for an effective organization-specific implementation method and infrastructure safeguarding success (Nicolay et al., 2012). Additionally, motivation and involvement of healthcare providers, support of data collection, leadership and behavioral change are factors with great influence (Nicolay et al., 2012; Taylor et al., 2013). As a result, increasing attention has been paid to provide explanations for these differences and to identify barriers or facilitators (Dixon-Woods et al., 2012).

Table 14.1 Content of 'Productive Ward: Releasing Time to Care™'

Productive ward module	Objectives
Executive Leader's Guide Project Leader's guide Ward Leader's Guide	Preparing the organization Getting the executive committee on board Project planning Creating commitment at all levels of the organization
Foundation modules: Knowing how we are doing	Development and visualization of ward based measures Shared-decision making Regular team huddle
Well organized ward	Redesign ward areas for improving efficiency of care
Patient status at a glance	Providing real-time patient information
Process modules	Redesign and streamline specific ward processes
Toolkit	Basic instructions and examples of (Lean) QI tools and methods

White and Waldron (2014); Wilson (2009)

The NHS Institute for Innovation and Improvement has translated QI methodologies in its Productive Series programs, including for example the 'Productive Ward—Releasing Time to Care™' program or Productive Ward (PW) program (Nicolay et al., 2012). The PW program is an example of adapting Lean-principles to the context of nursing wards within acute hospitals (White & Waldron, 2014). The overall aim of PW was to empower frontline staff to improve patient safety, experience of patients and staff, quality and reliability of care. The program has a modular approach and contains a self-directed learning QI toolkit (see Table 14.1).

A literature review performed by White and Waldron (2014) identified the effects and impact of Productive Ward. The three most important effects by nurses were improved empowerment, leadership and engagement. Empowerment and engagement of frontline staff, especially nurses, was a core principle behind this program (Robert et al., 2020). The use of PW was also based on aspects of authentic leadership style, with leadership support and facilitation skills by management and nurse leaders (White & Waldron, 2014). A multiple methods study published by Robert, Sarre, Maben, Griffiths, and Chable (2019) explored the legacies of this program 10 years after its implementation in six hospitals. An important observation was the benefit of involving frontline staff in the initial implementation of the Productive Ward program, the impact of adopting a quality culture with PDSA improvement cycles and providing staff a greater voice within QI. Hospitals with a far-reaching implementation approach, education program and project follow-up have translated this PW program in an organizational QI program. A longitudinal study about the impact of the PW program in a large 600-bed acute care university hospital, 2 years after implementation by Van Bogaert, Van heusden, et al. (2017), revealed positive impacts on the practice environment and aspects of empowerment such as decision latitude and social capital. Nursing staff at wards where PW was implemented, perceived a more favorable nurse-physician relationship. Overall, the Lean transformation of the hospital resulted in a higher agreement with statements about nurse management at unit level (e.g., physicians and working with nurses who are clinically competent); nurse managers consult with staff on daily problems and procedures and standardized policies, procedures and ways of doing things. The perceived workload appeared to be a strong point of attention in QI improvement projects, such as Productive Ward, because of the potential risk of increased staff exhaustion and decreased staff engagement. Studies indicated negative impacts because of insufficient resources (White, Wells, & Butterworth, 2014), too many projects and initiatives are going on (Van Bogaert, Peremans, et al., 2017) or change fatigue (White, 2015).

These results, obtained through the implementation of PW as a QI methodology, revealed the opportunities to empower nurses and clinical microsystems with the aim to improve quality and safety of patient care. However, organizations need to focus on adapting such methodologies to their local contexts. Kaplan, Provost, Froehle, and Margolis (2012) developed the Model for Understanding Success in Quality (MUSIQ) to gain insight into the various factors that explain the effectiveness and efficiency of quality improvement. In 2018, Reed and colleagues published an updated version of this framework. This model describes the mandatory contextual factors and skills at the external environment, organization, infrastructure, microsystem and improvement team level. A review of systematic reviews, based on this model, showed that factors at the microsystem level largely explained the success of quality projects (Kringos et al., 2015). More research is, however, needed to explore these factors in-depth and to determine the interactions within these complex social systems.

14.2.2 Personal Leadership in Balanced Work Systems

The unceasing drive to improve the quality of healthcare provision as well as the vast changes throughout the healthcare system call for strong leadership skills both at the intra- and interpersonal level. After all, influencing group activities and coping with change are the key aspects of the leadership role. The latter can be divided in two distinct, yet related, sub-roles that comprise both personal and interpersonal leadership. Personal leadership can be defined as an internal process of leading oneself. Working in clinical microsystems requires close interprofessional collaboration with team members of different disciplines. This close collaboration in often high workload environments entails that team members behavior can be influenced by emotions or affective states rather than a cognitive appraisal or objective facts and choices. Hence, the emotions experienced by individual health professionals directly influences safety behavior (Heyhoe et al., 2016). Consequently, the powerful influence of emotions in patient safety should be recognized in both research and clinical practice, and personal leadership skills including the ability to control one's emotions should be trained.

Personal leadership skills can be conceptualized using three crucial components: self-knowledge, self-awareness and self-control. Effective leaders have an overarching sense of purpose in combination with sufficient self-knowledge of their potential leadership assets (Goffee & Jones, 2000). Self-knowledge means knowing what drives you, developing a clear sense of purpose and strong values, and creating a sense of self that one feels comfortable with. Self-awareness goes beyond self-knowledge and can be summarized as being aware of what is happening at any moment within oneself. It encompasses being aware of ones' intentions, cognitions and emotions, and specifically how they interact with ones' (interpersonal) behavior and its related effects. The third component of personal leadership is self-control. Self-control is a type of dispositional capacity that can be developed and results in a more delayed but desirable outcome in reaction to immediate dominant responses or tendencies, thoughts and emotions which are short term oriented and create more negative outcomes in the longer run (De Ridder, Lensvelt-Mulders, Finkenauer, Stok, & Baumeister, 2012). Maintaining good self-control in challenging situations is necessary in order to maintain credibility as a leader.

Interpersonal leadership on the other hand is defined as something we do with other people (Goffee & Jones, 2000). The aim of leadership in healthcare organizations is to capitalize the diversity within the organization as a whole but also to align individual team members of a clinical microsystem with each other and the organization's goals. Various studies have shown that highly qualified healthcare workers, with direct patient responsibility, are rather autonomous and do not respond well to authoritarian leadership styles (Al-Sawai, 2013). Because of the complexity of healthcare organizations and the fact that many healthcare professionals view themselves as independent practitioners, acute care hospitals often have an inverted power structure (Ham, 2003). The leadership style of healthcare managers must adapt to these challenging environments to acknowledge and overcome the considerable barriers to change, resulting from this inverted power structure (Kumar, 2013). Today's healthcare leaders need to understand, translate and take the lead in complex healthcare changes through the application of innovation and principles of change (Ackerman et al., 2019). The leadership style suggested for overcoming resistance to change and developing ownership in quality improvement programs is referred to as '*authentic leadership*' (Alilyyani, Wong, & Cummings, 2018). Research from Laschinger, Wong, and Grau (2013) showed that authentic leadership results in nurses feeling empowered and supported in their work. Authentic leadership is defined as "*a process that draws from both positive psychological capacities and a highly developed organizational context, which results in both greater self-awareness and self-regulated positive behaviors on the part of leaders and associates, fostering positive self-development*" (Luthans & Avolio, 2003; p. 243). Authentic leaders possess personal leadership skills and can therefore facilitate higher quality relationships leading to active engagement of employees in workplace activities (Alilyyani et al., 2018). Factors such as a trusting relationship with the manager, job satisfaction, decision latitude, work environment factors including structural empowerment, work engagement and work group relationships, are all found to be positively related with authentic leadership (Alilyyani et al., 2018). Not surprisingly, this authentic leadership theory has gained more and more empirical support in nursing management literature (Laschinger, Borgogni, Consiglio, & Read, 2015).

Despite the growing body of scientific research addressing patient safety issues and the gap between evidence-based practice and daily practice, efforts to improve quality in healthcare appears to demonstrate predominantly inconsistent results. However, it is clear that single-bullet approaches usually do not produce consistent improvements. Improvement projects must therefore include complex and multifaceted interventions that are iteratively developed in response to unexpected and unintended effects (Taylor et al., 2013).

14.2.3 Nurse Practice Environment as Balanced Work Systems

Based on our previous work, we identified that *imbalanced* nurse work characteristics, including high perceived workload (or job demands), unfavorable perceived social capital (or limited experiences of peer support, shared values and mutual trust) and unfavorable perceived decision latitude (because of limited abilities to make decisions and the capacity to use and develop professional and personal leadership skills) are strongly associated with low morale. This latter state is characterized with feelings of burnout and limited engagement, which in turn negatively impacted nurse-reported outcomes such as job satisfaction and intention to leave the hospital as well as the profession; nurse-assessed quality of care at the unit and the last shift as well as in the hospital over the past year (Van Bogaert, Peremans, et al., 2017).

We, therefore, assume that *balanced* nurse work characteristics with favorably rated workload, favorable social capital and decision latitude are indicative and predictive for lower burnout and higher engagement levels, resulting in favorable reported nurse outcomes. It is, however, not clear to what extent the impact of such balanced work environments will have on burnout, engagement and reported outcomes. Hence, this study aimed to investigate associations between work characteristics, job satisfaction and perceived quality of care in a population of nurses and midwifes. Work environment characteristics included social capital, decision latitude and workload, but also entailed burnout and work engagement as potential explanatory variables. Job satisfaction needed to be self-rated by employees and studied as *very satisfied* in comparison with *satisfied or (very) dissatisfied*. The nurse-assessed quality of care at the unit was evaluated based on the rating of the participants and was assessed *as excellent* in comparison with *good, fair or poor*. Furthermore, demographic, educational and professional characteristics of participants were taken into account.

14.3 The Study

14.3.1 Methods

We performed a cross-sectional survey as a longitudinal study in two study hospitals in two periods (T1 and T2) including a first measurement period conducted in 2014 in study hospital 1 and 2015 in study hospital 2 (T1) and a second measurement period conducted in 2017 in study hospital 1 and 2018 in study hospital 2 (T2). Both hospitals are university hospitals located in two different large cities in Belgium; study hospital1 in the Dutch-speaking part of Belgium and study hospital2 in the Brussels-Capital Region, the latter largely French-speaking. Both hospitals are strongly committed to achieving and evaluating *supportive and productive work environments* resulting in improved patient outcomes, through conducting a survey each 2 years. One hospital was recently recognized as an ANCC Magnet Hospital and obtained an accreditation as an academic center by the Joint Commission International (Van Bogaert et al., 2018). We have invited all registered nurses and midwifes assigned to units to complete an online questionnaire at a voluntary basis (see Table 14.1). Response rates ranged from >50% to almost 70% with respectively 423 and 504 respondents and 326 and 330 respondents at the subsequent time points, in the respective hospitals.

Over the past 10 years, a set of study variables was developed through the adaptation and testing of several measurement instruments within the Belgian context. Variables were selected based on the results of a research program investigating associations using structural equation modeling and multilevel models (Van Bogaert & Clarke, 2018). Study variables were nurse work characteristics (Kowalski et al., 2010; Van Bogaert, Kowalski, Weeks, Van heusden, & Clarke, 2013), workload and decision latitude (Richter et al., 2000) and social capital (Ernstmann et al., 2009; Pfaff, Lutticke, Badura, Piekarski, & Richter, 2004). The Maslach Burnout Inventory Human Service Survey (MBI-HSS) was used to measure emotional exhaustion, depersonalization and personal accomplishment (Maslach, Jackson, & Leiter, 1996). Vigor, dedication and absorption were evaluated using the Utrecht Work Engagement Scale (UWES) (Schaufeli & Bakker, 2003); while nurse-reported quality of care at the unit and satisfaction with the current job (Aiken et al., 2001; Van Bogaert, Clarke, Vermeyen, Meulemans, & Van de Heyning, 2009) were evaluated both as single-item questions: quality of care at the unit with a 4-point Likert scale from excellent, good, fair to poor; satisfaction with the current job with a 4-point Likert scale from (very) satisfied to (very) dissatisfied . All variables, with the exception of workload, emotional exhaustion and depersonalization, were coded for analysis with higher scores indicating stronger agreement or more favorable ratings.

Hierarchical logistic regression analysis estimated the strength of associations with demographic characteristics (e.g., gender and having children (block-1)), professional characteristics (e.g., diploma, years in nursing, work schedule and type of unit (block-2)), hospital and period (block-3), work characteristics (block-4) and work engagement or burnout dimensions (block-5) as explanatory variables of high job satisfaction and excellent quality of care at the unit as outcome variables. A statistical significance level of $p < .05$ was set and the Statistical Package for the Social Sciences (SPSS Inc., Chicago; IBM SPSS statistics Armonk, NY) version 24.0 software was used for all analyses. In order to promote confidentiality, we did not attempt to match study results at the individual level nor did we try and track individual respondents between study periods. Approval from a qualified ethics review committee and institutional review board was obtained for each participating hospital.

14.3.2 Results

Table 14.2 summarizes demographic and study variables. The percentage of respondents that indicated to be very satisfied with their current job ranged across the hospitals from 19.7% in hospital 2 to 24.2% in hospital 1. The percentage of respondents whom rated the quality of care at the unit as excellent ranged from 15.8% in hospital 2 to 21.1% in hospital 1. We observed agreement (≥ 2.80) to high agreement (≥ 3.00) with the statements regarding social capital and decision latitude as well as an overall general agreement (>2.90) with statements on workload indicating that across all hospitals participants evaluated autonomy and social support but also a fairly high workload. Personal accomplishment (>4.80), vigor (>4.09), dedication (>4.92) and absorption (>3.96) were also rated relatively high comparing to reference values (Schaufeli & Bakker, 2003; Schaufeli & Van Dierendonck, 2000). A broader dispersion was noted although found to be relatively low in hospital 1 to somewhat higher levels in hospital 2 of emotional exhaustion ranging from 1.70 to 2.37 and depersonalization ranging from .78 to 1.20, respectively comparing to reference values (Schaufeli & Van Dierendonck, 2000).

The hierarchical regression model explained variances (see Table 14.3) were almost 40% for very satisfied with the current job and 20% for quality of the care at the unit rated as excellent for both burnout and engagement models. Nurse work characteristics explained > 20% of the variance in study outcomes with positive associations of social capital with odds ranging from 2.09 to 4.24 and decision latitude with odds ranging from 2.17 to 4.87. Negative associations with workload were observed with odds ranging from 25 to 68%. These models showed relevant positive associations between personal accomplishment and job satisfaction and between dedication and both outcome variables. Relevant differences in job satisfaction were noted between different types of units. Lower scores were observed for medical, surgical, geriatric and rehabilitation units as compared to ICU, PACU, OR and ER. The number of years working in the field of nursing was, however, positively associated with high job satisfaction. No effects were found for gender, having children, study hospital and study period on feeling highly satisfied with the job, excellent quality of care, burnout or engagement.

Table 14.2 Demographics and study variables

	Hospital 1 T1 n = 423		Hospital 1 T2 n = 504		Hospital 2 T1 n = 326		Hospital 2 T2 n = 330	
	n	%	n	%	n	%	n	%
Gender (Female)	355	85.1	427	86.1	249	76.9	248	75.8
Having children (Yes)	265	62.6	296	59.6	165	51.2	192	59.1
Day clinic – float pool	26	6.1	25	5.0	47	14.4	45	13.6
Medical, Surgical, Geriatric, Rehabilitation	179	42.3	208	41.3	155	47.5	150	45.5
Mother and Child	66	15.6	112	22.2	52	16.0	66	20.0
ICU, PACU, OR, ER	152	35.9	159	31.5	72	22.1	69	20.9
Bachelor in Nursing Sciences or Midwifery Sciences	369	87.2	436	88.3	270	84.1	271	83.6
Satisfied or very satisfied with the current job	378	89.8	442	88.6	277	85.5	278	85.3
Very satisfied with the current job	94	22.3	121	24.2	75	23.1	64	19.7
Quality of care unit good or excellent	359	85.1	419	84.3	281	86.5	264	80.2
Quality of care unit excellent	89	21.1	84	18.9	64	19.7	52	15.8
	Mean	SD	Mean	SD	Mean	SD	Mean	SD
Years in Nursing	15.7	11.5	15.9	12.2	12.9	10.7	12.3	10.7
Work schedule (%)	85.0	17.0	85.4	16.4	82.4	25.3	82.9	25.0
Social capital	3.09	.55	3.05	.53	2.95	.53	2.88	.59
Decision latitude	3.09	.30	3.12	.50	3.04	.54	3.04	.56
Workload	3.02	.54	3.07	0.44	2.91	0.52	2.91	.52
Emotional exhaustion	1.70	1.11	1.83	1.20	2.20	2.33	2.37	1.27
Depersonalization	.78	.71	.94	.88	1.21	1.11	1.31	1.20
Personal accomplishment	5.03	.74	5.07	.77	4.97	.77	4.84	.84
Vigor	4.46	1.15	4.36	1.31	4.38	1.22	4.09	1.30
Dedication	5.01	1.02	4.96	1.13	5.14	.93	4.92	1.18
Absorption	4.27	1.30	4.30	1.38	4.29	1.18	3.96	1.28

Social capital, decision latitude, workload range 1–4; work engagement and burnout range 0–6

Table 14.3 Hierarchical logistic regression analyses with personal characteristics (1) bachelor diploma, years in nursing, work schedule, type of unit (2) hospital, period (3), social capital, decision latitude and workload (4) and work engagement dimensions or burnout dimensions (5) (explanatory variables) and job satisfaction and quality of care at the unit (dependent variables)

Job satisfaction: very satisfied (1) versus satisfied or dissatisfied or very dissatisfied (0)

	B	SE	OR	95% C.I. Lower	95% C.I. Upper	adjR²		B	SE	OR	95% C.I. Lower	95% C.I. Upper	adjR²
Gender (male)	-.115	.226	.891	.572	1.388		Gender (male)	.173	.216	1.189	.779	1.816	
Children (yes)	-.345	.211	.708	.469	1.07	.012	Children (yes)	-.064	.20	.938	.634	1.387	.005
Bachelor (yes)	.193	0.277	1.213	.705	2.087		Bachelor (yes)	.282	.25	1.326	.812	2.166	
Years in nursing	-.015	.009	.985	.968	1.003		Years in nursing	-.007	.009	.993	.976	1.01	
Work schedule	.007	.005	1.007	.997	1.017		Work schedule	.001	.005	1.001	.992	1.01	
Type of unit			*				Type of unit			*			
Day clinic, float pool	.474	.335	1.607	.834	3.095		Day clinic, float pool	.352	.313	1.421	.77	2.624	
Medical, surgical, geriatric, rehabilitation	-.461	.225	.631*	.406	.98	.043	Medical, surgical, geriatric, rehabilitation	-.50	.214	.607*	.399	.922	.032
Mother and child	-.142	.248	.868	.534	1.41		Mother and child	-.073	.24	.93	.581	1.489	
Hospital (1)	-.257	0.202	0.773	.52	1.148		Hospital (1)	-.358	.183	.699	.488	1.000	
Period (T2)	.134	.169	1.144	.822	1.591	.060	Period (T2)	.008	.162	1.008	.734	1.385	.048
Social capital	.848	.184	2.34***	1.629	3.349		Social capital	.735	.176	2.09***	1.478	2.945	
Decision latitude	1.57	.299	4.80***	2.674	8.622		Decision latitude	1.584	.282	4.87***	2.801	8.474	
Workload	-.724	.204	.485***	.325	.723	.280	Workload	-1.139	.175	.32***	.227	.451	.267
Emotional exhaustion	-.769	.121	.464	.366	.587		Vigor	.252	.124	1.286	1.008	1.641	
Depersonalization	.094	.13	1.098	.851	1.419		Dedication	.928	.194	2.53***	1.729	3.700	
Personal accomplishment	.836	.157	2.31***	1.696	3.141	.391	Absorption	.246	.106	1.278	1.038	1.574	.398

	Quality of care unit: excellent (1) versus good or fair or poor (0)												
	B	SE	OR	95% C.I. Lower	95% C.I. Upper	adjR²		B	SE	OR	95% C.I. Lower	95% C.I. Upper	adjR²
Gender (male)	−.204	.226	.815	.524	1.269		Gender (male)	−.088	.217	.916	.599	1.40	.10
Children (yes)	.226	.199	1.253	.849	1.85		Children (yes)	.152	.19	1.164	.801	1.69	
Bachelor (yes)	.073	.243	1.075	.667	1.733		Bachelor (yes)	.011	.238	1.011	.634	1.611	
Years in nursing	.024	.008	1.024**	1.008	1.04		Years in nursing	.027	.008	1.027***	1.012	1.043	
Work schedule	−.002	.004	.998	.99	1.006		Work schedule	−.003	.004	.997	.989	1.005	
Type of unit						.015	Type of unit						
Day clinic, float pool	−.112	.325	.894	.473	1.691		Day clinic, float pool	−.036	.31	.965	.526	1.77	
Medical, surgical, geriatric, rehabilitation	−.06	.216	.942	.617	1.438		Medical, surgical, geriatric, rehabilitation	.024	.209	1.025	.68	1.543	
ICU,PACU,OR,ER	−.134	.242	.875	.544	1.405	.031	ICU, PACU, OR,ER	.045	.235	1.046	.661	1.657	.030
Hospital (1)	.023	.184	1.023	.713	1.68		Hospital (1)	.044	.172	1.045	.747	1.463	
Period (T2)	−.262	.158	.769	.565	1.048	.038	Period (T2)	−.253	.154	.777	.574	1.051	.035
Social capital	1.45	.18	4.24***	2.985	6.033		Social capital	1.417	.176	4.13***	2.92	5.825	
Decision latitude	.887	.272	2.43**	1.425	4.138	.198	Decision latitude	.774	.261	2.17**	1.298	3.618	.194
Workload	−.426	.189	.653*	0.451	.947		Workload	−.543	.159	.581**	.426	.793	
Emotional exhaustion	−.013	.096	.987	.817	1.192		Vigor	−.05	.100	.951	.782	1.157	
Depersonalization	−.142	.121	.867	.685	1.099		Dedication	.358	.14	1.43*	1.086	1.884	
Personal accomplishment	.159	.124	1.173	.92	1.495	.204	Absorption	−.071	.094	.932	.775	1.12	.204

OR, Odds Ratio 95% CI [lower and upper bound]; Adjusted R² reported additionally; Indicators: Female, No Children, Type of unit: ICU/PACU/OR/ER, No Bachelor, Hospital 2, Study Period T1; Social capital, decision latitude, workload, burnout and work engagement dimensions mean value

*P-value < .05; **P-value < .01; ***P-value < .001

14.3.3 Discussion

This multicenter study confirmed previous hypotheses that balanced work characteristics are associated with staff nurses and midwifes who are very satisfied with their job and rated the quality of care at the unit as excellent. Balanced nursing work characteristics entail favorably rated social capital expressed by support of peers, shared values and mutual trust. Furthermore, favorably rated decision latitude originating from abilities to make decisions and the capacity to use and develop professional and personal leadership skills along with feasible perceived workloads is also of importance. In addition, our study results showed that balanced nurse work characteristics or high rates of social capital and decision latitude and lower rates of perceived workload, were associated with personal accomplishment and dedication. These results confirmed previous findings in cross-sectional studies (Van Bogaert et al., 2013; Van Bogaert, Van heusden, Somers, et al., 2014; Van Bogaert, Peremans, et al., 2017). A cross-sectional study performed in a population of nursing, medical and allied health professionals at one of the study hospitals, confirmed the positive impact of balanced work characteristics on high ratings of current job satisfaction and quality of care at unit level. Moreover, dedication as a work engagement variable and emotional exhaustion and depersonalization as burnout variables also predicted our outcome variables of interest. We suggest that balanced nurse work characteristics are essential and strong indicators for leadership and inter-professional collaboration, as well as professional wellbeing and high performances to monitor and evaluate interventions and changes in organizations (Van Bogaert et al., 2018).

The design of work systems influences processes and in turn affects patient, care provider and organizational outcomes. An example of a comprehensive generic curriculum (Thomas, 2011) to improve work system is the PW-program developed by the NHS, which aims to eliminate waste in processes and increase benefit for patients by increased time for staff nurses' care delivery. However, studies evaluating the impact of such a PW-program showed inconsistent findings (White, 2015; White et al., 2014). Findings of one of our previous studies evaluating this program in an academic acute care center showed favorable impact on social capital and decision latitude, although an unfavorable impact was observed on workload with risks for lower morale and engagement (Van Bogaert & Clarke, 2018; Van Bogaert, Van heusden, et al., 2017). We assume that healthcare workers such as nurses, physicians and other professionals need a clinical work system that has the capacity to learn, adapt and improve and has the capacity to cope with their demands and responsibilities as an individual as well as an interprofessional team that has the necessary resources. An update of literature investigating the program relevance and effects revealed that "one size does *not* fit all" when it comes to how the program is implemented and managed. Furthermore, assessment of particular context characteristics (e.g., environment, readiness, leadership capabilities, QI conditions) greatly influences the success of implementation and its sustainability (White, 2018). These findings stress the importance of gaining an in-depth understanding of *each* particular work system, process and their stakeholders as a unique system within a broader context of a department or division, hospital or healthcare system.

Indirectly, the present study results also demonstrate the importance of strong leadership within healthcare organizations and clinical microsystems. After all, previous studies demonstrated that nurse work practice environment—including nurse management at the unit level as well as hospital management and organizational support had a direct impact on nurses' professional wellbeing which influenced ultimately their job satisfaction and nurse-assessed quality of care (for an overview, see Van Bogaert & Clarke, 2018). Authentic leadership contributes to people's professional development, professional self-esteem, decision latitude and decision-making skills (Alilyyani et al., 2018). A review of Haddad (2013) found structural empowerment as the only antecedent of authentic leadership and Gardner, Cogliser, Davis, and Dickens's (2011) review identified self-monitoring and psychological capital as antecedents. In general, present results combined with previous research data on authentic leadership indicate that authentic leaders promote elements of healthy work environments for staff and patients and hence may contribute to positive work organizations. However, very few studies have investigated relationship between authentic leadership and patient outcomes such as quality of care. Moreover, clinical work adapts to changes by becoming ambidextrous and combine production- and innovation-oriented processes, besides care delivery implementing improvements in care delivery processes such as evidence-based guidelines (Timmermans et al., 2012), will become more essential. Adopting innovations changes direct practices of the teams, but adopting radical innovations can change the clinical work systems from an internal orientation towards contributing to individual health as well as to the overall health of a population or even to creating a healthy region. Therefore, hospital leadership in their effort to achieve attractive and productive workplaces should monitor, evaluate and support interdisciplinary work systems in order to support and sustain state-of-the-art clinical outcomes such as low infection rates (e.g., central line bloodstream infections or urinary tract infections), pressure ulcers, patient falls with injury as well as patient-reported outcome and experience measures related to specific patient populations or care programs. Nevertheless, professionals' involvement is key, each in their capacities and their specific roles.

14.4 Conclusion

Balanced nurse work characteristics were found to be essential and strong indicators for professional wellbeing and reported outcomes such as job satisfaction and quality of care studied in burnout as well as engagement models. These models showed relevant positive associations between personal accomplishment and job satisfaction and between dedication and both outcome variables. Furthermore, these elements enabled healthcare professionals and teams to monitor and evaluate care interventions and changes in the organization. Changes are needed through quality improvements to provide excellent care that addresses needs of patients and their family as well as more radical innovations focusing on health.

14.5 Key Messages for Researchers (2–3 Points)

- Despite the strong growth of quality improvement initiatives, there is only limited knowledge about their effectiveness. For example, the effect of Team Resource Management skills training on quality of patient care is still unclear. More research is, however, needed to have an in-depth exploration of factors at the microsystem level and to determine the interactions within these complex social systems.
- Studies are needed to understand clinical microsystems' capacity to use feedback mechanisms in order to learn, adapt and improve their work system and processes through the monitoring and evaluation of care quality at individual and subgroup patient level.
- Moreover, to investigate the overall level of quality of care provided from a patient perspective, using a specific set of clinical and care-sensitive parameters such as infection rates, pressure ulcers, falls with injury as well as patient-reported outcome and experience measures related to specific patient populations or care programs, are recommended

14.6 Key Messages for Healthcare Delivery (2–3 Points)

- Balanced nurse work characteristics are essential and strong indicators for leadership and inter-professional collaboration, as well as professional wellbeing and high performances and strong indicators to monitor and evaluate interventions and changes in organizations
- Changes in healthcare are needed beyond incremental innovations such as patient safety initiatives but also in radical innovations with the focus on individual and population health instead of on disease treatment and management only.

References

Ackerman, M., Malloch, K., Wade, D., Porter-O'Grady, T., Weberg, D., Zurmehly, J., et al. (2019). The master in healthcare innovation: A new paradigm in healthcare leadership development. *Nurse Leader, 17*(1), 49–53.

Aiken, L. H., Clarke, S. P., Sloane, D. M., Sochalski, J. A., Busse, R., Clarke, H., et al. (2001). Nurses' reports on hospital care in five countries. *Health Affairs (Millwood), 20*, 43–53.

Alilyyani, B., Wong, C. A., & Cummings, G. (2018). Antecedents, mediators, and outcomes of authentic leadership in healthcare: A systematic review. *International Journal of Nursing Studies, 83*, 34–64. https://doi.org/10.1016/j.ijnurstu.2018.04.001

Al-Sawai, A. (2013). Leadership of healthcare professionals: where do we stand? *Oman Medical Journal, 28*(4), 285–287. https://doi.org/10.5001/omj.2013.79

Damschroder, L. J., Aron, D. C., Keith, R. E., Kirsh, S. R., Alexander, J. A., & Lowery, J. C. (2009). Fostering implementation of health services research findings into practice: a consolidated framework for advancing implementation science. *Implementation Science, 4*, 50.

de Ridder, D. T., Lensvelt-Mulders, G., Finkenauer, C., Stok, F. M., & Baumeister, R. F. (2012). Taking stock of self-control: a meta-analysis of how trait self-control relates to a wide range of behaviors. *Personality and Social Psychology Review, 16*(1), 76–99. https://doi.org/10.1177/1088868311418749

Dixon-Woods, M., McNicol, S., & Martin, G. (2012). Ten challenges in improving quality in healthcare: Lessons from the Health Foundation's programme evaluations and relevant literature. *BMJ Quality and Safety, 21*(10), 876–884.

Ernstmann, N., Ommen, O., Driller, E., Kowalski, C., Neumann, M., Bartholomeyczik, S., et al. (2009). Social capital and risk management in nursing. *Journal of Nursing Care Quality, 24*, 340–347.

Gardner, W. L., Cogliser, C. C., Davis, K. M., & Dickens, M. P. (2011). Authentic leadership: A review of the literature and research agenda. *Leadership Quarterly, 22*(6), 1120–1145.

Goffee, R., & Jones, G. (2000). Why should anyone be led by you? *Harvard Business Review, 78*(5), 62–70.

Haddad, L. M. (2013). *Generational differences in empowerment, professional practice environment, incivility, authentic leadership, job satisfaction, engagement and intent to leave in acute care nurses*. PhD diss., University of Tennessee.

Haegdorens, F., Van Bogaert, P., Roelant, E., De Meester, K., Misselyn, M., Wouters, K., et al. (2018). The introduction of a rapid response system in acute hospitals: A pragmatic stepped wedge cluster randomized controlled trial. *Resuscitation, 129*, 127–134.

Ham, C. (2003). Improving the performance of health services: the role of clinical leadership. *Lancet., 361*(9373), 1978–1980.

Heyhoe, J., Birks, Y., Harrison, R., O'Hara, J. K., Cracknell, A., & Lawton, R. (2016). The role of emotion in patient safety: Are we brave enough to scratch beneath the surface? *Journal of the Royal Society of Medicine, 109*(2), 52–58. https://doi.org/10.1177/0141076815620614

Holden, R. J., Carayon, P., Gurses, A. P., Hoonakker, P., Hundt, A. S., Ozok, A. A., et al. (2013). SEIPS 2.0: a human factors framework for studying and improving the work of healthcare professionals and patients. *Ergonomics., 56*, 1669–1686.

Johansen, M. Y., MacDonald, C. S., Hansen, K. B., Karstoft, K., Christensen, R., Pedersen, M., et al. (2017). Effect of an intensive lifestyle intervention on glycemic control in patients with type 2 diabetes: A randomized clinical trial. *JAMA, 318*(7), 637–646. https://doi.org/10.1001/jama.2017.10169

Jovanovic, B. (2005). Hospital accreditation as method for assessing quality in health care. *Archive of Oncology, 13*, 156.

Kaplan, H. C., Brady, P. W., Dritz, M. C., Hooper, D. K., Linam, W. M., Froehle, C. M., et al. (2010). The influence of context on quality improvement success in health care: A systematic review of the literature. *The Milbank Quarterly, 88*(4), 500–559.

Kaplan, H. C., Provost, L. P., Froehle, C. M., & Margolis, P. A. (2012). The Model for Understanding Success in Quality (MUSIQ): building a theory of context in healthcare quality improvement. *BMJ Quality & Safety, 21*, 13–20.

Kowalski, C., Ommen, O., Driller, E., Ernstmann, N., Wirtz, M. A., Köhler, T., et al. (2010). Burnout in nurses—the relationship between social capital in hospitals and emotional exhaustion. *Journal of Clinical Nursing, 19*, 1654–1663.

Kringos, D. S., Sunol, R., Wagner, C., Mannion, R., Michel, P., Klazinga, N. S., et al. (2015). The influence of context on the effectiveness of hospital quality improvement strategies: a review of systematic reviews. *BMC Health Services Research, 15*(1), 277. https://doi.org/10.1186/s12913-015-0906-0

Kumar, R. D. C. (2013). Leadership in healthcare. *Anesthesia and Intensive Care Medicine, 14*(1), 39–41.

Laschinger, H. K., Borgogni, L., Consiglio, C., & Read, E. (2015). The effects of authentic leadership, six areas of worklife, and occupational coping self-efficacy on new graduate nurses' burnout and mental health: A cross-sectional study. *International Journal of Nursing Studies, 52*(6), 1080–1089. https://doi.org/10.1016/j.ijnurstu.2015.03.002

Laschinger, H. K., Wong, C. A., & Grau, A. L. (2013). Authentic leadership, empowerment and burnout: a comparison in new graduates and experienced nurses. *Journal of Nursing Management, 21*(3), 541–552. https://doi.org/10.1111/j.1365-2834.2012.01375.x

Luthans, F., & Avolio, B. J. (2003). Authentic leadership: A positive developmental approach. In K. S. Cameron, J. E. Dutton, & R. E. Quinn (Eds.), *Positive organizational scholarship* (pp. 241–261). San Francisco: Barrett-Koehler.

Maslach, C., Jackson, S. E., & Leiter, M. P. (1996). *Burnout inventory manual* (3rd edn.). Mountain View, CA: Consulting Psychologists Press.

Nelson, E. C., Batalden, P. B., & Godfrey, M. M. (2011-01-14). *Quality By design.*

Nicolay, C. R., Purkayastha, S., Greenhalgh, A., Benn, J., Chaturvedi, S., Phillips, N., et al. (2012). Systematic review of the application of quality improvement methodologies from the manufacturing industry to surgical healthcare. *The British Journal of Surgery, 99*(3), 324–335.

Pfaff, H., Lutticke, J., Badura, B., Piekarski, C., & Richter, P. (2004). *Weiche' kennzahlenfur das strategische krankenhausmanagement. Stakeholderdinteressen zielgerichtet erkennen und einbeziehen.* Bern: Hans Huber.

Plsek, P. E. (2001). Complexity science: The challenge of complexity in health care. *British Medical Journal, 323*, 625–628.

Raisch, S., & Birkinshaw, J. (2008). Organizational ambidexterity: Antecedents, outcomes, and moderators. *Journal of Management, 34*, 375–409.

Reed, J. E., & Card, A. J. (2015). The problem with Plan-Do-Study-Act cycles. *BMJ Quality & Safety, 25*(3), 147–152. https://doi.org/10.1136/bmjqs-2015-005076

Reed, J. E., Kaplan, H. C., & Ismail, S. A. (2018). A new typology for understanding context: qualitative exploration of the model for understanding success in quality (MUSIQ). *BMC Health Services Research, 18*, 584.

Richter, P., Hermmann, E., Merboth, H., Fritz, S., Hänsgen, C., & Rudolf, M. (2000). Das Erleben von Arbeitsintensität und Tätigkeitsspielraum—Entwicklung und Validierung eines Fragebogens zur orientierenden Analyse (FIT). *Zeitschrift für Arbeits-und Organisationspsychologie.*

Robert, G., Sarre, S., Maben, J., Griffiths, P., & Chable, R. (2019). Exploring the sustainability of quality improvement interventions in healthcare organisations: a multiple methods study of the 10-year impact of the 'Productive Ward: Releasing Time to Care' programme in English acute hospitals. *BMJ Quality & Safety, 0*, 1–10. bmjqs-2019-009457.

Robert, G., Sarre, S., Maben, J., Griffiths, P., & Chable, R. (2020). Exploring the sustainability of quality improvement interventions in healthcare organisations: A multiple methods study of the 10-year impact of the 'Productive Ward: Releasing Time to Care' programme in English acute hospitals. *BMJ Quality & Safety, 29*(1), 31–40.

Schaufeli, W. B., & Van Dierendonck, D. (2000). *UBOS Utrechtse Burnout Schaal (UBOS): Manual (Duch)* Swets Test Publishers Lisse.

Schaufeli, W., & Bakker, A. (2003). *Utrecht work engagement scale: Preliminary manual.* Department of Psychology, Utrecht University, Utrecht, The Netherlands.

Shaw, C. D., Groene, O., Botje, D., Sunol, R., Kutryba, B., Klazinga, N., et al. (2014). The effect of certification and accreditation on quality management in 4 clinical services in 73 European hospitals. *International Journal for Quality in Health Care, 26*(Suppl 1), 100–107.

Soukup, T., Lamb, B. W., Aora, S., Darzi, A., Sevdalis, N., & Green, J. S. A. (2018). Successful strategies in implementing multidisciplinary team working in the care of patients with cancer: an overview and synthesis of the available literature. *Journal of Multidisciplinary Healthcare, 11*, 49–61.

Taylor, M. J., McNicholas, C., Nicolay, C., Darzi, A., Bell, D., & Reed, J. E. (2013). Systematic review of the application of the plan–do–study–act method to improve quality in healthcare. *BMJ Quality & Safety, 23*(4), 290–298. https://doi.org/10.1136/bmjqs-2013-001862

Thomas, E. J. (2011). Republished editorial: Improving teamwork in healthcare: current approaches and the path forward. *BMJ Quality & Safety, 20*(8), 647–650. https://doi.org/10.1136/bmjqs-2011-000117. Epub 2011 Jun 28.

Timmermans, O., van Linge, R., Van Petegem, P., & Denekens, J. (2012). Team learning and innovation in nursing; results of a comprehensive research project. *Journal of Nursing Education and Practice, 2*(4), 10–21.

Timmermans, O., Van Linge, R., Van Petegem, P., Elseviers, M., & Denekens, J. (2011). Team learning and team composition in Nursing. *Journal of Workplace Learning, 23*(4), 258–275.

Timmermans, O., Van Linge, R., Van Petegem, P., Van Rompaey, B., & Denekens, J. (2013). A contingency perspective on team learning and innovation in nursing. *Journal of Advanced Nursing, 69*, 363–373. https://doi.org/10.1111/j.1365-2648.2012.06014.x

Van Bogaert, P., & Clarke, S. (2018). Future steps in practice and research. In P. Van Bogaert & S. Clarke (Eds.), *The organizational context of nursing practice: Concepts; evidence and Interventions for improvements* (pp. 297–307). Cham: Springer.

Van Bogaert, P., Clarke, S., Vermeyen, K., Meulemans, H., & Van de Heyning, P. (2009). Practice environments and their associations with nurse-reported outcomes in Belgian hospitals: development and preliminary validation of a Dutch adaptation of the Revised Nursing Work Index. *International Journal of Nursing Studies, 46*, 54–64.

Van Bogaert, P., Kowalski, C., Weeks, S. M., Van heusden, D., & Clarke, S. P. (2013). The relationship between nurse practice environment, nurse work characteristics, burnout and job outcome and quality of nursing care: a cross-sectional survey. *International Journal of Nursing Studies, 50*, 1667–1677.

Van Bogaert, P., Peremans, L., Van heusden, D., Verspuy, M., Kureckova, V., Van de Cruys, Z., et al. (2017). Predictors of burnout, work engagement and nurse reported job outcomes and quality of care: a mixed method study. *BMC Nursing, 16*, 5.

Van Bogaert, P., Van heusden, D., Slootmans, S., Roosen, I., Van Aken, P., Hans, G. H., et al. (2018). Staff empowerment and engagement in a magnet® recognized and joint commission international accredited academic centre in Belgium: a cross-sectional survey. *BMC Health Services Research, 18*, 756.

Van Bogaert, P., Van heusden, D., Somers, A., Tegenbos, M., Wouters, K., Van der Straeten, J., et al. (2014). The Productive Ward program: a longitudinal multilevel study of nurse-perceived practice environment, burnout, and nurse-reported quality of care and job outcomes. *Journal of Nursing Administration, 44*, 452–461.

Van Bogaert, P., Van heusden, D., Timmermans, O., & Franck, E. (2014). Nurse work engagement impacts job outcome and nurse-assessed quality of care: model testing with nurse practice environment and nurse work characteristics as predictors. *Frontiers in Psychology, 5*, 1261.

Van Bogaert, P., Van heusden, D., Verspuy, M., Wouters, K., Slootmans, S., Van der Straeten, J., et al. (2017). The Productive Ward Program™: A two-year implementation impact review using a longitudinal multilevel study. *Canadian Journal of Nursing Research, 49*, 28–38.

White, M. (2015). How effective is productive ward? *Nursing Times, 111*, 22–25.

White, M. (2018). Productive Ward: Releasing time to care (a ward-based QI intervention). In P. Van Bogaert & S. Clarke (Eds.), *The organizational context of nursing practice: Concepts; evidence and Interventions for improvements* (pp. 119–137). Cham: Springer.

White, M., & Waldron, M. (2014). Systematic review: Effects and impacts of Productive Ward from a nursing perspective. *British Journal of Nursing, 8*, 419–426.

White, M., Wells, J. S., & Butterworth, T. (2014). The Productive Ward: releasing Time to Care (™)—what we can learn from the literature for implementation. *Journal of Nursing Management, 22*, 914–923.

WHO. (2018). *Fact sheet on non-communicable diseases*. http://www.who.int/mediacentre/factsheets/fs355/en/

Wilson, G. (2009). Implementation of releasing time to care - The productive ward. *Journal of Nursing Management, 17*(5), 647–654.

Chapter 15
Mindful Practice: Organizational Change and Health Professional Flourishing Through Cultivating Presence and Courageous Conversations

Michael S. Krasner and Ronald Epstein

> Looking back on my experience as a clinician, teacher, mentor, researcher, and family caregiver what stands out vividly are my memories of presence. By this I mean the intensity of interacting with another human being that animates being there for, and with, that person. Presence is a calling forward or a stepping toward the other. It is active. It is looking into someone's eyes, placing your hand in solidarity on their arm, speaking to them directly and with authentic feeling. Presence is built out of listening intensely, indicating that the person and their story matter, and explaining carefully so that you are understood. (Kleinman, 2017)
>
> Good patient care is found not in a computer screen but in being truly present with patients. (Verghese, 2016)

15.1 Mindful Practice: An Overview

Mindful Practice, a mindfulness-based program developed by a team of physicians at the University of Rochester School of Medicine and Dentistry (Rochester, New York, USA) was designed to enhance clinical health professionals' resilience and well-being, improve the clinician-patient relationship, and advance the quality of medical care they provide. This educational intervention, built on a strong biopsychosocial foundation, contains three major components—mindfulness

---

M. S. Krasner (✉)
Mindful Practice Programs, University of Rochester School of Medicine and Dentistry, Rochester, NY, USA
e-mail: Michael_Krasner@URMC.Rochester.edu

R. Epstein
Mindful Practice Programs, University of Rochester School of Medicine and Dentistry, Rochester, NY, USA

Center for Communication and Disparities Research, University of Rochester School of Medicine and Dentistry, Rochester, NY, USA

meditation, narrative medicine, and appreciative inquiry. These components are integrated in a series of theme-based modules to address key challenges facing clinicians and educators in a seamless experiential, interactive, and relational pedagogy (Epstein, 2014; Krasner, 2016; Krasner et al., 2009).

Mindful Practice as described by Epstein in 1999 refers to qualities of exemplary clinicians that transcend clinical specialty and clinical experience (Epstein, 1999): *moment-to-moment purposeful attentiveness to one's own physical and mental processes during every day work with the goal of practicing with clarity and compassion.* These same qualities, first identified as promotion of individual flourishing, also apply to qualities of organizations and leadership and can guide organizational change within the culture of medicine. Clinician distress, which contributes to burnout and lower quality of care (Shanafelt, 2003), is related to both individual and health systems factors (Montgomery, 2014), and thus, steps needed to promote clinician well-being must address individual vulnerability, as well as organizational structure, function, leadership and culture (Shanafelt et al., 2019). Applying the qualities that *Mindful Practice* focuses on within the culture of medicine at both the individual and organizational levels may be a useful approach for promoting positive change, a healthier working and learning environment, and improved quality of care (see Fig. 15.1).

The qualities central to *Mindful Practice*-attentive observation, critical curiosity, beginner's mind, and presence-not only inform the moment by moment lived experience of clinicians, but also that of the relationships among individuals and groups within the organization (Epstein, 2017). Those relationships occur at the intrapersonal, interpersonal, team, departmental and institutional levels, and include the sociopolitical environment that affects and is affected by the health care system, as well as the nested interactions among these levels within organizations. Mindfulness in organizations, thus, refers to the capacity of the members and of the

Fig. 15.1 Schematic of Mindful Practice as an intervention that connects together clinician well-being, quality of care, and quality of caring

organization themselves to have awareness of intrapersonal, interpersonal and environmental dynamics. Mindfulness, furthermore, enhances a universal capacity for clear thinking and open-heartedness through embodied awareness, contributing to a greater sense of emotional balance and well-being. Health professionals, leaders and educators world-wide have resonated with the goals, objectives and methods used in the *Mindful Practice* program; over the last decade more than a thousand of such individuals have participated in 2, 3 and 4-day *Mindful Practice* programs that have been held on every continent.

15.2 Challenges Facing Clinicians

> The context and the practice of medicine just seems to be accelerating, and the number of things competing for our attention is just incredible…David Hatem MD, Professor of Medicine, University of Massachusetts School of Medicine[1]
>
> The hustle and bustle of residency training, it's quite a fast pace, it's very grueling…Chiezetam Ekekeze MD, Chief Resident, Internal Medicine Residency Program, Brown University
>
> It is a relentless exposure to suffering…Frederick Marshall MD, Professor of Neurology, University of Rochester School of Medicine and Dentistry
>
> No matter what happens to you or your patients, or anything like that, that you're not allowed to, sort of, even have an emotion, let alone express it…Andrew Czuchwicki MD, Anesthesiologist, Queens Hospital, Adelaide, Australia

Recent epidemiologic studies suggest that clinician distress is common, that it is related to individual, micro-environmental and institutional issues, and that it is a precursor to the high levels of burnout reported among physicians, nurses and other health professionals. The first published reports describing burnout in the United States appeared in the mid-1970s (Freudenberger, 1975; Maslach, 1976). Since then, burnout has been defined as a work-related syndrome involving emotional exhaustion, depersonalization/cynicism, and a low sense of personal accomplishment, and epidemiologic studies suggest that burnout affects over half of physicians in training and practicing physicians, and over a third of nurses (McHugh, Kutney-Lee, Cimiotti, & Sloane, 2011; West, Dyrbye, & Shanafelt, 2018). The medical specialties most at risk for burnout are those on the "front lines" such as family medicine, general internal medicine, and emergency medicine (Shanafelt et al., 2012).

Affecting 25–55% of physicians worldwide, burnout has been linked to poorer quality of care, patient dissatisfaction, increased medical errors and lawsuits, and decreased empathic capacity (Shanafelt, 2003; Shanafelt et al., 2012). The consequences of burnout among practicing physicians include not only poorer quality of

---

[1]All quotes not otherwise noted in references are from: Mead, J. September 30, 2019. Mindful Practice for Medical Clinicians. https://www.youtube.com/watch?v=MGliZssn-Ps&fbclid=IwAR3ns0U8bfdmjD5lt4MV1i10HEdINYLaD89XkJ3t06hUzUbXUexqKLhEgkQ

care but also poorer quality of life, accidents, and suicide, as well as leaving clinical practice (Sinsky et al., 2017; Williams et al., 2001). There is concern that early retirement due to burnout will have a significant effect on patient access to health care services (AAMC, 2018; Bodenheimer, 2006; Treadway, 2008).

The factors contributing to physician burnout are complex and numerous. Throughout history, practitioners have often felt that their clinical tools were inadequate to address patients' health problems. Currently, though, structural and organizational factors within the healthcare environment threaten health professionals' identity, well-being and perceived effectiveness to a far greater degree (Zuger, 2004). These include the cumbersome information technology demands, burdensome administrative and documentation requirements, a pervasive sense of loss of control and meaning, and a lack of alignment of individual and organizational values (Dunn, Arnetz, Christensen, & Homer, 2007; Shanafelt & Noseworthy, 2017; Sinsky et al., 2016).

The problem of physician burnout seems an expected side-effect of contemporary medical practice. The pace, complexity, and ongoing challenges of the chronic and multiple medical conditions that physicians care for in which management requires not only a biomedical focus but increasingly psychological and socioeconomic considerations contribute significantly to the risks for burnout. Medical science has successfully addressed many of the public-health related diseases that once threatened one's survival or the survival of one's family. Now, stress-related maladies increasingly challenge modern medicine, which by their nature add complexity to diagnosis and treatment. Individuals and organizations of healthcare simultaneously struggle with these complexities as they attempt to address them for patients, for the public at large, and for the health of those working within the health care delivery system.

15.3 What Is Mindful Practice?

Mindful Practice® is an educational program designed for physicians and other health professionals that engages the physical, emotional and cognitive aspects of clinical experience through cultivating intrapersonal and interpersonal awareness. It supports collegial relationships and helps health professionals reflect on and learn from the most challenging clinical experiences in a manner that recognizes their intrinsic strengths and capacities for efficacy and quality in their work. It offers tangible skills that can be used at every level not only to build individual resilience but to change the health care system through awareness-building, from leadership down to the rank-and-file.

Mindful practice depends on developing a capacity for *mindfulness*. Mindfulness involves the awareness of the present moment that includes awareness of one's inner life (sensations, emotions, thoughts, feelings) as well as sensations and stimuli from the outside world. Mindfulness might incorporate experiences from the past and anticipating the future, but, importantly, the awareness of all of these experiences is grounded in the present moment—it can be described as being experienced in the unfolding *now*. Mindfulness is a human capacity that fosters clear thinking and receptivity and responsiveness to others' distress. Its historical role, that of relieving suffering and cultivating compassion, makes it a quality essential to medical care (Ludwig & Kabat-Zinn, 2008). We believe that mindfulness is a naturally occurring human capacity which can be cultivated in a variety of ways. Over the past 30 years, mindfulness has been closely associated with meditation practices and empirically validated and widely disseminated "mindfulness-based" interventions such as mindfulness-based stress reduction (MBSR) or mindfulness-based cognitive therapy (MBCT). We believe that there are many ways to cultivate mindfulness, including practices that can be incorporated into the workplace.

The *Mindful Practice* program at the University of Rochester School of Medicine and Dentistry was designed in 2005–2007 as a mindfulness-based intervention for medical students, physician trainees, practicing physicians and other clinicians to address burnout and build resilience through a contemplative, self-care-oriented approach. In addition to its effects on personal well-being, observational data suggest that clinician mindfulness is associated with greater patient safety and error reduction (Dierynck, Leroy, Savage, & Choi, 2017; Ludwig & Kabat-Zinn, 2008; Crosskerry, 2003; Sibinga & Wu, 2010; Vogus & Sutcliffe, 2007a, 2007b), as well as patients' assessments of physicians' communication skills and satisfaction with care (Beach et al., 2013). In addition, mindfulness is one quality that can help raise awareness of cognitive biases, such as avoiding or mitigating diagnostic and medical decision-making problems engendered by premature closure, and availability and anchoring biases (Crosskerry, 2003). Ron Epstein, who along with Mick Krasner designed the *Mindful Practice* program at the University of Rochester, outlined several core qualities of effective clinicians in his seminal 1999 JAMA article *Mindful Practice* (Epstein, 1999). For heuristic reasons, we have distilled the qualities of mindful practice to four attributes, or habits of mind: *attentive observation*, *critical curiosity*, *beginner's mind*, and *presence*. We chose these qualities because they are intuitively simple to understand, have relevance to medical practice, and are qualities thought to be teachable. For example, the concept of beginner's mind has to do with setting aside preconceptions and cultivating an openness to surprise; these qualities have been suggested as helpful in avoiding diagnostic bias and premature closure (Crosskerry, 2003). The *Mindful Practice* program endeavors to assist clinicians in cultivating these qualities, applying them to their practice of medicine, whether in the clinic, the operating room, or the board room, and has relevance for public health and leadership within health care organizations.

Three components that make up the core experience of *Mindful Practice* are:

- **Formal and Informal Mindfulness Practices:** Cultivation of an open, receptive, and non-judgmental orientation to one's present experience, which helps promote physical, emotional and cognitive stability. The formal practices—such as meditation—and what are called *informal practices*—such as strategically employing the breath or body awareness during the work day—are central to the skills used when building the qualities of attention, curiosity, openness, and presence.

- **Narratives from the Practice of Medicine:** Our approach to using narratives is informed by Rita Charon's transformative work on how the use of personal stories can enrich and humanize health care (Charon, 2001). In addition, we incorporate into narrative exercises some of the skills developed in formal and informal mindfulness practices. In these exercises, participants reflect on and share personal stories about significant challenges in clinical practice and in clinicians' professional development (e.g., meaningful experiences, errors, grief and loss, conflict, resilience and compassion). Particularly important is cultivation of a quality of deep listening that emphasizes curiosity and inquiry into the storyteller's experience, while avoiding providing advice, making judgments and comparing one's own stories to those of the speaker. Equally important is the cultivation of self-reflection and interpersonal awareness for the speaker while sharing their story. Thus, these narrative exchanges have a contemplative quality that deepens both the storyteller's self-awareness as well as the listener's understanding of the storyteller's experience. These experiences often help connect the clinicians with sources of professional satisfaction, meaning and personal capacities for managing the challenges of medical practice. While in the training workshops, participants practice sharing narratives in structured settings with the goal for participants to bring the same skills of self-awareness and deep listening to encounters with patients, to teaching venues and to administrative roles.
- **Appreciative Dialogues:** Based on Appreciative Inquiry (Cooperider, 2005), a strength-based approach to individual and organizational change that alters habitual patterns of thinking and behavior, appreciative dialogues are designed to help participants discover capacities and resources within themselves for positive potential. The dialogues are structured so as to incorporate an intentional focus on recognizing strengths of the clinician within the challenging experiences through the very act of discussing with a colleague. Participants are encouraged to bring the same skills of eliciting, naming and promoting individual strengths and capabilities to their work with patients, students and colleagues to complement the more common problem-oriented approaches in medical settings, to foster effective teamwork, and to increase patient motivation and self-reliance.

The *Mindful Practice* curriculum, taught in a modular fashion, presents themes of professional relevance and challenge as the ground upon which participants bring mindful attention and awareness as they reflect upon and then share clinical experiences that connect with the theme. Among the themes include the following (Epstein & Krasner, 2017):

- *Noticing*—improving clinicians' capacity for attentive observation, and increased awareness of blind spots and implicit biases.
- *Responding to suffering*—exploring how clinicians notice and respond to suffering in patients and themselves
- *Compassion*—the role of empathy and actions to relieve suffering, including the patient-clinician relationship

- *When things go wrong*—building awareness and resourcefulness when confronted with errors and bad outcomes
- *Grief and loss*—investigation of how clinicians' awareness of and responses to the inevitable experience of grief and loss in patient care, as well as their own attitudes toward their own illnesses and mortality can enrich their work
- *Resilience*—building skills, relationships and community resources to help clinicians flourish—being more effective in their work with patients and colleagues while also living a more balanced sustainable work life.
- *Uncertainty*—an examination of how clinical work can be enriched by adopting an improvisational stance when confronted with challenging situations
- *Professionalism*—consideration of training knowledge, skills, virtue, character, ethics and behavior in the culture of medicine

The acquisition of medical knowledge, assimilation of clinical information, and continued honing of manual skills are vital to professional competence. Likewise, the continual honing of interpersonal skills, steady development of increased intrapersonal and interpersonal awareness, and capacity to attend to patients with presence are also central tasks toward the goal of practicing high quality, relationship-centered medical care. A central objective of *Mindful Practice* has been the integration of these skills into the practitioner's clinical understanding and individual expression in much the same way that the understanding of organ systems and their physiology and pathology become integrated into an approach to solving problems in a clinical encounter.

Becoming Mindful: Getting Started in the Workplace
1. Take a moment to orient yourself to your workday as you arrive at work. Use the walk from arrival to the office from the parking lot bus or train to step into your life. Acknowledge where you are, where you are going, and inquire about your intention for the day
2. While sitting at your desk periodically pay attention to bodily sensations, noticing the state of tension or relaxation.
3. Bring awareness to transitions—from the office to the patient encounter, from the patient encounter to clinical workspaces, from the hallway into the exam room. Take a moment for a conscious breath when crossing the threshold into an exam room.
4. Close your door for 5 min at lunch, set your cell phone down, turn off the screen of the computer, and simply bring awareness to the moment
5. Practice **STOP**: **S**top, **T**ake a breath, **O**bserve, and **P**roceed as often as you can during the workday
6. Download and use cell phone apps like *Headspace* and *Insight Timer* to support contemplative practice
7. Consider further training such as those available through Mindful Practice (www.mindfulpratice.urmc.edu)

Mindful practice training for individuals and teams of health care providers (nurses, physicians, advanced practice providers, support staff) does not require large cultural or philosophical changes. Yet, developing habits of the informal and formal contemplative practices, sharing experiences using narratives, deep listening, awareness of one's own actions, biases and emotions all require practice and reinforcement. We believe that small adjustments in practice style through the incremental introduction of simple practices can lead to positive shifts in the lived experience of those delivering health care; when groups of colleagues share common experiences of practicing mindfully, it can change organizational culture and promote (and be promoted by) a collective vision that features the importance of self-awareness and self-care among all the stakeholders who are engaged in health care enterprise. Here, leadership, educational interventions and opportunities for reinforcement are key.

15.4 What Are the Effects of Mindful Practice?

The *Mindful Practice* program in its original form involved recruiting 70 primary care physicians to participate in a year-long study involving 8 weekly sessions with an all-day retreat after week 6, and 10 monthly sessions (Krasner & Epstein, 2010; Krasner et al., 2009). With grant support from the Physicians Foundation for Health System Excellence, we designed a program of individual modules, each of which addressed key aspects and challenges of professional life. Participants completed questionnaires at baseline, at the beginning of the program, at 8 weeks, at the end of the program, and at 3 months after completing the program. In general, participants were moderately burned out at baseline and showed significant and enduring improvements in physician well-being (lower burnout and mood disturbance), attentiveness (increased mindfulness), and attitudes toward clinical care (increased empathy, psychosocial orientation and interest in patients as people) (Krasner et al., 2009). We also noted that these changes were all mediated by changes in mindfulness, and, furthermore, noted personality changes—participants were more conscientious and experienced greater emotional stability, an unexpected finding in mid-career physicians (average age 46). This intervention has been repeated among primary care providers in Spain with similar results demonstrated on burnout, empathy, mood and mindfulness (Asuero, 2012).

A follow-up investigation of the participants in Rochester, designed to determine what aspects of this educational intervention contributed to participants' well-being and the care they provided, incorporated structured interviews and standard qualitative thematic analytic methods (Beckman et al., 2012). Participants reported three main themes: (1) the importance of a professional community: sharing personal experiences from medical practice with colleagues reduced professional isolation; (2) the importance of trainable skills: mindfulness skills improved the participants' ability to be attentive and listen deeply to patients' concerns, respond to patients more effectively, and to have sufficient resources to adapt to stressful circumstances;

and (3) the importance of physician self-care: while participants valued developing greater self-awareness and found it positive and transformative, they still had difficulty granting themselves permission to attend to their own personal growth.

Although the first two themes seem to have face-validity for this kind of intervention, this final theme was more unexpected. We attribute physicians' difficulty recognizing their vulnerability and need for self-care in the service of being more available to patients as reflecting the values of commitment to service, clinical excellence and altruism within the culture of medicine. These values when carried to a more extreme can lead to over-commitment, self-deprivation and perfectionism and can undermine physicians' well-being and clinical effectiveness. Since the publication of these findings, and as the link between health professional well-being and quality of care becomes stronger through empirical evidence (Dewa, Loong, Bonato, & Trojanowski, 2016; Linzer, 2018; Panagioti et al., 2018), there are now mandates from licensing bodies that undergraduate and graduate medical education address self-care and well-being of students and residents, and many health care organizations have developed wellness programs for practicing clinicians. With time, we are hopeful that organized medicine will address clinician burnout more systematically and make it more culturally normative for physicians and other health professionals to engage in activities that promote self-awareness and mindfulness.

Since its development, the *Mindful Practice* curriculum has been adapted to provide training experiences for health professionals in many different settings. The most prominent of these trainings involve 4 and 5-day intensive retreat-like experiences facilitated by the original developers along with additional clinician faculty who are experienced in mindfulness, narrative and appreciative interview practices and dedicated to promoting professional flourishing in healthcare. Advanced teacher training and internship opportunities have allowed *Mindful Practice* to reach physicians and other healthcare professionals in North and South America, Asia, Europe, Africa, the Middle East, and Australia. Participants include clinicians from all clinical specialties (and a few veterinarians), as well as those in healthcare administration, hospital executive suites, medical and nursing school deans' offices, malpractice insurance carriers, public health agencies, and government regulatory bodies.

15.5 Courageous Conversations and Conclusions

It does create this camaraderie and friendship and community which is so supportive and sustaining...Andrew Czuchwicki MD, Anesthesiologist, Queens Hospital, Adelaide, Australia

There's a lot of power in telling your own story, and that's so much of what we've been doing here at this retreat is strangers sharing their own stories, and then something magical happening where you feel like you're no longer strangers... ChiezetamEkekeze MD, Chief Resident, Internal Medicine Residency Program, Brown University

It allows me, I think, to embrace more of this human kind of vulnerability in a way that feels very courageous, so I see it now as more of a strength, as opposed to something that I kind of need to protect myself from...I think that enables me to actually engage in a different way, a way that's actually a little clearer, and I think really through Mindful Practice that's actually helped me to be a better physician... Joanna McDermid MD, Consulting psychiatrist, BC Children's Hospital, Vancouver, BC Canada

Mindful Practice has been well-received among participants from a wide-variety of medical specialties who have attended the training programs, as well as among participants in specific health-care teams who have invited Mindful Practice training within their organizations such as surgical teams. Leaders in health care are increasingly aware of the high costs due to attrition, early retirement and medical errors associated with burnout among health professionals in their organizations. By comparison, the cost of a mindfulness program or other programs to try to mitigate burnout is incredibly inexpensive. In 2017, Shanafelt et al clearly described a business case for interventions to reduce burnout (Shanafelt, Goh, and Sinsky, 2017).

Mindful Practice training cultivates qualities that most clinicians and educators recognize as qualities of excellent practitioners—attentiveness, self-monitoring, curiosity, beginner's mind, commitment, resilience, presence, empathy, acceptance and awareness of one's biases. However, while attention to these qualities has grown over the past 30 years, still, it is generally an afterthought in the formal education of health professionals. Mindfulness training, in whatever form, does present challenges. It requires exercising parts of oneself that have not been exercised for a long time. It involves awareness of—and questioning about—personal attitudes, values and blind spots that can be uncomfortable. When clinicians are very busy, distressed and burned out, the challenges of developing self-awareness can seem daunting; narrowly focused clinicians may find themselves unable to discern that self-care may be one of the best uses of their limited time and energies. Furthermore, health care teams, not just individuals, may benefit from the implementation of mindfulness training; yet team-based mindfulness training has not been rigorously studied. Recently, the popularity of mindfulness in the media has fostered preconceptions and distortions among the general public that mindfulness merely is an escape, a form of relaxation, only for the well-heeled and new age, or a luxury that they can ill-afford while they are struggling just to keep up. Here, education is essential. Finally, institutional support is key. Reports from Fortune 500 companies that have developed mindfulness programs demonstrate that in organizations where being mindful has positive valence and seen as a virtue, and where programs are offered, people are more likely to be drawn to it (Tan, 2012). Health care organizations should emphasize that even the busiest physicians are guided by principles of service and compassion, and endeavor to bring skill and wisdom to their work; that finding themselves struggling in their work, questioning the value of their efforts, or searching for professional meaning can bring a wide range of health professionals to recognize and find ways to address their needs; and that the organization values and supports the efforts of their constituencies to adopt practices that help them to be more mindful.

At a symposium in 2014 at Johns Hopkins University, Dr. John Kabat-Zinn, the founder of the Mindfulness-Based Stress Reduction program, offered an updated definition of mindfulness that included a more explicit ethical intention: Mindfulness is the awareness that arises by paying attention, on purpose in the present moment, non-judgmentally, *in the service of self-understanding, wisdom, and compassion* (Kabat-Zinn, 2014). This clarification mirrors a growing recognition within the medical community for the need to be more explicit about the professional ethics that not only support the provision of quality health care, but also support the needs of the providers of that care.

This ethical mandate has deep implications for the structure and systems within the medical culture. It calls on everyone involved in the enterprise of providing scientifically rational, ethically sound and exquisitely empathic care to communicate together, turning toward the most difficult issues while holding close the ideas of self-understanding, wisdom and compassion (Epstein, 2017). *Mindful Practice* asks participants to do just that. At its core is the fierce honesty of being able to see things not as we desire, but as they truly are, and then to ask, together, as a community, what capacities do we already have that can help us negotiate these turbulent waters? Whether it is a patient suffering deep loss and grief, a colleague challenged by fatigue and error, an administrator attempting to manage resources wisely and fairly, or a leader seeing threats to institutional existence looming while envisioning a better, safer, kinder and more effective learning and working environment.

Courage is required to initiate and engage in conversations that help individuals and organizations examine the ethical underpinnings of their work and implement behaviors and programs that support those ethical underpinnings. Once those conversations are underway, individuals and organizations require skills: skills of attentively observing what is, skills of applying critical curiosity to how things appear and are, skills at reframing and re-visioning the current situations with a beginner's mind, and skills of simply being present with acceptance and without judgment to the unfolding now, in the service of making the most skillful and effective decisions. This commitment to noticing, clear thinking, generosity and growth was the initial inspiration behind our work, and we believe that *Mindful Practice* offers a roadmap to move the conversations along a path of positive change.

> **Key Messages for Researchers**
> - Physician well-being and quality of care are strongly connected.
> - Further research, qualitative and quantitative, is required to evaluate the impact of investing in physician and health professional well-being.
> - Mindfulness-Based Interventions vary in so many aspects. For them to be compared, a research agenda for assessing efficacy should include a number of standard individual, team and systemic measures.
> - The ethical dimensions within healthcare are of great interest but are challenging to assess. Research should include explorations of this aspect
>
> (continued)

of physician and health professional well-being, institutional health, and the larger public health.
- One objective of continued research on mindfulness interventions designed to improve professional well-being and quality of care should be the identification of best practices and how these can be tailored to local environments.

Key Messages for Healthcare Delivery
- Physician and other health professional well-being should be considered a primary quality indicator within the healthcare system.
- Healthcare teams should consider reflections on patient narratives, as shared by members of the team, as a way of supporting meaning and purpose at work.
- Cultivating awareness of self, awareness of others, and awareness of relationship can assist health professionals to work effectively and flourish within the complex world of healthcare delivery.
- Social connectivity among health professionals support quality of care delivery, and mitigate the effects of isolation.
- Mindful Practice creates a growing and learning work environment that can translate into improvements in personal well-being, patient-centeredness, team function, and improved quality.

References

AAMC. (2018). *2018 update: The complexities of physician supply and demand: Projects from 2016-2030*. Washington, DC: Association of American Medical Colleges.

Asuero, A. (2012). *Effectiveness of an educational program on mindfulness to reduce burnout and improve empathy in primary care professionals*. Barcelona, Spain: Universidad Autónoma de Barcelona.

Beach, M., Roter, D., Korthuis, P., Epstein, R., Sharp, V., Ratanawongsa, N., et al. (2013). A multicenter study of physician mindfulness and health care quality. *Annals of Family Medicine, 11*(5), 421–428.

Beckman, H., Wendland, M., Mooney, C., Krasner, M., Quill, T., Suchman, A., et al. (2012). The impact of a program in mindful communication on primary care physicians. *Academic Medicine, 87*(6), 815–819.

Bodenheimer, T. (2006). Primary care—Will it survive? *New England Journal of Medicine, 355*(9), 861–864.

Charon, R. (2001). Narrative medicine: form, function, and ethics. *Annals of Internal Medicine, 134*(1), 83–87.

Cooperider, D. (2005). *Appreciative inquiry: A positive revolution in change*. San Francisco, CA: Berrett-Koehler.

Crosskerry, P. (2003). The importance of cognitive errors in diagnosis and strategies to minimize them. *Academic Medicine, 78*(8), 775–780.

Dewa, C., Loong, D., Bonato, S., & Trojanowski, L. (2016). The relationship between physician burnout and quality of healthcare in terms of safety and acceptability: a systematic review. *BMJ Open, 7*(6), e015141.

Dierynck, B., Leroy, H., Savage, G., & Choi, E. (2017). The role of individual and collective mindfulness in promoting occupational safety in Health Care. *Medical Care Research and Review, 74*(1), 79–96.

Dunn, P., Arnetz, B., Christensen, J., & Homer, L. (2007). Meeting the imperative to improve physician wellbeing: assessment of an innovative program. *Journal of General Internal Medicine, 22*(11), 1544–1552.

Epstein, R. (1999). Mindful practice. *Journal of the American Medical Association, 282*, 833–839.

Epstein, R. (2014). What will it take for physicians to practice mindfully? Promoting quality of care, quality of caring, resilience, and well-being. In A. Le, C. Ngnoumen, & E. Langer (Eds.), *The Wiley Blackwell handbook of mindfulness* (1st edn). Hoboken, NJ: Wiley.

Epstein, R. (2017). *Attending: Medicine, mindfulness, and humanity*. New York: Scribner.

Epstein, R., & Krasner, M. (2017). *Mindful practice workshop facilitator manual*, 3rd edn. Rochester, NY: University of Rochester School of Medicine and Dentistry.

Freudenberger, H. (1975). The staff burnout syndrome in alternative institutions. *Psychotherapy Theory Research and Practice, 12*, 72–83.

Kabat-Zinn, J. (2014). *Mindfulness and learning: An interdisciplinary symposium*. Baltimore, MD: Johns Hopkins University.

Kleinman, A. (2017). The art of medicine: Presence. *The Lancet*, 2466–2467.

Krasner, M. S. (2016). Teaching health care professionals. In D. McCown, D. Reibel, & M. Micozzi (Eds.), *Resources for teaching mindfulness: An international handbook* (pp. 391–407). Cham: Springer.

Krasner, M., & Epstein, R. (2010). *Mindful communication: Bringing intention, attention, and reflection to clinical practice: Curriculum Guide*. Rochester, NY: University of Rochester School of Medicine and Dentistry.

Krasner, M., Epstein, R., Beckman, H., Suchman, A., Mooney, C., & Quill, T. (2009). Association of an educational program in mindful communication with burnout, empathy and attitudes among primary care physicians. *Journal of the American Medical Association, 302*(12), 1284–1293.

Linzer, M. (2018). Clinician burnout and the quality of care. *JAMA Internal Medicine, 178*(10), 1331–1332.

Ludwig, D., & Kabat-Zinn, J. (2008). Mindfulness in Medicine. *Journal of the American Medical Association, 300*(11), 1350–1352.

Maslach, C. (1976). Burned out. *Human Behavior, 5*, 16–22.

McHugh, M., Kutney-Lee, A., Cimiotti, J., & Sloane, D. A. (2011). Nurses' widespread job dissatisfaction, burnout, and frustration with health benefits signal problems for patient care. *Health Affairs, 30*(2), 202–210.

Montgomery, A. (2014). The inevitability of physician burnout: Implications for interventions. *Burnout Research, 1*, 50–56.

Panagioti, M., Geraghty, K., Johnson, J., Zhou, A., Panagopoulou, E., Chew-Graham, C., et al. (2018). Association between physician burnout and patient safety, professionalism, and patient satisfaction: A systematic review and meta-analysis. *JAMA Internal Medicine, 178*(10), 1317–1331.

Shanafelt, T. (2003). The well-being of physicians. *American Journal of Medicine, 114*(6), 513–519.

Shanafelt, T., & Noseworthy, J. (2017). Executive leadership and physician well-being: Nine organizational strategies to promote engagement and reduce burnout. *Mayo Clinic Proceedings, 92*(1), 129–146.

Shanafelt, T., Boone, S., Tan, L., Dyrbye, L., Sotile, W., Satele, D., et al. (2012). Burnout and satisfaction with work-life balance among US physicians relative to the general US population. *Archives of Internal Medicine, 172*(18), 1377–1385.

Shanafelt, T., Goh, J., & Sinsky, C. (2017). The business case for investing in physician well-being. *JAMA Internal Medicine, 177*(12), 1826–1832.

Shanafelt, T., Schein, E., Minor, L., Trockel, M., Schein, P., & Kirch, D. (2019). Healing the professional culture of medicine. *Mayo Clinic Proceedings, 94*, 81556–81566.

Sibinga, E., & Wu, A. (2010). Clinician mindfulness and patient safety. *JAMA, 304*(22), 2532-2533.

Sinsky, C., Colligan, L., Li, L., Prgomet, M., Reynolds, S., Goeders, L., et al. (2016). Allocation of physician time in ambulatory practice: A time and motion study in 4 specialties. *Annals of Internal Medicine, 165*(11), 753–760.

Sinsky, C., Dyrbye, L. N., West, C., Satele, D., Tutty, M., & Shanafelt, T. (2017). Professional satisfaction and the career plans of US physicians. *Mayo Clinic Proceedings, 92*(11), 1625–1635.

Tan, C.-M. (2012). *Search inside yourself: The unexpected path to achieving success, happiness (and world peace)*. New York: HarperCollins.

Treadway, K. (2008). The future of primary care: Sustaining relationships. *New England Journal of Medicine, 359*(25), 2086.

Verghese, A. (2016, October). The importance of being. *Health Affairs*, 1924–1927.

Vogus, T., & Sutcliffe, K. (2007a). The impact of safety organizing, trusted leadership, and care pathways on reported medication errors in hospital nursing units. *Medical Care, 45*(10), 997–1002.

Vogus, T., & Sutcliffe, K. (2007b). The safety organizing scale: development and validation of a behavioral measure of safety culture in hospital nursing units. *Medical Care, 45*(1), 46–54.

West, C., Dyrbye, L. N., & Shanafelt, T. (2018). Physician burnout: contributors, consequences and solutions. *Journal of Internal Medicine, 283*, 515–529.

Williams, E., Conrad, T., Scheckler, W., Linzer, M., McMurray, J., & Schwartz, M. (2001). Understanding physicians' intentions to withdraw from practice: The role of job satisfaction, stress, mental and physical health. *Health Care Management Review, 26*(1), 7–19.

Zuger, J. (2004). Dissatisfaction with medical practice. *New England Journal of Medicine, 350*(1), 69–75.

Part IV
Towards Individual- and Organisation-Focused Interventions and Their Effectiveness

Chapter 16
Training as a Facilitator of Organizational Change in Health Care: The Input-Mediator/Moderator-Outcome-Input Model

Megan E. Gregory, Clayton D. Rothwell, and Ann Scheck McAlearney

16.1 Introduction

The healthcare industry is evolving rapidly to respond to changing conditions and demands. In order to keep pace, effective organizational change, defined as creating or responding to differences in structures, processes, and roles over time (Martins, 2011), is essential in healthcare. Many of the changes impacting the healthcare industry require clinicians to think and act in new ways. Thus, training is an important way to promote organizational change. In this chapter we will describe the role of training in the context of organizational change, and provide specific examples of teamwork training and cultural competency training. We will describe

---

M. E. Gregory (✉) · C. D. Rothwell
Department of Biomedical Informatics, The Ohio State University College of Medicine, Columbus, OH, USA

The Center for the Advancement of Team Science, Analytics, and Systems Thinking in Health Services and Implementation Science Research (CATALYST), The Ohio State University College of Medicine, Columbus, OH, USA
e-mail: megan.gregory@osumc.edu

A. S. McAlearney
Department of Biomedical Informatics, The Ohio State University College of Medicine, Columbus, OH, USA

The Center for the Advancement of Team Science, Analytics, and Systems Thinking in Health Services and Implementation Science Research (CATALYST), The Ohio State University College of Medicine, Columbus, OH, USA

Department of Family Medicine, The Ohio State University College of Medicine, Columbus, OH, USA

Division of Health Services Management and Policy, The Ohio State University College of Public Health, Columbus, OH, USA

© Springer Nature Switzerland AG 2020
A. Montgomery et al. (eds.), *Connecting Healthcare Worker Well-Being, Patient Safety and Organisational Change*, Aligning Perspectives on Health, Safety and Well-Being, https://doi.org/10.1007/978-3-030-60998-6_16

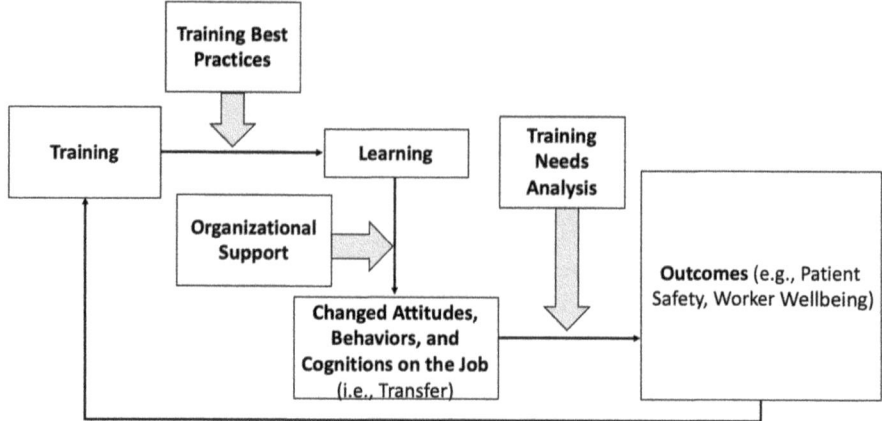

Fig. 16.1 Theoretical model of training in the context of organizational change, following the IMOI model

the outcomes that such training programs can achieve, how they can facilitate organizational change, and how they can impact patient safety and worker wellbeing.

The chapter is framed by the input-mediator/moderator-outcome-input (IMOI) model (modified from Ilgen, Hollenbeck, Johnson, & Jundt, 2005, who put forth the input-mediator-outcome-input model). This model posits that an input (e.g., training) leads to one or more mediators (e.g., changed attitudes, behaviors, and cognitions on the job, also known as transfer of training), that are impacted by moderators (e.g., conducting a training needs analyses, adhering to training best practices, and providing organizational support for training). This should then lead to outcomes (e.g., improved patient safety and worker well-being). Finally, the outcomes, in turn, feed into future inputs (e.g., continued organizational change through subsequent training). Figure 16.1 displays this process in full.

In the remainder of this chapter, we will discuss each section of this IMOI model in the context of organizational change. First, we will define the input of interest—training—and describe examples of two types of training intended to facilitate change in organizations: teamwork training and cultural competency training. Next, we will discuss the mediators, including learning and changed attitudes, behaviors and cognitions on the job (i.e., transfer of training). We will then discuss outcomes of training, with a particular focus on patient safety and worker wellbeing. Finally, we will discuss moderators in the model that facilitate subsequent training efforts (e.g., refresher training), including adherence to training best practices, organizational support, and the use of a training needs analysis. We conclude with an overall discussion and key messages for research and practice.

16.2 Input: Training

Broadly defined, training is "the systematic acquisition of attitudes, concepts, knowledge, rules, or skills that result in improved performance at work," (Goldstein, 1991, p. 508). Training can be provided for task and/or interpersonal skills related to a job, and can take various forms including traditional face-to-face training sessions, online modules (e.g., computer-based learning), or simulation (e.g., role playing, virtual reality). While there are various types of training that can influence organizational change, the current chapter focuses on two specific types that are distinct from each other yet very common in healthcare settings: (a) teamwork training, defined as "a learning strategy in which a learner or group of learners systematically acquire(s) teamwork KSAs [knowledge, skills, and attitudes] to impact cognitions, affect, and behaviors of a team" (Hughes et al., 2016, p. 1267); and (b) cultural competency training, which seeks to improve clinicians' KSAs around working with patients from different cultures (Gallagher & Polanin, 2015). Cultural competency training is often designed to increase awareness about healthcare disparities, defined as "a particular type of health difference that is closely linked with economic, social, or environmental disadvantage," (US Department of Health and Human Services, 2010) that are attributed to cultural differences and thereby can be used to address inequities in healthcare.

16.2.1 Teamwork Training: An Overview

As the number of clinicians and allied health professionals required to care for a single patient increases (e.g., Gawande, 2012), teamwork training is becoming increasingly necessary for organizations to effectively and safely accommodate this change. Teamwork training programs teach clinicians to engage in behaviors such as back-up behavior (e.g., providing task assistance and support), situation assessment, more effective communication, and focused efforts to prevent human error. As a result, teamwork training is associated with improved outcomes for hospitals (e.g., better safety climate, increased patient satisfaction, and lower mortality rates; Hughes et al., 2016). There is also evidence supporting the concept that there is a trickle-down effect such that training leads to learning, which impacts training transfer, and this ultimately yields improved outcomes such as those mentioned previously (Hughes et al., 2016). Popular choices for teamwork training programs in healthcare settings include crew resource management (CRM) and the Agency for Healthcare Research and Quality (AHRQ)'s publicly-available TeamSTEPPS® program (Agency for Healthcare Research and Quality, 2019). One study found that in 2015, over 1.5 million people had been trained on TeamSTEPPS® alone (Global Diffusion of Healthcare Innovation Working Group, 2015).

16.2.2 Cultural Competency Training: An Overview

In healthcare, implicit bias, defined as "associations outside conscious awareness that lead to a negative evaluation of a person on the basis of irrelevant characteristics such as race or gender" (FitzGerald & Hurst, 2017, p. 19), has been found to be correlated with lower quality of care and disparities in care provision (FitzGerald & Hurst, 2017). This correlation is likely due to the impact that these implicit judgments have on providers' behaviors towards and treatment decisions about different patients (Drewniak, Krones, Sauer, & Wild, 2016). Through cultural competency training, a type of training designed to reduce implicit bias and increase individuals' sensitivity to and knowledge about cross-cultural interactions (Betancourt, Green, Carrillo, & Ananeh-Firempong, 2003), the likelihood of these negative evaluations and their subsequent impacts on care quality may be reduced. Cultural competency training can be focused on individual or a combination of economic, social, or environmental factors such as race or ethnicity, religion, socioeconomic status, gender, age, mental health status, disability status, sexual orientation or gender identity. Interventions to improve cultural competency can be delivered at an individual or organizational level, thus the target of such training may be on health care providers, patients, hospitals, communities, or even government agencies (e.g., introduction of new policies; Chin, Walters, Cook, & Huang, 2007). Here we focus specifically on *training healthcare workers*. In this context, training to increase cultural competency around race and ethnicity in medical student and medical resident curricula has been proposed and implemented (Jacobs, Kohrman, Lemon, & Vickers, 2003; Smith et al., 2007; Vela, Kim, Tang, & Chin, 2008), as well as cultural competency training through continuing education programs for practicing physicians (Like, 2011). While cognitive knowledge and skills training are usually the focus of these curricula, including training focused on developing cultural competency can help to change cultural attitudes among these healthcare workers. For instance, incorporating experiential training such as a poverty simulation can increase awareness of and influence attitudes about socioeconomic disparities for healthcare workers who may need to address socioeconomic factors in providing care to their patients (Nickols & Nielsen, 2011).

16.3 Mediator: Learning, Changed Attitudes, Behaviors, and Cognitions on the Job

The goal of training is to impart new knowledge, skills, and/or attitudes (KSAs) onto workers (i.e., learning), with the intention that these new KSAs will be utilized by workers on the job (i.e., transfer of training). Outcomes targeted for improvement through training cannot be achieved if (a) the necessary KSAs are not learned in training, or (b) the KSAs are not used back on the job. While learning is a key proximal goal of training, not all training is effective—that is, not all training yields changes in KSAs. Similarly, not all KSAs that are learned are transferred back to the workers' job environments. We next describe moderators of these relationships.

16.3.1 Moderator: Adhering to Training Best Practices to Facilitate Learning

There are a number of best practices that should be employed to ensure that training is as effective as possible (Gregory, Feitosa, Driskell, Salas, & Vessey, 2013). As such, adherence to training best practices serves as a moderator, such that the degree to which trainees learn the intended KSAs is driven by the extent to which training is designed and delivered according to recommended practices. Specific best practices regarding instructional design and delivery include: (1) use of multiple delivery methods, including information (e.g., lectures, slides, handouts), demonstration (e.g., videos, in-person skits), and practice (e.g., role plays, simulations) (Salas & Cannon-Bowers, 2001); and, (2) gauging trainees' understanding and providing timely, specific feedback (both positive and negative) (Kluger & DeNisi, 1996).

16.3.2 Moderator: Organizational Support for Training Transfer

Another moderator that influences training effectiveness is organizational support. More specifically, the support the organization (including leadership, supervisors, and peers) provides (or does not provide) impacts the extent to which learned KSAs are transferred to and used in the job environment (Baldwin & Ford, 1988). This support comes in multiple forms, including both practical support (e.g., providing resources needed to use what was learned in training such as providing access to an interpreter service after training providers to be sensitive about the needs of non-English speaking patients), and culturally supporting the training in the practice setting (e.g., leaders and supervisors reinforcing the use of trained KSAs through verbal statements and rewards) (Hughes, Zajac, Spencer, & Salas, 2018).

16.4 Outcomes

While learning and transfer are more proximal outputs of training, the ultimate goal of training is to produce some type of change. In the context of healthcare, training that is intended to produce organizational change may be focused on improving outcomes for employees, and/or improving outcomes for patients. In this section, we will describe how training can positively impact both patient safety (a patient outcome) and worker wellbeing (an employee outcome).

16.4.1 Patient Safety

Patient safety, defined as "freedom from accidental or preventable injuries produced by medical care" (Agency for Healthcare Research and Quality Patient Safety Network), is one of the six domains of quality defined by the Institute of Medicine (2001). Patient safety incidents are complex and multi-causal; however, frequent contributors include medical error (e.g., diagnostic error), human factors (e.g., lack of attention), teamwork and coordination issues (e.g., miscommunication), environmental and equipment factors (e.g., malfunctions, missing equipment, disruptions), system issues (e.g., understaffing), patient-related issues (e.g., failure to follow medical advice) and training-related issues (e.g., lack of training, failure to recall) (Chaneliere et al., 2018; Joint Commission, 2016). As such, teamwork training designed to target such issues can help to reduce patient safety incidents. For instance, teamwork training (as defined previously, and inclusive of various programs such as TeamSTEPPS®, crew resource management, and Medical Team Training) has been shown meta-analytically to be associated with improved patient safety (Hughes et al., 2016). More specifically, in one study, Morey et al. (2002) implemented a teamwork training program in nine hospitals using a quasi-experimental, untreated control group design and found that clinical errors decreased 30.9% to 4.4% from pre- to post-teamwork training for the experimental group. Similarly, a teamwork training program implemented in a combat support hospital in Iraq was associated with significant reductions in communication-related errors, medication and transfusion errors, and needle stick incidents (Deering et al., 2011). Improved safety is likely due to the content that is taught in such training programs: communication, coordination, and assertiveness—concepts directly related to the contributors to patient safety, as mentioned above.

While evidence suggests a relationship between teamwork training and patient safety, research linking cultural competency training to patient safety outcomes is sparse (Shepherd, 2019). Nonetheless, it is likely that such training would have positive impacts on safety outcomes. For example, a core competency taught in many cultural competency training programs is that of reducing implicit bias. Implicit bias can influence decision making, which is an important precursor to the provision of safe care (Croskerry & Nimmo, 2011). While the link between implicit bias training and patient safety is understudied, research on training to reduce other types of biases (e.g., bias blind spot, confirmation bias, fundamental attribution error) has been shown to be effective in reducing bias in decision-making immediately after training and 2 months post-training for tasks similar to the training scenarios and generalizing to novel tasks that had a different format or context not present in the training (Morewedge et al., 2015). Further, there are theoretical reasons to believe that cultural competency training of healthcare workers can lead to improved patient safety. For instance, an analysis of adverse events across six hospitals compared adverse events for patients fluent in English to patients with low-English proficiency (Divi, Koss, Schmaltz, & Loeb, 2007). When patients with low-English proficiency experience an adverse event, it more often leads to physical harm, and the physical harm experienced is typically more severe. Communication errors contributed to the adverse events experienced by low-English proficiency patients more often than to events experienced by fluent patients, specifically disclosure (i.e., sharing care delivery and outcomes information) and assessment of patient needs. The possibility of harm can be reduced for patients with low-English proficiency when physicians and nurses are trained on how to identify language proficiency issues, to follow guidelines about when to use translation services, and to access and use the special services that are available to patients (Coren, Filipetto, & Weiss, 2009). Further, the type of interpreter used (i.e., professionally trained, paid interpreters, vs. ad hoc family members or hospital staff who speak the patient's language) has a clear impact on patient safety: professional interpreters are more effective at reducing clinically significant translation problems, compared to ad hoc interpreters (Flores, Abreu, Barone, Bachur, & Lin, 2012). Training for workers on how to use translation services including how to integrate an interpreter into the clinical encounter, or providing workers with experience in clinics serving these populations during medical school can improve patient safety and ultimately reduce disparities in care (Marion, Hildebrandt, Davis, Marín, & Crandall, 2008). In similar work related to cultural competency training, Lewin, Skea, Entwistle, Zwarenstein, and Dick (2001) conducted a systematic review of seventeen studies that trained providers to use more patient-centered communication techniques and concluded that such training programs can, in fact, enhance provider communication skills such that they are more inclusive of patient needs and preferences. This evidence supports the idea that it is possible to train providers to communicate with patients in a way that their unique needs (e.g., cultural needs/ preferences) are taken into account, and this can ultimately lead to safer care (Epstein & Street, 2007).

16.4.2 Worker Wellbeing

Worker wellbeing is a broad concept that includes concepts such as affect, mental health, emotional exhaustion, and satisfaction with work (Wright & Doherty, 1998). Within the scope of worker wellbeing, researchers have examined more specific constructs such as burnout (defined as "a psychological syndrome of emotional exhaustion, depersonalization, and reduced personal accomplishment" at work; Maslach, Jackson, Leiter, Schaufeli, & Schwab, 1986, p. 192), job stress (defined as "a perceived substantial imbalance between demand and response capability, under conditions where failure to meet demands has important perceived consequences;" McGrath, 1970, p. 20), job engagement (defined as "a high level of energy and strong identification with one's work;" Bakker, Demerouti, & Sanz-Vergel,

2014, p. 391), and job satisfaction (defined as "a positive (or negative) evaluative judgment one makes about one's job or job situation" (Warr & Nielsen, 2018; Weiss, 2002, p. 6). The job demands-resources model suggests that job demands (e.g., workload, emotional demands) can lead to poor wellbeing outcomes, while job resources (e.g., support, feedback) can improve motivation and other wellbeing outcomes (Bakker & Demerouti, 2017).

With increases in healthcare provider workload attributed to different causes including increased numbers of patient visits (Fu, Schwebel, & Hu, 2018) and consultations (Hobbs, Bankhead, & Mukhtar, 2016), as well as time demands related to the use of electronic health records (Arndt et al., 2017), worker wellbeing is becoming a major global issue in healthcare. Studies have found that almost half of physicians report burnout symptoms (e.g., Shanafelt et al., 2012; Soler et al., 2008), and recent estimates suggest that burnout costs healthcare organizations $7600 per physician per year (Han et al., 2019), or $4.6 billion nationally in the United States. The job demands-resources model (Bakker & Demerouti, 2017) suggests that providing workers with support and resources in their jobs can mitigate some of the negative effects of job demands (e.g., patient workload, electronic health record alerts), and training programs are one way to give workers the capacity to address job demands. For instance, Xanthopoulou et al. (2007) found that offering professional development opportunities to home healthcare workers buffered the negative effects of their job demands. This may be due to the new knowledge and skills built through training and professional development programs that enable workers to more efficiently and effectively complete job tasks. Teamwork training can similarly enhance knowledge and skills to improve efficiency and/or work conditions, and contribute to worker wellbeing. For example, interventions to improve team communication, such as communication between clinicians and staff members, can lead to increased clinician satisfaction (Linzer et al., 2015). Teamwork training programs have additionally been associated with lower turnover for nurses and with less sick leave time for nurse assistants (Meurling, Hedman, Sandahl, Felländer-Tsai, & Wallin, 2013), as well as with increased staff morale (West et al., 2012).

Cultural competency training, as a resource for providers, can also potentially serve to help providers better meet the demands of their jobs, yet studies disagree about the impact of these trainings on worker wellbeing. For instance, in practice, workers may view new training as another job demand. Further, as workers are already experiencing widespread levels of burnout and stress, cultural competency training will increase their awareness about expectations to deliver culturally competent care, but they may not feel appropriately supported to do so, thus adding to their stress and workload (Solberg, 2016). Also, workers may perceive that some factors contributing to care disparities are outside their control (Runyan, 2018); as a result, they may be frustrated and feel "that they cannot provide the good care they wish—and believe is their duty—to give" (Glasberg, Eriksson, & Norberg, 2007). However, in one study where clinicians were trained to increase their awareness about healthcare disparities and the factors that contribute to these disparities, they also learned about available community resources and how to screen patients to identify risk factors associated with these disparities (Tong et al., 2018). Although burnout was not specifically measured, the study found that providers modified the care they delivered based on the screenings and felt this improved their communication with patients. Thus, training that increases provider awareness about how to deliver culturally competent care for their patients may be able to build providers' skills to address risk factors related to economic, social, or environmental disadvantages, and potentially serve as a job resource to reduce burnout among these workers.

16.4.3 The Relationship Between Worker Wellbeing and Patient Safety

Research has identified important connections between worker wellbeing and patient safety. Using a longitudinal design, West et al. (2006) sought empirically to examine the directionality of the relationship between wellbeing and patient safety (i.e., does poor worker wellbeing lead to patient safety incidents, or do patient safety incidents lead to poor worker wellbeing?). They found that there was a reciprocal relationship between the two constructs such that being involved in a medical error led to reduced wellbeing, which subsequently led to an increased likelihood of being involved in another medical error. More recently, Tawfik et al. (2018) surveyed 6586 physicians and found that more than 10% of respondents reported a major medical error in the prior 3 months, and these rates were even higher among physicians who had symptoms of burnout (e.g., emotional exhaustion, depersonalization), even after adjusting for personal (e.g., age, sex, relationship status) and practice factors (e.g., specialty, practice setting, hours worked per week). In a meta-analysis of 21 studies linking burnout and patient safety, Panagioti et al. (2018) found that physician burnout was associated with twice the odds of being involved in a patient safety incident. Future work in this area should seek to examine the role training can play, including both training targeted at increasing worker wellbeing and at improving patient safety, as both would likely be beneficial.

16.4.4 Moderator: Training Needs Analysis

In order for a training program to get the outcomes it intends (including improved patient safety and worker wellbeing), a training needs analysis should be conducted prior to the development of training (Goldstein, 1991). The goal of a training needs analysis is to understand what content should be included in training, who should be trained, when and how training should occur, and the extent to which the organization is ready for and will support training (see Table 16.1). An appropriate training needs analysis can thus facilitate development of an effective training program. In practice, a training needs analysis is often a mixed-methods process that includes surveys and/or interviews and/or observations to understand (1) the organization's

Table 16.1 Example training needs analysis

Element of training needs analysis	Purpose	Methods
Organization	• To understand how a given training initiative will align with organizational goals and resources; • To determine the extent to which the organization will support training and transfer; and • To identify possible organizational barriers to success	Interviews and/or surveys of leaders and supervisors
Job/Task	• To inform training content by understanding which parts of a task or process require training; • To understand components of work that are independently performed vs. interdependent; and • To better understand the context and conditions of the environment in which the tasks are performed	Observations of work area, interviews and/or surveys of employees, cognitive task analysis
Person	• To identify which employees and work areas are best suited for the training by assessing employees' KSAs on the training content	Observations of job performance, tests (written and/or simulation), surveys of employees, review of employee records

support for training (e.g., understanding what resources they are willing to provide for workers to attend training; the extent to which attending training and using trained KSAs on the job will be rewarded; tangible support such as provision of materials and personnel [e.g., white boards for training on team briefs, interpreters for training on non-English speaking patients, etc.] in order to use trained skills); (2) the job environment and context (e.g., rapid-paced emergency room providing 24/7 staffing vs. rural primary care clinic with more traditional business hours); (3) tasks that workers perform independently, and/or interdependent tasks that team members work together to complete (to help identify where specific needs are for targeting training; e.g., it is not effective to focus training around handoff mnemonics when these are already frequently used); and (4) who the potential trainees are (e.g., perhaps a particular issue is most salient in intensive care, rendering the training of employees in ambulatory and medical-surgical units unnecessary). This process can also be used as an opportunity to increase buy-in from workers for the change that is desired to be achieved via training, and to allow them to help shape the direction of the change program—an approach recommended in contrast to a fully top-down change model (Tams, 2018). While a training needs analysis process should be the first step in developing a training initiative (Goldstein, 1991), its importance becomes evident after training has transferred. For instance, while training transfer may occur (i.e., employees use newly learned KSAs back on the job), this transfer will not yield improved outcomes if the training did not address the KSA needs of those employees (i.e., a needs analysis was not done to understand what training content was needed in order to improve the outcomes an organization wished to change.)

16.5 Input: Continued Organizational Change

Following the logic of the IMOI framework, the last link of the model in Fig. 16.1 depicts a recursive arrow feeding back to the input of training thus showing that training is not a one-time event. In order to ensure continued attention to organizational change efforts over time, training evaluation should be ongoing to monitor the need for refresher training or for training on new content as new issues and needs arise. This is necessary for multiple reasons including: (1) evidence shows that people do not retain much of the information learned in training over time (Arthur, Bennett, Stanush, & McNelly, 1998); and (2) new workers will continue to join the organization after the training takes place and thus will have not been exposed to it. In addition to providing refresher training, sustainment of trained KSAs on the job can be increased by provision of supervisor, peer, and organizational support (Hughes, Zajac, Woods, & Salas, 2019).

16.6 Discussion

In this chapter, we discussed the role of training to improve patient safety and worker wellbeing in the context of organizational change. Throughout the chapter we interwove specific examples of two training programs deployed in healthcare settings: teamwork training and cultural competency training. In so doing we reviewed the state of the science in these areas as they relate to our modified IMOI model. Broadly, both teamwork training programs and cultural competency training programs are associated with improvements in worker wellbeing and patient safety. However, while the science on teamwork training is relatively well-developed (e.g., Hughes et al., 2016; Marlow et al., 2017; Weaver, Dy, & Rosen, 2014), the evidence for cultural competency training is more limited with respect to its impact on worker wellbeing and patient safety.

16.6.1 Future Research

As previously noted, more research is needed to investigate the link between training and worker/patient outcomes. Overall, very few training programs are evaluated at this level; most evaluators collect simple participant reactions (Association for

Talent Development, 2009). We noted above the paucity of high-quality evidence linking cultural competency training with improved outcomes. Further, while the science of teamwork training is further developed, only 3% of healthcare teamwork training programs collect data on how the training impacts patient outcomes (Marlow et al., 2017). Future research on training to promote organizational change should assess the impact of training on both organizational (e.g., worker wellbeing) and patient (e.g., patient safety, patient satisfaction) outcomes. At the same time, although evidence linking cultural competency training to improved worker wellbeing is still emerging, it is unknown through what causal pathways (i.e., *how*) this may occur. More research should be done to investigate the causal mechanisms of these relationships so that future cultural competency training can be designed to achieve positive outcomes.

16.7 Conclusion

Training can be a key driver to produce organizational change that improves patient safety and worker wellbeing. However, many training programs do not achieve their intended outcomes and are unsuccessful in inducing organizational change (e.g., Vedantam, 2008). For instance, factors such as failure to align the training content with learners' training needs and desires (Tannenbaum & Yukl, 1992), suboptimal, passive delivery methods (e.g., death by PowerPoint) (Salas & Cannon-Bowers, 2001), failure to align training content with desired outcomes (Salas & Cannon-Bowers, 2001), and lack of organizational and/or supervisor support and resources for using trained KSAs (Rouiller & Goldstein, 1993) can contribute to less successful training efforts. We have presented a modified IMOI model positing that for training to achieve its goals, it must be designed in accordance with training best practices, be supported by the organization, and be grounded in a training needs analysis. As effective training is not a one-time event, it is important for organizations (and supervisors) to continue to support use of the trained KSAs on the job and provide refresher training over time to increase the likelihood that organizational changes to increase patient safety and wellbeing succeed.

16.7.1 Key Messages for Researchers

- Investigate the causal pathways that lead from training to improved outcomes; i.e., how does training change knowledge, skills, and attitudes on the job (e.g., via motivation, when effective interactive training methods are used, and when organizations/supervisors are supportive?).
- Evaluate training programs at multiple levels (e.g., learners' reactions, learning, transfer of training, outcomes/results): Invest in assessing the impact of training on organizational and patient outcomes.

16.7.2 Key Messages for Healthcare Delivery

- Conduct a training needs analysis before designing training in order to tailor training content and methods to the specific needs of the learners.
- Design training in accordance with training best practices; key tips include using multiple delivery methods (e.g., information, demonstration, practice), providing feedback, and ensuring training is provided when it is needed most.
- Organizations and supervisors should provide support for the training by providing time to complete training, and resources to support use of trained knowledge, skills, and attitudes on the job.

References

Agency for Healthcare Research and Quality. (2019). TeamSTEPPS 2.0. Retrieved from https://www.ahrq.gov/teamstepps/instructor/index.html

Agency for Healthcare Research and Quality Patient Safety Network. Patient safety. Retrieved from http://psnet.ahrq.gov/glossary.aspx#P

Arndt, B. G., Beasley, J. W., Watkinson, M. D., Temte, J. L., Tuan, W.-J., Sinsky, C. A., et al. (2017). Tethered to the EHR: Primary care physician workload assessment using EHR event log data and time-motion observations. *The Annals of Family Medicine, 15*(5), 419–426.

Arthur, W., Bennett, W., Stanush, P. L., & McNelly, T. L. (1998). Factors that influence skill decay and retention: A quantitative review and analysis. *Human Performance, 11*(1), 57–101.

Association for Talent Development. (2009). ASTD: New study shows training evaluation efforts need help. Retrieved from https://www.td.org/insights/astd-new-study-shows-training-evaluation-efforts-need-help

Bakker, A. B., & Demerouti, E. (2017). Job demands–resources theory: Taking stock and looking forward. *Journal of Occupational Health Psychology, 22*(3), 273–285.

Bakker, A. B., Demerouti, E., & Sanz-Vergel, A. I. (2014). Burnout and work engagement: The JD–R approach. *Annual Review of Organizational Psychology and Organizational Behavior, 1*(1), 389–411.

Baldwin, T. T., & Ford, J. K. (1988). Transfer of training: A review and directions for future research. *Personnel Psychology, 41*(1), 63–105.

Betancourt, J. R., Green, A. R., Carrillo, J. E., & Ananeh-Firempong, O. (2003). Defining cultural competence: A practical framework for addressing racial/ethnic disparities in health and health care. *Public Health Reports, 118*(4), 293–302. https://doi.org/10.1093/phr/118.4.293

Chaneliere, M., Koehler, D., Morlan, T., Berra, J., Colin, C., Dupie, I., et al. (2018). Factors contributing to patient safety incidents in primary care: A descriptive analysis of patient safety incidents in a French study using CADYA (categorization of errors in primary care). *BMC Family Practice, 19*(1), 121–134. https://doi.org/10.1186/s12875-018-0803-9

Chin, M. H., Walters, A. E., Cook, S. C., & Huang, E. S. (2007). Interventions to reduce racial and ethnic disparities in health care. *Medical Care Research and Review, 64*(5 Suppl), 7S–28S. https://doi.org/10.1177/1077558707305413

Coren, J. S., Filipetto, F. A., & Weiss, L. B. (2009). Eliminating barriers for patients with limited English proficiency. *The Journal of the American Osteopathic Association, 109*(12), 634–640.

Croskerry, P., & Nimmo, G. (2011). Better clinical decision making and reducing diagnostic error. *The Journal of the Royal College of Physicians of Edinburgh, 41*(2), 155–162.

Deering, S., Rosen, M. A., Ludi, V., Munroe, M., Pocrnich, A., Laky, C., et al. (2011). On the front lines of patient safety: Implementation and evaluation of team training in Iraq. *The Joint Commission Journal on Quality and Patient Safety, 37*(8), 350–356.

Divi, C., Koss, R. G., Schmaltz, S. P., & Loeb, J. M. (2007). Language proficiency and adverse events in US hospitals: A pilot study. *International Journal for Quality in Health Care, 19*(2), 60–67. https://doi.org/10.1093/intqhc/mzl069

Drewniak, D., Krones, T., Sauer, C., & Wild, V. (2016). The influence of patients' immigration background and residence permit status on treatment decisions in health care. Results of a factorial survey among general practitioners in Switzerland. *Social Science & Medicine, 161*, 64–73.

Epstein, R., & Street, R. (2007). *Patient-centered communication in cancer care: Promoting healing and reducing suffering*. National Cancer Institute; Bethesda. Retrieved from https://cancercontrol.cancer.gov/brp/docs/pcc_monograph.pdf

FitzGerald, C., & Hurst, S. (2017). Implicit bias in healthcare professionals: A systematic review. *BMC Medical Ethics, 18*(1), 19. https://doi.org/10.1186/s12910-017-0179-8

Flores, G., Abreu, M., Barone, C. P., Bachur, R., & Lin, H. (2012). Errors of medical interpretation and their potential clinical consequences: A comparison of professional versus ad hoc versus no interpreters. *Annals of Emergency Medicine, 60*(5), 545–553. https://doi.org/10.1016/j.annemergmed.2012.01.025

Fu, Y., Schwebel, D., & Hu, G. (2018). Physicians' workloads in China: 1998–2016. *International Journal of Environmental Research and Public Health, 15*(8), 1649.

Gallagher, R. W., & Polanin, J. R. (2015). A meta-analysis of educational interventions designed to enhance cultural competence in professional nurses and nursing students. *Nurse Education Today, 35*(2), 333–340. https://doi.org/10.1016/j.nedt.2014.10.021

Gawande, A. (2012). Big med. *The New Yorker*. Retrieved from https://www.newyorker.com/magazine/2012/08/13/big-med

Glasberg, A.-L., Eriksson, S., & Norberg, A. (2007). Burnout and 'stress of conscience' among healthcare personnel. *Journal of Advanced Nursing, 57*(4), 392–403.

Global Diffusion of Healthcare Innovation Working Group. (2015). *Global diffusion of healthcare innovation study: Accelerating the journey*. Retrieved from http://wish-qatar.org/summit/2015-summit/global-diffusion-of-healthcare-innovation

Goldstein, I. L. (1991). Training in work organizations. In M. D. Dunnette & L. M. Hough (Eds.), *Handbook of industrial and organizational psychology* (pp. 507–619). Palo Alto, CA: Consulting Psychologists Press.

Gregory, M., Feitosa, J., Driskell, T., Salas, E., & Vessey, W. (2013). Designing, delivering, and evaluating team training in organizations: Principles that work. In *Developing and enhancing high-performance teams: Evidence-based practices and advice*. San Francisco, CA: Jossey-Bass.

Han, S., Shanafelt, T. D., Sinsky, C. A., Awad, K. M., Dyrbye, L. N., Fiscus, L. C., et al. (2019). Estimating the attributable cost of physician burnout in the United States. *Annals of Internal Medicine*. https://doi.org/10.7326/M18-1422

Hobbs, F. R., Bankhead, C., & Mukhtar, T. (2016). On behalf of the National Institute for Health Research School for Primary Care Research. Clinical workload in UK primary care: A retrospective analysis of 100 million consultations in England, 2007–14. *Lancet, 387*(10035), 2323–2330.

Hughes, A. M., Gregory, M. E., Joseph, D. L., Sonesh, S. C., Marlow, S. L., Lacerenza, C. N., et al. (2016). Saving lives: A meta-analysis of team training in healthcare. *Journal of Applied Psychology, 101*(9), 1266–1304. https://doi.org/10.1037/apl0000120

Hughes, A. M., Zajac, S., Spencer, J. M., & Salas, E. (2018). A checklist for facilitating training transfer in organizations. *International Journal of Training and Development, 22*(4), 334–345.

Hughes, A. M., Zajac, S., Woods, A. L., & Salas, E. (2019). The role of work environment in training sustainment: A meta-analysis. *Human Factors, Online First*. https://doi.org/10.1177/0018720819845988

Ilgen, D. R., Hollenbeck, J. R., Johnson, M., & Jundt, D. (2005). Teams in organizations: From input-process-output models to IMOI models. *Annual Review of Psychology, 56*, 517–543. https://doi.org/10.1146/annurev.psych.56.091103.070250

Institute of Medicine. (2001). *Crossing the quality chasm: A new health system for the 21st century.* Washington, DC: National Academy Press.

Jacobs, E. A., Kohrman, C., Lemon, M., & Vickers, D. L. (2003). Teaching physicians-in-training to address racial disparities in health: A hospital-community partnership. *Public Health Reports, 118*(4), 349–356. https://doi.org/10.1093/phr/118.4.349

Joint Commission. (2016). Sentinel event statistics released for 2015. *The Joint Commission Online.*

Kluger, A. N., & DeNisi, A. (1996). The effects of feedback interventions on performance: A historical review, a meta-analysis, and a preliminary feedback intervention theory. *Psychological Bulletin, 119*(2), 254–284.

Lewin, S., Skea, Z., Entwistle, V. A., Zwarenstein, M., & Dick, J. (2001). Interventions for providers to promote a patient-centred approach in clinical consultations. *Cochrane Database of Systematic Reviews, 4.*

Like, R. C. (2011). Educating clinicians about cultural competence and disparities in health and health care. *The Journal of Continuing Education in the Health Professions, 31*(3), 196–206. https://doi.org/10.1002/chp.20127

Linzer, M., Poplau, S., Grossman, E., Varkey, A., Yale, S., Williams, E., et al. (2015). A cluster randomized trial of interventions to improve work conditions and clinician burnout in primary care: Results from the Healthy Work Place (HWP) Study. *The Journal of General Internal Medicine, 30*(8), 1105–1111. https://doi.org/10.1007/s11606-015-3235-4

Marion, G. S., Hildebrandt, C. A., Davis, S. W., Marín, A. J., & Crandall, S. J. (2008). Working effectively with interpreters: A model curriculum for physician assistant students. *The Medical Teacher, 30*(6), 612–617. https://doi.org/10.1080/01421590801986539

Marlow, S. L., Hughes, A. M., Sonesh, S. C., Gregory, M. E., Lacerenza, C. N., Benishek, L. E., et al. (2017). A systematic review of team training in health care: Ten questions. *The Joint Commission Journal on Quality and Patient Safety, 43*(4), 197–204. https://doi.org/10.1016/j.jcjq.2016.12.004

Martins, L. L. (2011). Organizational change and development. In S. Zedeck (Ed.), *APA handbook of industrial and organizational psychology, Vol 1: Building and developing the organization* (Vol. 3, pp. 691–728). Washington, DC: American Psychological Association.

Maslach, C., Jackson, S. E., Leiter, M. P., Schaufeli, W. B., & Schwab, R. L. (1986). *Maslach burnout inventory* (Vol. 21). Palo Alto, CA: Consulting Psychologists Press.

McGrath, J. E. (1970). A conceptual formulation for research on stress. *Social and Psychological Factors in Stress, 10*, 21.

Meurling, L., Hedman, L., Sandahl, C., Felländer-Tsai, L., & Wallin, C. J. (2013). Systematic simulation-based team training in a Swedish intensive care unit: A diverse response among critical care professions. *BMJ Quality & Safety, 22*(6), 485–494. https://doi.org/10.1136/bmjqs-2012-000994

Morewedge, C. K., Yoon, H., Scopelliti, I., Symborski, C. W., Korris, J. H., & Kassam, K. S. (2015). Debiasing decisions: Improved decision making with a single training intervention. *Policy Insights from the Behavioral and Brain Sciences, 2*(1), 129–140.

Morey, J. C., Simon, R., Jay, G. D., Wears, R. L., Salisbury, M., Dukes, K. A., et al. (2002). Error reduction and performance improvement in the emergency department through formal teamwork training: Evaluation results of the MedTeams project. *Health Services Research, 37*(6), 1553–1581.

Nickols, S. Y., & Nielsen, R. B. (2011). "So many people are struggling": Developing social empathy through a poverty simulation. *Journal of Poverty, 15*(1), 22–42.

Panagioti, M., Geraghty, K., Johnson, J., Zhou, A., Panagopoulou, E., Chew-Graham, C., et al. (2018). Association between physician burnout and patient safety, professionalism, and patient satisfaction: A systematic review and meta-analysis. *The Journal of the American Medical Association Internal Medicine, 178*(10), 1317–1331.

Rouiller, J. Z., & Goldstein, I. L. (1993). The relationship between organizational transfer climate and positive transfer of training. *Human Resource Development Quarterly, 4*(4), 377–390.

Runyan, C. N. (2018). Assessing social determinants of health in primary care: Liability or opportunity? *Families, Systems, & Health, 36*(4), 550–552.

Salas, E., & Cannon-Bowers, J. A. (2001). The science of training: A decade of progress. *Annual Review of Psychology, 52*, 471–499. https://doi.org/10.1146/annurev.psych.52.1.471

Shanafelt, T. D., Boone, S., Tan, L., Dyrbye, L. N., Sotile, W., Satele, D., et al. (2012). Burnout and satisfaction with work-life balance among US physicians relative to the general US population. *Archives of Internal Medicine, 172*(18), 1377–1385. https://doi.org/10.1001/archinternmed.2012.3199

Shepherd, S. M. (2019). Cultural awareness workshops: Limitations and practical consequences. *BMC Medical Education, 19*(1), 14. https://doi.org/10.1186/s12909-018-1450-5

Smith, W. R., Betancourt, J. R., Wynia, M. K., Bussey-Jones, J., Stone, V. E., Phillips, C. O., et al. (2007). Recommendations for teaching about racial and ethnic disparities in health and health care. *Annals of Internal Medicine, 147*(9), 654–665. https://doi.org/10.7326/0003-4819-147-9-200711060-00010

Solberg, L. I. (2016). Theory vs. practice: Should primary care practice take on social determinants of health now? No. *Annals of Family Medicine, 14*(2), 102–103. https://doi.org/10.1370/afm.1918

Soler, J. K., Yaman, H., Esteva, M., Dobbs, F., Asenova, R. S., Katić, M., et al. (2008). Burnout in European family doctors: The EGPRN study. *Family Practice, 25*(4), 245–265.

Tams, C. (2018). Why we need to rethink organizational change management. *Forbes*. Retrieved from https://www.forbes.com/sites/carstentams/2018/01/26/why-we-need-to-rethink-organizational-change-management/#53923035e93c

Tannenbaum, S. I., & Yukl, G. (1992). Training and development in work organizations. *Annual Review of Psychology, 43*(1), 399–441.

Tawfik, D. S., Profit, J., Morgenthaler, T. I., Satele, D. V., Sinsky, C. A., Dyrbye, L. N., et al. (2018). Physician burnout, well-being, and work unit safety grades in relationship to reported medical errors. *Mayo Clinic Proceedings, 93*(11), 1571–1580. https://doi.org/10.1016/j.mayocp.2018.05.014

Tong, S. T., Liaw, W. R., Kashiri, P. L., Pecsok, J., Rozman, J., Bazemore, A. W., et al. (2018). Clinician experiences with screening for social needs in primary care. *The Journal of the American Board of Family Medicine, 31*(3), 351–363. https://doi.org/10.3122/jabfm.2018.03.170419

US Department of Health and Human Services. (2010). Healthy people 2020. Retrieved from https://www.healthypeople.gov/2020/about/foundation-health-measures/Disparities

Vedantam, S. (2008). Most diversity training ineffective, study finds. *Washington Post*. Retrieved from http://www.washingtonpost.com/wp-dyn/content/article/2008/01/19/AR2008011901899.html

Vela, M. B., Kim, K. E., Tang, H., & Chin, M. H. (2008). Innovative health care disparities curriculum for incoming medical students. *The Journal of General Internal Medicine, 23*(7), 1028–1032. https://doi.org/10.1007/s11606-008-0584-2

Warr, P., & Nielsen, K. (2018). Wellbeing and work performance. In E. Diener, S. Oishi, & L. Tay (Eds.), *Handbook of well-being*. Salt Lake City, UT: DEF.

Weaver, S. J., Dy, S. M., & Rosen, M. A. (2014). Team-training in healthcare: A narrative synthesis of the literature. *BMJ Quality & Safety, 23*(5), 359–372. https://doi.org/10.1136/bmjqs-2013-001848

Weiss, H. M. (2002). Deconstructing job satisfaction: Separating evaluations, beliefs and affective experiences. *Human Resource Management Review, 12*(2), 173–194.

West, C. P., Huschka, M. M., Novotny, P. J., Sloan, J. A., Kolars, J. C., Habermann, T. M., et al. (2006). Association of perceived medical errors with resident distress and empathy: A prospective longitudinal study. *The Journal of the American Medical Association, 296*(9), 1071–1078.

West, P., Sculli, G., Fore, A., Okam, N., Dunlap, C., Neily, J., et al. (2012). Improving patient safety and optimizing nursing teamwork using crew resource management techniques. *The Journal of Nursing Administration, 42*(1), 15–20. https://doi.org/10.1097/NNA.0b013e31823c17c7

Wright, T. A., & Doherty, E. M. (1998). Organizational behavior 'rediscovers' the role of emotional well-being. *Journal of Organizational Behavior, 19*(5), 481–485.

Xanthopoulou, D., Bakker, A. B., Dollard, M. F., Demerouti, E., Schaufeli, W. B., Taris, T. W., et al. (2007). When do job demands particularly predict burnout? The moderating role of job resources. *Journal of Managerial Psychology, 22*(8), 766–786.

Chapter 17
Schwartz Center Rounds: An Intervention to Enhance Staff Well-Being and Promote Organisational Change

Jill Maben and Cath Taylor

17.1 Introduction

This chapter draws upon data from a UK National Institute for Health Research (NIHR) commissioned national evaluation of Schwartz Center Rounds® (Rounds) in the UK which aimed to examine how, in which contexts and for whom, participation in Rounds affects staff wellbeing at work, social support for staff and improved relationships between staff and patients (Maben, Taylor, et al., 2018). Rounds originated in Boston, USA in 1994 and were introduced to the UK in 2009 and Australia in 2017. They are now run in over 420 healthcare organisations in the US, over 200 healthcare organisations in the UK and Ireland and approximately 10 organisations respectively in Canada and Australia and New Zealand (Maben, Taylor, et al., 2018).

Rounds were inspired by the experiences of a 39-year old healthcare lawyer, Kenneth Schwartz, who when terminally ill with lung cancer wrote in the Boston Globe in 1995 (Schwartz, 1995) that "small acts of kindness made the unbearable bearable" noting the importance of caregivers showing empathy and engaging with him as a person. He noted some caregivers could do this and others couldn't and even those that did, could not do it every day. This led him to consider what it was like to work in an environment where people were regularly dying—what was the toll on healthcare staff and how could they be supported to remain engaged and compassionate? Before his death, he set up the Schwartz Center for Compassionate Care (SCCC) as a not-for-profit organisation where Rounds were developed and then implemented in North America over 20 years ago. Rounds were implemented in

---

J. Maben (✉) · C. Taylor
School of Health Sciences, University of Surrey, Guildford, Surrey, UK
e-mail: j.maben@surrey.ac.uk

© Springer Nature Switzerland AG 2020
A. Montgomery et al. (eds.), *Connecting Healthcare Worker Well-Being, Patient Safety and Organisational Change*, Aligning Perspectives on Health, Safety and Well-Being, https://doi.org/10.1007/978-3-030-60998-6_17

the UK, via the Point of Care Foundation[1] (PoCF), who have held the license with SCCC to run Rounds in the UK since 2009.

Rounds provide a regular, usually monthly, forum where structured time and a safe, confidential space is offered for staff to get together to discuss and share the emotional, social or ethical challenges of caring for patients and families. They are organisation-wide forums, open to all staff (clinical and non-clinical)—implicitly recognising that all staff within healthcare organisations are integral to the provision of compassionate patient care. They are intended to help improve staff wellbeing, effectiveness of communication and work engagement, and ultimately patient care. Thus the purpose of Rounds is to support staff and enhance their ability to provide empathic and compassionate care.

Each Round usually lasts for one hour and begins with a pre-prepared multidisciplinary panel presentation of a patient case by the team who cared for the patient, or a set of different stories based around a common theme. Up to four panellists each describe the impact on them of the difficult, demanding or satisfying aspects of the situation and the topic is then opened to the audience for group reflection and discussion. Trained facilitators (usually a senior doctor and psychosocial practitioner, e.g. a psychologist or social worker) then guide discussion of emerging themes and issues, allowing time and space for the audience to comment and/or reflect on similar experiences they may have had. Rounds are typically organised and managed by a steering group and championed by a senior doctor/clinician. The role of the steering group is to support the facilitator and clinical lead to source stories that will resonate with the wider organisation and its staff, and support panellists to tell their stories safely and succinctly. Consequently, staff with roles that give them organisational or departmental/faculty perspectives are often approached to be members. Attendance is voluntary and staff attend as many or as few Rounds as they are able. Food is provided, usually before the Round. Rounds take place during work hours and organisations typically experiment with the timing of Rounds (e.g. early morning to capture those finishing night shifts, lunchtimes, afternoons) in order to allow different types and members of staff to attend.

There had been few evaluations of Rounds prior to the study we report in this chapter (<15 empirical studies to date), though evidence from evaluations conducted in the USA and UK suggests that those attending Rounds perceive benefits to their wellbeing (e.g. reduced stress and improved ability to cope with psychosocial demands at work) and improved relationships with colleagues (e.g. better teamwork), and that Rounds attendance may lead to more empathic and compassionate patient care, and wider changes to institutional culture (Goodrich, 2012; Lown & Manning, 2010). The evidence base mostly consists of weak study designs including lack of control groups, and non-validated measures (e.g. self-report views/satisfaction with Rounds) (Taylor, Xyrichis, Leamy, Reynolds, & Maben, 2018). Only one previous study has included non-attender control

---

[1]The Point of Care Foundation was established in 2013 as an independent charity. Previously known as the Point of care programme established in 2007 and hosted at the King's Fund.

group comparisons (Reed, Cullen, Gannon, Knight, & Todd, 2015). Evidence shows Rounds to be highly valued by attenders and most studies reported positive impact on 'self' (e.g. improved wellbeing, improved ability to cope with emotional difficulties at work, self-reflection/validation of experiences) (Taylor et al., 2018).

17.2 Unique Features of Rounds Compared to Other Wellbeing Interventions

Healthcare organisations that wish to address the wellbeing needs of their workforce are faced with a plethora of interventions to choose from including those designed to reduce stress (e.g. stress management, relaxation, mindfulness programmes) through to those designed to restructure working conditions (e.g. flexible working policies). One way in which wellbeing interventions have been categorised is according to their intended purpose: primary (reduce/eliminate stressors); secondary (reducing individuals perceptions of or reactions to stressors); or tertiary (treating or 'rehabilitating' those who have poor wellbeing and intended scope (aimed at individuals, teams or whole organisations) (DeFrank & Cooper, 1987; deJonge & Dollard, 2002; Tetrick & Quick, 2011), and numerous authors have called for a "systems approach" to tackling poor wellbeing at work, that includes interventions addressing both individual and environmental/structural factors, and for preventing, reducing and treating poor wellbeing (Boorman, 2009; Goetzel & Pronk, 2010). However, systematic reviews of healthcare workforce wellbeing interventions have repeatedly highlighted the lack of interventions targeting organisational impact or change, with most targeting the individual (e.g. stress management, mindfulness courses etc.) (Graveling, Crawford, Cowie, Amati, & Vohra, 2008; Marine, Ruotsalainen, Serra, & Verbeek, 2006; NICE, 2009; Seymour & Grove, 2005). The focus on the individual, whilst important, risks placing the onus of responsibility for wellbeing solely on the individual ('blaming' them that they are not coping). As stated by Chambers and Maxwell over 20 years ago in an editorial in the British Medical Journal, but relevant to all healthcare professionals, "if the job is making doctors sick, why not fix the job rather than the doctors". (Chambers & Maxwell, 1996).

Rounds are a rare example of an intervention that targets wellbeing at an organisational level. They offer many of the same resources as other wellbeing interventions, such as a safe and confidential space for reflection and open, honest communication. Such features are key to many interventions designed to support healthcare workers manage the impact of their work on their wellbeing, including Critical Incident Stress Debriefing, After Action Reviews; and Clinical Supervision. However, a key purpose of these other interventions is to 'problem solve' or action plan: to use the patient case or event as the purpose of the discussion to challenge, explore and discuss what happened and what could be done (or felt) differently (Taylor et al., 2018). However, Rounds differ from these other types of reflective practice interventions, as solving problems or focusing upon the clinical aspects of patient care is not the intention, rather the focus is on the impact on staff of providing care for patients often in challenging emotional social or ethical circumstances, not the clinical case itself (Maben, Taylor, et al., 2018). Instead the stories (or cases) shared within a Schwartz Round are instead intended as trigger stories, to resonate with the audience and encourage reflection about their thoughts and feelings. Indeed they are prepared prior to the Round (in panel preparation, with the facilitator and ideally with the other panellists too) so that the essence of their stories and in particular those aspects that will most resonate with the audience are prioritised in the story told in the Round itself. The facilitator is trained to intervene if the audience attempt to question those sharing their stories, or to problem solve in relation to their story, instead directing the audience to reflect and share the resonance it has with them. This is important to ensure the psychological safety of those sharing their stories in Rounds (see below), as unlike these other interventions, Rounds are open to all staff, meaning the composition of the audience/group is different in every Round. This differs from the closed (or 'invited') membership of other interventions (such as Balint Groups or Critical Incident Stress Debriefing) that includes only staff involved in an incident or event or who have a relationship with each other for other purposes. The sharing of the 'story' or 'case' thereby has a very different purpose in Rounds compared to other interventions.

Schwartz Rounds are most similar to group interventions such as Balint Groups and Reflective Practice Groups, both of which are also designed to be ongoing programmes providing facilitated forums for staff to share experiences of delivering patient care, and have as core features the ability to offer and receive peer support in safe confidential environments. However, both have "closed" (e.g. invited) membership, are often uni-disciplinary (e.g. Balint Groups originated in primary care for General Practitioners), and thereby are not open to all staff in an organisation. Nor do they offer the opportunity for 'silent' participation—there would be an expectation that all members of the group would contribute and participate.

The size of the evidence base for comparative alternative interventions to Rounds is variable, ranging from being very sparse for some (less than five empirical evaluations within healthcare for Psychosocial Intervention Training, Peer-supported storytelling, Critical Incident Stress Debriefing and Caregiver Support Programme), with the most evidence available for Clinical Supervision and Balint Groups (Taylor et al., 2018). Akin to Schwartz Rounds, much of the evidence is low quality in relation to study design (e.g. cross-sectional studies; post-interventional evaluations lacking control comparisons); sampling (e.g. non-probability and small samples; many focused only on nursing workforce); used non validated outcome measures; and were heterogenous in relation to aims, content and format of interventions. However, across most interventions there is limited evidence of beneficial impact to the individual healthcare workers, in their relationships with others, and to the wider organisation, as found with Schwartz Rounds (Taylor et al., 2018).

Therefore key features that are unique to Schwartz Rounds, and that lead to them having unique and specific outcomes (see section below) include (a) that they are an ongoing intervention that is **open to all staff** in an organisation: they do not require sign-up or membership, and all staff are welcome—regardless of their seniority or role, including those in non-clinical roles); (b) they provide a space where there is **no expectation for contribution** (silent reflection is valued and acceptable); (c) where **storytelling** (of an event or patient case) **is used as a vehicle for resonance and reflection** in others rather than as an end in itself; and (d) their central purpose is to **focus on the impact of caregiving on the caregivers themselves**: other interventions may do this sometimes but not as a key feature.

17.3 The Research

We conducted a realist-informed mixed methods evaluation of Schwartz Rounds with data collected in 2015 and 2016. Realist Evaluation is a theory-driven approach to evaluation that involves identifying causal explanations of how Rounds work, for whom, and under which circumstances. Using this methodology allowed us to take account of the complexity of the intervention and its interaction with the organisational settings of our case study sites. The aim is therefore to understand the effect that Context (C) has on how an intervention works, in relation to enhancing or decreasing the effects of Mechanisms (M) in order to produce outcomes (O): $C + M = O$. Following an initial mapping phase where we undertook telephone interviews with Rounds leads and facilitators (45/76 59%) and surveyed all sites regarding implementation and resources (41/76 54%) (Robert et al., 2017) we sampled nine case study sites for in-depth realist evaluation using observation and interview methods. In addition, and due to the perceived need to also provide data on 'hard' outcomes from Rounds attendance, we sampled ten case study sites to participate in a longitudinal staff survey. Six sites participated in both.

17.3.1 *Longitudinal Staff Survey*

In ten sites (acute/mental health/community Trusts and hospices), following a pilot study in two sites, a staff survey was conducted with staff who had never attended Rounds, recruited either immediately prior to the start of a Round, or via a random sample of staff through an online survey. All were followed up 8 months later, resulting in completed surveys at both time points by 256 staff who had attended at least one Round by the time of the follow-up (51 classified as regular attenders, having attended at least half of the Rounds that had run in their site between baseline and follow-up surveys), and 233 who were non-attenders (controls, e.g. had never attended Rounds at Baseline or when re-assessed at follow-up). This longitudinal staff survey was administered to determine if Rounds have an impact on work engagement, wellbeing, as well as empathy, compassion and reflective practice. The questionnaire included validated measures of work engagement, psychological wellbeing, self-reflection, empathy, compassion, peer support and organisational climate for support, and questions about absenteeism and views on Rounds (see

Maben, Taylor, et al., 2018 for measures). The primary analysis compared regular attenders (defined as attending at least half of the Rounds held in the organisation in the 8 month period, n = 51) to non-attenders (n = 233); supplementary analysis examined the effects of attending different numbers of Rounds (thereby including the intermediary group of those that attended fewer than half of the Rounds available at their site).

17.3.2 Organisational Case Studies: Realist Evaluation

Concurrently, organisational case studies were undertaken in nine sites (acute/mental health/community Trusts and hospices: six were also survey sites). These were purposively sampled from all Rounds providers to provide maximum variation (such as size of institution, established and new Rounds and early and late adopters). The purpose was to understand (1) the mechanisms by which Rounds 'work' and result in outcomes and ripple effects regarding staff wellbeing and social support and outcomes for patients; and (2) staff experiences of attending, presenting at and facilitating Rounds.

We observed 42 Rounds, 29 panel preparation meetings and 28 steering group meetings and we undertook a large number of interviews with clinical leads, facilitators, panellists, and members of steering groups, audiences, organisation Boards and regular, irregular and non-attenders across the nine case studies (n = 177). Data were managed using NVivo, and analysed thematically to identify staff experiences and contextual variation of Rounds. Data were also analysed concurrently, using realist evaluation methods (Manzano, 2016; Pawson & Tilley, 1997), to identify causal explanations for how Rounds work (articulated as Context + Mechanism = Outcome (CMO) configurations) which were then tested and refined in subsequent interviews (Manzano, 2016) and two focus groups with Rounds mentors and key Point of Care Foundation (PoCF) stakeholders (Maben, Taylor, et al., 2018). This in-depth iterative process of simultaneous collection and analysis of data resulted in the development of nine interlinked programme theories explaining how and why Rounds produce outcomes:

(i) The importance of trust, psychological safety and containment;
(ii) Group interaction enhances reflection and sharing of stories;
(iii) Rounds provide a counter-cultural space for staff;
(iv) Rounds create an environment where staff are willing to self-disclose;
(v) Story-telling provides a vehicle for staff to talk about their experiences at work;
(vi) Staff role modelling vulnerability, courage and bravery reveals their humanity
(vii) Stories provide greater context to patient and staff experiences;
(viii) Stories shine a spotlight on hidden stories and roles; and

(ix) Rounds facilitate experiences to be shared through storytelling that resonate and trigger reflection (Maben, Taylor, et al., 2018).

17.4 How Rounds Work to Produce Outcomes

The use of realist evaluation methods in our organisational case studies identified how Rounds work to produce their outcomes by influencing individuals, teams and organisational change to impact on patient care (Maben, Taylor, et al., 2018).

Overall, through analysis of our observation of Rounds and interviews with Rounds participants, we identified that good facilitation and the creation of a safe space supported staff to disclose stories revealing difficult, demanding and satisfying aspects of their work. When staff showed their human and vulnerable side it broke down barriers between them, and created a level playing field for *all* staff. The group interaction and hearing multiple perspectives created a recognition of shared experiences and feelings, and provided greater insights into patient, carer and staff behaviours. Rounds shone a spotlight on hidden organisational stories and roles, and provided opportunities for reflection and resonance so staff could make sense of their experiences at work. Interviewees described Rounds as interesting, engaging and a source of support, valuing the opportunity to learn more about their colleagues, understand their perspectives and motivations and reflect and process work challenges. Rounds reportedly increased understanding, empathy and tolerance towards colleagues and patients. A few Rounds attenders interviewed described feelings of negativity associated with Rounds, including questioning the purpose of unearthing feelings of sadness, anger and frustration in work time and others found witnessing the anguish of others uncomfortable. Asked about 'unsuccessful' Rounds some suggested poor attendance, prolonged silences, strained discussions and perhaps a lack of personal interest in the Round topic defined whether they felt the Round was successful or not. Yet others felt silence was an important and unique aspect of Rounds that supported contemplation, and provided an alternative to their usual busy, noisy professional lives.

In-depth analysis of our interviews with clinical leads, facilitators, panellists, and members of steering groups and audiences across the nine case studies (n = 177) enabled us to identify the self-reported impacts of Rounds. Over time, Rounds have a cumulative effect (as illustrated by the arrows in Fig. 17.1). For example, a Schwartz-savvy audience develops (Rounds attenders who really understand the purpose of Rounds, know and follow the explicit and implicit rules of how to contribute appropriately and support each other in a non-judgemental way) who can support the facilitator to ensure safety and containment, build trust and a supportive community. Staff who attended Rounds reported attendance having a beneficial impact on them as an individual, on relationships with colleagues, on relationships and encounters with patients and on the organisation and its culture. Staff reported having increased empathy and compassion for colleagues and

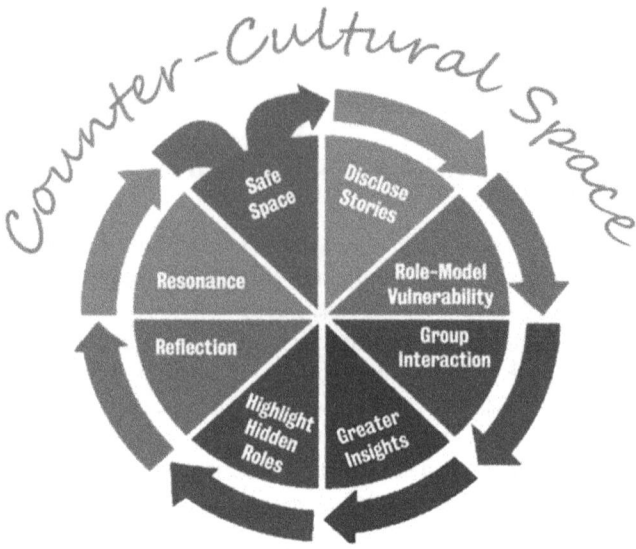

Fig. 17.1 Key components of Rounds that result in impact. Adapted from Understanding Schwartz Rounds: Findings from a National Evaluation film: https://youtu.be/C34ygCIdjCo

patients; reduced feelings of isolation; and improved teamwork and communication (see Table 17.1).

Our survey of Rounds attenders and non-attender control groups across the ten case study organisations (500 responses at time points 1 and 2) found a significant reduction in poor psychological wellbeing of staff as a result of attending Rounds. There was no significant impact of Rounds attendance on any of the other outcomes measured in the survey.

At the beginning of our study, a third of all staff in our survey (n = 32%) reported poor psychological wellbeing before attending any Rounds. Staff who did not attend any Rounds during the study (and who had never attended Rounds before: our control group) reported poorer baseline psychological wellbeing (37%) compared to attenders (25%), suggesting those that attend Rounds may be a self-selecting group with better well-being than non-attender peers. When we re-surveyed the same group 8 months later, there was little change in these staff who hadn't attend Rounds (37% at baseline 34% at 8 month follow-up). However, in staff who attended Rounds, the proportion with poor psychological wellbeing had halved over the same 8 months period from 25 to 12%. The odds ratio for this effect was 0.28 (95% CI 0.08–0.98) See Figs. 17.2 and 17.3 infographics below. The difference between the two groups at baseline should be acknowledged, however (a) the analysis controlled for baseline values so the change was the focus of the analysis; (b) the higher level of 'caseness' was found in the non-attenders group (where we found less change over time) ruling out any regression to the mean effects; (c) the effect of Rounds attendance was not limited to this one analysis, but was consistent

Table 17.1 Impacts of attending Rounds on self, team/colleagues, patient care and wider organisation derived from thematic synthesis of interview data

Impact of Rounds on self	Impact of Rounds on team/colleagues	Impact of staff attending Rounds on patient care	Impact of staff attending Rounds on culture/wider organisation
More EMOTIONAL ENGAGEMENT with patients—realisation that small things make a massive difference to patients	IMPROVED COMMUNICATION—more honest communication. GREATER TEAM COMMUNICATION—talking with each other, and discussing issues and being HONEST	Promotes more THOUGHTFUL PATIENT CARE—see things from patients' perspective—walking in their shoes.	A BETTER PLACE TO WORK: Having honest conversations makes the organisation A BETTER PLACE TO WORK
Encourages REFLECTION concerning: (a) rationale for decisions and (b) headspace to think and (c) helps you think about things differently	COLLEAGUES MORE APPROACHABLE—seeing someone present, more likely to approach them in workplace to discuss issues	GREATER EMPATHY (realisation that small things make a difference to patients—tissue/cup of tea)	CHANGED CONVERSATIONS: (softened the ground for things to grow) very different conversations to about a year ago)
PERSONAL DEVELOPMENT—learnt from others' expertise and experience and improved listening skills	CLOSER WORKING-Working a little bit more closely with the other panellists now. DEEPER/LESS SUPERFICIAL CONVERSATIONS between colleagues	More THOUGHTFUL/COMPASSIONATE patient care—more considerate interactions with patients	SYMBOLIC of VALUING STAFF: Presence of Rounds is symbolic (makes staff feel valued and says 'staff matter')
Experience VALIDATED, feeling they are NOT ALONE—found it very affirming to be able to share struggles and concerns (VULNERABILITY)	More UNDERSTANDING BETWEEN/TOWARDS COLLEAGUES—understand more of personal/life experiences; colleagues seen as human. Realise everyone is trying to do their best even if it doesn't initially appear that way. Mindful of INTERACTIONS	OPENESS—learning from others mistakes and willing to try something new to improve patient care	GREATER EMPATHY AND IMPROVED COMMUNICATION—Rounds will increase empathy and communication within the organisation
Way of COPING WITH STRESS sharing experience out loud and being heard	Increased VISIBILITY. Now have a better understanding of others' roles	SAFER Care—being open to challenge from others and being prepared to challenge colleagues. Sometimes people talk about their mistakes and by talking care is improve	LEARNING ORGANISATION: Through shared learning, organisation might move to one with a bit more compassion/learn from issues raised

(continued)

Table 17.1 (continued)

Impact of Rounds on self	Impact of Rounds on team/colleagues	Impact of staff attending Rounds on patient care	Impact of staff attending Rounds on culture/wider organisation
CLOSURE/UNBURDEN—(change how staff felt about the experience) it becomes a shared experience, not just one persons	IMPROVES TRUST: colleagues are more trusting of panellists having seen them present. (BETTER CONNECTIONS BETWEEN COLLEAGUES)—People talking to people they didn't talk to before. Improved RELATIONSHIPS with colleagues—creating friendships	CHANGING BEHAVIOUR TO IMPROVE PATIENT CARE: internalise what they've heard so even subconsciously they think they might try to do things a bit differently	MORE PATIENT-CENTRIC: the more staff ask how can they do better in a non-judgmental way—the more the organisation will become more patient centric
Recognition and FEELING LESS ALONE. Realisation of shared experience	GREATER INSIGHT/UNDERSTANDING OF COLLEAGUES supports cohesion—realise one's actions have implications for others and interconnectedness between staff. More HONEST DIALOGUE between colleagues	GREATER INSIGHT/UNDERSTANDING OF THE CONTEXT OF PEOPLE'S LIVES: helps people understand the more complex and more challenging cases and why people behave like they do allowing greater compassion for their behaviours/situation	Organisation is more REFLECTIVE: being a reflective and learning organisation starts to build outwards from Rounds
More HONEST to self—More likely to admit or talk about something you previously didn't want to admit	See the BIGGER PICTURE in terms of how the wider team/organisation functions after hearing colleagues	RECONNECTS STAFF TO THEIR VALUES that originally brought them into healthcare, which can become eroded over time and through the use of emotionally protective barriers, which Rounds help remove	ORGANISATIONAL CHANGES: revision of protocols based on Rounds discussions/new support groups reportedly set up when unmet staff needs were identified
NO IMPACT—experience was positive but it didn't change anything/don't do anything different, just probably more aware about communication. Broadly felt exactly the same (pre/post round)	NO IMPACT: Impact restricted because not all colleagues present due to other work commitments	NO IMPACT—I would treat patients well anyway	NO IMPACT because people of influence not present

17 Schwartz Center Rounds: An Intervention to Enhance Staff Well-Being and Promote...

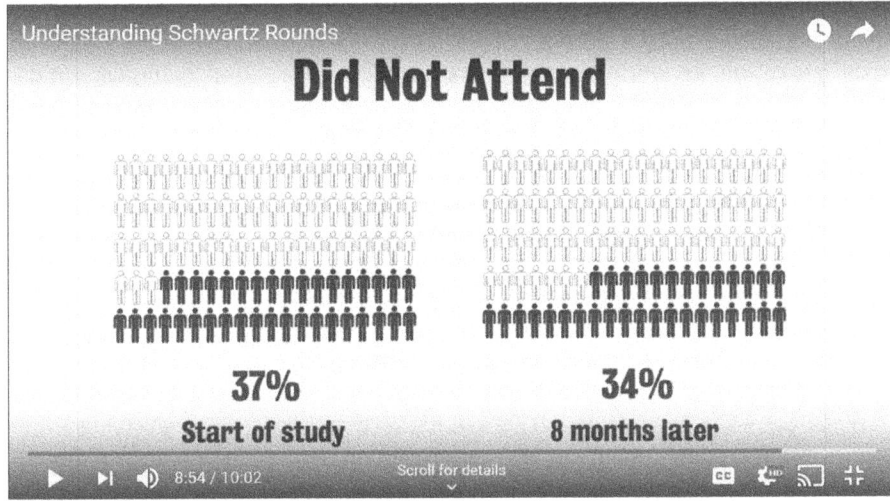

Fig. 17.2 Percentages of poor psychological well-being in sample of staff who did not attend Rounds as measured by GHQ-12

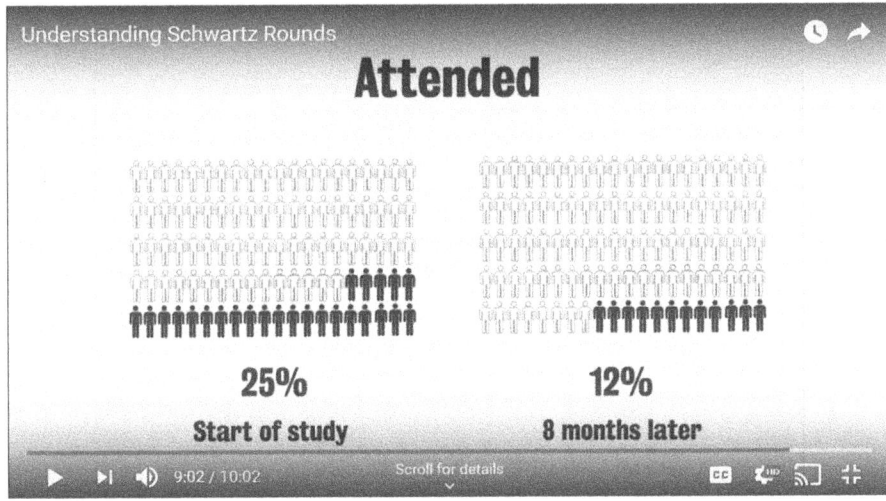

Fig. 17.3 Percentages of poor psychological well-being in sample of staff who attended Rounds regularly as measured by GHQ-12

across a range of effects (e.g. when using different definitions of regular attendance, or comparing any attendance with non-attendance).

So how is poor psychological well-being halved in regular Rounds attenders? Our study supported Wren's work (Wren, 2016) to suggest that Rounds offer a unique countercultural space by providing a psychologically safe contained space, where staff experience is the priority, emotional disclosure is encouraged, and staff support and listen to each other without judgement. Wren writes: "the process of Schwartz Round implementation is in many ways counter-cultural. Good Rounds shift an organisation and its workers away from their default position of urgent action, reaction and problem solving to an hour of stillness and slowness". (Wren, 2016: page 41). This is 'counter-cultural' because it differs very much from the usual healthcare culture in the UK where there is a busy, hierarchical, outcome-oriented environment, where stoicism is valued and where staff are exhorted to put patients (not their own well-being) first. In this counter-cultural Rounds space, hierarchies are flattened, defences are left at the door and staff humanity is revealed, supporting other to disclose, share experiences and make themselves more open and vulnerable creating a cycle of support and facilitating greater empathy and compassion for self, other staff and ultimately patients and carers, reducing poor psychological wellbeing in staff attenders.

While Schwartz Rounds do not set out to solve problems, or produce outcomes per se, we identified examples of changes in practice such as the revision of resuscitation protocols based on Rounds discussions as well as other ripple effects such as changes in types of conversations occurring in organisations (allowing more open conversations, or more wellbeing focussed, noting links between the importance of staff wellbeing for good patient care delivery), and new support groups were reportedly set up when unmet needs were identified.

17.5 What Are the Challenges of Implementing, Evaluating and Sustaining Rounds?

Rounds are a complex organisational intervention, with many interacting components that work to produce the outcomes described above. Aside from the complexity inherent to all interventions that include behavioural/human interaction, Rounds are a multi-stage intervention; we identified four stages to Rounds, with the Round itself only constituting one of those stages (Fig. 17.4).

Stage one is sourcing stories and panellists to tell the stories; stage two is preparing the panellists to tell their stories; then stage 3 is the Round itself, where staff tell their stories and the audience reflects and share further stories; then finally stage 4 is the post-Round after effects; the outcomes and ripple effects resulting from the Round and preparation for the next Round. Over time, stage four of one Round/series of Rounds, impacts upon the early stages of the next Round/Rounds to have cumulative effects and impact. This complexity in structure and process for Rounds lends itself to a variety of challenges in implementing, evaluating and sustaining Rounds.

Our evaluation highlighted key challenges relating to both the structure (personnel resources for running Rounds especially in relation to the core team: facilitators, clinical lead and administrators); and in relation to the process of running Rounds (particularly sourcing stories and panellists, preparing them adequately to ensure

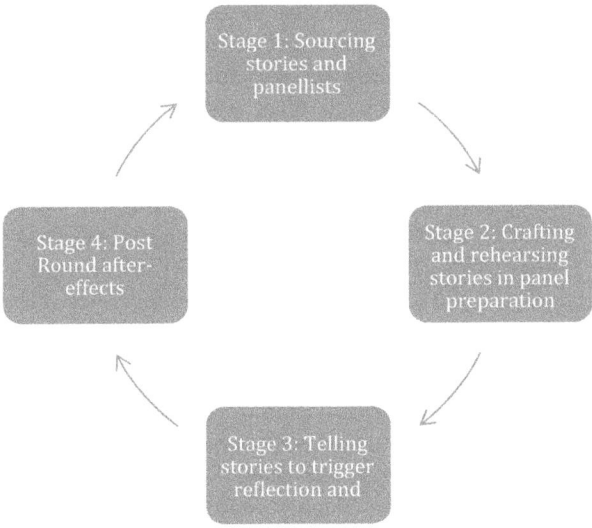

Fig. 17.4 Rounds stages, with cumulative effects [reproduced with permissions from NIHR journals (Maben, Taylor, et al., 2018)]

safety in Rounds, ensuring reach and accessibility to all staff, and evaluating and measuring outcomes from Rounds). We found that some Rounds sites were inadequately resourced either lacking administrative support or only having one facilitator. Furthermore, in many organisations the responsibility for running and sustaining Rounds rested on the shoulders of a few individuals with an apparent lack of senior organisational commitment and support.

Our key recommendations for implementing and sustaining Rounds based on findings from our evaluation (Maben, Leamy, et al., 2018) include:

(a) **Ensuring organisational support for Rounds:** This is a key feature built into the contract required by organisations wishing to run Rounds. In the UK, the Point of Care Foundation require a letter of support from the chief executive before they will issue a licence. This support is fundamental to the success of Rounds in relation to the provision of adequate resources (see below); supporting staff to implement initiatives to enable staff to attend Rounds; and actively demonstrating shared ownership and responsibility for the sustainability of Rounds. Ideally, we recommend identifying a Board member to share responsibility with the clinical lead and facilitator to implement and sustain Rounds.

(b) **Ensuring adequate resources for Rounds:** this includes the personnel required to run Rounds (appropriate amounts of time in job plans for facilitators, clinical leads and administrators; funding for facilitator training for sufficient numbers of facilitators); any room and publicity costs; and the provision of food at each Round (which is a contractual requirement). It is important to ensure that facilitators have appropriate skills to safely run Rounds (e.g. prior group facilitation knowledge, experience and skills in identifying and managing distress), and our data suggest that to keep Rounds psychologically safe there should always be at least two facilitators in each Round.

(c) **Ensuring adequate support for facilitators and clinical leads:** Running and sustaining Rounds can place considerable strain and burden on facilitators and clinical leads, both in terms of the sheer time it can take to organise and run Rounds, and in relation to the psychological impact of facilitating and providing emotional support to others. We found that facilitators were often at risk of burnout themselves due to lack of consideration given to the impact of running Rounds on them. The sustainability of Rounds therefore depends upon the provision of adequate support to mitigate these stressors. This should include:

  (i) Training sufficient numbers of facilitators (planning for sick leave, annual leave, succession planning);
  (ii) Ensuring the provision of administrative support for Rounds so that this is not an additional task taken on by facilitators (Rounds publicity, organising steering group meetings, booking rooms, organising food, coordinating sign-in and evaluation in Rounds, synthesising feedback to produce reports for internal and external use);
  (iii) Providing continued professional development (CPD) and supervision for facilitators and clinical leads to ensure they have a reflective space/psychological support that provides a sounding board (pre Rounds) and space for debriefing (post Rounds).
  (iv) Ensuring appropriate use of steering group members and active membership: appointing steering group members to cover a range of departments in the organisation; with clear roles that include attending Rounds and playing an active role in helping to sustain them (e.g. by helping to identify stories and panellists for Rounds). Rotating membership (e.g. every 6–12 months) can help with the sustainability of this and with spread to new parts of the organisation.

(d) **Raising awareness and understanding of Rounds:** It can be difficult to explain what a Round is to someone that has never attended one before, as they are unlike any other intervention that staff would be familiar with. In our evaluation, we interviewed staff that told us they had been to a Round but it was clear they were talking about something else; and other staff who had heard of Rounds but didn't think they were 'invited'. Overcoming these misconceptions is important to enhancing reach and accessibility: we recommend using multiple communication modes (not just relying on electronic forms) to let people know about Rounds, perhaps incorporating available resources such as films depicting real or re-enacted Rounds (via https://www.pointofcarefoundation.org.uk/our-work/schwartz-rounds/); and using more explanatory titles and information within publicity for Rounds (in particular emphasising that they are open to ALL staff and using titles that would spark interest and resonate across the organisation).

(e) **Encouraging attendance:** Rounds will not be felt as required—or useful to—all staff, but we found that there were groups of staff that were less able to attend Rounds due to practical barriers. This particularly applied to ward based nursing and support staff who were not able to leave their patients/wards for long enough to attend Rounds, which were often held at lunch times (one of the busiest times for those working on wards). Some organisations are trialling 'pop-up' Rounds where Rounds are taken to ward based staff—these Rounds tend to be shorter (30 min) and often uni-disciplinary (e.g. nursing staff) and these have yet to be evaluated. Further attention should be paid to potential solutions to this, either in relation to workable solutions to enable staff to attend (e.g. on a rotational basis with other staff covering their roles to enable this); or by providing alternative forms of Rounds (see section below about creative alternatives to Rounds). Other staff may be encouraged to attend if they receive accreditation for attending (e.g. CPD points, which some organisations were offering), and others built Schwartz Rounds into their in-house training programmes, though it is important for Rounds fidelity that attendance is voluntary, not mandatory.

(f) **The importance of panel preparation**: We uniquely identified this as a specific stage of Rounds (Stage 2), and found that it was a key aspect determining the success of a Round particularly in relation to psychological safety. Panel preparation enables panellists to shape their stories and to ensure that it is 'safe' to share; to hear about how the Round will run (and that their story may not be commented on by the audience, and not to take this personally); and to hear the other panellists stories. As well as ensuring safety and relevance, panel preparation also enables the facilitator to identify the themes that may come up in the Round itself. A key challenge is the time taken for this, in particular to meet with all panellists together in a group which was not always possible, but we recommend that at least one-to-one preparation occurs (even if by telephone).

(g) **Implementing creative adaptations of Rounds 'peripheral components'**: We identified that there were core (essential) components of Rounds that should not be adapted (Leamy, Reynolds, Robert, Taylor, & Maben, 2019), but that other aspects could potentially be modified to support adaptation to local contexts to support sustainability. Core components include: having senior clinical leadership; two facilitators (with appropriate skills as above) to maintain trust, safety and containment; that they are a group intervention; ongoing (not one-off) and not combined with other things; that food is provided; staff-only (not patients); that they use pre-prepared staff stories about the emotional impact of work to trigger audience reflection; and do not focus on the clinical detail or problem solving. Potentially adaptable components include the diversity of the audience (e.g. targeting specific staff rather than open to all); the source of stories (e.g. using filmed rather than live stories); having fewer panellists; and shortening the format (e.g. 'pop-up' Rounds (PoCF, 2016)) to reach those that cannot attend normally. These adaptations remain untested and may potentially dilute or change the outcomes.

(h) **Evaluating Rounds: Resisting the desire to demonstrate 'hard' outcomes from Rounds evaluation in single organisations**: We found an expectation in some organisations that it was both possible and desirable to measure 'outcomes' to demonstrate the effectiveness of Rounds—either outcomes for staff and or for patients and carers. This is unsurprising given the prevailing healthcare culture of monitoring and targets and evidence-based medicine. However, together with being in contrast to the 'counter-cultural space' that we argue Rounds sits within, we also argue that an individual organisation would rarely be able to undertake a robust quantitative evaluation with sufficient 'control group' data for staff outcomes (our quantitative evaluation required ten organisations, many of whom had to be 'new organisations' to provide us with sufficient participants). In addition, whilst we based our selection of survey measures on our initial programme theory about how Rounds work to produce outcomes (including for example the role of reflection and compassion), we now have a more comprehensive understanding of how and why Rounds work to produce outcomes and would argue that such measures do not capture the full effects of Rounds. Furthermore, as Rounds are open to all staff which can attend as many or as few as they like—linking individual staff attendees to specific patient experiences or outcomes is fraught with methodological difficulty. We did not feel we could deliver a robust evaluation at the patient level due to not being able to control for all the many confounders that may also affect patients and carer experiences and outcomes. Other evaluators have also not been able to achieve this despite trying. Rather we sought to evaluate Rounds impact on staff wellbeing, and reported impacts on self, colleagues, patients and the organisation, drawing on evidence that has identified the link between staff wellbeing at work and patient experiences of care (Maben et al., 2012). We therefore recommend that organisations instead should focus on reported experiences of Rounds attendance, and capturing any ripple effects (changes in practice, perhaps through an annual survey of attenders to capture these). Our data suggest that it is important to ensure clarity at Board level regarding the complexity of evaluation, and to confirm their expectations (if any) for reporting and "evidence", perhaps considering Schwartz Rounds steering groups reporting directly to the Board or a sub-committee.

17.6 Conclusions

Rounds are a complex intervention methodologically (e.g. comprising many interacting components, and non-linear causal pathways). They were developed in the USA and are now being taken up in other countries. Our national UK evaluation has identified how Rounds work to produce their outcomes creating ripple effects within and across organisations that facilitate cultural changes and changes in practice. In our study Rounds reduced poor psychological wellbeing for staff who regularly attended Rounds, and our in-depth qualitative case study data shed more light on how this happened and the mechanisms by which Rounds act as a counter-cultural space to have effects on individuals, teams, patients and the organisation. Key messages for researchers and for healthcare delivery are summarized below (Tables 17.2 and 17.3).

Table 17.2 Key messages for researchers

Identification and robust evaluation of interventions to promote wellbeing is required, particularly in relation to interventions aimed at organisational change/wellbeing
Evaluation of complex organisational-wide interventions requires a greater understanding of how such interventions work (or not) in different settings (context) to produce their outcomes using mixed methods that take context into account and allow for organisational adaptation
Future work could focus on evaluating the impact of Rounds on any changes to practice and organisational culture (e.g. annual surveys of ripple effects to capture these often elusive and unreported changes)

Table 17.3 Key messages for healthcare delivery

Rounds will not be for everyone and so to improve staff wellbeing organisations need to consider implementing a range of interventions on the spectrum from prevention through to treatment and those aimed at both organisational wellbeing as well as individually focussed for example, clinical supervision; stress reduction techniques; safe staffing programmes; mindfulness as well as Rounds and other reflective spaces; and good occupational health services
Healthcare organisations may consider implementing Schwartz Rounds as they offer a safe counter-cultural psychological space where staff come together to make sense of and emotionally process difficult experiences and feel heard. Telling stories can lead to closure, affirmation and the creation of alternative narratives. Hearing stories can lead to increased empathy and compassion for colleagues and patients and can increase work motivation and connection with own values, leading to improved staff wellbeing and staff feeling less alone and more connected to colleagues and patients
Successful implementation and sustainability of Rounds requires senior organisational support and strong steering group support for facilitators and clinical leads to facilitate sustainability

References

Boorman, S. (2009). *The final report of the independent NHS Health and well-being review*. London: TSO: Department of Health.

Chambers, R., & Maxwell, R. (1996). Helping sick doctors. *BMJ, 312*(7033), 722–723.

DeFrank, R. S., & Cooper, C. L. (1987). Worksite stress management interventions: Their effectiveness and conceptualisation. *Journal of Managerial Psychology, 2*, 4–10. https://doi.org/10.1108/eb043385

deJonge, J., & Dollard, M. F. (2002). *Stress in the workplace: Australian Master OHS and environment guide*. Sydney, Australia: CCH.

Goetzel, R. Z., & Pronk, N. P. (2010). Worksite health promotion: How much do we really know about what works? What works in worksite health promotion systematic review findings and recommendations from the Task Force on Community Preventive Services. *American Journal of Preventive Medicine, 38*, S223–S225. https://doi.org/10.1016/j.amepre.2009.10.032

Goodrich, J. (2012). Supporting hospital staff to provide compassionate care: Do Schwartz Center Rounds work in English hospitals? *JRSM, 105*, 117–122. https://doi.org/10.1258/jrsm.2011.110183

Graveling, R. A., Crawford, J. O., Cowie, H., Amati, C., & Vohra, S. (2008). *A review of workplace interventions that promote mental wellbeing in the workplace*. Edinburgh: Institute of Occupational Medicine.

Leamy, M., Reynolds, E., Robert, G., Taylor, C., & Maben, J. (2019). The origins and implementation of an intervention to support healthcare staff to deliver compassionate care: exploring fidelity and adaptation in the transfer of Schwartz Center Rounds® from the United States to the United Kingdom. *BMC Health Services Research, 19*, 457.

Lown, B. A., & Manning, C. F. (2010). The Schwartz Center rounds: Evaluation of an interdisciplinary approach to enhancing patient-centered communication, teamwork, and provider support. *Academic Medicine, 85*, 1073–1081.

Maben J., Peccei R., Adams M., Robert G., Richardson A., Murrells T., & Morrow, E. (2012). *Exploring the relationship between patients' experiences of care and the influence of staff motivation, affect and wellbeing*. Final Report: NIHR Service Delivery and Organisation Programme.

Maben J., Taylor, C., Dawson, J., Leamy, M., McCarthy, I., Reynolds, E., et al. (2018). A realist informed mixed methods evaluation of Schwartz Center Rounds® in England. *Health Services and Delivery Research, 6*(37). Published in November 2018, https://doi.org/10.3310/hsdr06370, https://www.journalslibrary.nihr.ac.uk/hsdr/hsdr06370#/abstract

Maben, J., Leamy, M., Taylor, C., Reynolds, E., Shuldham, C., Dawson, J., et al. (2018). *Understanding, implementing and sustaining Schwartz Rounds: An organisational guide to implementation*. London: King's College. https://www.surrey.ac.uk/content/schwartz-organisational-guide-questionnaire

Manzano, A. (2016). The craft of interviewing in realist evaluation. *Evaluation, 22*, 342–360. https://doi.org/10.1177/1356389016638615

Marine, A., Ruotsalainen, J. H., Serra, C., & Verbeek, J. H. (2006). Preventing occupational stress in healthcare workers. *The Cochrane Database of Systematic Reviews*, (4), CD002892. https://doi.org/10.1002/14651858.CD002892.pub2

National Institute for Health and Care Excellence (NICE). (2009). *Promoting mental wellbeing through productive and healthy working conditions: guidance for employers*. London: NICE.

Pawson, R., & Tilley, N. (1997). *Realistic evaluation*. London: Sage.

Point of Care Foundation. (2016). https://www.pointofcarefoundation.org.uk/event/training-pop-rounds/. Accessed 15/08/19.

Reed, E., Cullen, A., Gannon, C., Knight, A., & Todd, J. (2015). Use of Schwartz Center Rounds in a UK hospice: Findings from a longitudinal evaluation. *Journal of Interprofessional Care, 29*, 365–366.

Robert, G., Philippou, J., Leamy, M., Reynolds, E., Ross, S., Bennett, L., et al. (2017). Exploring the adoption of Schwartz Center Rounds as an organisational innovation to improve staff wellbeing in England, 2009-2015. *BMJ Open, 7*(1), 1–10.

Schwartz, K. (1995, July 16). A patient's story. *Boston Globe Magazine*.

Seymour, L., & Grove, B. (2005). *Workplace interventions for people with common mental health problems*. London: British Occupational Health Research Foundation.

Taylor, C., Xyrichis, A., Leamy, M., Reynolds, E., Maben, J. (2018). Can Schwartz Center Rounds support healthcare staff with emotional challenges at work, and how do they compare with other interventions aimed at providing similar support? A systematic review and scoping review. *BMJ Open, 8*, e024254. https://doi.org/10.1136/bmjopen-2018-024254n. https://bmjopen.bmj.com/content/8/10/e024254.full

Tetrick, L. E., & Quick, J. C. (2011). Overview of occupational health psychology: public health in occupational settings. In J. C. Quick & L. E. Tetrick (Eds.), *Handbook of occupational health psychology* (2nd edn., pp. 3–20). Washington, DC: American Psychological Association.

Wren, B. (2016). *True tales of organisational life*. London: Karnac.

Chapter 18
How Healthcare Worker Well-Being Intersects with Safety Culture, Workforce Engagement, and Operational Outcomes

Kathryn C. Adair, Kyle Rehder, and J. Bryan Sexton

Since 2001, the Job-Demands-Resources Model has accurately and repeatedly demonstrated that increasing demands without also increasing (or in some cases even reducing) resources creates strain on the workforce (Demerouti, Bakker, Nachreiner, & Schaufeli, 2001; Schaufeli & Bakker, 2004). This strain has been reflected in burnout, problems with well-being, low engagement, low safety culture, poor teamwork, and other concerning outcomes. Maslach describes a continuum between the negative experiences of burnout (exhaustion, cynicism, and inefficacy) and the positive experience of engagement (energy, involvement, and efficacy; Maslach & Leiter, 2016). The links between strain, burnout, and engagement are often underrecognized, yet they provide leaders with a clear path to bolster well-being and productivity in their workforces.

Unfortunately, the number and extent of demands placed on healthcare workers have risen in recent years (e.g., increased production pressure, additional administrative burdens, and complex EHR systems). Resources to meet these demands have not kept pace, leaving workers vulnerable to compromises in their well-being.

K. C. Adair (✉)
Duke Center for Healthcare Safety and Quality, Duke University Health System, Durham, NC, USA

K. Rehder
Department of Pediatrics, Duke University Children's Hospital and Health Center, Durham, NC, USA

Duke Center for Healthcare Safety and Quality, Duke University Health System, Durham, NC, USA

J. B. Sexton
Department of Psychiatry, Duke University School of Medicine, Durham, NC, USA

Duke Center for Healthcare Safety and Quality, Duke University Health System, Durham, NC, USA

© Springer Nature Switzerland AG 2020
A. Montgomery et al. (eds.), *Connecting Healthcare Worker Well-Being, Patient Safety and Organisational Change*, Aligning Perspectives on Health, Safety and Well-Being, https://doi.org/10.1007/978-3-030-60998-6_18

Fortunately, "resources" are not limited to staffing and budgets, but also include the broad range of physical, psychological, social and organizational aspects of ones' job (Van den Broeck, Vansteenkiste, Witte, Soenens, & Lens, 2010). For example, aspects of the job that support workers in achieving their goals and/or stimulate personal growth, learning, and development may also functionally reduce physical and mental demands of the job. Ultimately, to better address the demands and resources that account for strain, much more focus is needed on the social and organizational environment in which individuals work.

When health care workers (HCWs) experience significant strain, we see it reflected in measures of disengagement (the opposite of engagement), poor safety culture, burnout (the opposite of well-being), and poor operational outcomes (e.g., increased medical errors, lower quality of care, higher standardized mortality ratios; Aiken, Clarke, Sloane, Sochalski, & Silber, 2002; Cimiotti, Aiken, Sloane, & Wu, 2012; Shanafelt et al., 2010). As we will see in this chapter, these concepts overlap considerably, and while no studies (to our knowledge) look at all four simultaneously, this chapter will include published and ongoing work highlighting the relationships between well-being, safety culture, engagement, and outcomes. For our purposes in this chapter, we consider the following aspects as separate indicators of well-being which together comprise a multidimensional assessment: emotional exhaustion, work-life balance, depression, and subjective well-being (Andresen, Malmgren, Carter, & Patrick, 1994; Lyubomirsky & Lepper, 1999; Maslach & Jackson, n.d.; Sexton et al., 2017). Measures of each of these constructs were selected for brevity, strong psychometric properties, and responsiveness to interventions (Adair, Kennedy, & Sexton, 2019; Rehder et al., 2019; Sexton & Adair, 2019).

18.1 Burnout, Safety Culture, and Workforce Engagement Are Linked

In the early days of the patient safety movement, around the release of the Institute of Medicine's report "To Err is Human," in 2000 (Institute of Medicine (US) Committee on Quality of Health Care in America, 2000), compelling links between HCW burnout and safe delivery of care were hypothesized but untested. Anecdotal stories of struggling HCWs making more errors certainly seemed logical: when we are emotionally exhausted, feeling like we are no longer good at our jobs, and cynical to the current processes in place in healthcare, it is natural to expect the quality of our work to suffer. Decades later, we no longer need to be armchair theoreticians about these links. Numerous well conducted studies demonstrate that work settings with higher burnout also have lower levels of safety culture and engagement (e.g., Adair et al., 2018; Henson, 2016; Rehder et al., 2019; Sexton et al., 2018), as well as higher rates of negative operational outcomes (e.g., medical errors, infections, mortality; Aiken et al., 2002; Cimiotti et al., 2012; Shanafelt et al., 2010). Given the emphasis that contemporary healthcare has placed on improving HCW capacity to improve the care quality, we hope that this chapter will show that well-being acts as an overarching variable that influences ones' ability to feel engaged with their work (e.g., participate in quality improvement projects, effectively collaborate will colleagues), successfully achieve operational goals (e.g., reducing infection, increasing patient satisfaction), and contribute to a positive safety culture (e.g., discussing errors, speaking up about safety concerns).

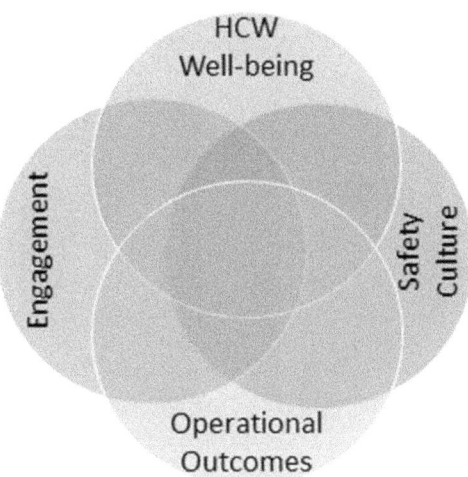

Advances in psychometrically sound safety culture and engagement measures, such as the SCORE (**S**afety, **C**ommunication, **O**perational **R**eliability, and **E**ngagement) survey, have helped health systems identify the extent of burnout throughout their entities, as well as which units are struggling the most (Sexton et al., 2018). The SCORE survey includes measures of safety culture, workforce well-being, and engagement. Early safety culture assessment from 1995 through 2005 did not include engagement or well-being metrics, but these metrics were integrated more deliberately as rates of burnout rose among HCWs. Today, integrated surveys of safety culture and engagement are much more common, and provide empirical evidence for the concepts in this chapter.

Using several large samples, we have demonstrated that the SCORE domains of safety culture, well-being, and engagement are considerably related. Across 31 hospitals in Michigan, we found medium to large correlations between safety culture domains and emotional exhaustion (r = .55 to .67; see Table 18.1; Sexton et al., 2017). Significant links between emotional exhaustion and engagement were also identified, although they varied by engagement domain, with associations ranging from .28 (advancement) to .61 (participation in decision-making). These correlations are not surprising to HCWs who have personally experienced emotional exhaustion up close and found that it can impair one's ability to consistently deliver optimal care. A relatively common comment from HCWs is "Of course burnout is linked to safety and engagement! Did you really need to conduct a study to show that?" and yet these data are invaluable when discussing the topic with reticent leaders who may believe that burnout is measured poorly, isn't their responsibility, or does not contribute to lower patient safety, and therefore they are not responsible for dealing with the issue.

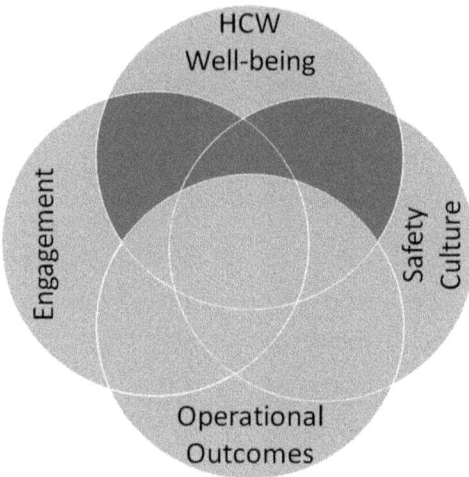

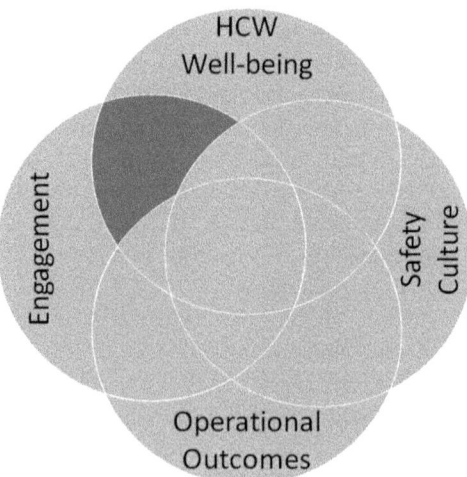

Table 18.1 Work setting level correlation matrix of safety culture and engagement domains across 829 work settings (Cronbach's alphas and ICCs in the diagonal)

Score domain	1	2	3	4	5	6	7	8	9	10	11	12
1. Improvement readiness	0.92, 0.16											
2. Local leadership	0.74	0.94, 0.17										
3. Teamwork climate	0.67	0.57	0.82, 0.19									
4. Safety climate	0.80	0.75	0.73	0.87, 0.17								
5. Personal burnout	−0.619	−0.59	−0.58	−0.64	0.92, 0.15							
6. Burnout climate	−0.62	−0.55	−0.67	−0.67	0.80	0.90, 0.26						
7. Advancement	0.39	0.35	0.34	0.40	−0.28	−0.27	0.89, 0.14					
8. Growth opportunities	0.70	0.62	0.58	0.71	−0.56	−0.56	0.49	0.92, 0.10				
9. Job uncertainty	−0.29	−0.30	−0.19	−0.27	0.33	0.29	−0.13	−0.30	0.88, 0.08			
10. Participation in decision-making	0.70	0.67	0.56	0.75	−0.61	−0.60	0.45	0.70	−0.29	0.88, 0.13		
11. Work-life climate	0.35	0.28	0.35	0.38	−0.51	−0.53	0.09	0.23	−0.23	0.31	3.82, 0.11	
12. Workload	−0.24	−0.26	−0.28	−0.27	0.56	0.53	−0.04	−0.20	0.15	−0.27	−2.50	0.84, 0.12

All correlations are significant at the p<0.01 level except the correlations between Advancement and Workload (r=−0.04, p=0.27) and Advancement and Work-life climate (r=0.09, p=0.02).
ICC, intraclass correlations.

Sexton, J. B., Adair, K. C., Leonard, M. W., Frankel, T. C., Proulx, J., Watson, S. R., ... Frankel, A. S. (2017). Providing feedback following Leadership WalkRounds is associated with better patient safety culture, higher employee engagement and lower burnout. BMJ Qual Saf, bmjqs-2016-006399. https://doi.org/10.1136/bmjqs-2016-006399
Note: The SCORE survey is comprised of two overarching domains (1) Safety Culture (subscales #1-6, and (2) Engagement (subscales #7-12). For more information about the constructs in this table see Adair et al. (2018); Rehder et al. (2019); Schwartz et al. (2019); Sexton et al. (2018); Sexton, Leonard, Frankel, & Adair, (2019)

We have identified links between HCW well-being and workforce engagement across a number of scales. In one large academic health system we collected SCORE's burnout climate domain (i.e., a measure of how emotionally exhausted you assess your colleagues to be), as well as personal emotional exhaustion and work-life balance (Schwartz et al., 2019). Separately, this health system also used the NDNQI (National Database of Nursing Quality Indicators; Montalvo, 2007) nursing engagement survey, which is required to qualify for prestigious Magnet recognition from the American Nurses Credentialing Center. When we aggregated responses for all surveys at the work setting level, we found medium to large negative correlations between all NDNQI domains (e.g., Staffing and Resource Adequacy, Leadership Access, Teamwork) and both burnout variables (see Table 18.2). It is clear that work settings reporting high levels of burnout are less engaged. Moreover, units with better work-life balance reported higher levels of nursing engagement across six out of the seven NDNQI domains. Since the work-life balance scale assesses frequencies of work-life infractions (e.g., skipping a meal, not taking breaks, getting home late, sleeping less than 5 h a night), these correlations suggest that work settings and organizations with cultures and policies that support work-life balance are more likely to have engaged workers.

Press Ganey is a commonly used company that administers and analyzes employee engagement surveys for healthcare settings in the US. In 2016 the health system in the prior analysis also used the Press Ganey work culture survey for assessing employee engagement (items included: "I like the work I do", "My entity makes every effort to deliver safe, error-free care to patients", and "I have confidence in senior

Table 18.2 Spearman correlations between HCW well-being domains, work culture, and national database of nursing quality indicators survey domains at the work setting level

	Burnout Climate	Emotional Exhaustion	Work-life Balance	Work Culture (Press Ganey)
NDNQI				
Staffing and Resource Adequacy	−.63*** N = 71	−.62*** N = 71	.32** N = 70	.71*** N = 58
Autonomy	−.50*** N = 71	−.52*** N = 71	.33** N = 70	.83*** N = 58
Quality Fundamentals	−.53*** N = 71	−.51*** N = 71	.28* N = 70	.81*** N = 58
Professional Relationships	−.52*** N = 70	−.50*** N = 70	.27* N = 69	.70*** N = 57
Leadership Access	−.51*** N = 71	−.52*** N = 71	.28* N = 70	.83*** N = 58
Professional Development	−.48*** N = 70	−.49*** N = 70	.31* N = 69	.82*** N = 57
Teamwork	−.50*** N = 70	−.42*** N = 70	.11 N = 69	.68*** N = 57

Note: Burnout climate, Emotional Exhaustion (Personal burnout) and Work-life balance were measured with the SCORE survey
*P < .05, **P < .01, ***P < .001

management's leadership"). This allowed us to examine Press Ganey's work culture survey's predictive ability with the NDNQI engagement measures. Assessments of work culture were highly correlated with the NDNQI domains (see Table 18.2). We found that better work culture was also correlated with lower levels of burnout climate (r = −.59, p < .001) and emotional exhaustion (r = −.54, p < .001), as measured by SCORE.

It is perhaps not surprising that surveys measuring seemingly similar constructs (work culture and engagement) would be highly correlated, but for those working to improve culture, these data indicate that their efforts are likely to return dividends in the form of higher engagement. The addition of the SCORE well-being domains indicates that other potential dividends are lower rates of emotional exhaustion and burnout climate, as well as better work-life balance. The integration of the safety culture, well-being, and engagement surveys was the beginning of a strong collaboration between Human Resources and Patient Safety/Quality Improvement within this health system.

18.2 Healthcare Worker Well-Being Is Related to Operational Outcomes

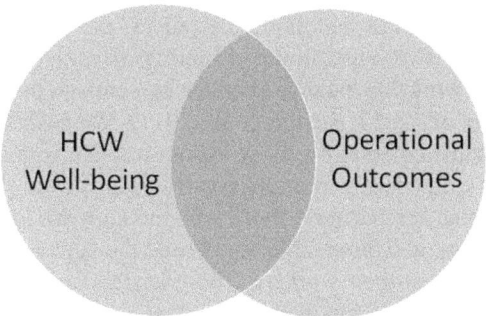

Healthcare leaders are intrigued by survey-to-survey correlations, but for many, the impact of burnout is only meaningful when it predicts operational outcomes. Several compelling studies have now established that higher healthcare worker burnout is associated with higher rates of turnover (Willard-Grace et al., 2019), healthcare acquired infections (Cimiotti et al., 2012), medication errors (Fahrenkopf et al., 2008), medical errors (Kang, Lihm, & Kong, 2013; Panagioti et al., 2018; Shanafelt et al., 2010), lower quality of care (Dyrbye et al., 2013; Panagioti et al., 2018; Shanafelt et al., 2012), lower patient satisfaction (Aiken et al., 2012; Panagioti et al., 2018), and higher standardized mortality ratios (Aiken et al., 2002). This body of research indicates that institutions can now predict which work settings are at higher risk for major medical errors based on their level of HCW burnout. These outcomes are not only emotionally devastating for patients and their families, as well as providers, but they are also incredibly costly.

A recent study estimated that the cost of physician burnout alone was approximately $4.6 billion annually in the US (Han et al., 2019). This figure is a conservative estimate, as it only accounts for the cost of physician turnover and reduced clinical hours due to burnout, leaving many of the expensive consequences of burnout out of the calculations (e.g., infections, mortality, hospitalizations, and lower hospital reputation due to poor patient satisfaction). Moreover, the study examined only physicians, and while they are quite expensive to turnover, they represent a small percentage of the healthcare workforce. For instance, nurses outnumber physicians four to one (Organisation for Economic Co-operation and Development, 2015), and rates of burnout in nurses range between 30 and 40% (Molina-Praena et al., 2018). The monetary cost of nurse burnout is likely much greater than $4.6 billion, and there is no price tag that can be put on the human toll that burnout is taking on HCWs, patients, and families.

In prior research we have found work-life balance behaviors (e.g. taking breaks, getting home on time, eating meals) are difficult for many in healthcare due to workload and demanding schedules (Sexton et al., 2017). Although work-life balance is typically discussed as an individual difference, we have found that work settings appear to have work-life balance norms, such that behaviors that support or detract from work-life balance (e.g., consistently working late, not eating lunch) become a part of local cultures that implicitly reflect "the way we do things around here". Statistically this is revealed in the clustering of variance at the work-setting level, suggesting that work-life balance operates as a climate that differs from group to group (Schwartz et al., 2019; Sexton et al., 2017). We suspect that work setting norms and expectations are behind why work-life balance is good in some groups, and terrible in others. Leaders play a disproportionate role in the development of norms and expectations. For instance, those who model work-life balance by taking breaks and leaving work at a reasonable hours send the behavioral message "It's ok to take care of yourself" to their workers. These leaders are likely to have workers who feel that it is then safe for them to engage in healthier work-life balance behaviors as well. When leaders model work-life balance, workers are also more likely to perceive that their well-being is genuinely supported, compared to groups where leaders verbally say that work-life balance is supported, yet will repeatedly send emails to their workers at 4:00 am.

Since work-life balance norms play a role in overall work culture rather than just for individuals, and since both are linked to emotional exhaustion (Tables 18.1 and 18.2), we expected to find that work settings with positive work-life balance scores and lower burnout scores (as measured with the SCORE survey), as well as positive work culture scores (as measured with the Press Ganey survey) would also experience lower rates of turnover and medication errors.

In our institutional data we found that work settings with better work-life balance reported lower rates of preventable medication related errors ($r = -.28$, $p < .05$; Table 18.3; Fig. 18.1), but work-life balance did not predict turnover. Work settings with lower emotional exhaustion scores reported fewer preventable medication related errors ($r = .41$, $p < .001$), and lower turnover ($r = .25$, $p < .05$). Surprisingly, Press Ganey's work culture survey did not predict either outcome. These differential findings reveal a truism about survey measures: surveys vary in terms of their psychometric strengths and their ability to predict outcomes. Across our analyses, we find that the Press Ganey work culture survey predicts responses to other survey

Table 18.3 Spearman correlations between HCW well-being domains, work culture, and operational outcomes at the work setting level

	Burnout Climate	Emotional Exhaustion	Work-life Balance	Work Culture Press Ganey
Turnover	.35**	.26*	−.14 (NS)	−.06 (NS)
	N = 69	N = 69	N = 69	N = 65
Preventable Medication Related SRS	.35**	.41***	−.28*	−.15 (NS)
	N = 68	N = 68	N = 68	N = 64

*P < .05, **P < .01, ***P < .001

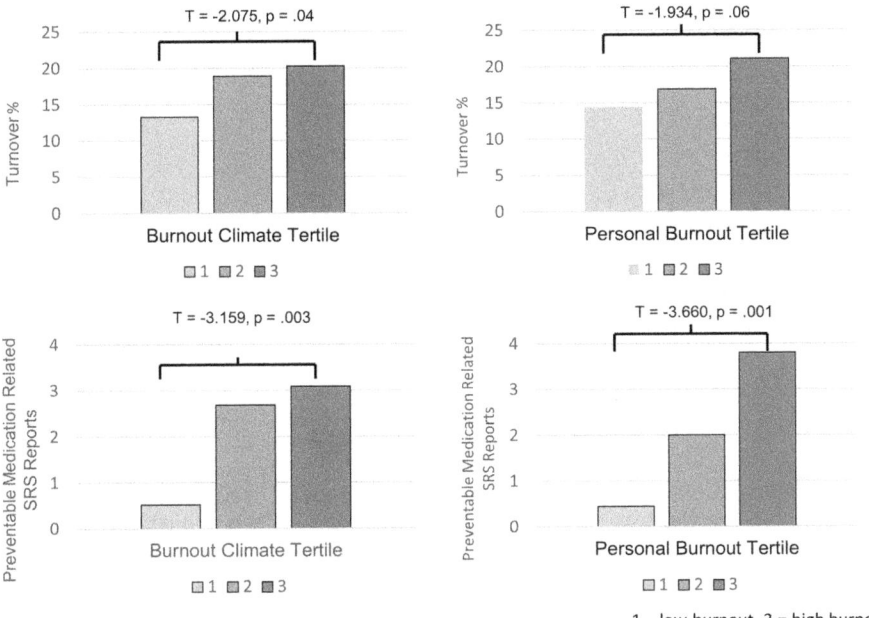

Fig. 18.1 Personal burnout and burnout climate's associations with turnover and preventable medication related SRS reports

metrics like NDNQI, while other surveys such as SCORE predict responses to NDNQI as well as operational outcomes. Emotional exhaustion, burnout climate, work-life balance, and work culture predict NDNQI survey responses, but only the SCORE domains of emotional exhaustion, burnout climate, and work-life balance predicted operational outcomes in this sample.

In a recently published study, we examined whether work settings with higher rates of emotional exhaustion have workers with greater intentions to leave their positions or report more frequent disruptive behaviors in their teams (see Figs. 18.2, 18.3, and 18.4; Doram et al., 2017; Rehder et al., 2019). In a sample of 7923 HCWs from 16 hospitals within a large health system, HCWs of all roles reported on their emotional exhaustion, intentions to leave their position, and the frequency of six disruptive behaviors[1] taking place in their work setting (e.g., workers turning their backs before a conversation is over).

Work settings higher in burnout had workers who were significantly more likely to report intentions to leave their position (Fig. 18.2). As reported earlier, turnover is incredibly costly to institutions (Han et al., 2019), and frequent vacancies and replacements significantly disrupt the flow of patient care within high turnover

---

[1] Note: The term "disruptive behaviors" is commonly used in the literature to refer to a set unprofessional actions ranging from prematurely turning one's back before a conversation is over to physical aggression.

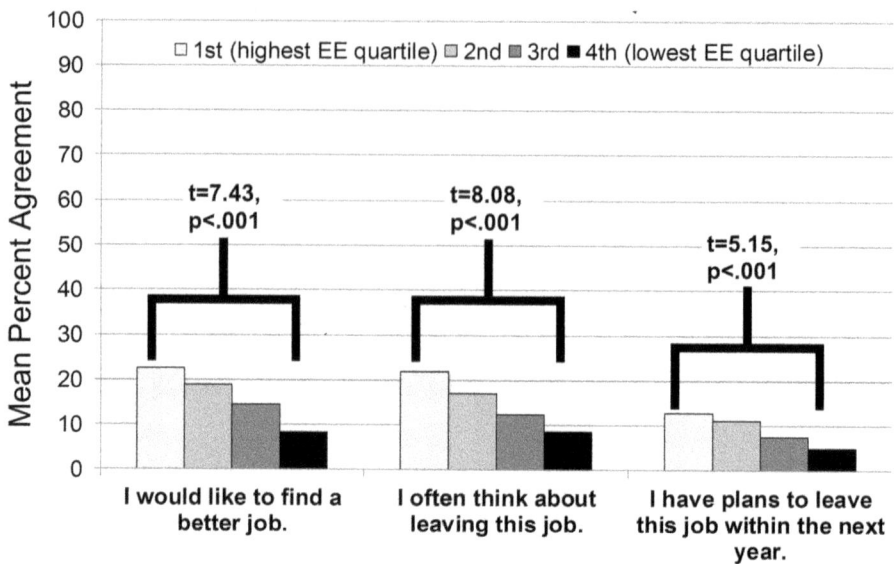

Fig. 18.2 Intention to leave rates across 319 work settings by emotional exhaustion quartiles

work settings. Building the trust, teamwork, and communication processes necessary for consistent patient care is impossible when staff are constantly leaving and joining teams.

We also found that 97.8% of work settings reported the presence of one or more of six disruptive behaviors (see Fig. 18.3 for disruptive behaviors distribution). Disruptive behaviors were significantly more common in work settings high in emotional exhaustion (Fig. 18.4). Individuals who are struggling may be more likely to act out in inappropriate and destructive ways. Unfortunately, disruptive behaviors can drastically destabilize the teamwork and psychological safety within teams and, in turn, undermine patient safety by increasing the risk of harm. Disruptive behaviors have been linked to more frequent adverse medical errors, decreased patient safety, lower quality of care, and higher patient mortality, in addition to organizational outcomes such as cost, staff turnover, and job dissatisfaction (Catron et al., 2016; Dang, Bae, Karlowicz, & Kim, 2016; Rawson, Thompson, Sostre, & Deitte, 2013; Rosenstein & Naylor, 2012; Rosenstein & O'Daniel, 2008).

18.3 Institutional Interventions to Improve Healthcare Worker Well-Being

Health systems, hospitals, and work settings with high rates of emotional exhaustion often have varied institutional approaches for addressing burnout. The leadership, cultures, and structures within these groups can drastically influence the direction of

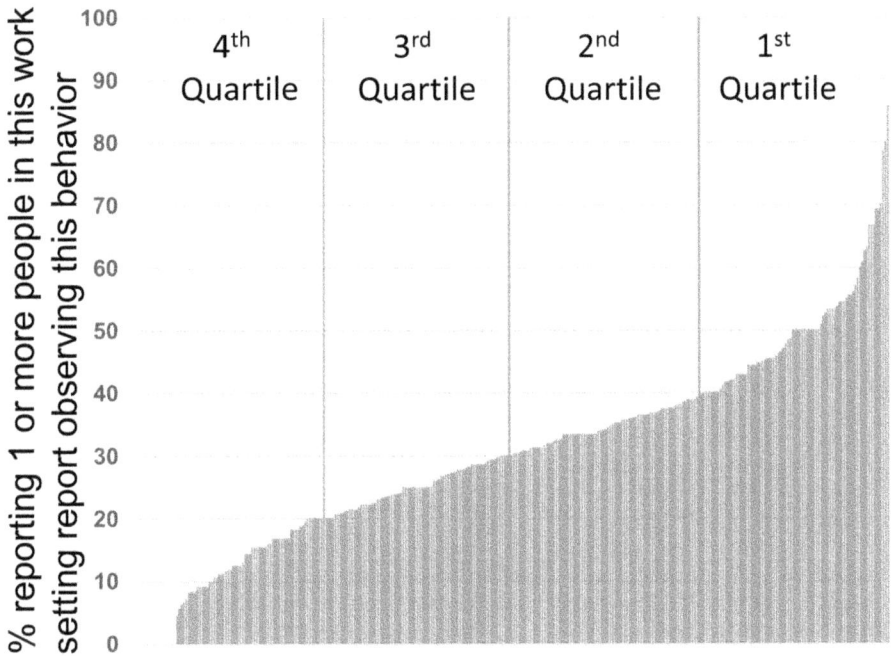

Fig. 18.3 Distribution of disruptive behaviors

the approaches taken. Research indicates that while there are effective, evidence-based approaches for both institutions and individuals to improve well-being, the data currently suggest that institutional interventions, on average, have a greater impact (Panagioti et al., 2017). Unfortunately, many of these institutional interventions are also resource intensive, which may affect an institution's willingness to implement or sustain such a program. Yet there is almost certainly a positive return on such an investment through improved patient and staff outcomes.

18.3.1 Institutional Changes to the Work Environment to Improve Well-Being

Within the large academic health system mentioned earlier, across a sample of 69 units, we found that work settings with higher rates of burnout (across role type) also have higher rates of staff turnover, as well as higher medication related errors (see Table 18.3). These findings have shifted this health system's priorities to include empowering work settings to improve HCW well-being. Health system leaders provided resources and supported work setting leaders to implement the well-being tools, strategies, and policies they deemed most useful for their groups (e.g., altering scheduling policies, hosting regular potlucks and celebrations). Even

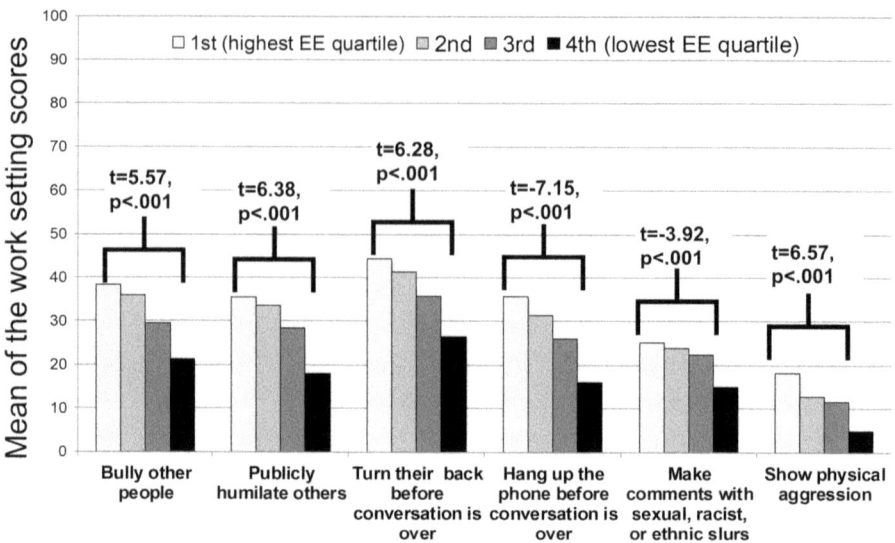

Fig. 18.4 Disruptive behavior rates across 319 work settings by emotional exhaustion quartiles. Figures 18.2, 18.3, and 18.4 are adapted from the dataset used in Doram et al. (2017); Rehder et al. (2019); Sexton et al. (2018)

greater focus was placed on work settings with particularly high emotional exhaustion scores. With these work settings, the typical first step was for well-being and patient safety leaders to hold focus groups (without local leaders present) to hear from the workers about problematic processes, or "pain points" that they felt were giving rise to burnout in their groups. The themes from the focus groups were then given to leaders to take action on what was heard. Importantly, leaders are asked to communicate "we heard you, and this is what we're doing to fix it" in departmental and local meetings after taking action on focus group findings. This health system's most recent culture survey indicates that these and other actions have been effective: 78% of the work settings that received this attention saw reductions in their emotional exhaustion scores between the 2017 and 2019 surveys.

Research has also demonstrated reductions in burnout as the result of workflow improvements and changing staffing models. Linzer et al. (2015) studied 34 primary care clinics, and using a cluster randomized control design found that changes to workflow were more powerful in reducing burnout than interventions aimed at improving communication and targeted quality improvement projects. Workflow changes at these cites varied, but included utilizing medical assistants to enter data into the EHR, improving patient flow through the clinic, pairing one medical assistant with each attending, and sharing information to make the clinic more efficient. In addition, a crossover pilot trial of two intensivist staffing models found that a shift work model (one intensivist working 7 day shifts, while other intensivist remained in the ICU at night) resulted in less burnout than the traditional model (one intensivist working 7 days and taking night call from home; Garland, Roberts, & Graff, 2012). Moreover, patient outcomes did not differ between these models, yet nurses reported more role conflict and house staff reported less autonomy and more supervision under the shift work model. Since this was a small pilot study, these effects should be replicated with a larger sample. This study and others do however demonstrate that improving the work environment can significantly reduce HCW burnout (Garland et al., 2012; Linzer et al., 2015; Lucas et al., 2012; Panagioti et al., 2017).

18.3.2 Institutional Interventions Aimed at Improving Individuals' Well-Being

There is a small but growing number of well-being interventions for individual HCWs being rolled out and tested at various institutions. One such initiative, a pilot study of professional coaching sessions for physicians across five months (3.5 h total), was found to significantly reduce emotional exhaustion and overall burnout compared to a randomized control group (Dyrbye, Shanafelt, Gill, Satele, & West, 2019). The program included thirty minutes of professional coaching sessions over the phone approximately every two to three weeks. Across the sessions, the following themes were discussed: integrating personal and professional life, optimizing meaning in work, building social support and community at work, improving work efficiency, building leadership skills, addressing workload, and engaging in self-care. Perhaps not surprisingly, physicians with higher burnout were more likely to enroll in the program, indicating it was more appealing to those with greater need. Although the pilot program reduced burnout, it was costly: US$1400 per physician.

Another promising intervention, the COMPASS program, gave physicians protected time to meet twice a month for one year, in groups of six to ten, to discuss well-being, stress, and professional fulfillment topics (West, Dyrbye, Satele, & Shanafelt, 2015). The goals of the program were to encourage collegiality, to boost mutual support, and to find greater meaning in work, as routes to reducing burnout. Using a randomized controlled design, the COMPASS program was found effective in significantly reducing emotional exhaustion, depersonalization, and overall burnout, while also improving meaning, empowerment, and engagement. Improvements in depersonalization, meaning and engagement were sustained 12 months after the end of the intervention. It appears that having HCWs connect and discuss meaningful work and well-being topics can be quite beneficial, yet the institutional cost of providing this much protected time, particularly for physicians, could be cost prohibitive.

18.4 Interventions Aimed at Individuals to Improve Well-Being

Although many institutions are beginning to invest in well-being interventions for their workers, many are simply not prepared to do so yet. For the workers lacking well-being resources in their institutions, there still is some good news: The field of positive psychology has found evidence that brief, uplifting activities and tools can meaningfully improve well-being. Researchers in healthcare have recently introduced such tools, such as the Three Good Things (3GT) tool, to HCWs (Seligman, Steen, Park, & Peterson, 2005). Originally conceived for depression patients, 3GT simply asks participants to record three good things (large or small) that happened that day each evening for one to two weeks. It is a remarkably brief (2–5 min), straightforward, and (based on evaluations) enjoyable activity that decreases depression symptoms and increase happiness (Seligman et al., 2005). In our research, we found that HCWs participating in 3GT reported reductions in emotional exhaustion and depression symptoms, and gains in work-life balance and happiness from pre to post, and that these gains were sustained at the 6 and 12 month follow-ups (Sexton & Adair, 2019). Moreover, a follow-up study has shown that the improvements are detectable after just two weeks, and still present 12 months later (Adair et al., 2019).

The Three Good Things tool is thought to improve well-being through several possible mechanisms. These include increasing the savoring of positive events while reflecting on them, anticipating having to complete the nightly tool and therefore being on the lookout for possible good things to note throughout the day, and becoming aware of the positive nature of events and experiences that had been previously taken for granted. We have identified these possible mechanisms as themes participants consistently express in open-ended questions posed to them about their experience with the tool. Across the days of participation, it is believed that attention paid to positive events in general grows, thereby boosting the frequency of positive emotions, as well as purpose, meaning, and fulfillment.

We recently rolled out an institution-wide initiative to encourage participation in the 3GT tool. A free online version of 3GT was built (see bit.ly/start3gt), and it sends nightly text messages or emails to prompt participation daily for 15 days. The link to enroll in the tool was widely shared among health system leaders and managers with an invitation to participate and or share with colleagues. A year later the health system surveyed all of its 12,716 workers on safety culture and well-being (72% response rate). Due to the timing of the 3GT tool and the system-wide survey, the question "I have participated in the "Three Good Things" intervention" (Yes/No/Not Sure) was added. Those who said they participated in 3GT reported large and significant differences across all survey domains, teamwork, safety climate, emotional exhaustion, and work-life balance, compared to those who said they did not participate in 3GT (see Fig. 18.5). Of course we cannot assume causation from these data, they are suggestive in so far as they reveal associations between participating in 3GT and better safety culture and well-being.

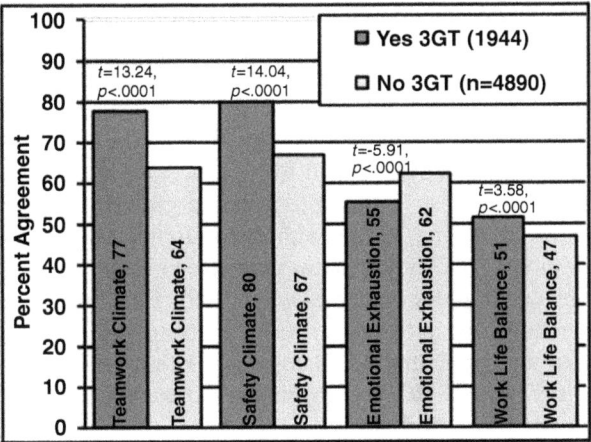

Fig. 18.5 Safety culture and well-being scores based on participation in three good things

18.5 A Possible Mechanism Behind Interventions' Effectiveness

In a field where such a large number of people are suffering from burnout, finding or creating effective interventions is essential. Moreover, identifying an underlying mechanism of action, or similar driving force behind the interventions' effectiveness would be quite valuable, as it would help refine current interventions to enhance that particular mechanism. This knowledge could also inspire and shape the development of future interventions to make them even more meaningful and effective.

The interventions listed above do share one key quality: participants are given the time to *pause and reflect* on what is going well, which can facilitate feeling greater purpose and meaning. Many healthcare workers struggle to find time to go to the bathroom or grab a bite to eat, so it is not surprising that taking the time to deliberately focus on what is going well is an underutilized practice. Research indicates that burnout actually predicts decrements in one's ability to pay attention to positive stimuli in the environment. Using eye-tracking technology, Bianchi and Laurent (2015) found that burnout was associated with increased attention to negative images, and decreased attention to positive images, meaning that those who would benefit most from enjoying positive images were exactly those who were least likely to look at them. Given this attentional bias, there is a large opportunity to deliberately boost positive emotions, purpose, and meaning through interventions designed to give HCWs time (even a small amount of it, as seen in 3GT) to pause and reflect on what is going well.

Awareness of good things, big and small, may help HCWs recalibrate their sense of how things are going, the impact that their work is having, and remind them of the aspects of their job that gives them greater purpose and meaning. By reconnecting with these aspects of their work, individuals are likely to feel more energy to improve themselves, as well as identify and work on areas for improvement in their institutions. The fields of clinical and positive psychology have repeatedly demonstrated the effectiveness of reflecting on the good to improve mental health issues and general well-being (Duckworth, Steen, & Seligman, 2005). Based on the studies and data presented throughout this chapter, we believe that institutions, HCWs, patients, and patients' families might reap tremendous benefits from institutional programs designed to give HCWs the chance to *pause and reflect* on the good (while also working to improve problematic process and policies). In other words, providing HCWs with opportunities to recharge their batteries offers them additional bandwidth that they can use to make meaningful differences, deliver safe care, and improve quality along the way. Luckily, this psychological practice can be incredibly low in cost (e.g., 3GT), brief, simple, and immediately enjoyable. Benefits from such programs would come in the form of lower rates of burnout and turnover, higher rates of HCW engagement and well-being, and ultimately safer and higher quality of care for patients and families.

18.6 Summary of This Chapter

Looking across the preponderance of empirical evidence presented here, there are a few overarching concepts that can be gleaned from the results. Well-being metrics such as emotional exhaustion and work-life balance have reliable and consistent relationships with safety culture, employee engagement, and operational outcomes. Emotional exhaustion (a key pillar of burnout) is moderately to strongly associated with less engagement through fewer perceived growth opportunities, less participation in decision making, and higher workload. Well-being metrics (emotional exhaustion, burnout climate, and work-life balance) as well as Press Ganey Work Culture scores are associated with self-reported nursing practice environment scales from NDNQI. Nevertheless, in our experience, we have consistently found that only well-being metrics are also associated with **both** the self-reported metrics like NDNQI practice environment domains, **as well as** costly operational outcomes like turnover, preventable harm, and disruptive behaviors by fellow HCWs.

Not only is emotional exhaustion costly due to higher rates of infections, medical errors, lower patient satisfaction, and turnover (at least $4.6 billion; Han et al., 2019), it is linked to much higher rates of incivility at work, such as more bullying behaviors, hanging up the phone or turning one's back before a conversation is over and even displays of physical aggression such as grabbing, throwing, hitting and pushing. Rates of incivility often doubled when comparing lowest quartile of emotional exhaustion to the highest. Similarly, emotional exhaustion was linked to both turnover and intentions to leave, with rates of intentions to leave more than double in the highest versus lowest quartile of emotional exhaustion.

The demonstrably higher costs of well-being deficits, their consequences for HCW mental and physical health, as well as operational outcomes are troubling. Fortunately, a growing body of empirical evidence suggests that the well-being of individuals and groups is responsive to interventions. Positive psychology tools such as 3GT (Sexton & Adair, 2019), as well as programs such HCW coaching (Dyrbye et al., 2019) and COMPASS (West et al., 2015) mentioned here each share a common element of pausing and reflecting on what is going well. Remarkably, these reflective practices go a long way toward improving well-being metrics such as emotional exhaustion, work-life balance, depression and subjective well-being (for more examples of resources please visit: www.hsq.dukehealth.org/tools). Ultimately, HCWs are vulnerable to compromises in well-being and have earned the right to have researchers, administrators and policy makers come together to engineer better systems of care delivery, and to provide more accessible and diverse resources to enhance well-being in general.

Key Messages for Researchers
 • Regular assessment (e.g. every 18 months) of well-being using psychometrically valid measures (e.g., emotional exhaustion, burnout climate, work-life balance) can identify work settings at higher risk for lower engagement and professionalism (e.g., intentions to leave, turnover, disruptive behavior), as well as higher patient safety risks (e.g., infections, medication errors)
 • Interventions designed to improve HCW well-being should be assessed for effectiveness using psychometrically valid measures, and ideally randomized control designs

---

Key Messages for Healthcare Delivery
 • Regular measurement of HCW well-being can identify work settings at greater risk for patient safety events. Leaders should use this information to target struggling units, help solve pain points in these groups, and provide ongoing well-being resources
 • Investment in effective well-being interventions, particularly those that include *pausing and reflecting on what's going well*, are likely to result in lower turnover, fewer disruptive behaviors, fewer errors, and better patient outcomes. These results make investments in well-being highly financially worthwhile

---

References

Adair, K. C., Kennedy, Lindsay, & Sexton, J. B. (2019). 3 Good tools: Positively reflecting backwards and forwards is associated with robust improvements in well-being across 3 distinct interventions. *The Journal of Positive Psychology*. https://doi.org/10.1080/17439760.2020.1789707

Adair, K. C., Quow, K., Frankel, A., Mosca, P. J., Profit, J., Hadley, A., et al. (2018). The Improvement Readiness scale of the SCORE survey: A metric to assess capacity for quality improvement in healthcare. *BMC Health Services Research, 18*(1) https://doi.org/10.1186/s12913-018-3743-0

Aiken, L. H., Clarke, S. P., Sloane, D. M., Sochalski, J., & Silber, J. H. (2002). Hospital nurse staffing and patient mortality, nurse burnout, and job dissatisfaction. *JAMA, 288*(16), 1987–1993. https://doi.org/10.1001/jama.288.16.1987

Aiken, L. H., Sermeus, W., Van den Heede, K., Sloane, D. M., Busse, R., McKee, M., et al. (2012). Patient safety, satisfaction, and quality of hospital care: Cross sectional surveys of nurses and patients in 12 countries in Europe and the United States. *BMJ, 344*(mar20 2), e1717–e1717. https://doi.org/10.1136/bmj.e1717

Andresen, E. M., Malmgren, J. A., Carter, W. B., & Patrick, D. L. (1994). Screening for depression in well older adults: Evaluation of a short form of the CES-D (Center for Epidemiologic Studies Depression Scale). *American Journal of Preventive Medicine, 10*(2), 77–84.

Bianchi, R., & Laurent, E. (2015). Emotional information processing in depression and burnout: An eye-tracking study. *European Archives of Psychiatry and Clinical Neuroscience, 265*(1), 27–34. https://doi.org/10.1007/s00406-014-0549-x

Catron, T. F., Guillamondegui, O. D., Karrass, J., Cooper, W. O., Martin, B. J., Dmochowski, R. R., et al. (2016). Patient complaints and adverse surgical outcomes. *American Journal of Medical Quality: The Official Journal of the American College of Medical Quality, 31*(5), 415–422. https://doi.org/10.1177/1062860615584158

Cimiotti, J. P., Aiken, L. H., Sloane, D. M., & Wu, E. S. (2012). Nurse staffing, burnout, and health care-associated infection. *American Journal of Infection Control, 40*(6), 486–490. https://doi.org/10.1016/j.ajic.2012.02.029

Dang, D., Bae, S.-H., Karlowicz, K. A., & Kim, M. T. (2016). Do clinician disruptive behaviors make an unsafe environment for patients? *Journal of Nursing Care Quality, 31*(2), 115–123. https://doi.org/10.1097/NCQ.0000000000000150

Demerouti, E., Bakker, A. B., Nachreiner, F., & Schaufeli, W. B. (2001). The job demands-resources model of burnout. *Journal of Applied Psychology, 86*(3), 499–512. https://doi.org/10.1037/0021-9010.86.3.499

Doram, K., Chadwick, W., Bokovoy, J., Profit, J., Sexton, J. D., & Sexton, J. B. (2017). Got spirit? The spiritual climate scale, psychometric properties, benchmarking data and future directions. *BMC Health Services Research, 17*(1), 132. https://doi.org/10.1186/s12913-017-2050-5

Duckworth, A. L., Steen, T. A., & Seligman, M. E. P. (2005). Positive psychology in clinical practice. *Annual Review of Clinical Psychology, 1*(1), 629–651. https://doi.org/10.1146/annurev.clinpsy.1.102803.144154

Dyrbye, L. N., Shanafelt, T. D., Gill, P. R., Satele, D. V., & West, C. P. (2019). Effect of a professional coaching intervention on the well-being and distress of physicians: A pilot randomized clinical trial. *JAMA Internal Medicine*. https://doi.org/10.1001/jamainternmed.2019.2425

Dyrbye, L. N., Varkey, P., Boone, S. L., Satele, D. V., Sloan, J. A., & Shanafelt, T. D. (2013). Physician satisfaction and burnout at different career stages. *Mayo Clinic Proceedings, 88*(12), 1358–1367. https://doi.org/10.1016/j.mayocp.2013.07.016

Fahrenkopf, A. M., Sectish, T. C., Barger, L. K., Sharek, P. J., Lewin, D., Chiang, V. W., et al. (2008). Rates of medication errors among depressed and burnt out residents: Prospective cohort study. *BMJ (Clinical Research Ed.), 336*(7642), 488–491. https://doi.org/10.1136/bmj.39469.763218.BE

Garland, A., Roberts, D., & Graff, L. (2012). Twenty-four–Hour Intensivist Presence: A pilot study of effects on intensive care unit patients, families, doctors, and nurses. *American Journal of Respiratory and Critical Care Medicine, 185*(7), 738–743. https://doi.org/10.1164/rccm.201109-1734OC

Han, S., Shanafelt, T. D., Sinsky, C. A., Awad, K. M., Dyrbye, L. N., Fiscus, L. C., et al. (2019). Estimating the attributable cost of physician burnout in the United States. *Annals of Internal Medicine, 170*(11), 784–790. https://doi.org/10.7326/M18-1422

Henson, J. W. (2016). Reducing physician burnout through engagement. *Journal of Healthcare Management, 61*(2), 86.

Institute of Medicine (US) Committee on Quality of Health Care in America. (2000). *To err is human: Building a safer health system*. L. T. Kohn, J. M. Corrigan, & M. S. Donaldson (Eds.). National Academies Press (US). http://www.ncbi.nlm.nih.gov/books/NBK225182/

Kang, E.-K., Lihm, H.-S., & Kong, E.-H. (2013). Association of intern and resident burnout with self-reported medical errors. *Korean Journal of Family Medicine, 34*(1), 36–42. https://doi.org/10.4082/kjfm.2013.34.1.36

Linzer, M., Poplau, S., Grossman, E., Varkey, A., Yale, S., Williams, E., et al. (2015). A cluster randomized trial of interventions to improve work conditions and clinician burnout in primary care: Results from the Healthy Work Place (HWP) Study. *Journal of General Internal Medicine, 30*(8), 1105–1111. https://doi.org/10.1007/s11606-015-3235-4

Lucas, B. P., Trick, W. E., Evans, A. T., Mba, B., Smith, J., Das, K., et al. (2012). Effects of 2- vs 4-week attending physician inpatient rotations on unplanned patient revisits, evaluations by trainees, and attending physician burnout: A randomized trial. *JAMA, 308*(21), 2199–2207. https://doi.org/10.1001/jama.2012.36522

Lyubomirsky, S., & Lepper, H. S. (1999). A Measure of subjective happiness: Preliminary reliability and construct validation. *Social Indicators Research, 46*(2), 137–155. https://doi.org/10.1023/A:1006824100041

Maslach, C., & Jackson, S.. (n.d.). *Maslach burnout inventory.*

Maslach, C., & Leiter, M. P. (2016). Chapter 43—Burnout. In G. Fink (Ed.), *Stress: Concepts, cognition, emotion, and behavior* (pp. 351–357). Academic Press. https://doi.org/10.1016/B978-0-12-800951-2.00044-3

Molina-Praena, J., Ramirez-Baena, L., Gómez-Urquiza, J. L., Cañadas, G. R., De la Fuente, E. I., & Cañadas-De la Fuente, G. A. (2018). Levels of burnout and risk factors in medical area nurses: A meta-analytic study. *International Journal of Environmental Research and Public Health, 15*(12) https://doi.org/10.3390/ijerph15122800

Montalvo, I. (2007). The National Database of Nursing Quality Indicators(TM) (NDNQI®). *Online Journal of Issues in Nursing, 12*, 3. https://www.questia.com/library/journal/1P3-1692234461/the-national-database-of-nursing-quality-indicators-tm

Organisation for Economic Co-operation and Development. (2015). *Health at a glance 2015: OECD indicators*. OECD Publishing. https://doi.org/10.1787/health_glance-2015-en

Panagioti, M., Geraghty, K., Johnson, J., Zhou, A., Panagopoulou, E., Chew-Graham, C., et al. (2018). Association between physician burnout and patient safety, professionalism, and patient satisfaction: A systematic review and meta-analysis. *JAMA Internal Medicine, 178*(10), 1317–1330. https://doi.org/10.1001/jamainternmed.2018.3713

Panagioti, M., Panagopoulou, E., Bower, P., Lewith, G., Kontopantelis, E., Chew-Graham, C., et al. (2017). Controlled interventions to reduce burnout in physicians: A systematic review and meta-analysis. *JAMA Internal Medicine, 177*(2), 195–205. https://doi.org/10.1001/jamainternmed.2016.7674

Rawson, J. V., Thompson, N., Sostre, G., & Deitte, L. (2013). The cost of disruptive and unprofessional behaviors in health care. *Academic Radiology, 20*(9), 1074–1076. https://doi.org/10.1016/j.acra.2013.05.009

Rehder, K. J., Adair, K. C., Hadley, A., McKittrick, K., Frankel, A., Leonard, M., et al. (2019). Associations between a new disruptive behaviors scale and teamwork, patient safety, work-life balance, burnout, and depression. *Joint Commission Journal on Quality and Patient Safety*. https://doi.org/10.1016/j.jcjq.2019.09.004

Rosenstein, A. H., & Naylor, B. (2012). Incidence and impact of physician and nurse disruptive behaviors in the emergency department. *The Journal of Emergency Medicine, 43*(1), 139–148. https://doi.org/10.1016/j.jemermed.2011.01.019

Rosenstein, A. H., & O'Daniel, M. (2008). A survey of the impact of disruptive behaviors and communication defects on patient safety. *Joint Commission Journal on Quality and Patient Safety, 34*(8), 464–471.

Schaufeli, W. B., & Bakker, A. B. (2004). Job demands, job resources, and their relationship with burnout and engagement: A multi-sample study. *Journal of Organizational Behavior, 25*(3), 293–315. https://doi.org/10.1002/job.248

Schwartz, S. P., Adair, K. C., Bae, J., Rehder, K. J., Shanafelt, T. D., Profit, J., et al. (2019). Work-life balance behaviours cluster in work settings and relate to burnout and safety culture: A cross-sectional survey analysis. *BMJ Quality & Safety, 28*(2), 142–150. https://doi.org/10.1136/bmjqs-2018-007933

Seligman, M. E. P., Steen, T. A., Park, N., & Peterson, C. (2005). Positive psychology progress: Empirical validation of interventions. *The American Psychologist, 60*(5), 410–421. https://doi.org/10.1037/0003-066X.60.5.410

Sexton, J. B., & Adair, K. C. (2019). Forty-five good things: A prospective pilot study of the Three Good Things well-being intervention in the USA for healthcare worker emotional exhaustion, depression, work–life balance and happiness. *BMJ Open, 9*(3), e022695. https://doi.org/10.1136/bmjopen-2018-022695

Sexton, J. B., Adair, K. C., Leonard, M. W., Frankel, T. C., Proulx, J., Watson, S. R., et al. (2018). Providing feedback following Leadership WalkRounds is associated with better patient safety culture, higher employee engagement and lower burnout. *BMJ Quality & Safety, 27*, 261–270. https://doi.org/10.1136/bmjqs-2016-006399

Sexton, J. B., Leonard, M., Frankel, A., & Adair, K. C. (2019). *Technical report: SCORE: Assessment of your work setting safety, communication, operational reliability, and engagement.*

Sexton, J. B., Schwartz, S. P., Chadwick, W. A., Rehder, K. J., Bae, J., Bokovoy, J., et al. (2017). The associations between work–life balance behaviours, teamwork climate and safety climate: Cross-sectional survey introducing the work–life climate scale, psychometric properties, benchmarking data and future directions. *BMJ Quality & Safety, 26*(8), 632–640. https://doi.org/10.1136/bmjqs-2016-006032

Shanafelt, T. D., Balch, C. M., Bechamps, G., Russell, T., Dyrbye, L., Satele, D., et al. (2010). Burnout and medical errors among American surgeons. *Annals of Surgery, 251*(6), 995–1000.

Shanafelt, T. D., Boone, S., Tan, L., Dyrbye, L. N., Sotile, W., Satele, D., et al. (2012). Burnout and satisfaction with work-life balance among US physicians relative to the general US POPULATION. *Archives of Internal Medicine, 172*(18), 1377. https://doi.org/10.1001/archinternmed.2012.3199

Van den Broeck, A., Vansteenkiste, M., Witte, H., Soenens, B., & Lens, W. (2010). Capturing autonomy, competence, and relatedness at work: Construction and initial validation of the Work-related Basic Need Satisfaction scale. *Journal of Occupational and Organizational Psychology, 83*(4), 981–1002. https://doi.org/10.1348/096317909X481382

West, C. P., Dyrbye, L. N., Satele, D., & Shanafelt, T. D. (2015). A randomized controlled trial evaluating the effect of COMPASS (COlleagues Meeting to Promote and Sustain Satisfaction) small group sessions on physician well-being, meaning, and job satisfaction. *Journal of General Internal Medicine, 30*(S89).

Willard-Grace, R., Knox, M., Huang, B., Hammer, H., Kivlahan, C., & Grumbach, K. (2019). Burnout and health care workforce turnover. *The Annals of Family Medicine, 17*(1), 36–41. https://doi.org/10.1370/afm.2338

Chapter 19
Mindfulness as a Way to Improve Well-Being in Healthcare Professionals: Separating the Wheat from the Chaff

Anthony Montgomery, Katerina Georganta, Ashvirni Gilbeth, Yugan Subramaniam, and Karen Morgan

19.1 Introduction

Mindfulness-based Interventions (MBIs) are increasingly employed in healthcare settings, even though the evidence to support their effectiveness is equivocal. The arguments in favour of mindfulness interventions emphasize that mindfulness, which involves reconnecting and enhancing meaning, has the potential to improve authentic awareness that arises through the paying of purposeful non-judgemental attention to the present moment (Connelly, 1999; Epstein, 1999; Kabat-Zinn & Hanh, 2009). Greater authentic awareness should enhance engagement (reduce feelings of burnout) and improve clinical practice.

The aforementioned seems to be supported by a number of meta-analyses. For example, meta-analyses of MBIs among healthcare professionals (HCPs) have concluded that; cognitive, behavioral, and mindfulness-based approaches are effective in reducing stress in medical students and practicing physicians (Regehr, Glancy, Pitts, & Le Blanc, 2014), MBIs have the potential to significantly ameliorate stress among HCPs (Burton, Burgess, Dean, Zoutsopoulou, & Hugh-Jones, 2017), and mindfulness-based interventions are effective in reducing distress and improving well-being (Spinelli, Wiserner, & Khoury, 2019). However, the aforementioned conclusions fail to present the major caveats of the MBIs research literature. A more fine-grained analysis of these meta-analyses indicates that the statistically significant effect sizes may be blinding us to the fact that the evidence base is very limited. In

---

A. Montgomery (✉) · K. Georganta
University of Macedonia, Thessaloniki, Greece
e-mail: antmont@uom.edu.gr

A. Gilbeth · Y. Subramaniam · K. Morgan
Perdana University Royal College of Surgeons in Ireland School of Medicine, Serdang, Selangor, Malaysia

the following chapter, we conduct a systematic review of meta-analyses of MBI's among healthcare professionals. Our review has three objectives; (1) to examine whether grouping MBIs together is scientifically meaningful, (2) to assess whether there is evidence that they affect employee wellbeing and clinical practice, and (3) to find out whether they are appropriate tools for healthcare professionals.

19.2 Systematic Review of the Literature

In this systematic review we searched PubMed, Web of Science, SCOPUS, ERIC, EBSCOhost and Cochrane databases for meta-analyses regarding mindfulness interventions and their impact on HCPs mental health and clinical practice from inception until April 2020. We used a combination of the key words mindfulness, systematic review, meta-analysis, stress, burnout, depression, anxiety, mood, mental-health and resilience to locate studies. In addition, we proceeded with hand searching the reference lists of all the papers included in the final list to identify any further meta-analysis for inclusion. Only studies published in English were included. Unpublished research was not included in this review. Studies were eligible if they included meta-analysis about mindfulness interventions for employees in the healthcare sector either exclusively or as part of wider study of different occupations. The definition of healthcare sector employee was broad and included nurses, physicians, psychologists, health care technicians, managers and other hospital employees. Mindfulness interventions were also broadly defined, thus in this review studies that included any type of mindfulness intervention, long and short term, practiced online, face to face, in the workplace or at home were included. In relation to outcomes we included all potential variables, for example stress, burnout, anxiety, and job engagement.

The returned data included 1598 studies (see Fig. 19.1). After removing duplicates, 890 studies remained. The search was conducted in three phases. During the first phase the data that were retrieved from the literature search were subjected to a screening process on the basis of their titles. At the end of this phase we identified and excluded 31 studies which were not reviews, 10 commentaries, 7 papers in languages other than English, 3 protocols, 2 retracted papers, 1 editorial, 1 erratum, 1 poster and 83 studies that were not related to mindfulness. At the second phase we reread the remaining titles and the abstract where necessary and we excluded 31 studies that did not include a mindfulness intervention review, 656 studies that were not about the workplace (most of them referred to mindfulness interventions for patients, students and adults outside of their workplace), 18 studies that did not include health care professionals, 3 studies that did not mention sample characteristics and 31 that did not include a meta-analysis. The first two phases resulted in 12 studies (see Table 19.1). For the third phase we read the full text of the papers. These 12 meta-analyses met the inclusion criteria and were subject to review and quality assessment.

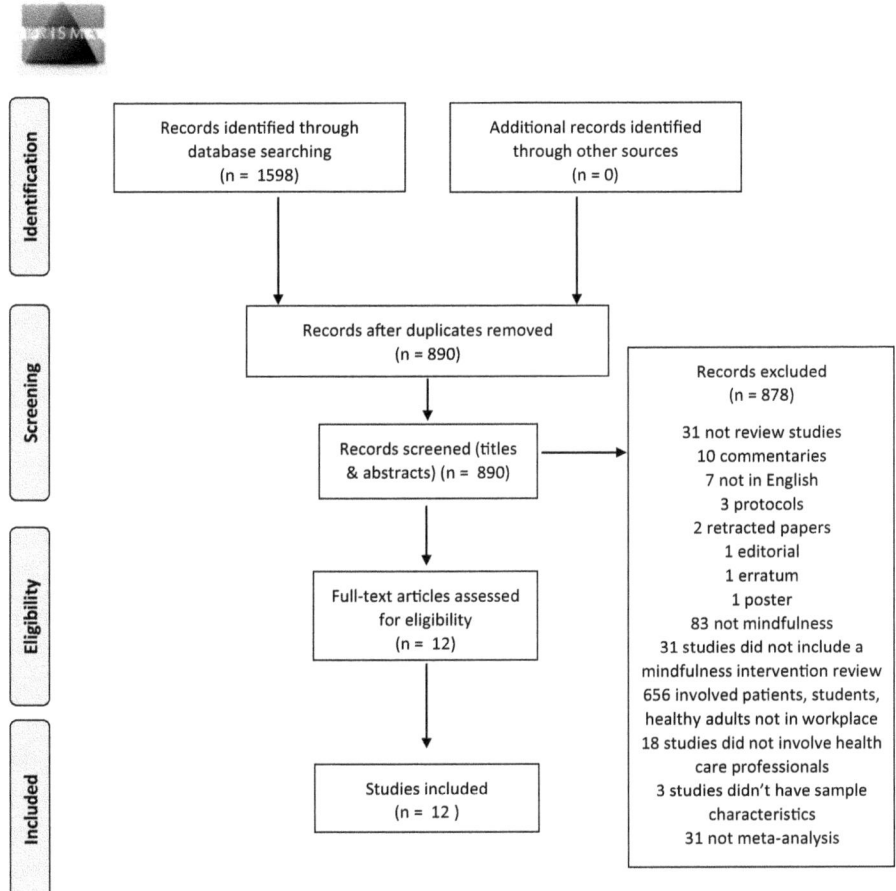

Fig. 19.1 PRISMA 2009 flow diagram. From: Moher D, Liberati A, Tetzlaff J, Altman DG, The PRISMA Group (2009). *P*referred *R*eporting *I*tems for *S*ystematic Reviews and *M*eta-*A*nalyses: The PRISMA Statement. PLoS Med 6(7): e1000097. doi:10.1371/journal.pmed1000097. For more information, visit www.prisma-statement.org

19.3 Findings and Discussion

Overall, the meta-analyses reported statistically significant effect sizes, but with the caveat that there was relatively little evidence of follow-up studies to track the impact over time. The variability as to what actually constitutes a mindfulness intervention and the quality of studies included in the reviews is problematic. In the Regehr et al. (2014) meta-analysis, involving physicians and medical trainees, it is not clear what type of MBIs were employed as the authors report that all of the included studies examined interventions that incorporated components of cognitive-, behavioral-, and/or mindfulness based techniques. Additionally, the authors report

Table 19.1 Study characteristics of MBI meta-analyses

	Study	Quality	Long-term effect	Most significant limitation reported	Length of Intervention Range	Sample size	HP Papers included
1	Bartlett et al. (2019)	Samples were mostly self-selected into the study in response to invitation campaigns, whereas the others were directed by their employers to participate	Beneficial effects for psychological distress, depression and anxiety and wellbeing also remained stable at 3 months follow up	No RCT evidence supporting mindfulness training for leadership or creativity, decision-making, citizenship behaviors, deviance, or safety. Men underrepresented (average 15%)	3–10 weeks	2290	6/23
2	Burton et al. (2017)	Studies were rated poorly on the use of an 'explicit theoretical framework', with only two studies clearly referring to a theoretical or conceptual framework	2 studies with follow up, but no detail	All studies used self-selected participants. For studies where gender information was provided, the number of female participants was greater than that of male participants	1 day – 4 weeks	284	9/9
3	Chiesa and Serretti (2009)	Low	Little or no evidence	Majority of samples were females, Caucasian, and undergraduate students	6–8 weeks	671	6/10
4	Dharmawardene, Givens, Wachholtz, Makowski, and Tjia (2016)	High variability in terms of study quality	None reported	Vast majority of studies enrolled female participants	4–8 weeks	Not reported	12/27
5	Heckenberg, Eddy, Kent, and Wright (2018)	The studies scored between 12 and 22 out of 26. Lack of follow-up measurements or blinding procedures, failing	2 studies with follow up, but no detail	Only five studies assessed engagement in the program. The majority of the samples were female (73.9%)	8–16 weeks	812	2/9

#	Author						
		to report randomization or having inadequate randomization, along with inadequate control groups					11/29
6	Khoury, Sharma, Rush, and Fournier (2015)	Heterogeneity in Quality assessment Median 4 (based on 1–7 score)	Lack of Long-term follow up	High heterogeneity among some study groups, most participants were female, Caucasian and relatively young, therefore results cannot be generalized to other populations	6–42 h	2668	11/29
7	Lomas, Medina, Ivtzan, Rupprecht, and Eiroa-Orosa (2019)	Most studies did not give sufficient details about their design. Most studies failed to deploy any kind of active control group	None reported	Most studies did not give sufficient details about interventions (e.g., the precise nature of the MBI) 74% women	Not reported	3090	13/35
8	Petrie et al. (2019)	Studies were very diverse, differing in intervention approach, delivery, and the outcomes assessed	Short-term follow-up, with few studies assessing physicians' mental health beyond 3–6 months after the intervention	Given the focus on suicide and mental health, no studies were examining organisation-level interventions	One off mailed intervention – 9 month intervention	1023	9/9
9	Regehr et al. (2014)	Not assessed	Not reported	Composition of the control groups in some studies may have represented a bias	90 min – 8 weeks	1034	12/12
10	Slemp, Jach, Chia, Loton, and Kern (2019)	Study quality was generally rated as poor	The length of last follow-up varied considerably, ranging from 1 month to 3 years	File drawer problems. Review shows that publication bias is inflating effects	Not reported	6044	18/119
11	Spinelli et al. (2019)	Out of a possible 14 points, quality scores ranged from	Most studies did not include follow-ups, making it	76% of participants were female	2.5–70 h	2505	38/38

(continued)

Table 19.1 (continued)

	Study	Quality	Long-term effect	Most significant limitation reported	Length of Intervention Range	Sample size	HP Papers included
		6 to 11 with an average of 8.10	difficult to interpret the long-term effects of interventions				
12	Virgili (2015)	Methodological quality did not bias the observed mean effect sizes	Effects obtained at posttreatment were largely maintained at follow-up, (Median = 5 weeks)	Little evidence to suggest that MBIs are more effective than similar stress management interventions, such as yoga and relaxation, for reducing psychological distress in working adults	4–12 weeks	1139	6/11

Note: *HP* healthcare professionals

that it is not clear if the reviewed MBIs are discernible from standard cognitive behavioural therapy. In the Burton et al. (2017) meta-analysis the MBIs included a wide range of approaches; smart phone mindfulness-based stress reduction applications, mindfulness-based stress reduction, an abbreviated mindfulness course, and mindfulness based cognitive attitude training workshops. Moreover, the authors reported a significant file drawer problem, in that only 44 non-significant studies would be needed to render the findings non-significant. Quality assessment of the papers in the Burton at al review, conducted as part of this review highlighted several methodological limitations, which draw the fidelity of the reported effects of the interventions into question. In the Spinelli et al. (2019) review there was considerable inconsistency in study measures and variations of intervention design, with moderate to high heterogeneity on some study outcomes.

Secondly, 75% of the studies reported that the majority of participants were women. The over-representation of women in MBI interventions has been noted in meta-analysis looking at the general working population (e.g., Heckenberg et al., 2018; Khoury et al., 2015). Additionally, it is likely that all participants represent a narrow range of people in terms of both socio-economic status and cultural variation. There is a broad movement in psychology that has detected biases when the vast majority of research is based on a single population demographic. This problem has been referred to as the bias of psychology research being dominated by WEIRD populations (Western, Educated, Industrialized, Rich, and Democratic), which account for 90% of psychology publications (Henrich, Heine, & Norenzayan, 2010).For example, when psychological studies have been conducted with non-WEIRD populations, researchers have discovered that presumed universal processes such as visual perception, spatial reasoning, and behavioral motivation related to fairness and cooperation have cultural variations (Henrich et al., 2010). Therefore, we are presently running the risk of overlooking the fact that the evidence pertaining to the effectiveness of MBIs is based on a very selective sample.

Thirdly, the majority of studies on mindfulness focus on outcome variables related to self-reported wellbeing. Apart from the problems associated with common method variance, the bigger problem is that research is not linking MBIs with healthcare practice. For example Spinelli et al. (2019) recommend linking MBIs with relevant skills, such as ambiguity tolerance, emotional intelligence, empathy, humility, leadership, resilience and diagnostic accuracy. In their review, physical health, cognitive performance, and clinical skills were not significantly affected by mindfulness training. Wellbeing should be the concern of healthcare organizations, but MBIs will not be taken seriously unless it can be demonstrated that they impact on clinical practice. Additionally, there is some evidence that MBIs benefit approach-coping versus avoidance coping in a sample of medical students, whereby MBIs (for approach coping) enables improved self-awareness and better emotional and behavioural self-regulation (Spinelli et al., 2019).

Fourthly, mindfulness requires significant levels of engagement and commitment. Is this method really the most appropriate for healthcare professionals? The Burton et al. (2017) review reported high attrition rates among studies, and this may simply reflect the fact that in healthcare such interventions are viewed as a burden or additional task. Support for this idea also comes from one of the few studies to explore intervention engagement through interviews and focus groups, reporting that the intervention was found to be enjoyable, but ongoing mindfulness practice outside of the intervention (advised to be between 10–40 min/day) would be difficult for health care professionals to implement and maintain (Foureur, Besley, Burton, Yu, & Crisp, 2013). Congruently, it was difficult to assess the context in which interventions were introduced. For example, it wasn't clear to which extent have MBIs been introduced as a primary intervention or explicitly for employees with elevated stress levels (as secondary/tertiary intervention). Knowing which contexts are more suitable for MBIs would help to differentiate their 'worth'.

Congruently, it may be that problems like psychological distress need an organizational solution that focuses on job-person fit rather than an individual approach that uses mindfulness to have a 'ripple effect' on quality and safety in a healthcare setting. Contemplative interventions are defined as practices originally rooted in Buddhist traditions and comprise a variety of cognitive-behavioural activities intended to produce sustained alterations in basic cognitive and affective processes, including the regulation of attention, affect, and distress, to support personal insight and well-being (Davidson et al., 2012). Slemp et al. (2019) in a meta-analysis of 119 studies assessing contemplative interventions in the general workforce found that the weakest effects were observed in health care, with regard to the impact of contemplative interventions on general psychological distress (Cohen's $d = 0.21$, 0.04, 0.38, k = 18). Encouraging healthcare professionals to be more mindful is desirable and the benefits seem obvious. But we need to be careful as to whether we are really advocating practices that dovetail with the tendency of physicians (in particular) to solve problems individually rather than advocating solutions that prompt people to reflect on team and work practices that challenge quality and safety.

19.4 Where Do We Go from Here with Mindfulness?

Systematic reviews and meta-analysis are an important step in the hierarchy of evidence, but they become less useful when they communicate mixed messages—such as evidence that MBIs can work but with caveats that significantly undermine the evidence presented. Reading the conclusions of methodologically sound meta-analyses about MBIs can mask the fact that the interventions reviewed can include a varied mix/combination of the following; mindfulness meditation, focused concentration, open awareness, body/internal focus, nature/external focus, yoga, tai chi, and qigong. Therefore, we should acknowledge that there is not yet enough evidence as to the effectiveness of MBIs in healthcare. This does not mean that an organization should not use them, but simply recognize that their use of these approaches entails an evaluation of them in parallel.

The basic idea of mindfulness, to be more aware of our surroundings, should be one that has the potential to improve both quality of care and patient safety.

However, attempts to 'crow-bar' it into daily practice in a healthcare setting are more likely to increase the work demands of an already exhausted workforce. There has to be the recognition that it is likely to be viewed as either alien or a luxury by healthcare professionals whose daily experiences involve heavy patient loads, work-arounds and little time for self-care (i.e., breaks, food). Randomized controlled trials of MBIs are only useful to the extent that the 'medicine' being evaluated is meaningful and applicable. Since the majority of interventions utilize cognitive and movement based aspects, and because there is substantial variation within each of these categories (e.g., mindfulness meditation, focused concentration, open awareness, body/internal focus, nature/external focus, yoga, tai chi, qigong), it may be useful for future studies to identify the beneficial outcomes associated with specific techniques, or the most appropriate target audiences for each technique (Dharmawardene et al., 2016).

Finally, it's important not to 'throw the baby out with the bathwater'. For example, approaches such as Mindful Practice (Krasner et al., 2009) which enable clinicians to apply qualities such as attentive observation, critical curiosity, beginner's mind, and presence to their practice of medicine are more likely to have face validity with healthcare workers. Mindfulness was adopted as a strategy on the basis that it had great potential to ameliorate stress and burnout, but its assimilation into the culture of medicine is dependent on its ability to demonstrate an impact on patient experience, claims reports, rehospitalisation rates and higher levels of psychological safety in among medical teams.

Key messages for researchers

The evidence concerning the efficacy of mindfulness based interventions among HCPs is limited and based largely on the experience of women participants in western populations

There is a significant lack of follow-up studies concerning the impact of mindfulness based interventions

The majority of outcomes that have been measured concern self-reported well-being measures, this needs to be supported by studies that demonstrate the impact of mindfulness based interventions on clinical outcomes

Key messages for healthcare delivery

The use of piloting prior to the use of mindfulness based interventions, and the use of exit interviews following implementation is strongly advised

Mindfulness based interventions need to be assessed for feasibility and acceptability before being employed in healthcare settings

Mindfulness based interventions should be part of a comprehensive approach that includes a combination of individual and organizational approaches

---

References

Bartlett, L., Martin, A., Neil, A. L., Memish, K., Otahal, P., Kilpatrick, M., et al. (2019). A systematic review and meta-analysis of workplace mindfulness training randomized controlled trials. *Journal of Occupational Health Psychology, 24*(1), 108–126. https://doi.org/10.1037/ocp0000146

Burton, A., Burgess, C., Dean, S., Zoutsopoulou, G. Z., & Hugh-Jones, S. (2017). How effective are mindfulness-based interventions for reducing stress among healthcare professionals? A systematic review and meta-analysis. *Stress & Health, 33*, 3–13.

Chiesa, A., & Serretti, A. (2009). Mindfulness-based stress reduction for stress management in healthy people: A review and meta-analysis. *The Journal of Alternative and Complementary Medicine, 15*(5), 593–600. https://doi.org/10.1089/acm.2008.0495

Connelly, J. (1999). Being in the present moment: developing the capacity for mindfulness in medicine. *Academic Medicine, 74*, 420–424.

Davidson, R. J., Dunne, J., Eccles, J. S., Engle, A., Greenberg, M., Jennings, P., et al. (2012). Contemplative practices and mental training: Prospects for American education. *Child Development Perspectives, 6*(2), 146–153.

de Vibe, M., Solhaug, I., Rosenvinge, J. H., Tyssen, R., Hanley, A., & Garland, E. (2018). Six-year positive effects of a mindfulness-based intervention on mindfulness, coping and well-being in medical and psychology students: results from a randomized controlled trial. *PLoS One, 13*, e0196053.

Dharmawardene, M., Givens, J., Wachholtz, A., Makowski, S., & Tjia, J. (2016). A systematic review and meta-analysis of meditative interventions for informal caregivers and health professionals. *BMJ Supportive & Palliative Care, 6*(2), 160–169. https://doi.org/10.1136/bmjspcare-2014-000819

Epstein, R. M. (1999). Mindful practice. *Journal of the American Medical Association, 282*, 833–839.

Kabat-Zinn, J., & Hanh, T. N. (2009). *Full catastrophe living: Using the wisdom of your body and mind to face stress, pain, and illness* (15th ed.). New York: Delta.

Foureur, M., Besley, K., Burton, G., Yu, N., & Crisp, J. (2013). Enhancing the resilience of nurses and midwives: Pilot of a mindfulness based program for increased health, sense of coherence and decreased depression, anxiety and stress. *Contemporary Nurse, 45*, 114–125. https://doi.org/10.5172/conu.2013.45.1.114

Heckenberg, R. A., Eddy, P., Kent, S., & Wright, B. (2018). Do workplace-based mindfulness meditation programs improve physiological indices of stress? A systematic review and meta-analysis. *Journal of Psychosomatic Research, 114*, 62–71.

Henrich, J., Heine, S. J., & Norenzayan, A. (2010). Most people are not WEIRD. *Nature, 466*(7302), 29–29.

Khoury, B., Sharma, M., Rush, S. E., & Fournier, C. (2015). Mindfulness-based stress reduction for healthy individuals: A meta-analysis. *Journal of Psychosomatic Research, 78*, 519–528.

Krasner, M., Epstein, R., Beckman, H., Suchman, A., Mooney, C., & Quill, T. (2009). Association of an educational program in mindful communication with burnout, empathy and attitudes among primary care physicians. *Journal of the American Medical Association, 302*, 1284–1293.

Lomas, T., Medina, J. C., Ivtzan, I., Rupprecht, S., & Eiroa-Orosa, F. J. (2019). Mindfulness-based interventions in the workplace: An inclusive systematic review and meta-analysis of their impact upon wellbeing. *The Journal of Positive Psychology, 14*(5), 625–640.

Petrie, K., Crawford, J., Baker, S. T. E., Dean, K., Robinson, J., Veness, B. G., et al. (2019). Interventions to reduce symptoms of common mental disorders and suicidal ideation in physicians: a systematic review and meta-analysis. *The Lancet Psychiatry, 6*(3), 225–234. https://doi.org/10.1016/S2215-0366(18)30509-1

Regehr, C., Glancy, D., Pitts, A., & Le Blanc, V. (2014). Interventions to reduce the consequences of stress in physicians: A review and meta-analysis. *Journal of Nervous and Mental Disease, 202*, 353–359.

Scheepers, R. A., Emke, H., Esptein, R. M., & Lombarts, K. M. J. H. (2019). The impact of mindfulness-based interventions on doctors' well-being and performance: A systematic review. *Medical Education, 54*, 138–149.

Slemp, G. R., Jach, H. K., Chia, A., Loton, D., & Kern, M. L. (2019). Contemplative interventions and employee distress: A meta-analysis. *Stress & Health, 35*, 227–225.

Spinelli, C., Wiserner, M., & Khoury, B. (2019). Mindfulness training for healthcare professionals and trainees: A meta-analysis of randomized controlled trials. *Journal of Psychosomatic Research, 120*, 29–38.

Virgili, M. (2015). Mindfulness-based interventions reduce psychological distress in working adults: A meta-analysis of intervention studies. *Mindfulness, 6*, 326. https://doi.org/10.1007/s12671-013-0264-0

Chapter 20
Using Transformative Learning to Develop Skills for Managing Conflict: Lessons Learnt over 10 Years

Eva Doherty

Incivility and conflict between healthcare workers is commonplace in hospitals and other healthcare environments. Learning how to manage conflict is not routinely taught in education and training programmes for either undergraduate or postgraduate health professionals perhaps because the educators themselves are conflict averse (Andrew, 1999). Psychologists have an important contribution to offer as there is a body of knowledge that they can utilise. This chapter will describe how a 1-day training programme was designed and delivered to equip doctors with the knowledge and skills to manage incivility and conflict in their workplace. An overview of research and evidence regarding the psychological impact of incivility on healthcare professionals' well-being and the implications for patient safety will be followed by a detailed description of the programme and learning activities. The programme has been delivered for 10 years at a national centre for postgraduate surgical training.

Incivility and rudeness in the workplace is due to a multitude of environmental and human factors. Lack of personnel, crowded departments and poor work and learning conditions all contribute (Montgomery, 2014; Panagioti et al., 2017). It is likely that the majority of health professionals do not intend to be difficult and may not have insight into how others feel after their interactions (Kline & Lewis, 2019). For example, junior doctors expect that they will have to accept being the target of rude, aggressive and dismissive behavior (Bradley et al., 2015; Coakley, O'Leary, & Bennett, 2019). Healthcare environments are commonly not psychologically safe resulting in fear of the possibility of a negative consequence which might follow an attempt to resist such behavior (Edmondson, 1999).

E. Doherty (✉)
National Surgical Training Centre, RCSI University of Medicine and Health Sciences, Dublin, Ireland
e-mail: edoherty@rcsi.ie

Conflict is related to a lack of trust and connectiveness amongst healthcare professionals which is observed in individuals experiencing burnout (Chan, Bakewell, Orlich, & Sherbino, 2014; Shanafelt & Noseworthy, 2017). Individuals who are not engaged are at risk of encountering difficult communication issues with colleagues (Pearson, Andersson, & Porath, 2005). It may follow that training junior doctors in the skills of managing conflict may lead to improvements in engagement with colleagues and reductions in burnout and lower levels of stress. Stress can be understood as equivalent to the emotional exhaustion component of burnout (Maslach & Leiter, 2017) and elevated emotional exhaustion scores on the Maslach Burnout Inventory (MBI; Maslach, Jackson, & Leiter, 1996) are the first signs that an individual may be at risk for eventual burnout.

While learning techniques to manage stress can potentially prevent individuals becoming burnt out, Christina Maslach and Michael Leiter have identified six toxic factors which when present in the work environments will trigger burnout (Leiter & Maslach, 2005). These toxic factors are: an unreasonable workload; lack of opportunities for personal autonomy at work; a lack of community and sense of trust in the workplace; evidence that personal values and ethics are not upheld; elements of the workplace which feel unfair and finally a lack of reward and recognition. These factors trigger frustration and stress and the acquisition of skills which facilitate the recognition and self-regulation of these strong emotions are key components of the ability to resolve conflict.

The ability to distinguish between oppositional behaviours that are incidents of conflict or of bullying is an important skill and bullying in the healthcare work environment is also a significant issue and is associated with threats to patient safety, absenteeism and poor performance (Cullati et al., 2019; Dewa, Loong, Bonato, & Trojanowski, 2017; Kline & Lewis, 2019; Porath & Pearson, 2013; Riskin et al., 2015; Shanafelt & Noseworthy, 2017; West et al., 2006). Workplace bullying has been defined as

> ...harassing, offending, socially excluding someone or negatively affecting someone's work tasks...it has to occur repeatedly and regularly...and over a period of time. Bullying is an escalating process in the course of which the person confronted ends up in an inferior position and becomes the target of systematic negative social acts. (Einarsen, Hoel, Zapf, & Cooper, 2003, p. 15).

Thus bullying differs from conflict in that the target of the bullying behaviour ends up in an inferior position whereas conflict can occur between two or more individuals who are equals. While responses to bullying require different strategies to those required to resolve a conflict, nevertheless, acquiring the skills of conflict resolution can help (Illing et al., 2013).

Jan Illing and colleagues have summarised the evidence for the effectiveness of conflict resolution training programmes in their report on bullying behaviour for the National Health Service (NHS) in the United Kingdom (UK) (Illing et al., 2013). The authors conducted a systematic review of the literature and found eight examples of conflict management programmes. None reviewed provide detail regarding the actual programme content but merely refer to the use of techniques such as role-plays, case studies and problem-solving. Only one intervention was evaluated by direct observation of behaviour in the workplace, the remainder relied on participants' self-reports of perceived benefits. The report concluded that while there was some evidence for a perceived improvement in conflict resolution skills, the evidence could not be considered robust. There is a scarcity of literature on this topic and even less information available regarding programme content to assist the educator. A Cochrane review of randomised and controlled studies of interventions to prevent bullying identified only five studies. Two of these known as the CREW studies and reported below were classified as interventions aimed at the organisational level and found improvements in self-reported civility by about 5% and a reported reduction in time off work by a third of a day per month. Two further studies were identified which delivered interventions at the individual level. One of these found a reduction in reported sense of victimisation and one did not find any changes in self-reported reports of victimisation or perpetration. Finally a programme which was aimed at both the individual level and also at the policies of five organisations failed to demonstrate improvements in self-reported victimisation or perpetration. The authors found that all studies were liable to a high degree of bias and concluded that they had failed to identify an intervention with strong evidence of proven efficacy (Gillen, Sinclair, Kernohan, Begley, & Luyben, 2017). Despite this lack of robust evidence for what works best, there is a reported need for training and intervention in conflict management (Kfouri & Lee, 2019). A number of leading interventions in the field are briefly reviewed below. These interventions have been chosen because the academic publications associated with them are highly cited.

Michael Leiter and colleagues have developed a specific programme called CREW which stands for Civility, Respect and Engagement at Work (Leiter, Laschinger, Day, & Gilin-Oore, 2011; Osatuke et al., 2009). The intervention uses a therapeutic model similar to that used in family therapy (Michael Leiter, personal communication 2019) and as such it is not possible to prescribe the programme in advance as it depends on the needs and goals of the participants. It has been well evaluated and there is some evidence for its efficacy as reported by the authors of the Cochrane review summarised above (Hodgins, MacCurtain, & Mannix-McNamara, 2019; Leiter, Day, Gilin-Oore, & Laschinger, 2012).

Another example of a highly cited intervention is the Vanderbilt model which targets bullying and disruptive behaviours and features 'graduated interventions: informal conversations for single incidents, nonpunitive "awareness" interventions when data reveals patterns, leader-developed action plans if patterns persist, and imposition of disciplinary processes if the plans fail' (Hickson, Pichert, Webb, & Gabbe, 2007, p. 1040). Chris Turner, a consultant Emergency Medicine doctor in Coventry, United Kingdom and author of the website www.civilitysaveslives.com is an advocate of this approach.

Finally, an example of a programme named a Bystander Intervention programme targets the problem of bullying in all its forms and is available as a one-hour intervention package designed and delivered by a commercial company (http://www.activebystander.co.uk/). Evidence for the effectiveness of the intervention has not been published however the programme has been delivered to 5000 healthcare workers at Imperial College, United Kingdom (https://www.imperial.ac.uk/engineering/staff/human-resources/active-bystander/).

A useful resource for more detailed course descriptions regarding teaching content and resources is MedEd Portal (https://www.mededportal.org/) which is a peer-reviewed, open-access online website/journal that promotes educational scholarship and dissemination of teaching and assessment resources in the health professions. At the time of writing, there were 11 programmes available under the search headings 'conflict resolution/conflict management'. Three of these describe three to four hour symposia and the remaining resources are case studies for use in training.

This brief review of examples of interventions serves to provide the reader with a sense of the landscape in advance of the description of the programme designed and delivered at the RCSI University of Medicine and Health Sciences, Dublin, Ireland. The programmes have advantages and varying levels of evidence however none were suitable for our specific requirements which was a 1 day training workshop which we could run in our educational facility and which would motivate and trigger learning and hopefully behaviour change. The aims of the programme are:

1. To explore the real life communication challenges faced by healthcare workers with their colleagues
2. To increase trainees' awareness of the detrimental effect that conflict and bullying can have on healthcare professionals and on patient safety.
3. To introduce the strategies and techniques which have been shown to be useful in high conflict situations
4. To allow trainees the opportunity to practice conflict resolution techniques using role play.
5. To introduce structured handover and discuss how structured handover can be supported within the confines of a busy workload

Our training programme follows a transformative learning theoretical model which informs all the human factors in patient safety training for doctors studying at RCSI. The model was chosen because it offers educators with a framework which they can use to develop strategies to promote experiential, practical and applied learning tailored to the learning preferences of doctors. The theory defines learning as a process which helps adult learners to transform their beliefs and feelings through reflection on the content and process by which they were learnt. Transformative learning means that the learner's paradigm undergoes radical change. Critical reflection and rational discourse are the primary processes used in learning. Learners should feel empowered and safe to uncover distorted assumptions and create new paradigms. To be successful, learners should feel supported by skilled facilitators who both challenge their existing beliefs and provide alternative perspectives. A transformative model recommends a variety of learning activities to promote the creation of new paradigms. These include rational discourse, role-playing, simulations and games, case studies, reflection exercises and experience with critical incidents and feedback. For more on this model, the reader is referred to Mezirow, Brookfield, and Candy (1990). Mindful of this model, it was clear that the day would require an element of rational discourse with some simulation and games to trigger emotional responses and a motivation to reconsider existing paradigms.

20.1 Course Components

The day is divided into three components:

- Introduction and discussion of personal experiences of conflict
- A conflict game, and description of a model of negotiation and human manipulation tricks
- Small group work using simulated conflict scenarios with skills rehearsal

The course takes place as one of three training days in the first year of the Human Factors in Patient Safety programme at RCSI. Trainees who are accepted to postgraduate training must attend these training days in addition to technical skills training days at the college. Trainees are on surgical, radiology and emergency medicine training programmes. In addition the programme includes trainees from the College of Surgeons and Physicians in Pakistan who come to Ireland for 2 years training. The Human Factors in Patient Safety programme is delivered over 8 years with 2–3 days training each year. This results in approximately 160 h of face-to-face training in small groups. Topics include, health communication, error and safety, stress management, decision-making, coping with an adverse event, open disclosure, leadership and teamwork. The name of the day in which conflict resolution is introduced for the first time in first year is 'Professional Interactions'. The topic is revisited during the 8 years in various other contexts in order to reinforce learning. Class size of the first training day on the topic is limited to 25 trainees. The mix of disciplines allows for reflection in real time on the conflicts which commonly arise between disciplines and professions. Anecdotally, trainees have reported that learning together in this way helps to forge good relationships outside the learning environment in the hospitals and that conflicts are uncommon between doctors who recognise each other from their 'human factors' classes.

The furniture in the training room is organised in a particular way. Tables are grouped together in what has come to be known as 'cabaret style' in the college. This results in ready-made small groups of approximately six trainees who are seated around four small desks and who can easily turn to each other for small group activities. Faculty always comprises of an expert in human behaviour, usually a psychologist and consultants representative of all disciplines.

20.2 Introduction and Discussion of Personal Experiences of Conflict

The introductions at the beginning of each day are regarded as an integral component of the desired learning environment. Faculty introduce themselves every day over the 8 years of the programme even when they know the trainees well. Trainees introduce themselves, the programme they are on and the hospital in which they are currently working. These introductions help to break the ice and model effective communication in agreement with the #hello my name is campaign initiated by Dr Kate Granger MBE. Dr Granger was a neurologist and a patient herself in the UK who started the movement on Twitter to bring attention to the lack of introductions which healthcare personnel offered her during her treatment (https://www.hellomynameis.org.uk/).

Objectives for the day are presented, confidentiality is assured and an amusing video is shown. An example is a clip from the British comedy group, Monty Python which makes fun of arguments (https://www.youtube.com/watch?v=xpAvcGcEc0k). The group's reaction to these videos gives a good indicator of the emotional energy in the room and helps to set the scene.

20.2.1 Personal Experiences

Following this, the trainees are invited to recount an experience of a conflict to each other in their small groups. The identity of the hospital and individuals are kept anonymous. A period of 20 min is given for this activity and then the experiences are debriefed. The focus of the debrief is to empathise with the impact on the individual and then to ask whether with hindsight, something could have prevented the conflict. Differing perspectives are made explicit and faculty discuss possible alternatives to resolution. This is particularly useful when the conflict concerned is one between a surgeon and an emergency medicine doctor or a radiologist as the consultants present can demonstrate how these perspectives can be resolved in the best interest of the patient concerned. Learning points encountered in this session are reiterated throughout the day. Frequently trainees will verbalise their perspectives and these will be reinforced. Insights which learners verbalise in the classroom are regarded as very powerful as they represent peer to peer modelling. Transformative learning theory advocates the facilitation of learners to come up with their own decisions (Mezirow et al., 1990).

Care is taken to distinguish between experiences which are examples of conflict between two equals and experiences which are an example of bullying in which one or more of the individuals are taking advantage of their status in order to attempt to control the victim. Bullying is addressed in the third phase of the day along with the section on manipulation techniques. As the debrief can be quite emotional and participants often need a time out, it is followed by a coffee break.

20.3 A Conflict Game, and Description of a Model of Negotiation and Human Manipulations Tricks

Following coffee, an exercise designed to demonstrate the importance of differing perspectives and also to demonstrate differing reactions to conflict is demonstrated. This exercise can be run with eight or ten trainees or the whole group. Trainees are asked to stand opposite each other with a small table in between them. A flip chart page is available on each table with one thick marker to share. Trainees are instructed that the exercise is to demonstrate non-verbal communication and so instructions will be distributed silently to each trainee. Once instructions are given, all verbal communication is not permitted. The written instructions invite the participants to draw an object using one marker between each pair. They are told that they may not lift the marker. One half of the pairs are told to draw a house and the other half is told to draw an elephant. Instructions should be collected quickly after they have been read in case trainees attempt to share the instruction sheets. Conflict is inevitable as each trainee in each pair attempts to draw something different. Participants frequently start to laugh as they realise the conflict. The rest of the group, the observers, are often confused about the purpose of the exercise but are amused by the laughing. A debrief follows which involves asking each member of each pair to speak about their experience and the resulting drawing can be held up for all to see. Frequently one trainee does not get to draw their object at all and this is an example of conflict avoidance. What is most common is some kind of a hybrid with features of both a house and an elephant and this is identified as collaboration. Sometimes the conflict can be quite intense and holes in the paper can result much to the amusement of the trainees and observers. Even if trainees correctly guess when they read the instructions that the exercise is a conflict, learning still results because this demonstrates the value of realising that differing perspectives may exist. This exercise was sourced from and is described here with kind permission of Dr. Ron Epstein from the University of Rochester School of Medicine, United States.

The Harvard model of the principles of successful negotiation is next presented using Powerpoint slides (Fisher & Ury, 1981; Ury, 1991). The potential for the application of the model to healthcare work environments is discussed with the group. The model was chosen as it is regarded to have the best applicability to the healthcare environment. It advocates four stages in the negotiation process and the authors recommend that each stage should be successfully negotiated before progression to the next stage is possible.

The first stage in the Harvard model is called *Separate the People from the Problem*. This refers to the stereotyping in which opponents can engage and applies well to the so called 'silos' in which healthcare professionals work. So nurses, doctors and healthcare workers often maintain negative stereotyped beliefs about each other which contribute to a negative bias before the interaction has even begun. The Harvard model advocates that these stereotypes and biases need to be addressed before opponents can progress to stage two which is called *Focus on Interests not Positions* which in healthcare is straightforward and will always be the patient. The third stage is called *Generate a Variety of Possibilities* and the fourth and final stage is called *Insist that the Result is based on some Objective Standard*. These last two stages are comparatively easy in healthcare and decisions made should be supported by evidence based medicine and available protocols.

The authors of the Harvard model emphasise the importance of never attempting a negotiation when angry and a short video is shown to demonstrate this principle. This video is an example of animal research and is described by psychologist Dr. Frans de Waal. The brief video depicts an experiment between two monkeys, one of whom is being treated unfairly in that she receives a less than favourable reward compared to the monkey in the adjacent cage, This amusing video also facilitates the learning point that when human beings are angry they are 'hijacked' by their limbic system (https://www.youtube.com/watch?v=meiU6TxysCg).

The next learning point concerns human manipulation tactics which can escalate conversations to become hostile. Manipulations are attempts by individuals to control another individual's behaviour by triggering the fear response. They work because human beings will automatically respond to reduce the feeling of fear. This is a concept well known and used by the advertising industry. The authority card e.g. *We have always Done it this Way*, *FUD* (Fear, Uncertainty, Doubt) e.g. 'This patient is very sick and needs attention immediately', are two of the most commonly used and usually result in a 'knee jerk' reaction which the individual who takes the bait subsequently regrets. It is particularly damaging to working relationships and the break in trust which results is often never repaired or addressed.

Other manipulations include statements which begin with; 'with respect or no offence but....'; forcing a choice when other options are available e.g. 'Look you are either for this or against this'; repeating the same sentence ('please come and see the patient, please come and see the patient...'); pointing out someone's mistake as a way of weakening their position and a number of others. With each manipulation, the recommended strategy is not to take the bait and to attempt to side step the manipulation. At times it may be appropriate to ask for evidence for the claim or to acknowledge the situations in which the individual's position may be the correct one. Care should be taken to avoid the use of the word 'but' in these conversations and to replace this word with the word 'and' which has the effect of including the opponent rather than dismissing their perspective. The content for this section was sourced from Pierce (2003).

When the conflict is regarded as bullying then different strategies are required. In the first instance, it may be necessary to call out what is happening by asserting oneself and pointing out the inappropriate nature of the behavior. This may be something that the victim of the bullying may have to work up to and may require support from others. Other strategies include reporting the behaviour to the Human Resources department or to a confidential helpline. If the bullying is more subtle then more subtle strategies may be necessary to distract from what is occurring. Examples of this might be pretending to take a phone call to break up the conversation or pretending that the insult has been misinterpreted in some way.

20.4 Indian Talking Stick

Steven Covey, an American educator developed this strategy to manage conflict. A three minute video explains the technique which he was taught by a Navajo American Indian (https://www.youtube.com/watch?v=7Jl0S6kTf2g). Essentially it requires the listener to repeat back what the speaker has just said before stating their own point of view. Participating in a negotiation using this technique demonstrates that listening is a skill in itself and one which is often not practiced when arguing. It also demonstrates how validating it is to hear one's view repeated back and how the validation experienced contributes to a preparedness to compromise. The exercise relies on the use of a neutral scenario which will trigger different perspectives and will not offend the audience. There are two narratives which have been found to work and to be inoffensive. The first story is about a veteran soldier who has fallen on hard times and eventually gets into a fight in a bar and kills another man. He is imprisoned for manslaughter and subsequently escapes before completion of the sentence but is recaptured and now needs to be sanctioned. The second story concerns a group of holiday makers travelling in a jeep who get stranded in the jungle and need to make their way back to safety. One option is treacherous but quick and the second option is safer but will take much longer and they have no food and very little water.

The stories can be embellished as desired and the group are asked to decide what they think is best. Individuals with opposing views are asked to come together in pairs to negotiate a solution using the Indian talking stick technique and then debriefed.

All of what has been described above can be completed in a four hour session. The afternoon session subsequently offers trainees the opportunity to rehearse the principles discussed in the morning. Three commonly occurring scenarios in addition to a discussion session (Scenario 4 below) have been tried and tested over the years. They require differing levels of fidelity and teachers may have to be creative in creating these scenarios in their own learning environments. Each scenario should run for ten minutes and debriefed by skilled facilitators for 20 min. Our facilitators are trained in the use of the *Advocacy –Inquiry* (AI) method of debriefing with *Good Judgement* (Rudolph, Simon, Rivard, Dufresne, & Raemer, 2007). The AI method focusses on eliciting the perspective of the learner which motivated the observed action. The AI model is based on the assumption that there is an explanation for every behavior and that it is necessary to elicit these perspectives in order to facilitate reflection and discussion. The class is divided into four groups and each group rotates around each scenario every 30 min. Following this a plenary session with the larger group to identify the principle learning points completes the day.

20.5 Small Group Work Using Simulated Conflict Scenarios with Skills Rehearsal

20.5.1 Scenario 1

In this scenario, a mock operating theatre is used as the background context. A model of a human head from a technical training skills laboratory is used with the body simulated with a duvet /blankets/pillows and operating theatre draping. A skin pad requiring suturing is used with a balloon secured behind the pad. Two volunteer trainees are instructed to suture the skin pad as best they can. The attending Anaesthesiologist (a confederate) is behind the 'blood-brain' barrier and plays the part of someone who is irritable about the number of patients remaining on the list for theatre. The Anaesthesiologist calls to the circulating nurse (also a confederate) to 'call for the next patient' and proceeds to put the trainee under pressure to hurry up. If the trainee gets flustered and attempts to speed up there is a possibility that the balloon will burst and the task will not be achieved. The debrief focuses on the skills of assertiveness with a senior colleague. Reactions are sought from the trainees in the 'hot seat' and also from the rest of the small group.

20.5.2 Scenario 2

In this scenario, a radiologist (played by a faculty member) refuses to agree to carry out a scan on a number of patients following a request from the junior doctor. Successful negotiation requires an empathic response and an explicit use of stage two of the Harvard model (i.e. what are the shared interests).

20.5.3 Scenario 3

In this scenario, trainees are instructed that they have been incorrectly allocated to work a weekend in a rota from which they have previously requested to be excluded. The reason is that they need to travel to their training college to sit a very important examination on the Monday morning. This scenario can trigger very strong emotional reactions in the group as it reflects real life experiences in the workplace and frequently the facilitator will opt not to run the role play. This models the principle that if one is angry, one should wait until the emotion has abated before attempting a negotiation. Sometimes there will be one trainee in the group who is not angry and who easily demonstrates the desired skills to reach the resolution. The debrief then focuses on this principle as advocated in the Harvard model and discussed at the earlier session.

20.5.4 Scenario 4

This scenario is designed to demonstrate the effectiveness of using a model for handover which minimises both the opportunities for misunderstanding as well as conflict. The Department of Health National Guideline on Handover (National Clinical Effectiveness Committee, Ireland, 2015) commissioned a systematic review of the literature and has advocated the use of the ISBAR$_3$ model. ISBAR$_3$ is an aide memoire and the letters stand for; Identify (i.e. self and patient); Situation (i.e. presenting problem); Background (i.e. history of presenting problem and other relevant information); Assessment (i.e. Diagnosis or assessment of the problem); Recommendation (i.e. what needs to be done); Read Back (i.e. recipient repeats a brief summary of what has been communicated so far); Risk (i.e. both parties agree on the factors which may threaten implementation of the recommendation). While most health professionals are familiar with the principle of ISBAR, few appreciate the value of the last two 'Rs' i.e. *Read Back and Risk*. *Read Back* requires the repetition of the information which has just been given and *Risk* refers to the identification of any risks to implementing the recommendations. We like to draw the analogy with what is practiced in many restaurants, where a food order is repeated back to check for errors. To trigger interest in the framework, two examples are given and discussed by a facilitator who is a consultant surgeon and this brings fidelity to the cases. The first case is a true story of a patient who died of sepsis following a series of lost opportunities for effective handover. The second case is a video from Australia depicting a phone call in the middle of the night to a consultant (https://www.youtube.com/watch?v=1Wl9qogPw1E). The junior doctor initially gives the information about the patient in a muddled fashion and when he encounters the consultant's irritable response, he quickly reverts to using ISBAR. Different jurisdictions and specialities use different frameworks for handover however the principle of repeating back what has been heard is associated with the best evidence. It also allows the reiteration of the principle of the 'Indian Talking stick' practiced in the morning session.

20.5.5 Plenary

The group are brought back together for a brief plenary and summary of take home learning points. The programme is consistently rated a mean satisfaction score of between 4 and 5 by participants on a 5 point scale. Ten years running this programme has demonstrated that participants both enjoy and learn from the activities. We aim to provide an appropriate and sensitive learning environment which will serve to enhance trainees' skills and equip them to manage conflict in their workplace. Obtaining the evidence of the programme's efficacy to improve doctors' well-being and patient safety is challenging given the competing forces of the work environments in which these doctors work. They are distributed across 26 hospital

Table 20.1 Key messages for researchers

• Acts of incivility in the workplace are a key element of stress and lack of engagement for health care workers. The evidence that skills training leads to a significant reduction in these behaviors is yet to be demonstrated. Outcome measures should include both participant reports of these behaviors and patient outcomes. Large scale surveys using valid measures of observed behaviors in the workplace should be conducted to evaluate change
• Providing support and skills training for healthcare workers to manage conflict is intuitively beneficial, however organizational change which is directed at incivility in the workplace would supplement and greatly enhance these skills

Table 20.2 Key messages for healthcare delivery

• Incivility in the workplace is associated with impaired performance and unsafe care for patients however detailed content of training programmes to address these behaviors are not available. Modelling good conflict resolution skills and empowering juniors to assert their views to seniors is important not only for doctors' well-being but also ultimately for patient safety
• The programme described has been delivered for 10 years in a postgraduate surgical college and can be easily adapted to suit the requirements of a team, department or organization. Many of the activities described are already in use in some institutions and are delivered in training programs of shorter duration

sites nationwide, and are rotated through these hospitals every 6 months. Small groups of them are attached to large medical and surgical teams each with their own demands and cultures. Notwithstanding this, we are optimistic that the working climate can improve through the consistent use of these strategies in tandem with changes to the organisational culture (Tables 20.1 and 20.2).

References

Andrew, L. B. (1999). Conflict management, prevention and resolution in medical settings. *Physician Executive, 25*, 38–42.
Bradley, V., Liddle, S., Shaw, R., Savage, E., Rabbitts, R., Trim, C., et al. (2015). Sticks and stones: Investigating rude, dismissive and aggressive communication between doctors. *Clinical Medicine London, 15*(6), 541–545. https://doi.org/10.7861/clinmedicine.15-6-541
Chan, T., Bakewell, F., Orlich, D., & Sherbino, J. (2014). Conflict prevention, conflict mitigation, and manifestations of conflict during emergency department consultations. *Academic Emergency Medicine, 21*, 308–313. https://doi.org/10.1111/acem.12325
Coakley, N., O'Leary, P., & Bennett, D. (2019). 'Waiting in the wings'; lived experience at the threshold of clinical practice. *Medical Education, 53*(7), 698–709. https://doi.org/10.1111/medu.13899
Cullati, S., Bochatay, N., Maître, F., Laroche, T., Muller-Juge, V., Blondon, K. S., et al. (2019). When team conflicts threaten quality of care: a study of health care professionals' experiences and perceptions. *Mayo Clinic Proceedings, Innovations, Quality & Outcomes, 3*(1), 43–51. https://doi.org/10.1016/j.mayocpiqo.2018.11.003
Dewa, C. S., Loong, D., Bonato, S., & Trojanowski, L. (2017). The relationship between physician burnout and quality of healthcare in terms of safety and acceptability: a systematic review. *BMJ Open, 7*(6), e015141. https://doi.org/10.1136/bmjopen-2016-015141

Edmondson, A. (1999). Psychological safety and learning behavior in work teams. *Administrative Science Quarterly, 44*, 350–383.

Einarsen, S., Hoel, H., Zapf, D., & Cooper, C.L. (2003). The concept of bullying at work: The European tradition. In S. Einarsen, H. Hoel, D. Zapf, & C. L. Cooper (Eds.), *Bullying and emotional abuse in the workplace: International perspectives in research and practice* (pp. 3–30). London: Taylor & Francis.

Fisher, R., & Ury, W. (1981). *Getting to yes*. Boston: Houghton Mifflin.

Gillen, P. A., Sinclair, M., Kernohan, W. G., Begley, C. M., Luyben, A. G. (2017). Interventions for prevention of bullying in the workplace. *Cochrane Database of Systematic Reviews*, (1), Art No: CD009778. https://doi.org/10.1002/14651858.CD009778.pub2

Hickson, G. B., Pichert, J. W., Webb, L. E., & Gabbe, S. G. (2007). A complementary approach to promoting professionalism: identifying, measuring, and addressing unprofessional behaviors. *Academic Medicine, 82*, 1040–1048. https://doi.org/10.1097/ACM.0b013e31815761ee

Hodgins, M., MacCurtain, S., & Mannix-McNamara, P. (2019). Workplace bullying and incivility: A systematic review of interventions. *International Journal of Workplace Health Management, 7*(1), 54–72. https://doi.org/10.1108/IJWHM-08-2013-0030

Illing, J., Carter, M., Thompson, N. J., Crampton, P. E. S., Morrow, G. M., Howse, J. H., et al. (2013). *Evidence synthesis on the occurrence, causes, consequences, prevention and management of bullying and harassing behaviours to inform decision-making in the NHS. Project Report*. London: HMSO.

Kfouri, J., & Lee, P. E. (2019). Conflict among colleagues: health care providers feel undertrained and unprepared to manage inevitable workplace conflict. *Journal of Obstetrics and Gynaecology, Canada, 41*(1), 15–20. https://doi.org/10.1016/j.jogc.2018.03.132

Kline, R., & Lewis, D. (2019). The price of fear: Estimating the financial cost of bullying and harassment to the NHS in England. *Public Money & Management, 39*(3), 166–174. https://doi.org/10.1080/09540962.2018.1535044

Leiter, M., Day, A., GilinOore, D., & Laschinger, H. K. S. (2012). Getting better and staying better: assessing civility, incivility, distress, and job attitudes one year after a civility intervention. *Journal of Occupational Health Psychology, 17*(4), 425–434. https://doi.org/10.1037/a0029540

Leiter, M. P., Laschinger, H. K. S., Day, A., & Gilin-Oore, D. (2011). The impact of civility interventions on employee social behavior, distress, and attitudes. *Journal of Applied Psychology, 96*, 1258–1274. https://doi.org/10.1037/a0024442

Leiter, M. P., & Maslach, C. (2005). A mediation model of job burnout. In A. S. G. Antoniou & C. L. Cooper (Eds.), *Research companion to organizational health psychology* (pp. 544–564). Cheltenham, UK: Edward Elgar. Retrieved from https://www.researchgate.net/publication/232511448_A_mediation_model_of_job_burnout

Maslach, C., Jackson, S., & Leiter, M. (1996). *Maslach burnout inventory manual* (3rd edn). Mountain View, CA: CPP.

Maslach, C., & Leiter, M. P. (2017). New insights into burnout and health care: Strategies for improving civility and alleviating burnout. *Medical Teacher, 39*(2), 160–163. https://doi.org/10.1080/0142159X.2016.1248918

Mezirow, J., Brookfield, S. D., & Candy, C. (1990). *Fostering Critical Reflection in Adulthood*. San Francisco, CA: Jossey-Bass.

Montgomery, A. (2014). The inevitability of physician burnout: implications for interventions. *Burnout Research, 1*, 50–56. https://doi.org/10.1016/j.burn.2014.04.002

National Clinical Effectiveness Committee. (2015). Communication (clinical handover) in acute and children's hospital services. National Clinical Guidelines No. 11. Ireland: Department of Health.

Osatuke, K., Mohr, D., Ward, C., Moore, S. C., Dyrenforth, S., & Belton, L. (2009). Civility, respect, engagement in the workforce (CREW): Nationwide organization development intervention at Veterans Health Administration. *Journal of Applied Behavioral Science, 45*, 384–410. https://doi.org/10.1177/0021886309335067

Panagioti, M., Panagopoulou, E., Bower, P., Lewith, G., Kontopantelis, E., Chew-Graham, C., et al. (2017). Controlled interventions to reduce burnout in physicians: A systematic review and meta-analysis. *Journal of the American Medical Association, Internal Medicine, 177*, 195–205. https://doi.org/10.1371/journal.pone.0196888

Pearson, C., Andersson, L., & Porath, C. (2005). Workplace incivility. In S. Fox & P. E. Spector (Eds.), *Counterproductive work behavior: Investigations of actors and targets*. Washington, DC: American Psychological Association. https://doi.org/10.1037/10893-008

Pierce, V. (2003). *Quick thinking on your feet*. Dublin: Mercier Press.

Porath, C., & Pearson, C. (2013). The price of incivility. *Harvard Business Review, 91*(1–2), 114–121, 146. PMID: 23390745.

Riskin, A., Erez, A., Foulk, T. A., Kugelman, A., Gover, A., Shoris, I., et al. (2015). The impact of rudeness on medical team performance: A randomized trial. *Paediatrics, 136*, 487–495. https://doi.org/10.1542/peds.2015-1385

Rudolph, J. W., Simon, R., Rivard, P., Dufresne, R. L., & Raemer, D. B. (2007). Debriefing with good judgement: combining rigorous feedback with genuine inquiry. *Anaesthesiology Clinics, 25*(2), 361–376. https://doi.org/10.1016/j.anclin.2007.03.007

Shanafelt, T. D., & Noseworthy, J. H. (2017). Executive leadership and physician well-being: nine organizational strategies to promote engagement and reduce burnout. *Mayo Clinical Proceedings, 92*(1), 129–146. https://doi.org/10.1016/j.mayocp.2016.10.004

Ury, W. (1991). *Getting past no: Negotiating with difficult people*. New York: Bantam Books.

West, C. P., Huschka, M. M., Novotny, P. J., Sloan, J. A., Kolars, J. C., Habermann, T. M., et al. (2006). Association of perceived medical errors with resident distress and empathy: A prospective longitudinal study. *Journal of the American Medical Association, 296*(9), 1071–1078. https://doi.org/10.1001/jama.296.9.1071

Chapter 21
Well-Being, Patient Safety and Organizational Change: Quo Vadis?

Anthony J. Montgomery

This book grew out of the WELLMED Network. WELLMED is devoted to examining the connection between well-being and performance in clinical practice. The WELLMED network conducts research aimed at exploring how burnout and wellbeing are related to different aspects of quality of care and patient safety, in terms of clinical decision making, communication in clinical practice, medical errors, civility at the workplace, and patient neglect. To date, WELLMED has held three international conferences, and this book evolved out of the many conversations between the participants over the three conferences. The aim of the book was to take stock of where the field stands, and signpost future areas for research. To this end, the book has provided comprehensive coverage of the myriad factors that influence the nexus between healthcare worker well-being, patient safety and organizational change. Each chapter provides key messages for researchers and healthcare delivery. Analysis of these recommendations provides us with an appropriate way to delineate the future directions for the field, and answer the call of *Quo Vadis*.

Part I was concerned with linking organizational factors to healthcare worker well-being and patient outcomes. The combined messages for future researchers are to work harder to define constructs more clearly and by doing so allow us to understand the relationship among the key variables. More specifically, the authors in this part identify areas for improvement. O'Connor, Hall and Johnson (2020) note that it is possible burnout is only associated with perceived safety, whereas wellbeing may be more strongly associated with actual safety behaviours. Teoh and Hassard (2020) warn us that there are differences in how these commonly understood constructs (i.e., organisational factors, workers' well-being, patient care) are defined and operationalised, and recommend that researchers should be clearer on how this is done and recognise any corresponding implications. Equally,

---

A. J. Montgomery (✉)
University of Macedonia, Thessaloniki, Greece

Kirwan and Matthews (2020) argue that observation methods are needed to examine more deeply if the rationing of nursing care is always a result of lack of time or resources or if other explanations are also possible. Finally, Zhou, Panagioti, and Esmail (2020) remind us that whatever interventions we develop there is still a need to undertake international evaluations that will provide evidence regarding their feasibility, acceptability and cost-effectiveness. The authors in this part remind us that while the problems are well established and accepted, there is significant room for improvement in terms of being able to outline a definitive evidence base. The messages regarding healthcare delivery include; a greater emphasis on prevention, the need to acknowledge the links between staffing levels and missed care, an avoidance of locating worker health and occupational safety in different silos, and a greater need to link worker health and patient safety to workforce planning policies.

Part II took a finer grained look at the healthcare context across the globe. The key messages for researchers concerned a more systemic look at work practices and work design. Byrne et al. (2020) advised us that future research should look at work-life boundaries and the relationship between the intensification and extensification of temporal experiences for hospital doctors and the impact this has on their working lives. Isaksson Rø, Rosta, Tyssen, and Bååthe (2020) advocated the use of interactive collaborative research, where researchers could over a prolonged time-horizon collaborate with clinicians and managers, and study how system changes (co-created by clinicians and managers) impact clinician well-being and quality of care, over time. Equally, Van Stolk and Hafner (2020) note that more research is required to identify what human resource management practices are associated with better staff engagement. Governance is considered to be a distal aspect of work design, but as noted by Bringedal, Bærøe, and Teig (2020) future research should explore more closely the scope of how non-clinical factors, such as governing instruments, impact on health care provision. Finally, Jones and Blake (2020) who reviewed the impact of a UK "Freedom to Speak Up Guardian" (FTSUG) role discovered that the UK health system is a need on considerable research on training and guidance related to dealing with bullying and harassment concerns. In terms of healthcare delivery, the aforementioned authors recommend; making work schedules less porous, the need for clinicians and managers need to engage in local system changes, understanding variability in staff engagement scores across departments, acknowledging that accountability can undermine quality of care and more joined-up thinking concerning connections between interpersonal problems and quality/safety failures.

Part III explored how cultural factors are important levers of organizational change. The chapters in this part discussed how the organization of work drives the cultures that we find in different healthcare settings. In terms of key messages for researchers, Rus, Vâjâean, Oțoiu, and Băban (2020) argue that it is important to examine when (i.e., during work and after work) and how (i.e., the mechanisms) different work recovery experiences lead to individual, team and organizational positive outcomes and reduce the negative ones in healthcare settings. Moreover, Van Bogaert, Timmermans, Slootmans, Goossens, and Franck (2020) suggests that studies are needed to understand clinical microsystems' capacity to use feedback mechanisms in order to learn, adapt and improve their work system. This is similar to the recommendation of West (2020) who suggests there is a need to develop and evaluate primary interventions focused on improving the workplace factors that influence staff stress and wellbeing. De Chant and Shannon (2020) highlight the need for researchers to develop more effective approaches to measuring the cost of burnout beyond turnover, and the return on investment of burnout reduction interventions. Congruently, Krasner and Epstein (2020) note that Mindfulness-Based Interventions vary in so many aspects. Therefore, for them to be compared, a research agenda for assessing efficacy should include a number of standard individual, team and systemic measures. In terms of healthcare delivery, the aforementioned authors recommend; supporting the use of replenishing activities to boost recovery, piloting approaches to enable mentoring styles of leadership, initiate compassionate care approaches from the top down, linking health worker health to population health policies, and designing work practices that increase the opportunities of social connectivity. Overall, the authors in this part advocate for formalizing the informal aspects of work that contribute to better well-being.

Part IV reviewed the potential for individual and organizational interventions to resolve the triple challenge of the book. The key messages for researchers concern the way that interventions are conducted. Gregory, Rothwell, and McAlearney (2020) recommend that we evaluate training programs at multiple levels (e.g., learners' reactions, learning, transfer of training, outcomes/results) and invest in assessing the impact of training on organizational and patient outcomes. Maben and Taylor (2020) suggest that future research could focus on evaluating the impact of rounds on any changes to practice and organisational culture (e.g. annual surveys of ripple effects to capture these often elusive and unreported changes). Adair, Rehder, and Sexton (2020) argue for more rigours measurement in the form of regular assessments (e.g. every 18 months) of well-being using psychometrically valid measures (e.g., emotional exhaustion, burnout climate, work-life balance) that can identify work settings at higher risk for lower engagement and professionalism (e.g., intentions to leave, turnover, disruptive behavior), as well as higher patient safety risks (e.g., infections, medication errors). Equally, Montgomery, Georganta, Gilbeth, Subramaniam, and Morgan (2020) in a review of mindfulness based interventions note that there is a significant lack of follow-up studies concerning the impact of mindfulness based interventions, which represents a significant gap in the knowledge base. Doherty (2020) reminds us that while acts of incivility in the workplace are a key element of stress and lack of engagement for health care workers, the evidence that skills training leads to a significant reduction in these behaviors is yet to be demonstrated. All authors agree on the need for better and valid research, and research designs that allow us to be more confident of recommending policies. In terms of healthcare delivery, the aforementioned authors recommend; training approaches that fits with needs of learners, providing formal and informal spaces for healthcare professionals to share stories, employing methods that allow us to identify and target struggling work units, assessing interventions for acceptability should be mandatory and correctly done, and building on what already works.

The appropriate conclusion to this review is to bring our focus back to the patient. We have accumulated enough evidence to suggest that expecting health professionals to deliver safe, efficient and patient-centered care, while they are getting more and more burnt-out, is not only ineffective but also costly and dangerous (Panagopoulou, Montgomery, & Tsiga, 2015). The authors in the book have provided recommendations as to how we can better integrate the perspective of patients into healthcare delivery and design. Zhou et al. (2020) argue that multicomponent interventions that will monitor and improve the organisational function of primary care and effectively engage health professionals and patients have the most realistic potential for improving workforce wellness. Isaksson Rø et al. (2020) suggest that the only long-term sustainable way to handle budgetary dilemmas is to improve the clinical care processes, i.e. the way people in healthcare work together, to meet the needs of patients. De Chant and Shannon (2020) put the patient experience as central and behooves us to prioritize efforts to design workflows that provide clinicians more time to directly engage with patients and less time engaged with administrative work. West (2020) reminds us that there us a symbiosis between compassionate care for patients and staff in terms of enhancing quality of care. Congruently, Maben & Taylor (2020) remind us that Schwartz rounds has the potential to share stories that can results staff feeling more connected to both colleagues and patients.

As noted by Richards (2019) health systems need to get better at collecting the experience of wide communities of patients and carers and to use this information to inform their decision making. In particular, there is a need to collect information from those who have the worst outcomes, rather than the 'typical' patient (i.e., white, educated, middle class) which the system is skewed towards. The perspective of patients and carers has the potential to be an indicator of organisational wellbeing, in terms of the organisational problems and burnout among healthcare staff. Finally, to paraphrase Nelson Mandela, healthcare (or a Nation) should not be judged by how it treats its highest citizens, but its lowest ones.

References

Adair, K. C., Rehder, K., & Sexton, J. B. (2020). How healthcare worker well-being intersects with safety culture, workforce engagement, and operational outcomes. In A. Montgomery, M. Van der Doef, E. Panagopoulou, & M. Leiter (Eds.), *Connecting health care worker well-being, patient safety and organisational change: The triple challenge* (pp. 299–318). Cham: Springer.

Bringedal, B., Bærøe, K., & Teig, I. L. (2020). Governing health care provision—clinicians' experiences. In A. Montgomery, M. Van der Doef, E. Panagopoulou, & M. Leiter (Eds.), *Connecting Health care worker well-being, patient safety and organisational change: The triple challenge* (pp. 131–144). Cham: Springer.

Byrne, J. P., Conway, E., McDermott, A., Costello, R. W., Prihodova, L., Matthews, A., & Humphries, N. (2020). Between balance and burnout: Contrasting the working-time conditions of Irish-trained hospital doctors in Ireland and Australia. In A. Montgomery, M. Van der Doef, E. Panagopoulou, & M. Leiter (Eds.) *Connecting health care worker well-being, patient safety and organisational change: The triple challenge* (pp. 75–90). Cham: Springer.

De Chant, P., & Shannon, D. (2020). Creating optimal clinical workplaces by transforming leadership and empowering clinicians. In A. Montgomery, M. Van der Doef, E. Panagopoulou, & M. Leiter (Eds.), *Connecting health care worker well-being, patient safety and organisational change: The triple challenge* (pp. 187–206). Cham: Springer.

Doherty, E. (2020). Using transformative learning to develop skills for managing conflict: Lessons learnt over ten years. In A. Montgomery, M. Van der Doef, E. Panagopoulou, & M. Leiter (Eds.) *Connecting health care worker well-being, patient safety and organisational change: The triple challenge* (pp. 331–344). Cham: Springer.

Gregory, M. E., Rothwell, C. D., & McAlearney, A. S. (2020). Training for patient safety and worker well-being in the context of organizational change. In A. Montgomery, M. Van der Doef, E. Panagopoulou, & M. Leiter (Eds.), *Connecting health care worker well-being, patient safety and organisational change: The triple challenge* (pp. 263–280). Cham: Springer.

Jones, A., & Blake, J. (2020). Speaking-up for patient safety in NHS England: is it a case of one step forward for organisational change but two steps back for staff wellbeing? In A. Montgomery, M. Van der Doef, E. Panagopoulou, & M. Leiter (Eds.), *Connecting health care worker well-being, patient safety and organisational change: The triple challenge* (pp. 145–164). Cham: Springer.

Isaksson Rø, K., Rosta, J., Tyssen, R., & Bååthe, F. (2020). Doctors well-being, quality of patient care and organizational change—Norwegian experiences. In A. Montgomery, M. Van der Doef, E. Panagopoulou, & M. Leiter (Eds.), *Connecting health care worker well-being, patient safety and organisational change: The triple challenge* (pp. 91–114). Cham: Springer.

Kirwan, M., & Matthews, A. (2020). Missed nursing care: the impact on patients, nurses and organizations. In A. Montgomery, M. Van der Doef, E. Panagopoulou, & M. Leiter (Eds.) *Connecting health care worker well-being, patient safety and organisational change: The triple challenge* (pp. 25–40). Cham: Springer.

Krasner, M. S., & Epstein, R. (2020). Mindful practice: Organizational change and health professional flourishing through cultivating presence and courageous conversations. In A. Montgomery, M. Van der Doef, E. Panagopoulou, & M. Leiter (Eds.) *Connecting health care worker well-being, patient safety and organisational change: The triple challenge* (pp. 247–260). Cham: Springer.

Maben, J., & Taylor, C. (2020). Schwartz Center Rounds: an intervention to enhance staff wellbeing and promote organisational change. In A. Montgomery, M. Van der Doef, E. Panagopoulou, & M. Leiter (Eds.) *Connecting health care worker well-being, patient safety and organisational change: The triple challenge* (pp. 281–298). Cham: Springer.

Montgomery, A., Georganta, K., Gilbeth, A., Subramaniam, Y., & Morgan, K. (2020). Mindfulness as a way to improve well-being in healthcare professionals: Separating the wheat from the chaff. In A. Montgomery, M. Van der Doef, E. Panagopoulou, & M. Leiter (Eds.), *Connecting health care worker well-being, patient safety and organisational change: The triple challenge* (pp. 319–330). Cham: Springer.

O'Connor, D. B., Johnson, J., & Hall, L. (2020). Job strain, burnout, wellbeing and patient safety. In A. Montgomery, M. Van der Doef, E. Panagopoulou, & M. Leiter (Eds.), *Connecting health care worker well-being, patient safety and organisational change: The triple challenge* (pp. 11–24). Cham: Springer.

Panagopoulou, E., Montgomery, A., & Tsiga, E. (2015). Bringing the well being and patient safety research agenda together: why healthy HPs equal safe patients. *Frontiers in Psychology, 6*, 211. https://doi.org/10.3389/fpsyg.2015.0021

Richards, T. (2019). Should patient advocates adopt guerilla tactics? *BMJ blog*. Retrieved at https://blogs.bmj.com/bmj/2019/11/26/should-patient-advocates-adopt-guerilla-tactics/

Rus, C. L., Vâjâean, C. C., Oțoiu, C., & Băban, A. (2020). Between taking care of others and yourself: The role of work recovery in health professionals. In A. Montgomery, M. Van der Doef, E. Panagopoulou, & M. Leiter (Eds.), *Connecting health care worker well-being, patient safety and organisational change: The triple challenge* (pp. 165–186). Cham: Springer.

Teoh, K., & Hassard, J. (2020). Linking organizational demands and patient care: Does healthcare workers' well-being matter? In A. Montgomery, M. Van der Doef, E. Panagopoulou, & M. Leiter (Eds.), *Connecting health care worker well-being, patient safety and organisational change: The triple challenge* (pp. 41–58). Cham: Springer.

Van Bogaert, P., Timmermans, O., Slootmans, S., Goossens, E., & Franck, E. (2020). Workforce and excellence in nursing care: Challenges for leaders and professionals. In A. Montgomery, M. Van der Doef, E. Panagopoulou, & M. Leiter (Eds.), *Connecting health care worker well-being, patient safety and organisational change: The triple challenge* (pp. 227–246). Cham: Springer.

Van Stolk, C., & Hafner, M. (2020). The relationship between employee engagement and productivity in the English National Health Service: A look at employee data in 28 healthcare organizations. In A. Montgomery, M. Van der Doef, E. Panagopoulou, & M. Leiter (Eds.), *Connecting health care worker well-being, patient safety and organisational change: The triple challenge* (pp. 115–130). Cham: Springer.

West, M. (2020). Compassionate leadership for cultures of high quality care. In A. Montgomery, M. Van der Doef, E. Panagopoulou, & M. Leiter (Eds.) *Connecting health care worker well-being, patient safety and organisational change: The triple challenge* (pp. 207–226). Cham: Springer.

Zhou, A., Panagioti, P., & Esmail, A. (2020). Burnout in primary care workforce. In A. Montgomery, M. Van der Doef, E. Panagopoulou, & M. Leiter (Eds.) *Connecting health care worker well-being, patient safety and organisational change: The triple challenge* (pp. 59–74). Cham: Springer.

GPSR Compliance
The European Union's (EU) General Product Safety Regulation (GPSR) is a set
of rules that requires consumer products to be safe and our obligations to
ensure this.

If you have any concerns about our products, you can contact us on

ProductSafety@springernature.com

In case Publisher is established outside the EU, the EU authorized
representative is:

Springer Nature Customer Service Center GmbH
Europaplatz 3
69115 Heidelberg, Germany

www.ingramcontent.com/pod-product-compliance
Ingram Content Group UK Ltd.
Pitfield, Milton Keynes, MK11 3LW, UK
UKHW022152230426
12049UKWH00003BA/59